Key Resources on Community Colleges

A Guide to the Field and Its Literature

Arthur M. Cohen
James C. Palmer
K. Diane Zwemer

Key Resources on Community Colleges

Jossey-Bass Publishers

San Francisco • London • 1986

KEY RESOURCES ON COMMUNITY COLLEGES
A Guide to the Field and Its Literature
by Arthur M. Cohen, James C. Palmer, K. Diane Zwemer

Copyright © 1986 by: Jossey-Bass Inc., Publishers
433 California Street
San Francisco, California 94104
&
Jossey-Bass Limited
28 Banner Street
London EC1Y 8QE

Library of Congress Cataloging-in-Publication Data

Cohen, Arthur M.
  Key resources on community colleges.

  (Jossey-Bass higher education series)
  "Published in cooperation with ERIC Clearinghouse for Junior Colleges"—Verso t.p.
  Includes indexes.
  1. Community colleges—United States—Bibliography.
I. Palmer, James C. II. Zwemer, K. Diane. III. ERIC Clearinghouse for Junior Colleges. IV. Title. V. Series.
Z5814.J8C58   1986   016.378′052′0973   86-45628
[LB2328]
ISBN 1-55542-020-6

Published in cooperation with ERIC Clearinghouse for Junior Colleges.

This publication was prepared with funding from the Office of Educational Research and Improvement (OERI), U.S. Department of Education under contract no. 400-83-0030. The opinions expressed in this publication do not necessarily reflect the positions or policies of OERI or the Department of Education.

Alkaline paper ∞   Manufactured in the U.S.A.

FIRST EDITION   JACKET DESIGN BY WILLI BAUM   *Code 8643*

The Jossey-Bass
Higher Education Series

Contents

Preface

This bibliography is designed to provide community college faculty members and administrators, as well as students of higher education, with an overview of the ideas that have shaped today's two-year colleges, insights into how college practitioners have approached pedagogical and administrative problems, and a sense of the areas that need further research. The bibliography is not exhaustive; our task was to select approximately 650 items from the thousands of works available on community colleges. The final product is thus a selection of the major literature that has contributed to the field over the past twenty years, augmented by the inclusion of earlier classic works that provide a historical foundation for the body of literature under consideration. Exclusion of a work from this bibliography is not necessarily a criticism of that work's value.

The publication of this bibliography marks the twentieth anniversary of the Educational Resources Information Center (ERIC) Clearinghouse for Junior Colleges. The clearinghouse was established in 1966 as one of the original components of the ERIC system. Since then, clearinghouse personnel have monitored the literature on two-year colleges, adding approximately 12,000 documents and journal articles to the ERIC data base. These items chronicle the development of community colleges from the growth years of the 1960s through the steady-state era of the early 1980s. Many of the works cited in this bibliography are available through the ERIC system and can be ordered through the ERIC Document

Reproduction Service in Arlington, Virginia, or obtained on microfiche at more than 650 libraries across the country. Those items available through the ERIC system are marked with an "ED" (ERIC Document) number. Further information on ERIC is provided in Chapter Thirteen.

  While it is not possible to list all significant works in a single volume, we hope that this bibliography will provide the reader with an overview of the major themes and findings that have appeared in the literature. The chapter introductions, as well as the annotated citations themselves, are designed especially for administrators, faculty, and other college practitioners who desire a brief summary of developments in the literature and who do not have the time for in-depth library research. Should the reader require further information, the final chapter provides a guide to additional resources.

Scope of Coverage

  Included in the bibliography are more than 680 books, monographs, journal articles, and research reports. These items were selected from three sources: (1) the documents listed since 1966 in ERIC's *Resources in Education;* (2) the journal articles indexed since 1969 in ERIC's *Current Index to Journals in Education;* and (3) the published monographs and books in the libraries of the University of California at Los Angeles (UCLA). The UCLA library is an excellent source of information on two-year colleges because the university has offered doctoral-level graduate work in community college education since the mid 1950s.

  Several evaluative criteria were used to select items for inclusion in the bibliography:

1. The usefulness of the information provided by the work for researchers and practitioners in the field (works applicable only to isolated institutional situations were not included)

2. The reception of the work by community college practitioners and by professors of community college education
3. The durability of the work over time
4. The quality of research results or other information presented in the work
5. The degree to which the work advances the boundaries of theory and practice in the field
6. The availability of the work through ERIC or other library channels

Given these criteria, certain types of works were (with a few exceptions) excluded out of hand, including dissertations, speeches presented at educational conferences, ERIC documents that describe educational practices or research at individual institutions, and state and institutional annual reports. Although valuable in their own right, these items are often relatively narrow in focus and of value to a limited and possibly scattered audience. Furthermore, it was simply not possible for us to review and do justice to the thousands of institutional research reports and dissertations that have been written about community colleges.

Another limitation of this bibliography is that while almost any work on education or administration is of potential value to community college practitioners, we included only those works that specifically focus on community colleges themselves. Although there are scores of works on management and planning techniques, for example, that could feasibly be put to use by two-year college administrators, we included only those works dealing with management and planning *at the community college.* Similarly, works dealing with teaching, administration, or other topics in their generic sense—without the community college as an institutional focus—are not included in this bibliography. Information on how to obtain materials beyond the scope of this bibliography is provided in Chapter Thirteen.

In the final analysis, the compilation of a selective bibliography necessarily involves some subjective judgments, and we acknowledge that the selection and arrangement of the works in this bibliography undoubtedly reflect our biases.

Overview of the Contents

The first of thirteen chapters in this bibliography provides a brief introduction and an overview of community college education and administration as a field of study. This introductory chapter examines how the field came to be, which key events and people have shaped it, where the field is today, and which areas within the field require further research. The final chapter provides a guide to the library resources that can be used to find further information on two-year colleges, including descriptions of reference tools that provide access to appropriate journal articles, ERIC documents, dissertations, and published statistical information.

The bibliographical citations themselves are published in the middle chapters, Chapters Two through Twelve. Chapter Two lists general works on the community college, such as Eells's classic *The Junior College* (no. 15). Chapters Three and Four list works on students and faculty, respectively. These are followed by chapters on administrators and administration (Chapter Five), finance (Chapter Six), instruction and instructional support (Chapter Seven), occupational education (Chapter Eight), remedial education (Chapter Nine), continuing education and community services (Chapter Ten), collegiate education (Chapter Eleven), and the social role of the community college (Chapter Twelve). Thus, the bibliography documents works on the people who play a role in the community college as well as on the functions of the community college as an educational institution.

Each chapter is divided into two or more subsections. Within each subsection, works are cited alphabetically by author. Entries for each of the cited works include (1) a complete bibliographical citation and (2) an annotation of up to 130 words. The annotation summarizes the type of information provided by the work, the main point or points that the author is trying to make, and (in many cases) how and for whom the work is useful. The length of the annotation is *not* an indication of a work's relative importance or quality.

The scope of some works overlaps two or more chapters. A survey report involving responses from both students and faculty, for example, could appropriately be included in both Chapters Three and Four. For these works, the full entry—including the annotation—is included in only one of the appropriate chapters; a shorter entry—without an annotation—is provided in the other chapter or chapters. Each shortened entry refers the reader to the full annotation.

Designation of Outstanding Works

Some of the entries in the bibliography are marked with a star to indicate that they were considered groundbreaking at the time of their publication and have stood the test of time or have since had a major impact on community college education. Such works date from Koos's first comprehensive textbook on the junior college in the 1920s (No. 22), to McCabe's work on educational reforms at Miami-Dade Community College (No. 629), which have served as models for similar efforts at institutions across the country in the 1980s. By identifying these seminal items, our intention is to provide a guide for those readers seeking the fifty or so works that have been the most influential in community college education.

Using the Bibliography

There are two ways to use this bibliography. The first is simply to browse; the classified arrangement of the bibliography allows the reader to scan the literature on broad topics such as students or career education. The second approach is to use the two indexes: the subject index and the author index. In the subject index, the numbered entries are listed under much more specific categories than the broad classifications found in the table of contents. The author index includes the names of authors and the names of organizations responsible for the production of reports.

Acknowledgments

Several persons assisted us in compiling this bibliography. Celia Cudiamat and Minh Tran of the ERIC Clearinghouse for Junior Colleges provided clerical support, as did Glenda Childress and Patricia Weisson of the Center for the Study of Community Colleges. Several of the annotations were written by Ronald Opp, Reed Markham, and Sandy Jahiel of the UCLA Graduate School of Education. Paul Astin rooted through the UCLA libraries, dusting off many an old book for our consideration.

Funds for the publication of this work were derived from two sources. The ERIC Clearinghouse staff is supported by the U.S. Department of Education, Office of the Assistant Secretary for Educational Research and Improvement. The Center for the Study of Community Colleges received a grant from the Exxon Education Foundation as partial support for the bibliography.

Various chapters herein were reviewed by knowledgeable writers who suggested additional works to include. We appreciate this contribution by James Wattenbarger, S. V. Martorana, Charles Doty, K. Patricia Cross, Richard Alfred, Richard C. Richardson, Jr., Gunder Myran, Steven Zwerling, George Vaughan, James Hammons, William Piland, and John Terry. Diane Pezzullo of UCLA's education and psychology library reviewed Chapter Thirteen.

Any errors or omissions, however, are our responsibility alone.

Los Angeles, California   Arthur M. Cohen
September 1986   James C. Palmer
                                                            K. Diane Zwemer

The Authors

Arthur M. Cohen is director of the Educational Resources Information Center (ERIC) Clearinghouse for Junior Colleges and professor of higher education at the University of California at Los Angeles. He received his B.A. degree (1949) and his M.A. degree (1955) in history from the University of Miami and his Ph.D. degree (1964) in higher education from Florida State University. Cohen currently sits on the board of directors of the American Association of Community and Junior Colleges; he has also played leadership roles within the Community College Humanities Association, the National Council for Research and Planning, the Council of Universities and Colleges, and the California Educational Research Association. Cohen has authored several works on two-year college education, including *Dateline 79: Heretical Concepts for the Community College* and, with Florence B. Brawer, *Confronting Identity: The Community College Instructor, The Two-Year College Instructor Today,* and *The American Community College.*

James C. Palmer is assistant director for user services at the ERIC Clearinghouse for Junior Colleges at the University of California at Los Angeles, and a staff associate at the Center for the Study of Community Colleges in Los Angeles. He received his B.A. degree (1975) in English and German from Pacific University and the Master of Library Science degree (1981) from the University of California at Los Angeles. He is currently a Ph.D. candidate at the

Graduate School of Education there. Palmer is the author of several bibliographical reviews published in *New Directions for Community Colleges,* the *Community College Review,* and the *Community Services Catalyst.*

K. Diane Zwemer is user services librarian at the ERIC Clearinghouse for Junior Colleges at the University of California at Los Angeles. She received her B.A. degree (1980) in anthropology from Occidental College and the Master of Library Science degree with a certificate in Gerontology (1984) from Syracuse University. Zwemer has contributed several bibliographical reviews to *New Directions for Community Colleges* and the *Community Services Catalyst.*

Key Resources
on Community
Colleges

*A Guide to the Field
and Its Literature*

1

The Development
of Community
College Literature

The literature pertaining to community junior colleges dates from the earliest years of the institution. In fact, calls for an institution standing between secondary schools and universities had been made as early as the middle of the nineteenth century, fifty years before the first junior colleges opened their doors. At that time, some university leaders sought institutions that would relieve the universities of the necessity for educating freshmen and sophomores who were considered too young, too immature, or too uncommited to follow a scholarly or professionally oriented line of study; they wanted to preserve the idea of the university for students seriously committed to higher learning. William Rainey Harper advocated separating universities from the weaker four-year colleges, suggesting that the colleges eliminate junior- and senior-year studies and dedicate themselves to postsecondary work that would terminate at the sophomore year. By so doing, he said, the weaker four-year colleges could become stronger preuniversity institutions (W. R. Harper. *The Trend in Higher Education in America*. Chicago: University of Chicago Press, 1905).

The idea of the college limiting itself to freshman and sophomore studies was also furthered by early-twentieth-century analysts, such as Lange (no. 23), who saw the common school

1

extending itself past the 12th grade to accommodate students through age eighteen or nineteen. In their view, high school districts should begin offering postgraduate work that would strengthen student preparation for jobs that did not demand university education. They also saw the need for course work that would carry young people through their teens, fitting them with skills for living. These would be general education courses in the nature of finishing-school work, courses that would prepare youth for civic and home responsibilities. Home economics and civics would be the centerpiece of such institutions.

Both sets of ideas were articulated by authors writing in the early years of the century; both stimulated public school districts to organize postgraduate studies and church groups to organize junior colleges. These writings were cited by legislators sponsoring bills that authorized or funded junior college extensions of the high schools and, eventually, separate junior college districts. However, a literature about community colleges themselves dates only from around 1920, when the American Association of Junior Colleges was formed. Prior to then, most discussions of two-year colleges were embedded in writings about secondary schools and universities; after junior college educators became aware of themselves as a group, the literature became more self-conscious. In the mid 1920s, Koos (no. 22) provided the first sizable compendium of the status of the junior college. His analysis was followed quickly by authors describing the development of these institutions in those states that were early to accept the idea. By 1931, Eells was able to cite numerous studies in his general work (no. 15). The *Junior College Journal*, published continuously since 1930, provided an ongoing forum for those who would write about these rapidly expanding institutions.

The literature about the two-year colleges grew along with the institutions. Prior to 1940, the number of institutions increased rapidly as the idea of the junior college spread throughout the states. Because federal policy of the time was to leave the development of schools and colleges to the states and to private groups, the literature tracks the development of junior colleges across the land from state to state. Those pre-1940 colleges were many, numbering around 600, but small, averaging around 400 students each. They followed the model set down by the turn-of-the-century writers, offering terminal general education for young people who would go no further with their formal schooling, precollegiate studies for the few who would attend senior institutions but who, for a variety of reasons, preferred beginning in the junior college, and a small number of occupational programs preparing those who would enter careers for which baccalaureate or higher degrees were not required. The journal literature and books of that era reflect these junior college purposes and describe the organization and operation of institutions that would serve them. The same set of purposes was also recounted in the so-called feasibility studies that promoted the establishment of junior colleges in the various states.

Rapid growth came to the junior colleges in the latter 1940s and extended through the 1960s. In that era, colleges were organized in all states, and individual institutions became larger. The idea of the comprehensive community college took root. The institutions expanded the number and variety of their occupational programs and, accordingly, attracted students desiring entry to the job market. As the World War II baby boomers reached maturity, the colleges grew larger by serving as institutions to take the overflow, the students for whom university attendance was not an option. The colleges also provided the first two years of baccalaureate studies for students who would not or could not enter the universities as freshmen but who were directed toward eventual transfer. In addition, they began community service activities, providing short courses and ad hoc studies for people who wanted further education in any subject imaginable.

The literature of that era reflects this expansion of functions and exhibits a sense of worthiness on the part of community college leaders and advocates. It is anchored on one end by the President's Commission on Higher Education and on the other by the Carnegie Commission on the Future of Higher Education. The 1947 president's commission (no. 52) recommended providing college opportunities for up to half the population, and the Carnegie commission in 1970 (no. 41) urged maintaining community college comprehensiveness and availability. The colleges had gained a firm foundation in the scope of

American education, and their advocates applauded their growth, spread, and services.

By 1970, there were nearly 1,100 such institutions, serving 2.5 million students. But some changes in function were appearing. The colleges had begun enrolling higher percentages of part-time than full-time students. This function of serving students who held jobs or other responsibilities preventing them from participating in full-time study was applauded by many authors who saw it as a natural evolution. Since the colleges had always been designed for people other than those who would go straight through high school and into universities on their way toward the more prestigious professions or social positions, the enrollment of part-timers was considered evidence of the community college's commitment to democratic or populist ideals. Here was an institution for the masses: the colleges would serve everyone. These same sentiments led also to the vociferous claims that the colleges serve people of any age or ability—adults whose education had been suspended earlier or who needed additional jobs skills or courses for their personal interest, members of minority groups and others whose prior academic achievements did not qualify them for selected institutions, and people already working who desired further training to upgrade themselves in their careers.

The Developing Literature on Two-Year Colleges

The most significant factors affecting the development of the literature about community colleges include high school graduation rates, the universities' posture, the press of underrepresented groups, and demands of professional and occupational groups. High school graduation rates increased steadily from the turn of the century to the latter 1960s. Since one of the main outcomes of each year of schooling is a ticket of admission to the next year, the increase in percentage of the population completing grade 12 gave rise to increased demands to enter grade 13. The percentage of the college-age population enrolled in college went from 1.6 in the year 1900 to 5.8 in the year 1940; by 1980, the percentage had increased to 42. And whereas, in 1950, 43 percent of the 1.2 million high school graduates entered college, by 1978, 77 percent of the 3.1 million graduates enrolled. Since the community colleges took a large proportion of this increase, the prevailing position came to be that growth was positive and that the colleges must do all they could to attract increasing numbers. Medsker and Tillery's *Breaking the Access Barriers* (no. 26) and Knoell's *Through the Open Door* (no. 79) are examples of this view.

The second major factor, the increase in students continuing their university education beyond the freshman and sophomore years, resulted in a continuing theme in the literature, with descriptions and promotion of efforts at postsecondary education different from that carried on at the traditional colleges. Although there were some short-lived experiments with upper-division universities (institutions that first admitted students at the junior year) in Texas, Florida, and Illinois, the idea of universities without freshmen and sophomores did not spread. Hence, the community college developed as an adjunctive institution, one that could enroll students wishing to enter traditional college programs but whose major growth areas were in nontraditional curricula. Had the universities generally abandoned the lower division, the literature of the community college would have been more directed toward issues of articulating curricula between secondary schools and universities. As it is, articulation and transfer have occupied much of the attention of the community college writers, but a significantly greater proportion of the literature is directed toward its other-than-collegiate functions. Harlacher's *The Community Dimension of the Community College* (no. 841) and Gleazer's *The Community College: Values, Vision, and Vitality* (no. 18) are examples of this literature.

The press of underrepresented groups for admission is another major influence on the literature. Adults, members of minority groups, and numerous others whom the university could not accommodate have been described by authors who felt that those groups deserved a chance at education beyond the high school and that the community college was the most readily available point of entry for them. Over the years, proponents of the colleges have justified and defended them by pointing to the numbers of the underrepresented groups that they serve. And indeed, by the end of the 1970s, community colleges were enrolling nearly 40 percent of the ethnic minority students attending college in the United States. Olivas's *The Dilemma of Access* (no. 162) presented data on the ethnic groups served and challenged the colleges to do more for them.

Occupational groups have increasingly demanded more schooling of those applying for admission to their ranks. The root causes of these demands are the increased knowledge necessary to practice in many technologies and the increased professional status of jobs that require more years of formal education. Accordingly, the literature from the 1940s on is filled with program descriptions and exhortations for new programs in hundreds of occupational areas. Harris and Grede offered guidelines for program development in their *Career Education in Colleges* (no. 717), while Lombardi traced the rise of career studies in general in his *Resurgence of Occupational Education* (no. 703).

Categorizing the Literature

Who writes on the community college? The institutions have not been examined by many analysts. Most of the writers have been affiliated with the colleges as administrators or program directors. Some university professors, never more than a hundred at any one time and nearly all of them based in schools of education, have directed their attention to community colleges. A small number of sociologists, economists, and political analysts have also looked at the colleges. And graduate students preparing for careers in community colleges have contributed.

A more useful way of categorizing the literature is by the types of writings that have dominated it. One such category is *descriptive*. Here the articles range from explanations of the system in general to the specifics of curricular, managerial, and instructional operations at single institutions. This literature is written by college-based program coordinators, administrators, counselors, and instructors. It tends to be uncritical and often self-congratulatory. It appears in many sections in this bibliography, especially in the chapter on instruction and instructional support (Chapter Seven).

Although the concept of *institutional research* has never been widely adopted in community colleges, there is a thread of literature prepared by community college institutional research directors. Much of this attends to the students who are being served: demographics, sources, and follow-ups. During the 1950s and 1960s, numerous institutional research studies compared grades earned by students at community colleges and those at senior institutions. More recently, community surveys comparing the demographics of students with the characteristics of the population at large have become prominent. Institutional researchers have also considered curricular and managerial issues, but most of the institutional research literature appears in the chapter on students (Chapter Three).

Educational *experiments* with community college operations have been reported. Frequently done by instructors or graduate students preparing for careers in administration, these studies relate one group of students to another within the context of different instructional or curricular patterns. They are rarely experimental, with all the controls that the word implies; more often they are naturalistic investigations in which students participating in one or another instructional program are compared with students outside that program. Most of these studies are conducted with small samples at individual institutions and are thus not listed in this bibliography. Information on how such studies can be obtained through the ERIC data base is provided in Chapter Thirteen.

Much of the literature can best be described as *exhortation*. Here, writers from many areas point to what the community colleges should be doing for adult students, members of minority groups, handicapped persons, and various industrial or professional groups. Invariably, the writers point to the social, political, or humanistic gains to be made by colleges that direct more of their resources toward serving these various constituencies. They also frequently plead for more support for their favored functions. Their works appear throughout, but especially in the chapters on students (Chapter Three) and lifelong learning (Chapter Ten).

There has been a sizable amount of writing on questions of *identity*. What is the community college? What should it be?

Many of these authors take a defensive posture, saying that the colleges deserve more recognition and appreciation for what they are doing. Their writings cluster in the chapters on general works (Chapter Two) and governance and administration (Chapter Five).

Program review occupies another portion of the literature, with writers describing how and why programs were organized, numbers of people served, curricular and managerial patterns, instructional forms, and program outcomes. This literature is scattered; a review of the programs in one college or in one state is rarely made in the context of reviews of similar programs in other colleges or states. It is concentrated in the chapters pertaining to curriculum: those on career education (Chapter Eight), remediation (Chapter Nine), and the collegiate function (Chapter Eleven).

Many authors consider *temporal problems,* issues that have short life but are of intense concern. Over the years, the advent of collective bargaining for the faculty in the community colleges in one or another state has yielded much writing, most of it speculation as to the effects of negotiated contracts. Similarly, a funding crisis, tuition increase, or impending change in admissions requirements or institutional control yields a flurry of speculation on underlying motives and anticipated outcomes. This literature appears throughout.

One category must be reserved for *zealotry.* Authors of these papers are so convinced of the value of the community college that they seek to export the idea to other states, other nations. Their zeal stems from their belief that the community college answers numerous questions of access to education and enhances the human capital of any region in which the institutions are located. Many of the general works (Chapter Two) take this position, and it is also found in the chapters on the various curricular operations, especially lifelong learning (Chapter Ten).

Criticism encompasses a sparse but intense group of writings. The authors of works in this category question college effects, usually from an economic or sociological perspective, but sometimes from the standpoint of the educational outcomes themselves. Their works cluster in the chapter on the community college social role (Chapter Twelve). However, the few works of criticism only point up the fact that the colleges have rarely been so examined. They have not captured the attention of analysts from within the institutions, and too few outsiders have been concerned with them. This dearth probably relates to the lack of a substantive literature of criticism of education in general and also the colleges' recent arrival and phenomenal growth rate. The word in the 1960s was "We must be good. Look how the students are flocking to our doors." In the 1980s, it became "Curing social ills is expensive but worth the cost. Send the funds, and we will put them to good use." Because nearly all the literature derives from people with a vested interest in perpetuating the institution, little of it takes a neutral view. Nonetheless, it does reflect internal efforts at enhancing program quality.

How Can the Literature Be Improved?

The literature of community colleges would become more balanced if there were more critical analyses. A *dialogue* in which reviewers participate using the perspectives of the social sciences would be a welcome expansion of the writings. Instead of competitive exhortations, this could offer a forum for considered opinion. *Outcome measures* offer a second area of welcome expansion. To what degree does the community college enhance the well-being of its community? of its students collectively? Very few carefully tailored examinations have been reported. Relative *effectiveness* is a third missing dimension. What teaching technique, what management style, what program dimensions, what curriculum patterns are most effective? Little in the literature would lead one to believe that these questions are seriously considered by authors knowledgeable in the rigors of educational research. Last, more reliable *data and definitions* are needed. It is difficult to evaluate anything, from an attack on college outcomes to the assertions of a proponent for one or another curricular form, without comprehensive local, state, and national data sets. How many students transfer? How many obtain jobs in the field for which they were prepared? The data are not available. What is an "adult student"? an "effective program"? The definitions are as varied as the reports.

A more precise assessment of community colleges awaits commonly accepted definitions and uniformly derived data. For now, the dominant theme in the literature is description. Numerous reports recount the demographics of students and faculty, the role of administrators, trustees, and state agencies. Instructional programs are described and curricular changes documented. This literature itself is educative; people in one institution can compare themselves and their activities with those operative elsewhere. This serves the function of bringing together the practitioners in colleges across the nation, of sharing ideas among colleagues. It has contributed to attitudes of collegeality and to a sense of identity among the staff in these newly evolved colleges. But it is not sufficient for answering questions of institutional efficacy.

2

General Resources on Two-Year Colleges

This chapter cites those works that attempt a comprehensive analysis of the two-year college. Included are citations to previously published bibliographies covering the broad scope of two-year college education and administration (nos. 1–6), textbooks and studies that provide a comprehensive picture of the two-year college (nos. 7–39), and works discussing the community college mission (nos. 40–56). These items are a logical starting point for those studying any aspect of the two-year college.

Bibliographies

There are relatively few stand-alone bibliographies of the community college literature (nos. 1–6). The first (no. 3) was compiled in 1930 by Walter Crosby Eells, who, throughout the 1930s and early 1940s, was the outstanding bibliographer of the field. Eells's 1930 bibliography lists 1,600 items (mostly published books and journal articles) covering the years 1887 through 1930. Supplements to this bibliography appeared regularly in the *Junior College Journal* from its inception in 1930 through the April 1946 edition. These supplements list an additional 3,990 items extending the coverage of the original bibliography up through the mid 1940s. Eells's bibliographical efforts, then, provide an invaluable resource for persons examining the junior college literature prior to and during World War II.

The remaining five bibliographies cited in this section are considerably less extensive and provide only scattered coverage of the literature. For further bibliographical listings, the reader should turn to the general texts and studies cited on the following pages (nos. 7–39). Of particular note and usefulness are the extensive bibliographies provided by McDowell (1919, no. 24), Proctor (1927, no. 31), Eells (1931, no. 15), Hillway (1958, no. 21), Cohen, Brawer, and Lombardi (1971, no. 13), Monroe (1972, no. 27), Palinchak (1973, no. 30), and Cohen and Brawer (1982, no. 12). Together, these works can be used to chart the bibliography of the two-year college literature from the early 1900s through the early 1980s.

Comprehensive Texts and Studies

The first comprehensive monograph on the two-year college—McDowell's *The Junior College* (no. 24)—was published in 1919. Since then, several general monographs and textbooks have been published that, when read sequentially, chronicle the changing role of the junior college during the past six decades. Earlier authors, including Lange (no. 23) and Koos (no. 22), depict the junior college as an upward extension of secondary education; they make little or no mention of continuing or community education functions. Authors of the post–World War II era, however, provide extensive analyses of continuing education and community services; Bogue (no. 8) and Gleazer (nos. 16 and 18) are particularly strong advocates of these college roles. Most post–World War II authors also examine the role of occupational education in the two-year institution, as well as the status of the transfer and remedial functions. Thus, the general works cited in this chapter reflect the development of two-year colleges from strictly collegiate institutions providing instruction at the 13th- and 14th-grade levels to comprehensive institutions providing career, compensatory, and community education.

The reader wishing to delve further into the history and development of the American two-year college may want to consult any one of several histories that have been written about two-year colleges in particular states. Such histories, not listed in this bibliography, appear usually as dissertations and occasionally as monographs published by state university presses. Many of these histories are cited in the general texts and studies mentioned above.

Analyses of the Community College Mission

The post–World War II expansion of the two-year college mission fostered a great debate surrounding the appropriate role of the colleges. The thread of this debate can be followed in the last seventeen works cited in this chapter (nos. 40–56). On the one hand, the President's Commission on Higher Education (no. 52) and the Carnegie Commission on Higher Education (no. 41) have urged a comprehensive institutional role encompassing collegiate, occupational, and community studies. Other authors, however, have questioned the ability of colleges to be all things to all people and have called for a more defined mission that eschews noncollegiate tasks (Cohen and Brawer, no. 43; Frankel, no. 48; Cohen and Associates, no. 42; and Cohen and Lombardi, no. 44). This debate is a major theme in the literature and continues to be the focus of a growing body of research encompassing opinion surveys of the general public and of community college practitioners themselves (Gillo, Landerholm, and Goldsmith, no. 50; Field Research Corporation, no. 47; Cross, no. 46; Gallup Organization, no. 49; and Smith and Beck, no. 53). Further studies of this nature—not listed in this bibliography—have been conducted at the institutional level, analyzing how faculty, students, and others at single colleges differ in their opinions as to the appropriate institutional role. These institutional studies are available through the ERIC data base (the scope and use of which are discussed in Chapter Thirteen).

Bibliographies

1   Boss, Richard, and Anderson, Roberta (eds.). *Community/ Junior College: A Bibliography.* Corvallis: Division of Continuing Education, Oregon State System of Higher Education, 1967. 179 pages. (ED 020 724)

This unannotated bibliography of junior college literature focuses on the period from 1956 up to 1967. It contains citations to journal articles, conference proceedings, research reports, books, and state and national reports, dividing the literature into fifteen broad subject areas: related bibliographies; general works; historical development; purposes and characteristics; administration and organization; financing; curricula; guidance; the student; teachers and teaching; physical plants; accreditation; libraries; research; and serials. It also lists films and filmstrips pertaining to adult/ extension education, career opportunities, junior colleges in general, and vocational education.

2   Burnett, Collins W. (ed.). *The Community Junior College: An Annotated Bibliography with Introductions for School Counselors.* Columbus: College of Education, Ohio State University, 1968. 122 pages.

This selective annotated bibliography of the junior college journal literature from 1961 to 1967 presents eight chapters, each containing an introduction, a few book references, and journal citations with short (one- or two-sentence) annotations. Separate sections of the bibliography cover (1) community/junior college history; (2) philosophy and objectives of the junior college; (3) functions of the junior college; (4) organization and administration, including legislation, governance, planning, finance, and public relations; (5) the teaching and learning environment, including curriculum, instructional media, and the library; (6) student personnel programs; (7) trends and developments reflecting changes in philosophy, curriculum, and the development of colleges within individual states; and (8) research and evaluation activities centering on junior college education. The work includes over 700 citations from twenty professional journals.

★**3**   Eells, Walter Crosby. *Bibliography on Junior Colleges.*
         Office of Education Bulletin no. 2. Washington, D.C.: U.S.
         Government Printing Office, 1930. 167 pages.

This work provides an annotated listing of 1,600 published and
unpublished works covering the years 1887 through 1930. It
emphasizes published book and periodical literature but also lists
master's and doctoral dissertations "as far as they could be
secured" (p. vii). It includes a thorough subject and author index,
thus making the bibliography an excellent guide to the first four
decades of the junior college literature. (Note: supplements to this
bibliography appeared regularly in the *Junior College Journal*
from 1930 through April 1946, extending the coverage of the
bibliography up through the World War II years.)

4   Morrison, Duncan G., and Martorana, S. V. *The 2-Year
         Community College: An Annotated List of Studies and
         Surveys.* U.S. Office of Education Bulletin no. 14. Wash-
         ington, D.C.: U.S. Government Printing Office, 1958. 33
         pages.

This publication provides an annotated bibliography of over 200
research studies on the two-year college that were identified in a
1957 survey of educators and researchers. It includes references to
projects completed as of 1953 and to those identified as still under
way, dividing the entries into the following categories: regional
studies; institutional research studies; research on instruction;
relations with the public and with other institutions; organization
and finance; student personnel services; the library; advanced
academic study; vocational programs; general education; and
curriculum design and evaluation. The work, which includes only
dissertations, state documents, and institutional reports, is useful
as a listing of the fugitive literature produced in the late 1940s and
early 1950s.

★ This symbol signifies classic works throughout this volume.

5   Rarig, Emory W. (ed.). *The Community Junior College: An Annotated Bibliography*. New York: Teachers College Press, 1966. 114 pages.

This publication lists journal articles, monographs, and unpublished reports dealing with the history, functions, and organization of junior colleges as of the mid 1960s. It includes a particularly good listing of journal articles and books tracing the development of the junior college idea in American education from the late nineteenth century. It also cites works dealing with the functions and purposes of the junior colleges, college organization and administration, students, college programs, administrators and faculty, junior college facilities, and institutional research. It is useful primarily for those investigating the junior college literature of the late 1950s and early 1960s.

6   Trent, J. W., and others. *The Study of Junior Colleges*. Vol 1: *Roles and Realities of Community Colleges: An Analysis of the Literature*. Los Angeles: Center for the Study of Evaluation, University of California, 1972. 306 pages. (ED 077 507)

This comprehensive review of the literature on junior colleges draws heavily upon materials collected by the ERIC Clearinghouse for Junior Colleges as of 1972. Topics covered in the review include (1) characteristics of junior college students and the low achievers among them, (2) disadvantaged students and the programs designed to meet their needs, (3) student attrition, (4) career education and the remedial component of that curriculum, (5) innovative programs, including individualized instruction and technological innovations, (6) counseling services, and (7) the role and characteristics of junior college faculty. It also examines literature on the roles and responsibilities of administrators and on the needs of communities. It serves as a concise review of the junior college literature generated in the late 1960s.

Comprehensive Texts and Studies

★7   Blocker, Clyde E.; Plummer, Robert H.; and Richardson, Richard C., Jr. *The Two-Year College: A Social Synthesis.* Englewood Cliffs, N.J.: Prentice-Hall, 1965. 289 pages.

This comprehensive analysis of the functions and constituencies of two-year colleges focuses on the social forces that are shaping their development. It examines the two-year college as a product of American culture and then discusses the different types of two-year colleges in existence, the socioeconomic forces that affect the colleges, and the control and financing of the institutions. It also presents separate chapters on two-year college students, faculty-college relationships, administrative structures and functions, curriculum and instruction, and student personnel services and concludes with suggestions for the colleges' future development. It serves as a concise synthesis of the social, political, and economic factors shaping the growth and identity of the community college in the 1950s and 1960s.

★8   Bogue, Jesse P. *The Community College.* New York: McGraw-Hill, 1950. 390 pages.

This work analyzes the status of two-year colleges as of 1950, emphasizing their expanding role as comprehensive, community-based institutions. It examines the educational and social forces giving impetus to the junior college movement during the early decades of the twentieth century and discusses the varied missions assigned to the colleges in the immediate post–World War II era. Individual chapters discuss the organization and administration of the colleges and their role in general, technical, and adult education. The work provides the present-day reader with insights into the hopes that educational leaders had for the community colleges in the late 1940s and the origins of the colleges' expanded role in areas beyond traditional 13th- and 14th-grade education.

9   Brick, Michael. *Forum and Focus for the Junior College Movement: The American Association of Junior Colleges.* New York: Teachers College Press, 1963. 222 pages.

This publication traces the development of the American Association of Junior Colleges from its inception in 1920 through its forty-second annual meeting in 1962. It recounts the leadership role played by the association, especially in establishing a code of ethics for the colleges and in communicating information to assist them in forming their own identity as institutions not wholly a part of American secondary or higher education. It also discusses association activities on behalf of federal education legislation and reviews convention agendas and association-sponsored projects related to curriculum, faculty, students, and administration, illustrating the major role played by the association in the growth and development of the junior college movement.

10   Bushnell, David S. *Organizing for Change: New Priorities for Community Colleges.* New York: McGraw-Hill, 1973. 237 pages.

This work reports the findings and implications of Project Focus, a comprehensive national study of community colleges undertaken in the early 1970s. It draws upon a national survey of community college constituencies and a review of the literature to assess (1) the characteristics of students, faculty, and administrators, (2) their perceptions of institutional goals and priorities, (3) change strategies to align desired goals with actual practices, (4) barriers to change, and (5) social and demographic forces influencing the future direction of community colleges. It provides a comprehensive look at community colleges as of 1970 and a good examination of the factors that made the 1970s a decade of consolidation and stability.

11   Cohen, Arthur M. *Dateline '79: Heretical Concepts for the Community College.* Beverly Hills, Calif.: Glencoe Press, 1969. 234 pages.

The author argues that the community college should embrace a defined-outcomes approach to curriculum and instruction and that colleges should be valued only insofar as they produce demonstrable increases in student learning. He presents a paradigmatic picture of a community college built around this philosophy, stressing the need for (1) core general education courses with specified behavioral objectives; (2) the division of courses into short-term units that allow the student to stop in or stop out; (3) the employment of different instructional techniques to match varying student learning styles; and (4) the development of faculty as recognized professionals in student learning. He contrasts these ideals with actual instructional and administrative practices, noting that, as the colleges grow older, they become ends unto themselves, with little regard for the effects on students and the community, and concludes with a discussion of how defined instructional objectives can be utilized to effect institutional accountability.

★**12**   Cohen, Arthur M., and Brawer, Florence B. *The American Community College.* San Francisco: Jossey-Bass, 1982. 445 pages.

This work presents a comprehensive overview of community college education in the United States as of the early 1980s. The authors discuss the expanding community college mission, increases in the number and diversity of students, strategies used by faculty to cope with these changes, and issues related to governance, administration, finance, instruction, and student services. They also explore curricular issues and present separate analyses of career education, compensatory education, community education, collegiate education, and general education. They conclude with a critical analysis of the social role of the community college as it has been viewed in the literature. This work serves primarily as an evaluative textbook that introduces the reader to the issues and controversies surrounding the community college during the past twenty years.

13   Cohen, Arthur M.; Brawer, Florence B.; and Lombardi, John. *A Constant Variable*. San Francisco: Jossey-Bass, 1971. 238 pages.

This work reviews a substantive body of literature under three headings: institutional personality, people, and curriculum and instruction. It challenges traditional concepts in curriculum, noting that, because most students do not take courses in sequence, different ways of conceptualizing curricula should be adopted. Separate chapters treat vocational education and black studies. The book concludes with an analysis of the unstated functions of the community college, including those related to sorting and certifying, custodial overseeing of students, and social equality. It includes a bibliography of several hundred items.

14   Deegan, William L.; Tillery, Dale; and Associates. *Renewing the American Community College: Priorities and Strategies for Effective Leadership*. San Francisco: Jossey-Bass, 1985. 340 pages.

This book presents thirteen essays by well-known community college experts who examine factors that will be central to the future development of the American community college. It starts with a discussion of the various stages of the evolution of the community college and an examination of the problems encountered in determining future missions and priorities and continues with additional chapters on student characteristics, faculty leadership, effective programs for developmental education, revitalizing student services, institutional commitment to community services, establishing linkages with other education providers, and problems related to governance, state and local collaboration, institutional finance, and strategic planning. The book serves as a useful introduction to the controversies facing contemporary community college practitioners.

★**15** Eells, Walter C. *The Junior College*. Boston: Houghton Mifflin, 1931. 833 pages.

This comprehensive text on the junior college as of 1930 discusses (1) junior college development, reviewing data on numbers, enrollments, and curriculum; (2) the growth of the California junior colleges and developments in other states; (3) issues relating to standards and accreditation; and (4) the junior college role in increasing access to higher education, providing transfer education, providing terminal education, and providing student guidance services. It also outlines issues and data relating to organization and administration, governance, administrative personnel, instructional staff, physical facilities, the library, the curriculum, finance, state legislation, standardized tests, and student activities, with numerous citations for further reading. This is one of the classic texts on the early junior college.

16 Gleazer, Edmund J., Jr. *This Is the Community College*. Boston: Houghton Mifflin, 1968. 151 pages.

This work serves as a general introduction to the public community college of the 1960s and presents the rationale for higher education in a community context. It defines the assignment of the community college in expanding access to higher education, reviews the role of occupational education in meeting the needs of those students who do not transfer, and discusses the expanded role of the community college in serving as a center for continuing education and community service. It outlines the functions of various college staff members, including trustees, administrators, and staff. The work not only serves as an introductory textbook on the community college but also provides insights into how the author—a long-time president of the American Association of Community and Junior Colleges—viewed community colleges during the growth era of the 1960s.

17   Gleazer, Edmund J., Jr. *Project Focus: A Forecast Study of Community Colleges.* New York: McGraw-Hill, 1973. 239 pages.

This book, which reports impressions gained from surveys of students and staff at ninety-six colleges and visits to thirty colleges, focuses on the function and mission of the two-year college, college roles in community development, cooperation with other community agencies, lifelong learning, legislative policies, finance, institutional control, and leadership. It is useful as a reflection of the personal impressions gained by a long-time national spokesperson for community colleges, though no attempt is made by the author to tie his comments to the history of community colleges, theories of education, or a general body of knowledge about education.

18   Gleazer, Edmund J., Jr. *The Community College: Values, Vision, and Vitality.* Washington, D.C.: American Association of Community and Junior Colleges, 1980. 190 pages.

The author of this work argues that the purpose of the community college should be "to encourage and facilitate lifelong learning, with community as process and product" (p. 16). He shows how changing student populations and the need to provide services that do not fit traditional transfer and occupational program categories require that colleges organize themselves as agencies of community development. He demonstrates how colleges can improve local government, provide technical assistance to social service agencies, and help solve community problems; questions whether local flexibility can be maintained in the face of a trend toward state-level financing; and argues that a specially trained staff is necessary to operate a college dedicated to lifelong education.

19   Godfrey, Eleanor P., and Holmstrom, Engin I. *Study of Community Colleges and Vocational-Technical Centers, Phase I.* Washington, D.C.: Bureau of Social Science Research, 1970. 357 pages. (ED 053 718)

The publication provides an in-depth comparative analysis of the students, faculty, and graduates at four types of two-year colleges: branch campuses of universities, junior colleges offering transfer and terminal occupational programs, technical institutes, and vocational centers. It draws upon surveys of colleges in seven states to compare (1) students, in terms of demographic characteristics, educational experiences, and occupational goals; (2) graduates, in terms of personal characteristics, educational and employment status, and aspirations; and (3) faculty, in terms of demographic characteristics, employment experiences, and attitudes toward school services and policy. It is useful in understanding the differing milieus of the various types of two-year colleges that have been established in the United States.

★20   Henry, Nelson B. (ed.). *The Public Junior College.* Fifty-fifth yearbook of the National Society for the Study of Education. Part I. Chicago: National Society for the Study of Education, 1956. 347 pages.

Fifteen essays by predominant educators on the status of public junior colleges as of the mid 1950s include discussions of the personal and societal needs that led to the growth of public two-year colleges after World War II; the objectives and scope of college efforts in the areas of transfer studies, vocational education, general education, and community services; program development and improvement; student personnel services; preservice and in-service faculty training; the influence of legislators and accrediting agencies on the colleges; financial problems; and guiding principles in the establishment of new colleges. The work provides the reader with insights into how educational leaders of the time (including Paul Dressel, B. Lamar Johnson, James Thornton, James Reynolds, Leland Medsker, and Grace Bird) viewed the emergence of the public junior college.

21　　Hillway, Tyrus. *The American Two-Year College.* New York: Harper & Row, 1958. 276 pages.

This work summarizes, in textbook form, the milestones of two-year college development up through the mid 1950s and the evolution of the colleges' major functions. It includes individual chapters on the goals of the two-year college; student characteristics, organizations, and athletics; curricular components; legal status and accreditation; and teachers and administrators. It provides the reader with a brief and concise analysis of the status of two-year colleges in the aftermath of the President's Commission on Higher Education (no. 52).

★22　　Koos, Leonard V. *The Junior-College Movement.* Boston: Ginn, 1925. 436 pages.

This comprehensive examination of the community college movement as of the 1920s by one of its earliest proponents discusses the types of junior colleges, their geographical distribution, and their democratizing role. It details the training, experience, teaching load, and remuneration of instructors and examines trends related to older students, enrollment increases, and changes in students' occupational goals. It explores the problem of overlapping course work between high schools and colleges and proposes solutions on where to locate junior colleges and how to provide an appropriate financial base. This book serves as a historical overview of the early junior college movement.

23　　Lange, Alexis Frederick. *The Lange Book: The Collected Writings of a Great Educational Philosopher.* (Arthur H. Chamberlain, ed.) San Francisco: Trade, 1927. 302 pages.

This publication reproduces the collected writings of Alexis Frederick Lange, long-time dean of the Department of Education at the University of California at Berkeley and one of the early leaders of the junior college movement in the state. It includes four essays (pp. 87–128) devoted to the mission of the junior college and its place within the American system of education. The work provides the reader with insights into Lange's vision of the junior college as the capstone of public secondary education rather than as a junior partner to colleges and universities and helps in understanding why many early junior colleges were established as appendages to local high schools rather than independent institutions of higher education.

24 McDowell, F. M. *The Junior College.* Bureau of Education Bulletin no. 35. Washington, D.C.: U.S. Government Printing Office, 1919. 139 pages.

Drawing upon national surveys and an extensive literature review to examine the early history of junior colleges and to detail their status as of 1919, this publication reviews the several influences leading to the development of the junior college idea, including (1) influences originating in the university, (2) the transformation of state normal schools to colleges or junior colleges, (3) the demand for an extended period of secondary education, and (4) the movement to convert the large numbers of small and financially strapped four-year institutions into two-year colleges. It also presents a statistical profile of the junior colleges in operation at the time and surveys methods used to accredit these institutions. This is the first comprehensive analysis of the junior college to appear in the literature.

★**25** Medsker, Leland L. *The Junior College: Progress and Prospect.* New York: McGraw-Hill, 1960. 367 pages.

Reporting the results of a nationwide study of the two-year college that was conducted in 1960, the author outlines the strengths and weaknesses of the junior college, characteristics of students, and the makeup of the instructional program. He discusses the transfer and terminal functions, including data on the academic performance and retention of transfer students in selected states; details faculty attitudes regarding the purposes and organizational characteristics of two-year colleges; provides information from a number of states on problems of development and finance; and describes costs, state responsibilities, and standards that will affect the future role of the two-year college. This book serves primarily as a historical resource that places the junior college movement in relation to other segments of higher education as of the end of the 1950s.

26   Medsker, Leland L., and Tillery, Dale. *Breaking the Access Barriers: A Profile of Two-year Colleges.* Carnegie Commission on Higher Education Series. New York: McGraw-Hill, 1971. 183 pages.

This review of available junior college data as of 1970 analyzes major concerns and recommends directions for future development. Individual chapters cover (1) the growth of two-year colleges through the 1960s, enrollment projections, and the demand for new colleges; (2) student characteristics, including differences between two-year and four-year college students and the contrasts between students in vocational and academic programs; (3) the components of the comprehensive community college mission; (4) college responses to urban problems; (5) faculty characteristics, attitudes, work load, compensation, and training; (6) state control, internal governance, and financial support; and (7) special problems of the private junior college. The work concludes with policy recommendations concerning mission identification, the role of two-year colleges in higher education, state governance, financial support, student financial aid, and faculty development.

27   Monroe, Charles R. *Profile of the Community College: A Handbook.* San Francisco: Jossey-Bass, 1972. 435 pages.

This review of the history and characteristics of the community college examines, in textbook fashion, the historical evolution of the colleges; their commitment to open admissions and the comprehensive curriculum; the general, transfer, and occupational components of the curriculum; and student and faculty characteristics. It combines findings from an extensive review of the literature with personal insights gleaned from the author's long career in community college education.

28 O'Connell, Thomas E. *Community Colleges: A President's View*. Urbana: University of Illinois Press, 1968. 172 pages.

This publication evaluates the strengths and weaknesses of the community college as of the mid 1960s. It examines distinguishing characteristics of community college faculty and students, provides insight on how to start community colleges, and describes the transfer, career, and adult programs provided by most public two-year institutions. It also discusses how the multipurpose community college has changed the traditional meaning of *college* and elaborates on quantity versus quality in higher education and on the differences between two-year institutions and universities. The book provides—from a founding president's point of view—an analysis of the issues facing community college leaders in the boom years of the early 1960s.

29 Ogilvie, W. K., and Raines, M. R. (eds.). *Perspectives on the Community-Junior College: Selected Readings*. East Norwalk, Conn.: Appleton-Century-Crofts, 1971. 635 pages.

Ninety-three essays on the community college by a variety of individuals and agencies cover such topics as the purpose and mission of the community college, its historical background, the social context within which the colleges operate, student characteristics, student services, curricular functions, community services, faculty characteristics and role, and organizational structure and control. Contributors include Leland Medsker, Joseph Cosand, John Gardner, B. Lamar Johnson, James Wattenbarger, Edmund Gleazer, Leonard Koos, Raymond Schultz, Dorothy Knoell, Dale Tillery, John Lombardi, and other well-known community college experts. The book provides a wide-ranging interpretive and evaluative look at community colleges as of 1970.

30 Palinchak, Robert. *The Evolution of the Community College*. Metuchen, N.J.: Scarecrow Press, 1973. 364 pages.

Drawing upon a 750-item bibliography to provide a comprehensive text on the history of the community college, its students, and its faculty, this publication considers (1) the evolution of the institution and its curriculum, (2) the identity and missions of the colleges, and (3) student and faculty characteristics. The author notes that traditional colleges could not resolve problems of mass higher education in a technological society and that it remains for the community colleges to demonstrate that they can do so. This work provides historians of the community college with an exhaustive analysis of the issues surrounding the identity of the community college in American higher education.

31   Proctor, William Martin (ed.). *The Junior College: Its Organization and Administration.* Palo Alto, Calif.: Stanford University Press, 1927. 226 pages.

A series of thirteen essays (many of them written by California junior college presidents) examines the status of the junior college as of the mid 1920s and provides insights into what educational leaders of the time hoped the junior college would accomplish. The work includes discussions of the history of the junior college movement; the junior college curriculum, faculty, and organization; the administrative problems of small and large junior colleges; the place of the junior college in the American educational system; and the academic achievement of junior college transfers at Stanford University. It concludes with a ninety-item bibliography compiled by Walter Crosby Eells.

32   Seashore, Carl E. *The Junior College Movement.* New York: Holt, Rinehart & Winston, 1940. 160 pages.

This publication critically analyzes the status of the junior college movement as of 1940, arguing that two-year institutions should emphasize terminal rather than transfer education. The author maintains that only about 80 percent of junior college students have the ability or inclination to do university work and that efforts to increase baccalaureate attainment rates will lead many students to disillusionment and disappointment. The book provides the reader with insights into the school of thought that saw the junior college as an institution serving the needs of those "average" students who allegedly fall in the middle of an ability continuum ranging from the less able students who enter relatively unskilled trade occupations to students whose academic talent affords entrance to the university.

33 Starrak, James A., and Hughes, Raymond M. *The Community College in the United States.* Ames: Iowa State College Press, 1954. 114 pages.

The authors detail a proposed system of community colleges for the state of Iowa, analyzing factors contributing to the need for community colleges and outlining standards relating to location, size, accessibility, financial support, organization and administration, student body, curriculum, cooperative education, and guidance and personnel services, concluding with a proposed bill for the establishment of community colleges in Iowa. This work serves as a good example of the planning processes that led to the expansion of community colleges in the 1950s and 1960s.

34 Thornton, J. W., Jr. *The Community Junior College.* New York: Wiley, 1972. 304 pages.

An introductory textbook for staff members in preservice and inservice programs, this work covers all aspects of community college operations, with sections on history, curriculum, organization, support, and administrative responsibility. It makes the case for public support for higher education, placing community colleges within higher education and justifying these institutions as a natural extension of the free, public elementary and secondary school systems in America. It provides a particularly strong emphasis on the history of the two-year college and its curriculum. The book is useful as a reflection of community colleges as they were viewed during their period of greatest expansion in the 1960s.

35 Trent, James W., and others. *The Study of Junior Colleges.* Vol. 2: *Diverse Dimensions of Community Colleges: Case Studies of 15 Institutions.* Los Angeles: Center for the Study of Evaluation, University of California, 1972. 222 pages. (ED 077 508)

This work presents case studies of fifteen junior colleges that vary in terms of location, type of community served, age of institution, enrollment size, type of governance, ethnic composition, curricular program emphasis, and other variables. It draws upon data from surveys and interviews conducted at these institutions to assess student, faculty, and counselor characteristics and to examine administrator opinions concerning the goals of education, major institutional problems, community relations, counseling services, and college relations with governmental agencies. It provides researchers with an in-depth view of community colleges as they existed in 1970 and with an exhaustive study of the concerns of students, faculty, and administrators.

36 Vaughan, George B. *The Community College in America: A Short History.* (Rev. ed.) Washington, D.C.: American Association of Community and Junior Colleges, 1985. 33 pages. (ED 255 267)

The author briefly chronicles the events shaping the development of the American community college. He traces the roots of the community college movement to the Morrill Act of 1862 and then outlines milestones relevant to the establishment of the comprehensive mission in the post–World War II era and to the growth of community college education in the boom years of the 1960s. He concludes with an outline of factors that characterize the contemporary community college scene in terms of leadership, governance, services, and mission. This work serves as a historical sketch that can be used in conjunction with other, more comprehensive works on the community college.

37   Vaughan, George B., and Associates. *Issues for Communi-*
         ty College Leaders in a New Era. San Francisco: Jossey-
         Bass, 1983. 275 pages.

Twelve essays explore problems faced by community colleges in
terms of students, curricular functions, and institutional management, with discussions of the conflict between traditional transfer
education and growing demands for adult continuing education,
educational access for the poor, the college role in moving women
into the mainstream of society, underlying assumptions and
practices of remedial education, and the revitalization of general
education. The authors also examine the community college role
in baccalaureate education, model student services programs,
educational leadership in the community college, faculty and staff
commitment to the college, and college links with business and
industry. The book provides a comprehensive analysis of the
challenges facing community colleges in the 1980s.

38   Whitney, Frederick Lamson. *The Junior College in*
         America. Colorado Teachers College Education Series, no.
         5. Greeley: Colorado State Teachers College, 1928. 258
         pages.

This publication details the findings of a nationwide study of
junior colleges undertaken in the late 1920s to provide information
for Colorado educators who were considering the development of
state-subsidized two-year institutions. It draws upon a national
survey of colleges, a review of extant state laws on junior colleges,
an examination of junior college standards from twenty-four
states, and an analysis of fifty junior college catalogues. Separate
chapters cover (1) the number and types of existing junior colleges,
(2) the objectives of junior colleges, (3) the legal authorization and
definition of junior colleges, (4) entrance requirements and
curricula, (5) costs and sources of revenue, (6) college standards
and accreditation, and (7) criteria for the organization of new
public junior colleges. The book is useful primarily as an
exhaustive statistical abstract of data available on junior colleges
in the 1920s.

39   Yarrington, Roger (ed.). *Junior Colleges: 50 States/50 Years*. Washington, D.C.: American Association of Junior Colleges, 1969. 306 pages. (ED 034 514)

This collection of essays recounts the historical development of two-year colleges in each of twenty-eight states—Missouri, Maryland, Arizona, Oregon, Florida, North Carolina, Massachusetts, New Jersey, Washington, Michigan, Ohio, Alabama, Texas, Pennsylvania, California, New York, Illinois, Iowa, Hawaii, Minnesota, Montana, Colorado, Kansas, Oklahoma, Virginia, Connecticut, Georgia, and Mississippi—and presents synopses of the history of two-year colleges in each of the remaining twenty-two states. It provides historians of the two-year college with insights into the factors leading to the growth of junior colleges in the 1960s.

Analyses of the Community College Mission

40   Boyer, Ernest L. "The Future of Two-Year Colleges." *International Association of Universities Bulletin*, 1973, *21* (2), 104–108.

The author argues that the traditional transfer and vocational curricula of the community college do not meet emerging educational needs, noting that (1) lifelong learning is replacing the traditional pattern of completing all formal studies before employment; (2) youth are stopping in and out of college rather than completing four consecutive years; and (3) there is an increased questioning of the premise that a baccalaureate degree should be required for employment. He suggests, therefore, that colleges abandon their emphasis on curricula that prepare students only for immediate employment or further study and urges the provision of a "new transition degree programme" that would allow the majority of college-age youth to begin work at an earlier age while at the same time allowing them to continue their studies later on.

★**41**   Carnegie Commission on Higher Education. *The Open-Door Colleges: Policies for Community Colleges. A Special Report and Recommendations by the Carnegie Commission on Higher Education.* New York: McGraw-Hill, 1970. 74 pages.

This publication briefly traces the historical roots of the community college and recommends policies for its future development. It discusses the need for new community colleges and urges that they remain comprehensive rather than specialized. It maintains that graduates should be given full transfer rights, that occupational programs should be upgraded to meet changing manpower needs, that open access should be preserved, and that little or no tuition should be charged. The work emphasizes the need for more occupational guidance, greater commitment to enriching the cultural life of college service districts, and closer college-community relations and discusses optimal institutional size and the need for federal start-up grants for additional colleges. This is a historically important synopsis of the views of the Carnegie commission on the community college role in higher education.

42   Cohen, Arthur M., and Associates. *College Responses to Community Demands: The Community College in Challenging Times.* San Francisco: Jossey-Bass, 1975. 190 pages.

This book examines community college responses to new social forces in the 1970s and discusses the resultant expansion of institutional mission into the area of community development. It reviews institutional adjustments to external pressures emanating from increased state control, collective bargaining, governmental pressures to impose higher tuition, and affirmative action requirements; describes three college responses to shifting enrollment patterns: reductions in force, the expansion of the community services function, and the development of experimental colleges; and reviews research on faculty characteristics, job satisfaction, and performance evaluation. The book concludes that continued expansion of the college mission leads to diminishing returns and to a lack of institutional flexibility.

43   Cohen, Arthur M., and Brawer, Florence B. "The Community College in Search of Identity." *Change*, 1971-72, *3* (8), 55-59.

This article argues that, in the struggle to gain financial support, community colleges have been quick to seize upon every apparent new function and offer to fulfill it. It notes that these functions have included screening out low-ability students from collegiate studies; training students for jobs; and serving a custodial function for youth. The authors maintain that the community college cannot possibly succeed in fulfilling all that has been expected of it and urge community college leaders to identify and focus on specific goals. They suggest that the colleges should center their efforts on improving classroom instruction and leave other tasks to other agencies. The article provides the reader with insights into the dilemma faced by community colleges, which—in the absence of a long tradition in higher education—need to forge an institutional identity.

44   Cohen, Arthur M., and Lombardi, John. "Can the Community Colleges Survive Success?" *Change*, 1979, *11* (8), 24-72.

This article summarizes trends in the 1970s that led to the expansion of career, compensatory, and community education at the expense of the transfer function. The authors argue that the community colleges' power to attract nontraditional students was not matched by the ability to organize and sustain new programs, and they also suggest that the public will be reluctant to support a community college whose leaders imply that its greatest value lies in providing marginally educative pursuits and in acting as an agency for transfer payments. The article provides historians of the community college with a critical analysis of the expansion of the community college mission into areas outside the traditional scope of baccalaureate education.

45 Cosand, Joseph P. "The Community College and Its Critics in the 1980s." *AGB Reports,* 1980, *22* (1), 42-47.

The author outlines curricular and other factors that will affect the institutional integrity of community colleges in the 1980s. He discusses the continuing need to define the college mission and to find a middle ground between those who see the college as a social welfare institution providing an array of community development services and those who would confine the college to traditional academics and examines further the implications of the increased competition for students, the need to maintain high-quality academic programs while at the same time serving nontraditional students, the problems posed by part-time faculty, and the challenge posed by growing numbers of academically deficient students. This article provides a succinct overview of the factors affecting the image of community colleges as quality educational institutions.

46 Cross, K. Patricia. "Community Colleges on the Plateau." *Journal of Higher Education,* 1981, *52* (2), 113-123.

The author assesses the opinions of various college constituencies about the mission and purpose of the community college, basing her findings on a study in which faculty, administrators, trustees, students, and local citizens at eighteen geographically dispersed community colleges were asked to fill out the Community College Goals Inventory, an instrument that requires respondents to rank order institutional goal statements in terms of "what is" and "what should be." She notes that faculty and administrators feel that the goal of increased educational access has been accomplished and that institutional efforts should place greater emphasis on teaching those who are already admitted. She concludes that the egalitarian ideals that coalesced the community college movement of the 1960s are gone and that new ones have yet to be developed.

47   Field Research Corporation. *A Survey of California Public
         Attitudes Toward the California Community Colleges.*
         San Francisco: Field Research Corporation, 1979. 125
         pages. (ED 194 152)

This publication summarizes findings of a public opinion survey
commissioned by the California community colleges during fall
1979 to assess popular attitudes toward the colleges and to
determine the need for adult vocational education. The work
examines (1) the rate of community college attendance among
adults and their reasons for enrolling, (2) opinions concerning the
relative importance of community college functions and the
effectiveness with which the colleges perform those functions, (3)
evaluations of the effectiveness with which colleges use public
funds, (4) ratings of the colleges' instructional quality, (5) the
extent of public support for charging tuition, and (6) the perceived
need for adult vocational education and the extent to which
colleges were seen as appropriate places to provide this education.
It provides an in-depth analysis of how California citizens view
their two-year colleges.

48   Frankel, Joanne. *The Do Everything College.* Topical
         Paper no. 43. Los Angeles: ERIC Clearinghouse for Junior
         Colleges, 1974. 42 pages. (ED 094 814)

This publication documents the growth of the comprehensive
community services role of the community college, tracing the
development of the two-year college from an institution providing
vocational and lower-division academic education to one meeting
the needs of diverse community groups. It describes expanding
community college programs for new students, including the aged,
young children, members of the armed forces, prison inmates, drug
abusers, people living in rural areas, and the physically handicapped, and concludes that community colleges should establish
clear and compatible purposes and not overextend their efforts.

49   Gallup Organization. *A Gallup Study of the Image of and Attitudes Toward America's Community and Junior Colleges, 1981*. Princeton, N.J.: Gallup Organization, 1981. 66 pages. (ED 213 452)

This publication details responses of a nationally representative sample of 1,540 adults who were surveyed in 1981 to determine (1) why adults who were not in school might return to the classroom, (2) the type of school they would be likely to attend and who would pay for their education, (3) opinions concerning the quality and cost of a community college education, and (4) public perceptions of the primary functions of the community college. The responses reveal, among other findings, that 27 percent of the respondents would attend a community college if they were to return to school; 48 percent saw transfer education as the college's primary function, while only 22 percent indicated vocational education, and 10 percent indicated community services. The study provides an indication of the traditional academic role that the public feels community colleges should play.

50   Gillo, Martin W.; Landerholm, Merle; and Goldsmith, David N. "Goals and Educational Trends in Community Colleges." *Journal of Higher Education*, 1974, *45* (7), 491–503.

Reporting the findings of a survey conducted in the state of Washington to compare the perceived goal priorities of faculty, administrators, and board members at the state's twenty-six community colleges, this article reveals that there was close and consistent agreement among the three groups in placing highest emphasis on vocational programming for a limited number of students and favoring a de-emphasizing of academic transfer programs and open-door policies. Using the survey findings, the authors conclude that community colleges are moving toward a specialized identity that is in conflict with the more comprehensive role favored by legislatures, universities, and communities.

51   Kerr, Clark. "Changes and Challenges Ahead for Community Colleges." *Community and Junior College Journal*, 1980, *50* (8), 4–10.

The author comments on the continually changing role of community colleges as they assist American society in numerous ways, including preparing people for higher levels of occupational skills, generating better ideas and scientific research, involving people in intellectual and cultural pursuits, and enhancing the creative and performing arts. He considers that, although the academic function in community colleges may decline, programs in general education, occupational studies, life skills, cultural and recreational activities, counseling, community services, and other noncollegiate areas will increase, and he urges the further development of youth service programs that assist people in making the transition from school to work.

★52   President's Commission on Higher Education. *Higher Education for American Democracy.* Vol. 3: *Organizing Higher Education*. Washington, D.C.: President's Commission on Higher Education, 1947. 74 pages.

This work examines the organizational structure of the American higher education system, noting the respective roles of community colleges, colleges of arts and sciences, teachers' colleges, universities and professional schools, and proprietary institutions. The commission urges a rapid increase in the number of two-year colleges as a means of satisfying increased demand for expanded educational opportunity at the 13th- and 14th-grade levels and suggests that the term *community college* be applied to these institutions and that they should serve a variety of instructional purposes, including transfer, adult, and vocational education. This publication constitutes a milestone in the transformation of two-year institutions from collegiate-oriented junior colleges to comprehensive community colleges.

53   Smith, Milton L., and Beck, John J. "Image of the Community College During the 1970s: A Study of Perceptions." *Community/Junior College Quarterly of Research and Practice*, 1984, *8* (1–4), 233–241.

This article describes the changing image of the community college as perceived by college presidents, public school superintendents, state administrators, professors of community college education, and other educational leaders who participated in a national survey. It examines the respondents' perceptions as they relate to (1) the quality of teaching and the effect of growing numbers of part-time faculty, (2) changes in the composition of the student body, (3) the expansion of community colleges and changes in college administration, (4) changes in the relative importance of various college programs, and (5) factors precipitating change. Among the findings are that the perceived importance of the transfer function has declined, that the student body has become more diverse, and that the need to provide accessible, community-oriented programs was the most frequently mentioned change agent.

★**54**   Vaughan, George B. (ed.). *Questioning the Community College Role*. New Directions for Community Colleges, no. 32. San Francisco: Jossey-Bass, 1980. 117 pages. (ED 195 318)

This sourcebook presents nine articles that question the community college's fulfillment of its educational and social roles, including discussions of the prominent writings of community college critics; the "cooling-out" function; the negative social impacts often attributed to the community college; "elite" community college students who transfer to and graduate from selective senior institutions; the impact of funding patterns on the college mission; the relationship between social stratification and education; and the influence of older, nontraditional students on community colleges. The book serves as a guide to the social analyses of prominent community college observers, including Burton Clark, David Riesman, David Breneman, Susan Nelson, and Steven Zwerling.

55　　Young, Robert B. "The Identity Crisis of the Community
College: A Dilemma in Dialectic." *Journal of Higher
Education,* 1977, *48* (3), 333–342.

This article examines the identity of the community college
through a dialectical analysis of two institutional models: the
egalitarian model and the elitist model. The author describes the
egalitarian college as one that is responsive to the local community, tied to the public secondary education system, and committed
to the goals of accessibility and curricular comprehensiveness,
whereas the elitist model posits a miniature university in which
the transfer curriculum dominates and all but the most able
students are weeded out. He concludes that community colleges
actually fall somewhere between the two models: the open door
provides access for all (an egalitarian function), but only a
homogeneous group of more academically able students persists
through the program.

56　　Zigerell, James J. "The Community College in Search of
an Identity." *Journal of Higher Education,* 1970, *41* (9),
701–712.

Maintaining that the community college is still in the throes of an
identity crisis that affects teachers, students, and the curriculum,
the author of this article points out that part of the crisis stems
from the community college's awkward position in American
education, sandwiched between high school and university. He
identifies the main problem, however, as the commitment of
community colleges to vocational-technical education, a vague
term that refers to a curricular grab bag, and argues that certain
kinds of vocational training should be conducted on the job or
should be carried out by other agencies and that general or liberal
education should still remain the prime goal of the community
college. He concludes that community colleges should be concerned with careers rather than jobs; that is, with providing a life-
enhancing education through instructional innovations.

3

Students

Two-year colleges are the point of entry for millions of students in higher education. The American Association of Community and Junior Colleges reports that 4,836,819 students were enrolled in two-year college credit programs during fall 1984 and that an additional 3,723,629 students enrolled in noncredit programs during 1983–84. These students vary greatly in terms of age, ability, aspirations, socioeconomic status, and reasons for attending college. The works cited in this chapter of the bibliography report on student characteristics and abilities (nos. 57–97), student outcomes and achievement (nos. 98–133), enrollment trends and influences (nos. 134–150), minorities and the economically disadvantaged (nos. 151–168), and the special needs of nontraditional students (nos. 169–188).

Student Characteristics and Abilities

Most student research focuses on descriptive analyses of those served by two-year colleges. Of particular note are those studies based on large national or state samples, including:

- Baird, Richards, and Shevel (no. 62), who analyze the college experiences of 4,009 second-year students at a sample of twenty-nine colleges;
- Garbin and Vaughn (no. 74), who profile the characteristics of 5,000 vocational students at sixty institutions;

41

- The Massachusetts State Transfer Articulation Committee (no. 83), which surveyed approximately 15,000 students attending public and private two-year colleges in spring 1972;
- Knoell and others (no. 79), who assessed the backgrounds, characteristics, goals, and outcomes of students at thirty-two California community colleges;
- Lenning and Hanson (no. 81), who drew upon a longitudinal study involving thousands of community college students to examine the differing characteristics of students in four age groups;
- Adams and Roesler (no. 57), who profiled the first-time students entering the Virginia community colleges;
- Nickens (no. 88), who surveyed 4,631 community services students in Florida;
- Templin, Daniel, and Shearon (no. 95), who contrasted the characteristics of North Carolina community college students with the state's population as a whole;
- Alden and Sieferth (no. 58), who assessed the role of race and sex stereotyping in the career decision-making processes of 1,488 Illinois community college students;
- Dennison, Forrester, and Jones (1982; no. 70), who studied 7,997 students in university transfer programs at British Columbia community colleges;
- Morante and others (no. 86), who assessed the basic skill competencies of first-time students in the New Jersey community colleges;
- Sheldon (no. 93), who conducted a longitudinal analysis of 6,500 students entering the California community colleges;
- Dennison, Forrester, and Jones (1983; no. 71), who surveyed 8,500 students entering vocational programs in British Columbia;
- Riley (no. 92), who assessed the liberal arts knowledge of 8,026 students in four urban community college districts; and
- Astin, Green, Korn, and Maier (no. 61), who examined the characteristics and aspirations of first-time, full-time freshmen entering a national sample of two-year colleges.

These studies reveal the wide range of socioeconomic, demographic, and psychological characteristics of two-year college students and the varied educational objectives that students bring with them to the college. Some of them also point up the limitations of using college-inspired definitions to describe the students. For example, Dennison, Forrester, and Jones (no. 70) note the large numbers of students who enroll in transfer programs to pursue a personal, intellectual interest and who have no intention of transferring. Similarly, Riley (no. 92) found that only 27 percent of the students enrolled in transfer courses in four urban community college districts actually intended to transfer; many were enrolled for personal interest or for job-related reasons. As for students enrolled in occupational programs, Sheldon (no. 93) found that only a minority actually intended to complete a certificate or associate degree; some students were enrolled intermittently to upgrade present job skills or to maintain professional licenses. Surveys of student educational intent, then, have made it increasingly obvious that traditional measures of success (for example, degree attainment and transfer) are inappropriate for understanding the behavior of a large percentage of the two-year college clientele.

Student Outcomes and Achievement

College leaders nonetheless recognize that it is imperative to assess student outcomes and the effectiveness of the college in meeting stated or implicit aims. The establishment of a transfer curriculum presupposes the goal of transfer and subsequent baccalaureate degree attainment. Similarly, the occupational curriculum incorporates the goal of student employment in training-related jobs. College mission statements—usually printed in college brochures and catalogues—also imply less tangible goals related to the affective development of students as good citizens and educated persons.

The items cited in the second part of this chapter (nos. 98–133) chronicle the efforts of educational researchers to assess these outcomes. Only one of these works (Alfred, no. 99) focuses on affective outcomes in terms of college impacts on student attitudes and behaviors. Most of the other works utilize follow-up research designs to examine the employment success of former students and the academic success of those students who have transferred to four-year colleges or universities. Of particular note are the large-scale follow-up studies conducted in Florida (nos. 109, 110, 124, 123), Illinois (nos. 101, 102, 103, 113, 114, 118, 119, 122), New Jersey (no. 121), Arizona (no. 128), Maryland (no. 129), North Carolina (no. 100), Oregon (no. 126), and British Columbia (no. 108). These studies are among the largest longitudinal examinations of two-year college students. In one study (no. 114), for example, the Illinois Community College Board assessed—over a four-year period—the objectives, educational experiences, and employment success of 27,663 first-time freshmen who enrolled in occupational programs at the Illinois community colleges during fall 1974.

These follow-up studies, however, vary greatly in terms of methodology and, thus, reliability. Many researchers, for example, survey only graduates (those who have earned an associate degree) and ignore the large number of students who leave college without fulfilling graduation requirements. Low response rates are a particularly pervasive problem, and, in addition, many researchers do not control for student input variables, such as academic ability or prior employment experience. Student follow-up studies, then, must be viewed in light of their considerable limitations, most of which the authors readily admit to.

What can be concluded from these studies? The findings are mixed. Most of the statewide follow-up studies cited above conclude that the community colleges do a good job in preparing students for employment or transfer. Despite the obvious lack of criteria indicating how many community college students *should* transfer or obtain training-related employment, these studies document the fact that large numbers of former students are doing well at the university or on the job. Other researchers are less sanguine. Astin (no. 104) and Clowes and Levin (no. 107) provide evidence that high school graduates who start their baccalaureate education at community colleges have a lower probability of obtaining the bachelor's degree than students who start out at four-year colleges or universities. Wilms and Hansell (no. 132) indicate that the success of vocational students in obtaining training-related employment varies by field of study and that large proportions of students are not successful at all.

Enrollment Trends and Influences

The third section of this chapter presents a selection of the relatively few authors who analyze changing trends and patterns in community college enrollment. Several themes emerge in the studies, including:

- the effect of college accessibility on enrollment (nos. 134, 135, 147);
- the "reverse transfer" phenomenon caused by growing numbers of students transferring from four-year to two-year institutions (nos. 138, 140, 141);
- declining enrollment in transfer programs and an upsurge of enrollments in vocational curricula (nos. 136, 142, 143, 144);
- the tendency of students to "stop out" and "stop in" on an intermittent basis (no. 150); and
- growing student consumerism (nos. 137, 148).

These studies document, among other trends, the growing emphasis of vocationalism in two-year colleges and the growing tendency of students to attend on an intermittent, part-time basis.

Minorities and the Economically Disadvantaged

A large proportion of all minority students in higher education are enrolled in the nation's two-year colleges. Of the works cited in this section of the chapter (nos. 151–168), three are landmark efforts in describing the special needs of these students: (1) Knoell's (no. 157) 1970 national study of black youth; (2) Morrison and Ferrante's (no. 161) survey of special programs for minority and educationally disadvantaged students; and (3) Olivas's (no. 162) exhaustive review of available data on the status of black, Hispanic, Asian, and Native American students. Each provides evidence that the opportunity to participate in higher education through enrollment in a community college—though significant in and of itself—has not greatly reduced educational inequities between the races. Olivas maintains that, because minorities are overrepresented in two-year colleges and because public two-year colleges spend less money per student than senior institutions, the educational system is in fact inequitable. This theme has been taken up more forcefully by several sociologists whose works (listed in Chapter Twelve) posit that the community college helps perpetuate an inequitable class structure. The counterargument, though, is that the community colleges have provided access to many students who might not otherwise have gone to college anywhere.

The Special Needs of Nontraditional Students

The term *nontraditional student* has become a catchall phrase for several groups of students who, like minorities, have been underrepresented at two-year colleges. The literature focusing on such students includes works on elderly students (nos. 177, 183), female students (nos. 179, 180, 186, 187), and adults beyond the traditional college-going age (nos. 175, 182, 184). Some also include foreign students in this category (nos. 169, 172, 176, 178, 185). Most authors stress the need to provide special services that will allow nontraditional students to take full advantage of college offerings. Large-scale efforts, for example, have been undertaken to recruit women in technical vocational programs (such as electronics) that are dominated by men (nos. 180, 181). Few of the authors, however, provide any evidence pertaining to the effectiveness of such efforts.

Sources of Further Information

The researcher looking for further information on community college students should consult the general texts cited in Chapter Two of this bibliography. Those texts providing extensive sections on the two-year college student include Henry (no. 20), Hillway (no. 21), Medsker (no. 25), Blocker, Plummer, and

Richardson (no. 7), Godfrey and Holmstrom (no. 19), Cohen, Brawer, and Lombardi (no. 13), Medsker and Tillery (no. 26), Ogilvie and Raines (no. 29), Monroe (no. 27), Bushnell (no. 10), Palinchak (no. 30), and Cohen and Brawer (no. 12). The bibliographies provided by the authors also serve as excellent sources of further information.

A second resource is, of course, the ERIC data base, which includes a wealth of relevant documents. The researcher turning to ERIC will find, among other items, the following: state and national compilations of statistical data on two-year college students (including enrollment and demographic data); numerous student follow-up studies conducted by individual colleges; and reports describing the efforts of individual colleges to provide for the special needs of nontraditional students. Numerous dissertations have also been written on two-year college students; these can be located through *Dissertation Abstracts International*. Chapter Thirteen provides further information on how to find statistical data, ERIC documents, and dissertations on topics related to two-year college education and administration.

Student Characteristics and Abilities

57 Adams, June J., and Roesler, Elmo D. *A Profile of First-Time Students at Virginia Community Colleges, 1975–76.* Richmond: Virginia State Department of Community Colleges, 1977. 58 pages. (ED 153 694)

This publication provides data on the demographic, socioeconomic, and academic characteristics of the first-time students entering the Virginia community colleges in 1973–74, 1974–75, and 1975–76. Trends noted over the three-year period studied include the growth in the proportion of female students, the increased number of black students, the increased median age of students, the decline in the proportion of students who plan to earn a bachelor's degree, and the increase in the proportion of students who have no degree aspirations at all. The authors point out, however, that these changes are relatively slight and that the overall characteristics of first-time students remained stable. The work is useful as a descriptive analysis of Virginia community college entrants during the mid 1970s.

58   Alden, Elaine F., and Sieferth, Berniece B. "Sex and Race as Career Choice Determinants in the Technologies." *Journal of Studies in Technical Careers,* 1980, *2* (3), 575–588.

This article reports findings of a student survey conducted to assess the role of sex and race stereotyping in the career decision-making process of young adults. It details the responses of 1,488 students at sixteen Illinois community colleges who were asked (1) to indicate the race and sex of acquaintances trained or working in the career field of their choice; (2) to classify each of thirty occupations as appropriate for men, women, or both; and (3) to classify those same occupations as appropriate for whites, minorities, or both. Among the findings is that women and minority respondents shared and supported traditional sex-role and racial occupational biases. The authors call for "a campaign of career information addressed to those persons perceived by students as most influential in the decision-making process . . ." (p. 587).

59   Allen, Kenneth. "Student and Faculty Attitudes." *Library College Journal,* 1970, *3* (4), 28–36.

Please see no. 650 for the full annotation.

★60   American College Testing Program. *The Two-Year College and Its Students: An Empirical Report.* Iowa City, Iowa: American College Testing Program, 1969. 157 pages.

This publication details various research projects conducted by the American College Testing (ACT) Program at two-year colleges, providing information on such institutional characteristics as cultural affluence, technological specialization, age, size, transfer emphasis, and business orientation. It compares two-year college students with four-year college students, finding the former less able in terms of academic potential and prior academic achievement and concluding that occupational education tends to attract students with low aptitude and high family socioeconomic status or with high aptitude and low socioeconomic status. The work reports that ACT scores predict specific course grades at two-year colleges about as well as they do at four-year colleges.

61   Astin, Alexander W.; Green, Kenneth C.; Korn, William S.; and Maier, Mary Jane. *The American Freshman: National Norms for Fall 1984.* Los Angeles: Higher Education Research Institute, University of California, 1984. 178 pages.

The authors detail the findings of a survey of a large national sample of first-time, full-time freshmen enrolled in colleges and universities during fall 1984. The study compares two-year college respondents with respondents from other types of institutions in terms of demographic and socioeconomic characteristics, high school background, educational and career objectives, reasons for selecting the college in which enrolled, probable college major, sources of financial support, and political and social attitudes. It provides one of the few sources of comparative data analyzing the differences between two-year and four-year college students. (Note: this survey has been conducted and published annually since 1966.)

62   Baird, Leonard L.; Richards, James M., Jr.; and Shevel, Linda R. "A Description of Graduates of Two-Year Colleges." *ACT Research Reports* no. 28. Iowa City, Iowa: American College Testing Program, 1969. 28 pages.

This article reports findings of a survey of 4,009 students who were completing their second year of study at a national sample of twenty-nine two-year colleges, including information on students' backgrounds, their purposes in attending college, their evaluations of teachers, their participation in campus extracurricular life, their future plans, their satisfaction with the college experience, methods used by students to finance their education, the amount of commuting done by students, and their allocation of time. It notes the small number of students who transfer and argues that two-year college practitioners should encourage students to think more realistically about their future.

63   Brawer, Florence B. *New Perspectives on Personality Development in College Students.* San Francisco: Jossey-Bass, 1973. 232 pages.

The author argues that college students need to be understood as individuals with complex personalities and not simply categorized on the basis of traditional intelligence and academic achievement measures. She utilizes data gathered in a survey of 1,876 freshmen at three community colleges to study students on the basis of "functional potential," a psychological construct "which describes the degree to which a person is able to tolerate ambiguity, delay gratification, exhibit adaptive flexibility, demonstrate goal directedness, relate to self and others, and have a clear sense of personal identity" (p. 34). She finds that measures of "functional potential" are not related to such common characterizations of students as ethnic background or marital status and examines the implications of the study findings for the conceptualization of student development at the community college.

64   Brue, Eldon J.; Engen, Harold B.; and Maxey, E. James. *How Do Community College Transfer and Occupational Students Differ?* Iowa City, Iowa: Research and Development Division, American College Testing Program, 1971. 31 pages. (ED 049 723)

This publication examines the personality differences between students enrolled in transfer and those enrolled in vocational curricula at three Iowa two-year colleges during spring 1968. Utilizing data from several personality inventories, the authors assess differences in such areas as vocational preference, academic aptitude, educational aspirations, interpersonal competence, and self-ratings of ability on various skills. Among their findings is that, while there were many differences between male students in occupational and transfer programs, female students in the two curriculum groups were very much alike. The work includes little information on the validity of the tests used but provides at least some insight into the personality differences of a sample of vocational and transfer students.

65 Cohen, Arthur M., and Brawer, Florence B. "Chapter Six: Instruction: Old Methods and New Media." In Arthur M. Cohen and Florence B. Brawer, *The American Community College*. San Francisco: Jossey-Bass, 1982, pp. 147–168.

For an annotation of the work in its entirety, please see no. 12.

66 Cohen, Arthur M., and Brawer, Florence B. "Chapter Two: Students: Greater Numbers, More Diversity, Varied Purposes." In Arthur M. Cohen and Florence B. Brawer, *The American Community College*. San Francisco: Jossey-Bass, 1982, pp. 29–65.

For an annotation of the work in its entirety, please see no. 12.

67 Cohen, Arthur M., and Brawer, Florence B. (eds.). *The Humanities in Two-Year Colleges: A Review of the Students*. Los Angeles: Center for the Study of Community Colleges and ERIC Clearinghouse for Junior Colleges, 1975. 64 pages. (ED 108 727)

Drawing upon an extensive review of the literature to provide a description of students in humanities courses at two-year colleges, the authors stress the great variety of students served by two-year colleges and assess the impact of eight types of community college students on humanities programming: (1) students who intend to transfer; (2) terminal students, who do not intend to go beyond two years of postsecondary study; (3) pragmatic students, who choose their colleges for practical reasons, such as closeness to home, low cost, and the types of courses available; (4) honors students; (5) minority students; (6) adult students; (7) senior citizens; and (8) working and married students. They illustrate how the diversity of

the student body places special demands on humanities curricula
at two-year colleges.

68   Cohen, Arthur M.; Brawer, Florence B.; and Lombardi,
         John. "Chapter Five: The Students in Review" and
         "Chapter Six: Studying the Students." In Arthur M.
         Cohen, Florence B. Brawer, and John Lombardi, *A
         Constant Variable*. San Francisco: Jossey-Bass, 1971, pp.
         63–98.

For an annotation of the work in its entirety, please see no. 13.

69   Cross, K. Patricia. *The Junior College Student: A Research
         Description*. Princeton, N.J.: Educational Testing Service,
         1968. 56 pages.

The author draws upon a number of research studies conducted in
the mid 1960s to profile the characteristics of the junior college
student and establish hypotheses for further research, utilizing
these studies to summarize what is known and unknown about the
academic characteristics of students, their socioeconomic backgrounds, their self-concepts, their interests and personality traits,
their reasons for attending college, and their educational and
occupational aspirations. She makes several comparisons between
junior college students and their counterparts at four-year colleges
and universities. This work serves primarily as an interpretive
summary of the student data collected in large-scale national
studies conducted during the 1960s.

70   Dennison, John D.; Forrester, Glen; and Jones, Gordon.
         "A Study of Students from Academic Programs in British
         Columbia's Community Colleges." *Canadian Journal of
         Higher Education*, 1982, *12* (1), 29–41.

This article summarizes the results of a survey of 7,997 students
who enrolled in university transfer programs at British Columbia
community colleges but did not continue their study at a university. The authors review findings (based on a 56 percent response
rate) as to original reasons for enrolling in the academic program,

factors in the choice of a community college over other institutions, reasons for not transferring to a university, employment status while enrolled, and opinions concerning the college experience and quality of teaching provided. They note that many adults pursue academic courses for personal interest only, that the teaching reputation of the colleges attracts only a small percentage of students, and that college attendance is positively related to the existence of a college within the region in which a student lives.

71 Dennison, John D.; Forrester, Glen C.; and Jones, Gordon. "An Analysis of Students Enrolling in Career Technical Programs in the Colleges and Institutes of British Columbia." *Canadian Vocational Journal*, 1983, *18* (4), 24–27.

Reporting the findings of a survey of 8,500 students who entered vocational programs at British Columbia postsecondary institutions in fall 1981, the authors outline the demographic characteristics of the students, their educational and employment backgrounds, their objectives in enrolling, and their future plans. They note that the survey is only the first phase of a major longitudinal study that will monitor the performance of the students from the time of their enrollment until they have been actively employed for a period of two years after graduation. This constitutes one of the most comprehensive longitudinal analyses of postsecondary vocational students.

72 Faulkner, Gary L.; Garbin, Albeno P.; Wimberley, Ronald C.; and Vaughn, Derrald. "Socioeconomic Status and Prestige of Vocational Occupations Among Junior College Students." *Journal of Industrial Teacher Education*, 1976, *13* (4), 80–83.

This article surveys vocational-technical students from sixty two-year colleges throughout the nation to assess student perceptions of the prestige of the jobs for which they are being trained. Drawing upon responses from 5,170 students, the authors note that those from lower socioeconomic backgrounds tend to attribute more prestige to the jobs for which occupational training is provided than do students from middle- and upper-status backgrounds. They argue, therefore, that mobility into more prestigious occupations is more problematical for youths who have been socialized in lower-status families.

73 Friedlander, Jack. *Student and Faculty Ratings of Academic Abilities of Community College Students.* Los Angeles: Center for the Study of Community Colleges, 1981. 14 pages. (ED 202 510)

The author examines student academic abilities as perceived by a sample of instructors and students at a large urban multicampus district. He details the instructors' perceptions of their students' ability or inability to perform a series of fourteen skills, the students' ratings of their confidence in those skills, and the degree of correspondence between student and instructor ratings. Among his conclusions is that there is a consensus among students and their instructors "that a high percentage of students . . . have some difficulty in performing activities that require reading, writing, speaking, solving problems . . . , understanding science, identifying biases in research reports, and engaging in independent inquiry." He suggests that the existing practice of allowing students to enter and complete courses without first having to demonstrate mastery of basic skills should be discontinued.

74 Garbin, Albeno P., and Vaughn, Derrald. *Community-Junior College Students Enrolled in Occupational Programs: Selected Characteristics, Experiences, and Perceptions. Final Report.* Columbus: Center for Vocational and Technical Education, Ohio State University, 1971. 280 pages. (ED 057 196)

This descriptive analysis of approximately 5,000 community college vocational students from sixty separate institutions across the United States draws upon responses to a survey administered in 1968 to profile the students in terms of demographic and socioeconomic characteristics, self-esteem and success orientation, high school background and grades, parental interest and influence, immediate post–high school experiences, factors influencing college and program enrollment, and opinions concerning the adequacy of the college program. It includes comparative break-downs of data by sex, race, program of study, and other variables, providing a rare insight into the characteristics, motivations, and goals of a large national sample of vocational students in the late 1960s.

75 Godfrey, Eleanor P., and Holmstrom, Engin I. *Study of Community Colleges and Vocational-Technical Centers, Phase I.* Washington, D.C.: Bureau of Social Science Research, 1970. 357 pages. (ED 053 718)

Please see no. 19 for the full annotation.

76 Johnson, Alan, and Avila, Don. "Community Colleges: Miniuniversities or Opportunity Centers?" *Community/ Junior College Research Quarterly*, 1977, *1* (2), 109–116.

Please see no. 115 for the full annotation.

77 Julian, Augusta A. *Utilizing Telecommunications for Non-Traditional Instruction in the North Carolina Community College System: Project Final Report.* Durham: Durham Technical Institute and North Carolina Consortium for Instructional Telecommunications, 1982. 148 pages. (ED 224 957)

Please see no. 584 for the full annotation.

78 Kintzer, Frederick C., and Wattenbarger, James L. *The Articulation/Transfer Phenomenon: Patterns and Directions.* Horizons Monograph Series. Washington, D.C.: Council of Universities and Colleges, American Association of Community and Junior Colleges; Los Angeles: ERIC Clearinghouse for Junior Colleges, 1985. 80 pages.

Please see no. 932 for the full annotation.

79   Knoell, Dorothy, and others. *Through the Open Door: A Study of Enrollment and Performance in California's Community Colleges.* Report 76-1. Sacramento: California State Postsecondary Education Commission, 1976. 82 pages. (ED 119 752)

This work reports on a landmark study of students at thirty-two California community colleges conducted between 1972 and 1976 in an effort to ascertain educational origins, personal characteristics, goals, patterns of performance and persistence, and activities after leaving the colleges. It shows the heterogeneity of community college students and points out how enrollments grew rapidly during the 1970s as the colleges developed special programs for the educationally and economically disadvantaged, the physically handicapped, women, senior citizens, and displaced-worker students. The study reveals that two-thirds of the California students at the time it was conducted were part-timers who were older than traditional college-age students and who enrolled only intermittently. The authors conclude that continuing education for part-time adult students has become the dominant function in the California system, and they recommend that college policies affecting the award of grades and credit be modified to accommodate part-time students dropping in and out of the institutions according to their particular goals. They also suggest guidelines for better student record keeping.

80   Koos, Leonard V. *The Community College Student.* Gainesville: University of Florida Press, 1970. 580 pages.

Synthesizing several hundred studies dating from the 1920s on junior college and university students and on adolescents in general, the author presents data on the physical, mental, personal, and social development of adolescents, their sexual and dating behavior, and occupational and recreational interests. He discusses aptitude, social and personal characteristics, and attitudes and interests of college students, presents implications for the curriculum and for college student personnel services, and shows how colleges can enhance personal development in students through an increased emphasis on student activities. Chapter summaries provide useful synopses of findings from numerous studies of college students.

81   Lenning, Oscar T., and Hanson, Gary R. "Adult Students at Two-Year Colleges: A Longitudinal Study." *Community/Junior College Research Quarterly,* 1977, *1* (3), 271–287.

This article draws upon data collected by the American College Testing Program in a longitudinal study of community college students to assess the differing characteristics and needs of students in four age groups: nineteen or younger, twenty to twenty-four, twenty-five to thirty-nine, and forty or older. It summarizes findings from three surveys conducted in the longitudinal study: (1) the base-year survey of 17,137 students who entered a national sample of two-year colleges in 1970, (2) a survey of 7,933 of those students two years after initial enrollment, and (3) a survey of 2,594 of the participating students conducted in spring 1975. Differences were found at each stage between younger and older respondents in terms of abilities, achievement, motivation, self-concept, goals, values orientation, out-of-class activities, expressed need for help, and other variables.

82   London, Howard B. *The Culture of a Community College.* New York: Praeger, 1978. 181 pages.

Please see no. 970 for the full annotation.

83   Massachusetts State Transfer Articulation Committee. *Study of Massachusetts Two-Year College Students: Implications for Massachusetts Four-Year Colleges and Universities.* Amherst: Massachusetts State Transfer Articulation Committee, 1972. 43 pages. (ED 068 081)

This survey of approximately 15,000 students attending public and private junior colleges in Massachusetts during spring 1972 assesses the students' demographic characteristics, aspirations, reasons for attending college, living arrangements, plans for transfer, financial aid requirements, needs for vocational counseling, and major fields of study. Among the findings are that only 25 percent of the respondents indicated that they did not plan to transfer and that the state's four-year colleges should be prepared to accept growing numbers of transfer students. The work is useful for understanding the characteristics and educational aspirations of Massachusetts junior college students in the early 1970s.

84   Medsker, Leland L. "Chapter Two: The Junior College Student." In Leland L. Medsker, *The Junior College: Progress and Prospect.* New York: McGraw-Hill, 1960, pp. 29–50.

For an annotation of the work in its entirety, please see no. 25.

85   Monroe, Charles R. "Chapter Ten: Students." In Charles R. Monroe, *Profile of the Community College: A Handbook.* San Francisco: Jossey-Bass, 1972, pp. 181–206.

For an annotation of the work in its entirety, please see no. 27.

86   Morante, Edward A., and others. *Report to the Board of Higher Education on Results of the New Jersey College Basic Skills Placement Testing and Recommendations on Instruction and Curriculum, May 20, 1982–September 23, 1982.* Trenton: New Jersey Basic Skills Council, 1982. 54 pages. (ED 232 716)

This report summarizes composite scores earned by the 51,135 New Jersey college students who took the New Jersey College Basic Skills Placement Test in 1982. It compares data for four groups of students: those at public two-year colleges, those at New Jersey state colleges, those at Rutgers University, and those at the New Jersey Institute of Technology; within each of these four categories, scores are also compared by sex, enrollment status (full-time/part-time), and year of high school graduation. The report provides insights into how New Jersey community college students compare with students at other higher education institutions in terms of competency in verbal skills, computation, and elementary algebra.

87 Murphy, Peter J. "Factors Affecting an Adult's Attendance at a Community College in the Evening." *Manitoba Journal of Education*, 1973, *8* (2), 66–72.

Drawing upon a survey of attending students, dropouts, and faculty from the evening division of a Canadian community college, the author assesses the factors affecting the attendance and persistence of adult students. Among other findings, he determines that adult students do not have adequate opportunities to discuss learning difficulties and personal problems with faculty. He also notes that insufficient time for study significantly affects the adult student's progress and that attendance is strongly motivated by the desire to learn vocational skills for job advancement. The article provides a useful example of one college's effort to better understand the motivation and problems of evening students.

88 Nickens, John M. "Who Takes Community Service Courses and Why." *Community/Junior College Research Quarterly*, 1977, *2* (1), 11–19.

This study of the demographic characteristics of 4,631 community service students in Florida and their reasons for enrolling in community service courses reports that students have diverse reasons for taking community service courses, ranging from employment-related goals to those dealing with personal interests or hobbies. The author recommends that course objectives be communicated prior to the beginning of the course and that teacher qualifications be examined in some areas of community service programs. He concludes that greater effort should be made to serve all types of citizens in the community, although that may require financial support through fee waivers, financial aid, or state support.

89   Ogilvie, William K., and Raines, Max R. (eds.). "Part Four: The Student Population." In William K. Ogilvie and Max R. Raines (eds.), *Perspectives on the Community Junior College*. New York: Appleton-Century-Crofts, 1971, pp. 175–221.

For an annotation of the work in its entirety, please see no. 29.

90   Ommen, Jerome L.; Brainard, Stephen R.; and Canfield, Albert A. "Learning Preferences of Younger and Older Students." *Community College Frontiers*, 1979, 7 (3), 29–33.

This article compares younger and older students in a suburban community college in terms of course preferences, preferred learning style, and expectancy of success. Drawing upon the findings of a survey in which the Learning Styles Inventory was administered to 1,760 students aged twenty or younger and to 1,064 students who were twenty-five years of age or older, the authors conclude that learning environments for younger students should be structured differently from learning environments for older students.

91   Palinchak, Robert. "Chapter Four: The Student Clientele." In Robert Palinchak, *The Evolution of the Community College*. Metuchen, N.J.: Scarecrow Press, 1973, pp. 186–209.

For an annotation of the work in its entirety, please see no. 30.

92   Riley, Michelle. *The Community College General Academic Assessment: Combined Districts, 1983–84*. Los Angeles: Center for the Study of Community Colleges, 1984. 59 pages. (ED 246 959)

This publication examines the liberal arts knowledge of a large sample of urban community college students ($N = 8,026$) as revealed in their scores on the General Academic Assessment, an instrument specially designed to assess student competency in five areas: the humanities, sciences, social sciences, mathematics, and

English usage. It details mean scores in each area and presents tabular breakdowns of these means by age, number of college units completed, location of the high school from which the student graduated, highest degree held, anticipated date of receiving the associate degree, reason for attending college, ethnicity, native language, and self-ratings of academic ability. It provides insights into what students know about the liberal arts and how this knowledge varies with differing personal backgrounds.

★93   Sheldon, M. Stephen. *Statewide Longitudinal Study: Report on Academic Year 1978–81*. Part 5: *Final Report*. Woodland Hills, Calif.: Los Angeles Pierce College, 1982. 268 pages. (ED 217 917)

This report details the methodology and findings of a three-year longitudinal study of a sample of 6,500 students who entered fifteen California community colleges for the first time in fall 1978. It examines the characteristics, enrollment patterns, and goal achievement of different prototypes of students falling under three broad categories: (1) those who assumed that they would eventually transfer, (2) those who wanted to find new employment or improve their job skills, and (3) those who had enrolled to fulfill a personal interest. It provides valuable insights into the ways that standard categorizations of students belie actual student intent, noting, for example, that many so-called vocational students actually plan to attain a baccalaureate degree.

94   Stones, Ivan D.; Beckmann, Milton W.; and Stephens, Larry J. "Factors Influencing Mathematical Competencies in Two-Year College Students." *Community/Junior College Research Quarterly*, 1980, 5 (1), 31–36.

Utilizing an in-class survey of 338 students in precalculus courses at six community colleges, this article examines the relationship of competency in mathematics with four variables: sex of student, high school size, high school mathematics background, and attitude of the student toward mathematics. The authors determine that the students' sex or high school class size had no relationship to measured mathematics competency but that competency was significantly related to the number and type of courses taken in high school and to the personal attitudes of students toward mathematics. They provide evidence contradicting other research indicating that female students are more likely to be math anxious than male students.

95 Templin, Robert T.; Daniel, David E.; and Shearon, Ronald W. "Are Community Colleges Truly the 'People's College'?" *Community College Review*, 1977, *4* (4), 7–14.

This article examines the demographic and socioeconomic characteristics of a sample of 10,174 North Carolina community college students to determine whether the colleges are serving a representative cross section of the population at large. Comparing the student sample with the population of North Carolina as a whole in terms of age, sex, race, prior educational attainment, and income, the authors note that credit programs include disproportionately large numbers of younger college-age males and that noncredit programs include disproportionately large numbers of affluent females. They also find that the elderly and those with little formal education are underrepresented in both types of programs. The article provides useful insights into what segments of the general public are served by the community college.

96 Thornton, James W. "Chapter Eleven: The Community College Student." In James W. Thornton, *The Community Junior College*. New York: Wiley, 1972, pp. 145–156.

For an annotation of the work in its entirety, please see no. 34.

97 Warren, Jonathan R. "Chapter Three: The Changing Characteristics of Community College Students." In William L. Deegan, Dale Tillery, and Associates, *Renewing the American Community College: Priorities and Strategies for Effective Leadership*. San Francisco: Jossey-Bass, 1985, pp. 53–79.

For an annotation of the work in its entirety, please see no. 14.

Student Outcomes and Achievement

98   Alba, Richard D., and Lavin, David E. "Community
          Colleges and Tracking in Higher Education." *Sociology
          of Education,* 1981, *54* (4), 223–237.

This article compares the academic progress of two student cohorts
entering the City University of New York (CUNY) in 1970: (1)
students who applied to and were accepted at CUNY four-year
institutions and (2) students who applied to a CUNY four-year
institution but who were assigned instead to one of five CUNY
community colleges. It shows that the community college students
generally were less likely to attain the baccalaureate degree, even
when an impressive array of background variables were controlled
for. The authors warn, however, that the effects of attending a two-
year college rather than a four-year institution were modest and
varied from one two-year college to another. They conclude that
community colleges do not seem to function as a separate track in
higher education but that "too little is known about characteristics
of community college environments and their effects on students"
(p. 236).

99   Alfred, Richard L. *Impacts of Community and Junior
          College on Students.* Iowa City, Iowa: American College
          Testing Program; Los Angeles: ERIC Clearinghouse for
          Junior Colleges, 1975. 103 pages. (ED 108 792)

Integrating research and theory in a comprehensive study of
community/junior college impact on student attitudes and
behaviors, the author provides a review of the literature on college
impact, focusing on its relevance to the two-year college, and then
describes an empirical model for the analysis of impact in the
community/junior college. He isolates and identifies key variables
that account for impact in the community colleges, as well as
alternative strategies for maximizing impact, and finds that
community colleges have only minimal impact on students,
because student and institutional value orientations are often
nonintersecting and sometimes even conflicting. The work
provides a theoretical framework and specific guidelines for

educators interested in maximizing the positive impact of college programs.

100 Allred, Marcus D., and Wingfield, Julian C., Jr. *Follow-Up Study of 1979–80 Students: North Carolina Community College System.* Raleigh: Division of Planning and Research Services, North Carolina State Department of Community Colleges, 1982. 40 pages. (ED 217 924)

This publication reports findings of a follow-up survey conducted in 1981 to assess the employment and educational status of 53,045 occupational curriculum students who left the North Carolina community colleges in 1979–80, drawing upon responses from 46.1 percent of the former students to examine their opinions concerning (1) the degree to which their educational objectives had been met, (2) reasons for leaving the college, (3) current educational activities or plans for continuing education, (4) current job and relationship of employment to training, and (5) the usefulness and quality of the training provided at the community college. The report details findings for graduates, early leavers, and dropouts, thus providing insights into the comparative success of students who had not earned a degree or certificate.

101 Anderson, Ernest F. *Three-Year Comparison of Transfer and Native Student Progress at the University of Illinois at Urbana-Champaign, Fall, 1973 Group.* Research Memorandum 77-9. Urbana: Office of School and College Relations, University of Illinois, 1977. 63 pages. (ED 149 820)

This publication details findings of a study conducted at the end of spring 1976 to compare the academic progress and success of three groups of students at the University of Illinois: (1) students who transferred from community colleges in fall 1973; (2) students who had transferred to the university from a four-year institution; and (3) "native" university students, including all 1973 fall-term continuing juniors who had begun their baccalaureate work at the university. It compares the three groups of students on a semester-by-semester basis in terms of attrition, grade-point average, academic standing, and graduation rates. This work is useful as a descriptive analysis of the academic achievement of a large cohort of community college transfers, although study limitations preclude "inferences concerning the independent effects of type of institution attended on academic achievement" (p. 3).

102 Anderson, Ernest F., and Beers, Philip G. *Two-Year Comparison of Transfer and Native Student Progress at the University of Illinois at Urbana-Champaign: Fall, 1977 Group*. Research Memorandum 80-6. Urbana: Office of School and College Relations, University of Illinois, 1980. 89 pages. (ED 203 955)

This publication details the findings of a two-year longitudinal study undertaken at the University of Illinois to compare the academic progress of three student groups: (1) 786 students who transferred to the university from Illinois community colleges in fall 1977; (2) 4,220 "native" students who were enrolled at the university as continuing juniors in fall 1977; and (3) 676 students who transferred to the university in fall 1977 from four-year colleges. It provides a semester-by-semester analysis of the grade-point averages, academic status, and retention and graduation rates for each of the three student cohorts and also compares the grades earned by the students during the study period in twelve academic areas. The work serves as a descriptive analysis of the academic progress made by a large cohort of community college transfer students.

103 Anderson, Ernest F., and DeGray, Judith. *Comparison of Transfer and Native Student Progress at the University of Illinois at Urbana-Champaign, Fall, 1973 Group.*Research Memorandum 76-8. Urbana: Office of School and College Relations, University of Illinois, 1976. 45 pages. (ED 128 062)

This publication compares the academic progress of three categories of students enrolled at the University of Illinois: (1) "native" students who had begun their baccalaureate studies at the university, (2) students who had transferred to the university from another four-year institution, and (3) students who had transferred to the university from a junior college. It examines several indices of academic progress, including university grade-point average and persistence two years after transfer, grade-point averages earned in twelve subject areas during the 1973–74 and 1974–75 academic years, and the comparison of pretransfer with posttransfer grades. The authors conclude that two-thirds of the junior college transfers are successful at the university but that they have lower achievement rates than four-year transfers or native students.

104 Astin, Alexander W. *Four Critical Years: Effects of College on Beliefs, Attitudes, and Knowledge.* San Francisco: Jossey-Bass, 1977. 293 pages.

The author utilizes longitudinal data collected by the Cooperative Institutional Research Program to examine the effects of college on student beliefs and behavior. He examines findings as they relate to college impacts on attitudes, beliefs, and self-concept; academic achievement and educational attainment; and career development. He also examines behavior changes over the college years, student satisfaction with the college environment, and the permanence of college effects. Among his conclusions is that community colleges may not serve the best interests of students who begin their baccalaureate education directly out of high school, because their chances of attaining the baccalaureate degree are diminished by attending a two-year rather than a four-year institution. This book thus presents one of the most challenging criticisms of the community college transfer function.

105 Baird, Leonard L. (ed.). *Assessing Student Academic and Social Progress.* New Directions for Community Colleges, no. 18. San Francisco: Jossey-Bass, 1977. 118 pages. (ED 140 900)

This sourcebook, offering six essays examining techniques used to assess student progress, presents a taxonomy of student characteristics that potentially can be changed by college instruction and then discusses (1) a model of student learning that can be applied to decisions in admissions, selection, placement, further education, and program modification; (2) assessment measures that predict the academic success of community college students who transfer; (3) assessment of the impact of vocational programs; and (4) college impact on social mobility. The work demonstrates that assessment of student progress can improve guidance, counseling, and community college planning and administration.

106 Clark, Burton R. "The 'Cooling-Out' Function in Higher Education." *American Journal of Sociology,* 1960, *65* (6), 569–576.

Please see no. 965 for the full annotation.

107 Clowes, Darrel A., and Levin, Bernard H. "How Do Two Year Colleges Serve Recent High School Graduates?" *Community College Review,* 1980, 7 (3), 24–35.

The authors utilize data collected in the National Longitudinal Study of the High School Class of 1972 to examine (1) the differences between high school graduates who attend two-year colleges and those who attend four-year colleges and (2) the differences in achievement rates between those starting out at a two-year college and those starting out at a four-year college. Among other findings, they note that, while two-year colleges are effective in meeting the needs of students who aspire to a two-year degree, they are less effective in helping students who want to earn a bachelor's degree.

108 Dennison, John D.; Jones, Gordon; and Forrester, Glen C. *A Longitudinal Follow-Up Survey of Students from Career/Technical Programs in British Columbia Community Colleges and Institutions: Summary Report.* Vancouver, B.C.: B.C. Research, 1983. 34 pages. (ED 238 473)

This publication summarizes the findings of a follow-up study of 9,941 former full- and part-time students who had been enrolled in vocational programs at British Columbia two-year colleges but who did not re-enroll in fall 1982. Utilizing responses from 48 percent of the former students, it analyzes their reasons for attending college, their reasons for not completing graduation requirements (if applicable), their current employment and/or educational activities, their satisfaction with various aspects of the college experience, and their plans for further education. The work provides insights into the motivations of two-year college vocational students, although the data are rendered questionable by a low response rate (a characteristic problem of most vocational follow-up studies).

109 Florida Community Junior College Inter-institutional Research Council. *Where Are They Now? A Follow-Up Study of First Time in College Freshmen in Florida's Community Junior Colleges in Fall 1966.* N.p.: Florida Community Junior College Inter-institutional Research Council, 1969. 58 pages. (ED 035 396)

This publication details the findings of a survey conducted in 1969 to assess the educational progress and opinions of those individuals who entered the Florida community colleges as first-time freshmen in fall 1966. Utilizing responses from a stratified random sample of the students, it profiles the average respondent in terms of current residence, length of time between high school graduation and junior college matriculation, educational achievement, and opinions concerning the value of the junior college experience. Among the findings is that the majority of students in the sample had not received an associate degree or transferred to a senior institution in the time period covered. The study concludes that, while these students had not met the traditional measures of educational success, further research is needed to determine whether the colleges are assisting students in other, less tangible ways.

★110 Florida Department of Education. *Articulation.* Tallahasse, Fla.: Division of Community Colleges, Department of Education, 1975. 61 pages. (ED 116 721)

This work provides information on the characteristics and academic progress of 26,742 students who transferred from a

Note: N.p., "no place," is used when the publisher's location is not specified in the work.

Florida community college and were enrolled in one of the universities of the Florida State University System during fall 1973. Included are data on (1) personal characteristics, such as sex, race, age, year of university entrance, and number of credit hours transferred, (2) the university grade-point averages of the transfer students, and (3) the relationship between Florida Twelfth Grade Test scores earned by the transfer students and their university grade-point averages. Among the findings is that there was no relationship between the students' Twelfth Grade Test scores and their academic success at the university. The study suggests, therefore, that junior college students who have earned the associate degree should be admitted to the university without regard to earlier test scores.

111 Francis, John B., and Jones, Griffith, III. *Education (—?—) Employment: Comprehensive Follow-Up Study of Two-Year College Graduates in New York State, Phase II.* Buffalo: Department of Higher Education, State University of New York, 1976. 101 pages. (ED 156 273)

This publication assesses the effectiveness of vocational education in New York State's public two-year colleges through a follow-up survey of 1970–71 and 1973–74 graduates, examining (1) the success of graduates in job placement or university transfer; (2) salary and job-mobility patterns; (3) graduates' opinions of the training they received while at college; (4) employers' attitudes concerning graduates' training and work performance; and (5) graduates' use of college placement offices. It also provides a literature review covering college placement services, the organization and staffing of the placement function, and follow-up study methodologies. The work provides the reader with insights into the difficulties associated with vocational follow-up research and into one state's efforts to overcome those difficulties.

112 Gragg, William L., and Stroud, Patricia M. "Do Community Colleges Help Salvage Late-Bloomers?" *Community College Review,* 1977, *4* (3), 37–41.

Please see no. 927 for the full annotation.

113 Illinois Community College Board. *A Statewide Follow-Up Study of Fall 1973 Transfer Students from Illinois Public Community Colleges (Phase III Progress Report).* Vol. 2, no. 11. Springfield: Illinois Community College Board, 1977. 54 pages. (ED 140 894; available in microfiche only)

This publication details the findings of a study conducted in 1975 to assess the retention and academic performance of 10,145 students who transferred from the Illinois public community colleges in fall 1973 to public and private four-year colleges and universities in the state. Among the findings is that 77.5 percent of the transfer students either graduated or were enrolled in good standing as of the end of spring 1975. The work also points out that the students' grade-point average at the end of two years after transfer was the same as the grade-point average earned by the students at the community college level prior to transfer. This study is useful as a quantitative analysis of the semester-by-semester achievement and retention of a large statewide cohort of community college transfers.

114 Illinois Community College Board. *Illinois Public Community Colleges Statewide Occupational Student Follow-Up Study: Final Report of a Three Year Longitudinal Study of Fall 1974 New Students Enrolled in Occupational Programs.* Springfield: Illinois Community College Board, 1979. 72 pages. (ED 169 958)

This publication details the findings of a four-year longitudinal study conducted to examine the objectives, educational experiences, and employment success of 27,663 first-time freshmen who enrolled in occupational programs at the Illinois community colleges during fall 1974. It summarizes data pertaining to the reasons students enrolled in occupational programs, the extent to which former occupational students achieved their objectives, the enrollment patterns of occupational students, and the educational and employment status of former students. Among the findings are that only 56 percent of the students matriculated with the intent of preparing for employment in new career areas and that many enrolled with objectives that could be met by completing one or two courses. The study is useful primarily as an illustration of the diverse goals and enrollment patterns of vocational students.

115 Johnson, Alan, and Avila, Don. "Community Colleges: Miniuniversities or Opportunity Centers?" *Community/ Junior College Research Quarterly,* 1977, *1* (2), 109–116.

This article compares the academic success of students enrolled in two types of community colleges: (1) "miniuniversities," those with traditional, punitive grading systems and academic probation policies, and (2) "opportunity centers," those with pass/no-pass grading systems. The authors trace the academic progress of first-time, full-time students who enrolled in the transfer curricula at four community colleges, two classified as "miniuniversities" and two as "opportunity centers." They note that a larger percentage of "opportunity center" students (52 percent) transferred to senior institutions than did "miniuniversity" students (25 percent). They also find that the grade-point averages of the "opportunity center" transfers were higher than those of the "miniuniversity" students. They conclude that the "weeding out" process of the "miniuniversity" does not result in a more highly able cohort of community college transfers.

116 Kastner, Harold H., Jr. "Instructional Accountability and the Systems Approach." *Community College Review,* 1974, *2* (1), 35–41.

Please see no. 434 for the full annotation.

★**117** Knoell, Dorothy M., and Medsker, Leland L. *From Junior to Senior Colleges: A National Study of the Transfer Student.* Washington, D.C.: American Council on Education, 1965. 102 pages.

This work reports the results of a national study of the achievement of transfer students, focusing on degree attainment, outcomes for dropouts who enrolled elsewhere, grade-point average, and comparisons with native student populations. The authors discuss the factors affecting transfer student performance, analyze student views on their performance, and review problematical practices involving grades. They also examine state and institutional differences in the performance of transfer students; the curricular, counseling, and economic factors that affect transfer students; and problems in articulation. They conclude that junior colleges have a fine record in preparing students for transfer but suggest areas for improvement. The work serves as an in-depth analysis of the transfer function as it existed in the early 1960s.

118 Lach, Ivan J., and Kohl, Peggy L. *Follow-Up Study of FY 1979 Occupational Non-Graduate Completers.* Springfield: Illinois Community College Board, 1981. 28 pages. (ED 213 453)

The authors present the findings of a study conducted in 1980 to follow up all students who were enrolled in occupational programs at the Illinois community colleges and who completed all of the required skills courses but did not graduate with a degree or certificate. They examine survey responses related to (1) satisfaction with community college services, (2) impact of college attendance on students, (3) degree of success in achieving goals, (4) plans for further education, (5) employment status, (6) job satisfaction and relation of job to college program, and (7) the helpfulness of the college in job placement. The work provides an in-depth analysis of the growing number of students who attend community colleges with no apparent aim of attaining a degree or certificate.

119 Lach, Ivan J.; Kohl, Peggy; and Wellman, Fred. *Follow-Up Study of FY 1978 Occupational Graduates of the Illinois Public Community Colleges.* Springfield: Illinois Community College Board, 1979. 34 pages. (ED 176 823)

The authors detail the findings of a survey conducted in 1979 to follow up the 7,773 students who graduated from occupational programs at the Illinois community colleges in 1978. Utilizing responses from 53 percent of the graduates, they examine (1) their employment status, placement rates, and salaries, (2) job location,

(3) job satisfaction, (4) graduates' evaluation of community colleges, (5) degree of graduates' success in achieving occupational goals, and (6) impact of community college attendance on students. Among other findings, they note that library services, instruction, and veterans' services were rated highly by the graduates, while job placement and career counseling services received the highest percentage of "poor" and "very poor" ratings. The work provides insights into how a large cohort of vocational-program graduates view their community college experience.

120 Medsker, Leland L. "Chapter Five: Performance and Retention of Transfer Students." In Leland L. Medsker, *The Junior College: Progress and Prospect*. New York: McGraw-Hill, 1960, pp. 119–140.

For an annotation of the work in its entirety, please see no. 25.

121 Miller, Howard F.; Janawsky, Robin; and Katz, Adolf. *The Academic Achievement of Two-Year College Graduates in New Jersey Four-Year Colleges*. Research Report 77-2. Trenton: New Jersey State Department of Higher Education, 1977. 19 pages. (ED 143 397)

The authors review the findings of a study undertaken at the end of spring 1975 to assess the academic achievement of 1,523 community college students who transferred to New Jersey senior institutions in fall 1974. They evaluate the transfers' academic performance in four ways: (1) by comparing their pretransfer and posttransfer grade-point averages, (2) by comparing their university grade-point averages with those earned by native students, (3) by determining the percentage of transfers who earned a *C* average or above at the university, and (4) by comparing the number of units attempted by the transfers during spring 1975 with the number of units they actually completed. The study provides insights into the academic performance of community college transfers as a group, although attrition rates are not considered.

122 Moughamian, Henry; Lach, Ivan J.; Kohl, Peggy L.; and
Wellman, Fred L. *A Statewide Follow-Up Study of
Students Who Transfer from Illinois Public Community
Colleges to Illinois Four-Year Colleges and Universities.
Fall 1973 Transfer Students Followed Through Spring
1976.* Springfield: Illinois Community College Board,
1978. 61 pages. (ED 160 146; available in microfiche only)

This publication details the findings of a three-year longitudinal
study conducted to examine the pretransfer characteristics,
mobility, achievement, and persistence of the 10,504 students who
transferred during fall 1973 from Illinois public community
colleges to Illinois four-year colleges and universities. It examines
the tendency of students to transfer to nearby institutions; the
American College Testing Program scores of the students and their
pretransfer grade-point averages; the percentage of students who
transferred with or without an associate degree; and the semester-
by-semester academic progress of the students in terms of academic
standing, attrition rates, graduation rates, and grade-point
averages. The authors conclude that the Illinois community
colleges are successfully performing the transfer function, although several study limitations are noted.

123 Nickens, John. "Community College Dropout Redefined."
College and University, 1976, *51* (3), 322–329.

The author argues that community college dropout rates are
inflated, because attrition studies ignore the educational objectives
of dropouts and their plans to continue their education. He
supports this argument with data from a survey of 976 former
students from fifteen Florida community colleges: 57.7 percent
reported that they had reached their educational goals, and only
1.4 percent indicated that they had not attained their goals and
that they had no further plans to do so. He concludes that it is
wrong to apply the "dropout" label to former students who have
no intention of earning a credential or who leave college with the
intent of returning in the future.

124 Nickens, John. "The Effect of Attendance at Florida Junior Colleges on Final Performance of Baccalaureate Degree Candidates in Selected Majors at the Florida State University." *College and University*, 1970, *45* (3), 281–288.

This article compares the senior-year grade-point averages (GPAs) of two groups of Florida State University (FSU) students who received the baccalaureate degree in 1968: (1) those who had transferred to the university from a Florida junior college and (2) those native students who had started their college program at FSU and had attended no other college. The author determines that, for each of eighteen academic majors, the final academic performance of transfer and native students was not significantly different after adjustments were made for differences in initial ability, as measured by the Florida Twelfth Grade Tests. He concludes that the transfer students in the sample were not at a disadvantage for having attended a junior college, but he notes the limitations of confining the study to students actually attaining the baccalaureate degree.

125 Noeth, Richard J., and Hanson, Gary. "Occupational Programs Do the Job." *Community and Junior College Journal*, 1976, *47* (3), 28–30.

This article reports the results of a survey conducted by the American College Testing Program to assess the success of community college students five years after matriculation. The survey covered a national sample of 2,594 subjects, consisting of (1) males and females who originally enrolled in business and marketing, accounting, science, social science, and arts and humanities programs; (2) males who originally enrolled in electrical engineering technology and auto mechanics programs; and (3) females who originally enrolled in nursing programs. The article assesses the occupational status of the respondents five years after initially enrolling, the relationship of the respondents' jobs to their programs of study, and the respondents' attitudes toward their experiences at the two-year college. The authors conclude that most were employed in training-related jobs and felt that the college experience had a positive impact on their lives.

126 Oregon State Department of Education. *Follow-Up of 1980 Community College Vocational Program Graduates and Early Leavers and Their Employers.* Salem: Division of Vocational Education, Oregon State Department of Education, 1982. 33 pages. (ED 216 749)

This report details the findings of a follow-up study conducted in spring 1981 to assess the employment and educational activities of those students who graduated or dropped out from community college vocational programs in Oregon during 1979–80. It examines the job and educational activities of the students, their incomes, and the opinions of their employers concerning their mathematics skills, technical knowledge, work attitudes, work quality, and abilities in reading, writing, and speaking, drawing comparisons by educational status (dropout or graduate), by sex, and by race. The report provides the reader with insights into the occupational success of students who drop in and out of community college vocational programs without earning a degree or certificate.

127 Phlegar, Archie G.; Andrew, Loyd D.; and McLaughlin, Gerald W. "Explaining the Academic Performance of Community College Students Who Transfer to a Senior Institution." *Research in Higher Education,* 1981, *15* (2), 99–108.

Using a sample of 361 community college students who transferred to a large state university in 1974 to identify predictors of posttransfer academic performance, the authors find that community college GPA is the best single predictor of university GPA and suggest that students who complete more course requirements prior to transfer earn higher university grades. The article presents predictor equations for students in three curricular majors.

128 Richardson, Richard C., Jr., and Doucette, Donald S. *Persistence, Performance and Degree Achievement of Arizona Community College Transfers in Arizona's Public Universities*. Tempe: Department of Higher Education and Adult Education, College of Education, Arizona State University, 1980. 140 pages. (ED 197 785)

This report compares the academic persistence and degree attainment of three groups of students at Arizona universities: (1) students who transferred into the university after completing two years at a community college, (2) students who transferred into the university after completing one year at a community college, and (3) native university students. Findings are based on a semester-by-semester analysis of grade-point averages, retention rates, college credits earned, and graduation rates. Among other findings, the authors conclude that students who transfer to the university after completing two years at a community college perform as well as native students but that students who transfer after only one year at the community college do not do as well. The work includes a bibliography and in-depth explanations of study methodology and limitations.

129 Tschechtelin, James D., and MacLean, Abby D. *Student Follow-Up of Entrants and Graduates: Maryland Community Colleges*. Annapolis: Maryland State Board for Community Colleges, 1980. 55 pages. (ED 195 312)

This publication assesses the degree to which the Maryland community colleges help students achieve their educational and career goals, drawing upon responses from students who entered college in fall 1974 and from another cohort of students who graduated in 1978 to examine (1) the educational goals of the respondents and the proportion of students who achieved their goals, (2) reasons for college choice, (3) graduation rates of entrants, (4) reasons for discontinuing attendance, (5) employment status and job satisfaction, (6) the impact of community college training on employment success, (7) the transfer rate among those who desired transfer, (8) the relationship of studies pursued by transfers at the junior and senior institutions, and (9) student satisfaction with the community college experience. The publication provides insights into how Maryland students view the helpfulness of their community college education.

130 Vogler, Daniel E., and Asche, F. Marion. "Surveying Employer Satisfaction with Occupational Education: State of the Art." *Journal of Studies in Technical Careers*, 1981, *3* (2), 135–140.

Please see no. 740 for the full annotation.

131 Williams, William G., and Snyder, Fred A. "The Status of Community College Follow-Up: Some Ideas for Improvement." *American Vocational Journal*, 1974, *49* (1), 40, 42–43.

Please see no. 741 for the full annotation.

132 Wilms, Wellford W., and Hansell, Stephen. "The Dubious Promise of Postsecondary Vocational Education: Its Payoff to Dropouts and Graduates in the U.S.A." *International Journal of Educational Development*, 1982, *2*, 42–59.

Please see no. 742 for the full annotation.

133 Wray, Frederick E., and Leischuck, Gerald S. "Predicting Academic Success of Junior College Transfers." *College and University*, 1971, *47* (1), 10–16.

This article describes a study conducted to predict the posttransfer academic success of 474 Alabama junior college students who transferred to the state university between 1966 and 1968. It reveals that junior college GPA was the strongest predictor of posttransfer academic success but warns that more accurate predictive equations could be obtained by using a larger sample of transfers and by subdividing them by program of study and junior college attended.

Enrollment Trends and Influences

134 Anderson, C. Arnold; Bowman, Mary Jean; and Tinto, Vincent. *Where Colleges Are and Who Attends: Effects of Accessibility on College Attendance.* Carnegie Commission on Higher Education Series. New York: McGraw-Hill, 1972. 299 pages.

This work examines the effects of college accessibility upon the enrollment of college-aged youth in institutions of higher education, comparing the college-going rates of high school graduates in communities with differing college-access profiles. The authors conclude that academic ability and family socioeconomic status far outweigh the geographical proximity of colleges in explaining variance in college attendance rates. They suggest further that the expansion of junior college systems will have to be justified on grounds other than the argument that proximity contributes to educational equality for youth. The work constitutes a formidable challenge to the thesis that college proximity increases the participation rates of recent high school graduates in higher education.

135 Andrews, Alice C. "Some Demographic and Geographic Aspects of Community Colleges." *Journal of Geography,* 1974, *73* (2), 10–16.

This article examines the growing number of community colleges from a geographical standpoint. The author provides three maps of the United States, detailing state-by-state differences in average enrollment per public two-year college, the ratios of public two-year college enrollment to total population, and the actual percentage of the population enrolled in public two-year colleges as of October 1972. She points out regional variances in college quality and accessibility, concluding that community college development should be studied on a region-by-region basis.

136 Baron, Robert F. "The Change from Transfer to Career Education at Community Colleges in the 1970s." *Community/Junior College Quarterly of Research and Practice,* 1982, 7 (1), 71–87.

Please see no. 687 for the full annotation.

137 Bender, Louis W. "It Pays to Advertise . . . Truthfully." *Community College Review,* 1975, *3* (2), 32–39.

This article reports a study of college catalogues and other publications, showing how they may tend to mislead prospective students. The author notes that many such documents make false promises regarding the amount of money a student can expect to earn after graduation, the types of careers that he or she may be qualified for, the extent of credit that can be earned, the college's accreditation status, the cost of attending college, the time it takes to obtain a degree or certificate, and institutional quality and environment. He concludes that such misleading claims violate Federal Trade Commission regulations that are applied to proprietary schools and cautions that such regulations could be applied to the public sector if colleges do not reduce the number of misleading statements in their promotional material.

138 Brimm, Jack, and Achilles, C. M. "The Reverse Transfer Student: A Growing Factor in Higher Education." *Research in Higher Education,* 1976, *4* (4), 355–360.

This article surveys a sample of 195 reverse transfer students to assess their perceptions of the institutional characteristics that foster academic success and determine whether students who drop out of a university, enroll in a community college, and then return to the same four-year institution improve in academic performance. Among the findings are that students received higher grades at the two-year colleges than at the four-year institution; that these higher grades were attributed to smaller classes, improved study routines, and a less competitive atmosphere at the two-year college; and that respondents who returned to the four-year college earned higher grades during their second go-around at the senior institution than during their first go-around. The findings suggest that community colleges perform a salvage function for reverse transfers.

139 Hyde, William, and Augenblick, John. *Community College Students, Costs and Finances: A Review of Research Literature.* Denver, Colo.: Education Finance Center, Education Commission of the States, 1980. 121 pages. (ED 192 841)

This publication draws upon a review of the literature and ongoing research to provide a composite profile of the enrollment and financial status of the nation's community colleges. The authors discuss prospective student enrollment behavior and educational needs as determined through needs assessment surveys and econometric models that identify enrollment influences through regression analysis. They also examine (1) reasons for attending a community college as opposed to other institutions of higher education, (2) problems involved in using surveys and models to predict enrollment, (3) available financial aid data and the distribution of financial aid to community college students, (4) criteria for assessing community college financial systems, (5) tuition policies, (6) community service funding patterns, and (7) the impact of tax limitations. The work provides an extensive synthesis of research on enrollment and finance.

140 Kuznik, Anthony E.; Maxey, E. James; and Anderson, Duane D. "Reverse Transfers: A Survey." *Community and Junior College Journal,* 1974, *44* (5), 25–27.

This article reports the results of a survey conducted during 1969–70 of reverse transfer students in all two-year colleges in Iowa. These results indicate that the relatively high tuition rates of four-year institutions were not the primary cause of the reverse transfer phenomenon; the authors suggest that more powerful forces were the academic problems experienced by the students while at the four-year institution, as well as the impersonal nature of the senior colleges. The article also details the future plans of the reverse transfers, pointing out that 95 percent of those enrolled in arts and sciences programs hoped to earn a baccalaureate degree. It is useful in understanding the motivations of those who transfer from a four-year college to a two-year institution.

141 Lee, Robbie. "Reverse Transfer Students." *Community College Review*, 1976, *4* (2), 64–70.

The author reviews the literature on reverse transfer students, noting areas that require further research. She cites studies examining the characteristics of reverse transfer students, the reasons they have for leaving four-year colleges, and the evidence (pro and con) that community colleges "salvage" these students by giving them a second chance to succeed. She concludes that our understanding of reverse transfer is limited, because (1) data have heretofore been gathered from small samples, (2) the definitions of reverse transfers are not consistent, and (3) assumptions concerning the background and aspirations of these students have not been challenged.

142 Lombardi, John. *Riding the Wave of New Enrollments.* Topical Paper no. 50. Los Angeles: ERIC Clearinghouse for Junior Colleges, 1975. 58 pages. (ED 107 326)

This publication analyzes demographic, economic, political, and social causes of community college enrollment trends and examines the effects on enrollment of (1) proximity and low cost, (2) the reclassification of existing institutions to two-year college status, (3) community college usurpation of services formally provided by other institutions, (4) the new majority of part-time students, (5) the drift toward serving *all* persons over seventeen years of age, and (6) strategies to attract and retain students. The author notes the tendency to replace dwindling numbers of traditionally aged college students with older, nontraditional constituencies and discusses the threat that this tendency poses to the educational integrity of the colleges. The work provides a comprehensive analysis of enrollment trends in the mid 1970s.

143 Lombardi, John. *Resurgence of Occupational Education.* Topical Paper no. 65. Los Angeles: ERIC Clearinghouse for Junior Colleges, 1978. 41 pages. (ED 148 418)

Please see no. 703 for the full annotation.

144 Lombardi, John. *The Decline of Transfer Education.* Topical Paper no. 70. Los Angeles: ERIC Clearinghouse for Junior Colleges, 1979. 37 pages. (ED 179 273)

Please see no. 897 for the full annotation.

145 Marks, Joseph L. "Understanding the Dynamics of Change: The Case of the Humanities." *Community College Review*, 1981, *9* (1), 6–11.

Please see no. 899 for the full annotation.

146 Patton, Douglas A., and Carine, Edwin T., Jr. "Changing Patterns in Two-Year College Admissions Offices." *College Board Review*, 1979, (112), 26–29.

This article investigates the status of community college admissions offices in terms of staffing, responsibilities, relationships with other departments, and special problems, drawing upon interviews with administrators at twenty-six colleges, as well as the findings of a survey of staff at sixty-seven additional institutions. Among other observations, the authors note that the responsibilities of admissions officers have increased over the years, although the size of admissions staffs has remained constant; colleges have responded to the dwindling number of traditional college-age students by increasing the recruitment of adults; and administrator concerns about attrition rates are not matched by appropriate concern for attrition research, to which administrators assign a relatively low priority. They argue that community college admissions offices face greater challenges but that many are conducting business as usual and not adequately responding to changing times.

147 Tinto, Vincent. "The Distributive Effects of Public Junior College Availability." *Research in Higher Education,* 1975, *3* (3), 261–274.

This article details a study conducted to determine the effect of the presence of a public junior college within a community on the types of colleges attended by local high school graduates. The author utilizes data gathered on the postsecondary experiences of approximately 8,000 Illinois high school students who graduated in 1966 to compare the college attendance patterns of persons with and without a junior college in their community. He concludes that the local availability of a public junior college serves largely to alter the patterns of college going by substituting local attendance for attendance elsewhere (particularly at four-year colleges) in a manner inversely related to social status. He notes the implications of this trend, including the hypothesis that the establishment of community colleges may further "exacerbate differences between the educational opportunities of persons from different social-status backgrounds" (p. 274).

148 Vaughan, George B.; Elosser, Bonnie; and Flynn, R. Thomas. *Consumerism Comes to the Community College.* Topical Paper no. 55. Los Angeles: ERIC Clearinghouse for Junior Colleges, 1976. 38 pages. (ED 118 205)

The authors review the issues and problems surrounding student consumerism in community colleges, arguing that students are consumers of higher education and that the educational market-place needs to be concerned with fair-practice policies, just as business and industry are. They note the factors that have created consumerism problems at the community college (such as hard-sell recruitment techniques) and present a rationale for committing institutional resources to deal with these problems. They examine college responses to growing student consumerism and present a step-by-step description of the efforts undertaken by Monroe Community College (New York) to write an educational prospectus that answers student concerns such as "Will I find a job if I enroll in a career program?" and "What percentage of entering students actually graduate?"

149 Wattenbarger, James L.; Cage, Bob N.; and Arney, L. H. *The Community Junior College: Target Population, Program Costs and Cost Differentials.* Gainesville: Institute of Higher Education, University of Florida, and National Education Finance Project, 1970. 163 pages. (ED 045 068)

Please see no. 474 for the full annotation.

150 Willet, Lynn H. " 'One-Stop or Stop-Out?' A Five-Year Longitudinal Analysis of Community College Attendance." *Community/Junior College Quarterly of Research and Practice,* 1983, 7 (4), 333–341.

This article examines the attendance flow over a four-year period of a cohort of 3,159 full-time and part-time freshmen at a public community college in the Midwest, noting that at the end of the five-year period, only 13 percent had completed the requirements of a certificate or an associate degree. It also points out that 29 percent were "one-shot" students who attended for one semester only; 50 percent were "stop-out" students who had attended one semester, dropped out during the subsequent term, and then re-enrolled at a later date; and 8 percent were still enrolled at the college. It provides insights into the irregular attendance patterns of community college students.

Minorities and the Economically Disadvantaged

151 Astin, Alexander W. *Minorities in American Higher Education: Recent Trends, Current Prospects, and Recommendations.* San Francisco: Jossey-Bass, 1982. 263 pages.

Drawing upon a variety of data sources to examine the status of blacks, Puerto Ricans, Chicanos, and American Indians in American higher education, this work provides a descriptive analysis of these minority groups in terms of access to higher education, choice of institution, field of study, and degree attainment. It also examines factors that influence the access and educational attainment of minority students, concluding, among other findings, that many minority students are denied equal educational opportunity because they are disproportionately enrolled in community colleges and thus have reduced chances of persisting to the baccalaureate degree. The author suggests that community colleges need to improve their track record in moving students—especially minorities—through the educational pipeline.

152 Beckwith, Miriam M., and Edwards, Sandra J. *Ethnic Minorities in Two-Year Colleges: Report to the Higher Education Research Institute.* Los Angeles: Center for the Study of Community Colleges, 1979. 107 pages. (ED 176 831)

This work reviews research on the participation of minorities in community college education, discussing enrollment patterns, attrition rates, special programs for minorities, the effect of selectivity standards in occupational programs, and barriers to college enrollment in general. It also examines institutional practices that may hinder or encourage minority participation, such as special admissions procedures, differential tuition and fee charges, and evening classes, concluding with an analysis of articulation/transfer issues. The work provides community college officials with a thorough review of the issues surrounding minority access.

153 de los Santos, Alfredo G., Jr.; Montemayor, Joaquin; and Solis, Enrique, Jr. "Chicano Students in Institutions of Higher Education: Access, Attrition, and Achievement." *Aztlan,* 1983, *14* (1), 79–110.

This article provides an analysis of national, state, and institutional data related to the enrollment, retention, and degree completion of Hispanic students in higher education. The authors discuss the comparability and compatibility of data from different sources and summarize data related to the participation of Hispanics in higher education, attrition rates, the reasons for attrition, and degree attainment rates, including both junior college and university statistics. They conclude with recommendations for improved data-collection efforts, including studies that examine enrollment, attrition, and transfer rates of Hispanic students.

154 Ericson, David P., and Robertshaw, Dianne. "Social Justice and the Community College." *Community/Junior College Quarterly of Research and Practice*, 1982, *6* (4), 315-341.

Please see no. 980 for the full annotation.

155 Gilbert, Fontelle (ed.). *Minorities and Community Colleges: Data and Discourse*. Washington, D.C.: American Association of Community and Junior Colleges, 1979. 29 pages. (ED 171 345)

This publication provides six articles describing the accomplishments of community colleges in serving minority populations, including brief essays on the importance of community colleges for blacks, the developmental studies program at El Centro College (Texas), programs for Indian students at Haskell Indian Junior College, the efficacy of community colleges for minorities, the past and future relationship between minorities and the two-year colleges, and the special needs of minorities. It also provides minority enrollment data for 1978 and discusses barriers to minority participation in higher education, including language problems, testing and admissions criteria, finances, and poor academic preparation.

156 Knoell, Dorothy M. *Toward Educational Opportunity for All*. Albany: Office of Executive Dean for Two-Year Colleges, State University of New York, 1966. 234 pages. (ED 011 454)

Please see no. 969 for the full annotation.

157 Knoell, Dorothy M. *People Who Need College: A Report on Students We Have Yet to Serve*. Washington, D.C.: American Association of Junior Colleges, 1970. 204 pages. (ED 041 573)

This publication details the methodology and findings of a national study undertaken by the American Association of Junior Colleges (AAJC) to gain information about black youth who might be recruited by local community colleges. The author examines (1) the high school records, college-going rates, and socioeconomic backgrounds of a large sample of black and white students who graduated from high school in 1968, (2) the scores earned by these students on standardized tests taken while in high school, (3) the outcomes of interviews with approximately 1,000 black high school graduates who did not go on to college, and (4) the scores earned by a sample of black high school graduates on a variety of nontraditional cognitive tests. She summarizes the college-going rates of black versus white high school graduates, the future plans of non-college-goers, and their attitudes toward education. This work represents a landmark effort by the AAJC to better understand potential black students, although only limited implications are drawn between the study findings and college recruitment practices.

158 Levin, Bernard H., and Clowes, Darrel A. "Realization of Educational Aspirations Among Blacks and Whites at Two- and Four-Year Colleges." *Community/Junior College Research Quarterly*, 1980, *4* (2), 185–193.

The authors utilize data collected in the National Longitudinal Study of the High School Class of 1972 to investigate the contribution of two-year colleges to educational equality. They find that (1) low-ability blacks are overrepresented in four-year colleges rather than in two-year institutions; (2) blacks aspiring to the baccalaureate degree are less likely to attain it than are whites, although blacks and whites aspiring to only two years of college are equally successful in meeting their goal; and (3) initial attendance at a two-year college significantly reduces the probability of attaining a baccalaureate degree four years after high school.

Although failing to interrelate the implications of the three findings, they note that the third provides strong evidence in support of Astin's conclusions in *Four Critical Years* (no. 104).

159 Monroe, Charles R. "Chapter Seven: Programs for the Disadvantaged." In Charles R. Monroe, *Profile of the Community College: A Handbook*. San Francisco: Jossey-Bass, 1972, pp. 103–127.

For an annotation of the work in its entirety, please see no. 27.

160 Moore, William, Jr. *Community College Response to the High-Risk Student: A Critical Reappraisal*. Horizons Monograph Series. Los Angeles: ERIC Clearinghouse for Junior Colleges; Washington, D.C.: American Association of Community and Junior Colleges, 1976. 60 pages. (ED 122 873)

This work critically examines the community college response to disadvantaged, high-risk students, arguing that community colleges are not the teaching-oriented, student-centered institutions they claim to be. The author questions the commonly accepted belief that poor achievement can be traced to the social, family, economic, and motivational background of the student; he also questions the extent to which counseling and remedial programs have assisted low-achieving students, concluding that community colleges are actually conventional institutions that value students who are "college material" and do not accommodate the special needs of high-risk students. He calls for further research on the effects of instruction, teacher attitudes, and other institutional factors that impinge on the achievement of nontraditional students.

161 Morrison, James L., and Ferrante, Reynolds. *Compensatory Education in Two-Year Colleges.* Report no. 21. University Park: Center for the Study of Higher Education, Pennsylvania State University, 1973. 60 pages. (ED 078 818)

Please see no. 784 for the full annotation.

★**162** Olivas, Michael A. *The Dilemma of Access: Minorities in Two-Year Colleges.* Washington, D.C.: Howard University Press, 1979. 259 pages.

The author reviews available data on the status of black, Hispanic, Asian, and Native American students in the American school and college system. He traces the progress of minorities through the system, demonstrating that most of those who go on to higher education attend a community college. He takes the position that the educational system is inequitable, because public two-year colleges spend less money per student than senior institutions, and he recommends special federal funding for two-year colleges, better data-collection procedures regarding minority students, a review of state policies that place disproportionately large numbers of minorities in two-year colleges, aggressive affirmative action programs to attract minority faculty to two-year colleges, better transfer policies between two-year and four-year institutions, enhanced academic advising for minority students, and an increased emphasis on basic skills instruction in secondary schools. The work includes numerous data tables and an extensive bibliography.

163 Palola, Ernest G., and Oswald, Arthur R. *Urban Multi-Unit Community Colleges: Adaptation for the '70s.* Berkeley: Center for Research and Development in Higher Education, University of California, 1972. 129 pages. (ED 068 096)

This publication discusses the organization of urban community colleges in multiunit districts and reports the findings of a study conducted to assess the performance of six urban multiunit districts in serving disadvantaged students. The authors analyze four problem areas: increased minority enrollment, faculty ignorance about the plight of educationally disadvantaged ghetto students, traditional budgeting methods that do not meet the special needs of urban campuses, and conflict about the extent of local control over inner-city campuses. They describe the scope of college services for the disadvantaged and analyze the features of successful recruitment and community development programs, concluding that three barriers hinder urban colleges in fulfilling their missions: lack of commitment to developmental education, inadequate financial support, and rigid districtwide organizational structures.

164 Pulliams, Preston. "Black Students Feel Left-Out." *Community College Review*, 1977, *5* (1), 11–15.

The author of this article studies black students in a community college to determine the relationship between their self-concepts and their success in school, finding that failing black students have lower self-concepts than successful black students and suffer from a general lack of orientation to the college. He recommends using the Human Potential Seminar Process, a structured activity designed to aid participants in reaching higher self-regard, as a way of increasing their chances for success. He also recommends the use of black peer counselors and more black staff members at all levels.

165 Southern Regional Education Board. *The Black Community and the Community College: Action Programs for Expanding Opportunity. A Project Report.* Atlanta, Ga.: Institute for Higher Educational Opportunity, Southern Regional Education Board, 1970. 60 pages. (ED 046 380)

This publication briefly describes several efforts undertaken by junior colleges in the South to improve the recruitment of black students and to provide the special support services needed by many black students to succeed. It includes descriptions of recruitment efforts that involve outreach into local high schools and into the community at large and also examines supplementary support services related to precounseling and preparation at the admissions office, compensatory or remedial programs, and counseling and tutorial services, drawing upon these programs to outline guidelines for recruitment and assistance efforts that are designed to expand educational opportunity for blacks. It is useful as a brief analysis of how junior colleges in the South sought to improve services for blacks in the late 1960s.

166 Templin, Robert G., Jr. "Chapter Two: Keeping the Door Open for Disadvantaged Students." In George B. Vaughan and Associates, *Issues for Community College Leaders in a New Era.* San Francisco: Jossey-Bass, 1983, pp. 39–54.

For an annotation of the work in its entirety, please see no. 37.

167 Tschechtelin, James D. *Black and White Students in Maryland Community Colleges.* Annapolis: Maryland State Board for Community Colleges, 1979. 20 pages. (ED 175 513)

This work draws upon a follow-up survey (conducted in 1978) of first-time students who enrolled in the Maryland community colleges during fall 1974 to compare the goals and goal achievement of black and white students. The author notes that considerable differences were found between the characteristics and educational experiences of the two student groups: (1) blacks were more likely to be female, to attend full time, and to be in business and commerce programs; (2) black students completed fewer credits and were less likely to earn the associate degree; and (3) blacks did not achieve their transfer goals as often as whites. He points out, however, that there were no differences between blacks and whites in the area of employment goal achievement. The work serves as a cursory overview of differences between the educational experiences of black and white students in the Maryland community colleges.

168 West, Russell F., and Shearon, Ronald W. "Differences Between Black and White Students in Curriculum Program Status." *Community/Junior College Quarterly of Research and Practice,* 1982, *6* (3), 239–251.

Please see no. 989 for the full annotation.

The Special Needs of Nontraditional Students

169 Breuder, Robert L. *A Statewide Study: Identified Problems of International Students Enrolled in Public Community/ Junior Colleges in Florida.* Tallahassee: Department of Higher Education, Florida State University, 1972. 73 pages. (ED 062 977)

This publication details findings of a survey conducted during fall 1971 to identify the problems experienced by foreign students enrolled in the Florida community colleges and to compare the perceived problems of those students with those of foreign students enrolled in Florida State University. The author summarizes survey data by sex of respondent, by length of time the student had been enrolled (less than twelve months, more than twelve months), and by proficiency in English. He notes, among other findings, that most problems were perceived in the areas of financial aid, English language usage, placement, and admissions. He also determines that the problems perceived by foreign students in the junior colleges were not significantly different from those perceived by undergraduate foreign students in the university setting. The work is useful as a descriptive analysis of the problems faced by foreign students, although few implications for practice are discussed.

170 Chickering, Arthur W. "Adult Development: Implications for Teaching and Learning." *Community Services Catalyst,* 1979, *9* (2), 4–10.

The author urges community colleges to take account of the various developmental stages of their adult students so that a sufficient variety of programs and instructional methods may be employed. He argues that higher education in the past has recognized only a limited array of human abilities, centering on reading, writing, and other verbal skills, and has failed to recognize other types of competencies that must be applied to various social problems, interpersonal relations, and personal development. He suggests that, because students are at different developmental stages, an institution cannot pitch its educational program at a particular stage or limit it to a particular area.

171 Clarke, Johnnie R. *Commitment to the Nontraditional Student.* Topical Paper no. 51. Los Angeles: ERIC Clearinghouse for Junior Colleges, 1975. 18 pages. (ED 107 327)

This publication provides guidelines for developing community college programs that meet the needs of nontraditional students. The author discusses institutional commitment to the nontraditional student and ways to translate that commitment to specific actions in the areas of recruitment and admissions, course registration, counseling, academic planning, and student activities. The work is useful as a step-by-step guide to administrative practices that can make the college more responsive to nontraditional students.

172 College Entrance Examination Board. *The Foreign Student in United States Community and Junior Colleges: A Colloquium Held at Wingspread, Racine, Wisconsin, October 18–20, 1977.* New York: College Entrance Examination Board, 1978. 86 pages.

This work presents a series of essays that examine the impact of foreign students enrolled in community colleges and the efforts that might be undertaken to improve the quality of their educational experiences. It discusses (1) why foreign students attend community colleges and what happens to them in the community college setting, (2) the demographic characteristics of foreign students, and (3) issues related to planning and implementing community college programs for foreign students. It concludes with a public statement dealing with the purpose of international education in community colleges, the role of foreign students in promoting international education, and suggested administrative guidelines for the development of special foreign student programs. It provides useful background information for student personnel administrators facing increased enrollments of foreign students.

173 Cross, K. Patricia. *Beyond the Open Door: New Students to Higher Education.* San Francisco: Jossey-Bass, 1971. 200 pages.

The author draws upon secondary analyses of large-scale student surveys to assess the characteristics and educational needs of "new students," those who fall in the lowest third on tests of academic ability and for whom the school experience has been one of accumulated failure. She compares these students with their more academically able peers on the basis of interests, attitudes toward education, occupational aspirations, and post-school experiences, presenting separate analyses of women and minorities who fit the "new student" profile. She emphasizes that increased access does not ensure academic success and that alternative educational programs need to be established to meet the interests of "new students" and help overcome their fear of academic failure.

174 Cross, K. Patricia. *Accent on Learning: Improving Instruction and Reshaping the Curriculum.* San Francisco: Jossey-Bass, 1976. 291 pages.

Please see no. 563 for the full annotation.

175 Cross, K. Patricia. *Adults as Learners: Increasing Participation and Facilitating Learning.* San Francisco: Jossey-Bass, 1981. 300 pages.

The author draws upon an extensive review of available research to examine the characteristics and motivations of adult learners. Individual chapters discuss (1) the root causes of increased adult participation in education, (2) the arguments of those who see dangers in the growing pressures on adults to participate in education, (3) the characteristics of adult learners, (4) research findings on the motivations for and deterrents to adult learning, and (5) studies about how adults learn. The book also provides an explanatory model "of the motivation behind adult participation in learning activities" (p. xiii) and presents a framework for understanding "the interaction between learners and their environments" (p. xiv). It serves as an easily understood synthesis of research on adult participation in formal learning activities.

176 Davis, James M. "Foreign Students in the 2-Year College." *International Educational and Cultural Exchange*, 1971, 7 (2), 25–32.

The author notes characteristics of the two-year college that pose problems for foreign students and suggests procedures to facilitate their enrollment. He emphasizes that the lower-division, comprehensive curriculum of the community college may not be appropriate for many foreign students but points out that the presence of foreign students on campus enriches the educational experiences of the native students, boosts faculty interest, and enhances the image of the United States abroad. He warns administrators to provide prospective foreign students with accurate information about the community college and briefly outlines suggestions for admissions, orientation, housing, advising, on-campus programming, and other factors that need to be considered in recruiting international students.

177 DeCrow, Roger. *Older Americans: New Uses of Mature Ability*. Washington, D.C.: American Association of Community and Junior Colleges, 1978. 32 pages. (ED 154 859; available in microfiche only)

This work draws upon a national survey of two-year institutions to provide a brief descriptive account of community college programs and services for the elderly. It describes four types of activities: (1) senior employment services that provide career counseling, job placement, and job development; (2) volunteer service programs that recruit, organize, and manage senior volunteers in federally sponsored and community-based activities; (3) occupational and job-skills training; and (4) efforts to overcome age discrimination and other barriers to the employment of seniors. It also provides a seventy-four-item bibliography of materials related to aging and the education of older adults. It provides the reader with insights into how community colleges have gone beyond traditional education programs to provide outreach services for disadvantaged community constituencies.

178 Diener, Thomas. "Foreign Students and U.S. Community Colleges." *Community College Review,* 1980, 7 (4), 58–65.

Please see no. 618 for the full annotation.

179 Dziech, Billie Wright. "Chapter Three: Changing Status of Women." In George B. Vaughan and Associates, *Issues for Community College Leaders in a New Era.* San Francisco: Jossey-Bass, 1983, pp. 55–75.

For an annotation of the work in its entirety, please see no. 37.

180 Eliason, Carol. *Women in Community and Junior Colleges: Report of a Study on Access to Occupational Education.* Washington, D.C.: American Association of Community and Junior Colleges, 1977. 64 pages.

This publication reports findings of a study conducted by members of the American Association of Women in Community and Junior Colleges to determine enrollment patterns of women students in occupational programs. The author examines the types of programs in which women enroll, personal characteristics of the students, and interview information gained from 400 students on anticipated sex discrimination in jobs, previous and concurrent employment experience, and knowledge of available careers, concluding that enhanced recruitment and counseling will be needed if sizable numbers of women are to be attracted to programs that prepare for employment in careers other than female-dominated occupations, such as secretarial, nursing, and child-care work. The work includes a list of exemplary community college programs attracting women into new occupational areas.

181 Eliason, Carol. *Equity Counseling for Community College Women.* Washington, D.C.: American Association of Community and Junior Colleges, 1979. 291 pages. (ED 187 369)

Please see no. 756 for the full annotation.

182 Eliason, N. Carol. *Adult Part-Time Learners in the Eighties.* Washington, D.C.: American Association of Community and Junior Colleges, 1980. 24 pages. (ED 188 715)

The author addresses numerous issues and questions related to the adult part-time student, beginning with a comparison of the demographic characteristics of adults in and out of college and then pointing to several subpopulations that might be better served by the community college (for example, women, the aging, minorities, and blue-collar workers). She considers the educational needs of adult learners and provides insights into the issues of (1) organizational structures, such as internal college services, interinstitutional consortia, educational brokerages, and cooperative agreements; (2) the institutional changes needed to meet the needs of adult populations; (3) methods of delivering services; (4) restructuring of financial aid; (5) funding options and budgeting priorities; and (6) the benefits of continuing education for the adult learner. The work concludes with a 106-item bibliography that is particularly useful as a source of further information.

183 Glickman, Lillian L.; Hersey, Benjamin S.; and Goldenberg, I. Ira. *Community Colleges Respond to Elders: A Sourcebook for Program Development.* Washington, D.C.: National Institute of Education, 1975. 66 pages. (ED 115 332)

This work describes the educational needs of older adults and surveys some of the programs carried out in response to those needs by community colleges. The authors develop an inclusive model of educational program development for elders, with step-by-step directions on how to set up a core curriculum, form alliances, assess needs, select program content, ensure program effectiveness, and secure staffing, financing, and other needed resources, listing federal, state, and other resources on which a community college can draw for assistance in program development. They conclude that community colleges will need to offer a wider spectrum of activities for elders, including programs that prepare people for second careers and provide options for the use of leisure time.

184 Mangano, Joseph A., and Corrado, Thomas J. *Responding to the Needs of Re-entry Adults in Two-Year Colleges.* Albany: Two-Year College Student Development Center, State University of New York, 1979. 18 pages. (ED 180 564)

This publication briefly analyzes issues surrounding the community college role in serving adult re-entry students, focusing on (1) the state of the art in lifelong learning; (2) the characteristics of adult re-entry students in terms of age, objectives, employment backgrounds, sex, educational objectives, and preferences for learning sites and school schedules; (3) the responsiveness of community colleges, through open-door policies, to adult learners; and (4) ways of integrating lifelong learning into the two-year college. It also discusses the findings of a project undertaken to determine the relative importance of selected educational needs to adult re-entry students and to assist two-year colleges in providing programs and support services for these nontraditional students.

185 Matthewson, Douglas E., Jr. *A National Survey of International Students and Programs in Community Junior Colleges in the United States.* Washington, D.C.: Junior College Committee, National Association for Foreign Student Affairs, 1968. 190 pages. (ED 024 362)

The author reviews the findings of a survey conducted in the late 1960s to examine the provisions made by junior colleges for the enrollment and support of foreign students. He draws upon usable responses from 410 (out of 850) institutions to detail (1) general information, such as the number of colleges that have foreign students and the number that have a foreign student program; (2)

admissions and housing information, such as the existence of special admissions procedures and the provision of housing; (3) financial information, such as the provision of financial aid; and (4) enrollment information. He also provides information on English proficiency problems and on the respondents' philosophies regarding the enrollment of foreign students. The work serves as a statistical profile of foreign student services and enrollment in the mid 1960s.

186 Mezirow, Jack, and Marsick, Victoria. *Education for Perspective Transformation: Women's Reentry Programs in Community Colleges.* New York: Center for Adult Education, Columbia University, 1978. 63 pages. (ED 166 367)

The authors draw from a national field study of women's re-entry programs at community colleges to relate these programs to theories of adult development and to discuss program administration. They describe how re-entry programs facilitate a developmental process of "perspective transformation," by which students critically examine sex stereotypes and work to overcome culturally induced dependency roles. They also present a classification of various types of re-entry programs and discuss their goals, their integration into the college community, and their staffing requirements. They conclude with a description of an evaluation guide that can be used by administrators of re-entry programs for determining how staff, students, and other constituencies differ in terms of their perceptions of program goals and services. The work provides directors of community college women's programs with useful analysis of the theoretical and administrative underpinnings of re-entry programs.

187 Nichols, Donald D. "Women's Programs at Public Community Colleges." *Community and Junior College Journal,* 1976, *46* (4), 7–8.

The author surveys 577 community college deans of students to identify the types of programs and services offered for female students and community members. He examines types of special courses offered, financial support, publicity, the women's resource center, perceived degree of concern for women students at the college, and the need for a national clearinghouse on community college women's programs. He concludes that community colleges are on the way toward meeting the special needs of women students but that future expansion depends upon available funds, administrative commitment, and the degree to which women articulate their needs.

188 Walsh, Patricia Ann (ed.). *Serving New Populations.* New Directions for Community Colleges, no. 27. San Francisco: Jossey-Bass, 1979. 114 pages. (ED 175 520)

This sourcebook examines community college programs, activities, and services for older adults, the handicapped, and women. It provides insights into the development of emeritus colleges, gerontology centers, interinstitutional consortia for older adults, and support services for the handicapped. It also analyzes the concept of re-entry education and provides detailed descriptions of an industrial-technology program for women, a special program for rural women, and a program for women who are returning to the workplace after an extended absence. It serves as a basic sourcebook for administrators charged with the task of developing services for these special populations.

4

Faculty

During fall 1984, 252,269 full-time and part-time faculty members were employed by the nation's two-year colleges. The works cited in this chapter of the bibliography deal with the attitudes, backgrounds, and personal and professional characteristics of those instructors. The entries in this chapter are arranged under the categories of faculty characteristics (nos. 189–235), the faculty as professionals (nos. 236–270), faculty relations with the college (nos. 271–304), and part-time faculty (nos. 305–314).

Faculty Characteristics, Attitudes, and Instructional Practices

The literature includes several state and national faculty studies that provide a wealth of information on the characteristics of community college instructors and on their attitudes and instructional practices. Specific topics examined in these studies include:

- the characteristics and instructional practices of faculty within individual disciplines (nos. 192, 193, 195, 198, 205, 206, 207, 209, 210, 212, 213, 221, 222, 224);
- instructor job satisfaction (nos. 194, 197, 200, 216, 235);
- personal values and psychological traits (nos. 196, 201, 227);
- attitudes toward educational innovations and toward the educational role of the community college (nos. 189, 191, 199, 214, 223, 229); and
- the alienation of community college faculty from colleagues at four-year colleges and universities (nos. 217, 218).

A major theme of this literature is the difficulty that faculty have in adjusting to the community college, especially after an extended period of graduate work. London (no. 217), for example, argues that many community college instructors are demoralized by the large numbers of students needing remedial help and by the lack of opportunity to conduct scholarly research. Seidman (no. 263), on the other hand, uses a broader sample and reaches a more balanced conclusion regarding the satisfactions and frustrations that teachers experience.

It should be pointed out that the literature on two-year college faculty focuses primarily on those teaching transfer courses. Godfrey and Holmstrom (no. 211) are an exception; they provide comparative data on faculty at community colleges and at vocational-technical institutions.

The Faculty as Professionals: Preservice Education, In-Service Faculty Development, and Faculty Evaluation

During the growth era of the 1960s, considerable attention was paid to preservice education for community college faculty. Many observers foresaw the problems involved in hiring instructors whose graduate education had prepared them for research rather than teaching. During this era, literature on the professional status of faculty included discussions of instructor credentialing (no. 246), teaching internships for graduate students (no. 245), nontraditional graduate degrees, such as the doctor of arts (no. 270), and the pros and cons of hiring Ph.D. graduates (nos. 248, 266).

Enrollment stabilization in the 1970s, however, curbed faculty hiring rates and, concomitantly, concern for preservice faculty training. Writers increasingly turned to the problems of in-service faculty development, addressing such issues as the management and evaluation of staff development programs (nos. 249, 254, 255, 256, 262), common practices in staff development (nos. 240, 242, 250, 260, 264, 268), and the assessment of staff development needs (nos. 237, 238, 243, 261, 269). Handbooks on staff development also appeared. Significantly, though, the literature on faculty development offers little information on the effectiveness of program efforts.

Closely related to the issue of faculty development is the ongoing problem of faculty evaluation. Several authors, including Cohen (no. 247) and Mark (no. 257), have examined the conflicting goals of evaluation: to gather evidence for employment termination and to provide a mechanism for faculty self-improvement, growth, and development. Other themes emerging in the literature on faculty evaluation include the efficacy of various evaluation methods (no. 252) and the desirability of basing evaluation on student learning rather than on the instructor's personality (no. 247). The literature is bereft, however, of analyses of the effects of evaluation procedures on faculty morale or teaching effectiveness.

Faculty Relations with the College: Collective Bargaining, Reductions in Force, Tenure, and Work Load

More literature has been devoted to the status of faculty as institutional employees than to the status of faculty as teaching professionals. This is largely the result of the widespread occurrence of faculty unionization and collective bargaining at two-year colleges. The literature on collective bargaining is relatively extensive, providing analyses of:

- faculty and administrator attitudes toward collective bargaining (nos. 274, 293);
- the root causes of collective bargaining (nos. 271, 273);
- the differences between colleges with and those without collective bargaining (nos. 282, 300);
- contract provisions and the procedures for grievance arbitration (nos. 273, 277, 279, 286, 287, 288);
- the effects of collective bargaining on the faculty role in governance and on faculty salaries (nos. 272, 283, 289, 295, 298);
- the effect of collective bargaining on the centralization of state authority (no. 294); and
- variations in collective bargaining practices (no. 273).

Clearly, collective bargaining has been one of the most controversial and talked-about subjects in the two-year college literature, at least during the era when.it was imminent and spreading.

Other issues surrounding faculty employment have received less extensive coverage. Lombardi (nos. 284, 285) provides the most extensive analyses available on faculty work load and reductions in force. Tenure has been examined by the College and University Personnel Association (no. 302) and by Smith (no. 301).

Part-Time Faculty

According to the latest data from the American Association of Community and Junior Colleges, part-timers made up 57 percent of all faculty members at the nation's two-year colleges. While many of these adjunct instructors have full-time careers elsewhere, a growing number can be classified as "permanent part-time faculty" who, as reported by Fryer (no. 307), are hired year after year on a part-time basis and may hold two or more part-time positions at once. Much of the literature on part-time faculty centers on the second-class status of adjunct instructors (nos. 306, 307), on their remuneration and the resultant cost savings accrued to colleges (nos. 308, 311, 314), and on personnel policies governing part-timers (nos. 305, 309, 310). Extensive analyses of the part-time faculty issue are provided by Lombardi (no. 311) and by Parsons (no. 312). Further research, however, is needed to study the relationship between part-timers and institutional quality.

Further Information on Two-Year College Faculty

The general texts cited in Chapter Two are the logical starting point for those studying the characteristics and contributions of two-year college faculty. Extensive analyses of the faculty are provided by Henry (no. 20), Hillway (no. 21), Medsker (no. 25), Blocker, Plummer, and Richardson (no. 7), Godfrey and Holmstrom (no. 19), Cohen, Brawer, and Lombardi (no. 13), Medsker and Tillery (no. 26), Ogilvie and Raines (no. 29), Monroe (no. 27), Thornton (no. 34), Bushnell (no. 10), Palinchak (no. 30), Cohen and Brawer (no. 12), and Vaughan and associates (no. 37). These works also include several citations that may lead the reader to further information.

The ERIC data base also includes thousands of documents that provide information on two-year college faculty. These documents include:

- state and national compilations of statistical data on the number and demographic characteristics of faculty;
- descriptions of faculty development and evaluation programs that have been established at individual colleges;
- opinion papers presented by faculty at professional conferences; and
- discussions of efforts undertaken at individual institutions to integrate part-time faculty into the mainstream of the college community.

The use of ERIC as an informational resource is discussed in Chapter Thirteen.

Faculty Characteristics

189 Alderman, Donald L., and Mahler, William A. "Faculty Acceptance of Instructional Technology: Attitudes Toward Educational Practices and Computer-Assisted Instruction at Community Colleges." *Programmed Learning and Educational Technology,* 1977, *14* (1), 77–91.

The authors draw upon a survey of 300 faculty members at six community colleges to investigate instructor attitudes toward computer-assisted instruction and to test the hypothesis that teacher resistance thwarts the adoption of new instructional technologies. Among their findings is that faculty feel comfortable with computer-assisted instruction in remedial classes dealing with basic skills and memory work but that they disagree on the value of computer usage in more advanced courses or in classes involving creativity. They conclude that faculty at two-year colleges are no more receptive to computer-assisted instruction than faculty at four-year colleges.

190 Allen, Kenneth. "Student and Faculty Attitudes." *Library College Journal,* 1970, *3* (4), 28–36.

Please see no. 650 for the full annotation.

191 Barshis, Donald. "The Art of Teaching Versus Teaching the Arts." In Stanley F. Turesky (ed.), *Advancing the Liberal Arts.* New Directions for Community Colleges, no. 42. San Francisco: Jossey-Bass, 1983, pp. 55–62.

For an annotation of the work in its entirety, please see no. 548.

192 Beckwith, Miriam M. *Science Education in Two-Year Colleges: Interdisciplinary Social Sciences.* Los Angeles: Center for the Study of Community Colleges and ERIC Clearinghouse for Junior Colleges, 1980. 69 pages. (ED 181 955)

Please see no. 871 for the full annotation.

193 Beckwith, Miriam M. *Science Education in Two-Year Colleges: Mathematics.* Los Angeles: Center for the Study of Community Colleges and ERIC Clearinghouse for Junior Colleges, 1980. 80 pages. (ED 176 386)

Please see no. 872 for the full annotation.

194 Benoit, Richard J., and Smith, Al. "Demographic and Job Satisfaction Characteristics of Florida Community College Faculty." *Community/Junior College Research Quarterly,* 1980, *4* (3), 263–276.

The authors analyze changes over time in the demographic and job-satisfaction profiles of full-time certified staff in the Florida community colleges, comparing the findings of two statewide surveys—one conducted in 1968 and one conducted in fall 1977—that collected data on age, sex, marital status, salaries, educational backgrounds, teaching and/or administrative experience, participation in in-service programs, and factors contributing to job satisfaction and dissatisfaction. Among their findings is that, though there was a 71 percent increase in the number of certified staff employed at the colleges between 1968 and 1977, there was only a 3 percent increase in the proportion of staff made up by women. They also conclude that staff perceptions about factors contributing to job satisfaction had not significantly changed over the years.

195 Brawer, Florence B. *The Humanities in Two-Year Colleges: The Faculty in Review.* Los Angeles: ERIC Clearinghouse for Junior Colleges and Center for the Study of Community Colleges, 1975. 52 pages. (ED 111 469)

The author draws upon an extensive literature review to examine the characteristics of community college faculty who teach the humanities. She summarizes research findings on the educational backgrounds of these instructors, the in-service programs that are available to them, and factors affecting the work environment, including work loads, salaries, the lack of opportunities to do research, approaches to instruction, and the transition from graduate school to community college teaching. Among her conclusions is that the usual preparation for specialized competence in a humanities field (that is, graduate work leading to a Ph.D. degree) is frequently regarded as inappropriate preparation for two-year college instructors. She argues, nonetheless, that the faculty seem to be developing professional competence along disciplinary lines as they gradually seek to take control of their working conditions.

196 Brawer, Florence B. *Functional Potential: A New Approach to Viewing Faculty.* Topical Paper no. 57. Los Angeles: ERIC Clearinghouse for Junior Colleges, 1976. 48 pages. (ED 128 049)

This paper examines community college faculty on the basis of "functional potential," a variable that describes the ability of a person to tolerate ambiguity, delay gratification, exhibit adaptive flexibility, demonstrate goal directedness, relate to self and others, and have a clear sense of personal identity. It draws from a nationwide survey of two-year college faculty to derive a functional potential index for humanities and nonhumanities instructors and correlates functional potential measures with faculty attributes such as age, future career plans, attitudes about students, and involvement in professional activities. It suggests that functional potential provides a better picture of college faculty than the simple demographic information provided in institutional and government reports.

197 Brawer, Florence B. *Satisfaction and Humanities Instructors in Two-Year Colleges.* Topical Paper no. 56. Los Angeles: ERIC Clearinghouse for Junior Colleges, 1976. 46 pages. (ED 128 048)

This paper reports the results of a nationwide survey designed to examine the relationship between job satisfaction of humanities faculty and demographic variables, grouping respondents into high-, medium-, or low-satisfaction groups on the basis of responses to questionnaire items designed as a job-satisfaction index. The author subsequently examines relationships between job satisfaction and such faculty characteristics as ethnicity, age, sex, and full- and part-time status. She suggests that the construct of job satisfaction is as much a function of the person as it is a reaction to the workplace. She also reviews the literature on job satisfaction and provides a bibliography.

198 Brawer, Florence B. (ed.). *The Humanities in Two-Year Colleges: Trends in Curriculum.* Los Angeles: ERIC Clearinghouse for Junior Colleges and Center for the Study of Community Colleges, 1978. 162 pages. (ED 156 285)

Please see no. 875 for the full annotation.

199 Coder, Ann. "Why Do Community College Faculty Resist Media as an Instructional Delivery System?" *Educational Technology,* 1983, *23* (5), 7–11.

This article analyzes the resistance of community college faculty to the use of instructional television. The author argues that some of the major reasons for such resistance are a pervasive belief that instructional media are more suited for elementary and secondary schools, a perceived threat to faculty control over what is being taught, a fear that classroom autonomy will be quashed, and a fear of the deprofessionalization of the teacher, who essentially would become a "system manager." She concludes that the increased use of media in the community college classroom will come about through active involvement of faculty, not through administrative coercion.

200 Cohen, Arthur M. "Community College Faculty Job Satisfaction." *Research in Higher Education,* 1974, *2* (4), 369–376.

This article reports findings of a study conducted to identify the factors that contribute to the job satisfaction and dissatisfaction of community college faculty. It details responses of 222 instructors from twelve colleges who were asked to relate aspects of their work that led them to feel satisfied and aspects that led them toward dissatisfaction. The study reveals that satisfaction was gained primarily from student learning or interaction with students, while dissatisfaction resulted from administrative or organizational difficulties. The author discusses implications for collective bargaining, administrative action, and faculty professionalism.

★201 Cohen, Arthur M., and Brawer, Florence B. *Confronting Identity: The Community College Instructor.* Englewood Cliffs, N.J.: Prentice-Hall, 1972. 257 pages.

This publication offers a psychology-oriented approach to viewing community college instructors by postulating two major concepts: identity (defined as awareness of self) and maturity (defined as integrated functioning within a social context). The authors note that a professional, mature, self-aware faculty is essential if the community college is to optimally serve its constituency and the field of higher education, positing that a professional faculty operates autonomously, polices its own ranks, sets its own employment standards, and judges itself by its effects on student learning. They classify faculty functions around three categories (model, mediator, and manager) and discuss teacher development, faculty influence on students, and student influence on the instructor's personal development. They also examine faculty evaluation, stressing the differences between practices that measure faculty performance and those that measure effects on learning. The book includes a 280-item bibliography.

202 Cohen, Arthur M., and Brawer, Florence B. *The Two-Year College Instructor Today.* New York: Praeger, 1977. 174 pages.

This report on the findings of a nationwide survey of 1,998 faculty and department heads in humanities departments at 156 colleges considers faculty attitudes, values, satisfaction, concern for students, research orientation, preparation, and personal development. Among the findings are that faculty members were generally satisfied with their position, that younger instructors tended to be most concerned for their students, and that instructors with a high research orientation looked to university professors as their reference group. The authors criticize the practices of employing part-time faculty members and of giving salary increments to instructors with doctoral degrees. They argue for the professional development of community college instructors and for integrating the humanities into occupational, remedial, and community education programs.

203 Cohen, Arthur M., and Brawer, Florence B. "Chapter Three: Faculty: Coping with Changing Conditions." In Arthur M. Cohen and Florence B. Brawer, *The American Community College.* San Francisco: Jossey-Bass, 1982, pp. 66–92.

For an annotation of the work in its entirety, please see no. 12.

204 Dennison, John D.; Tunner, Alex; Jones, Gordon; and Forrester, Glen C. *The Impact of Community Colleges: A Study of the College Concept in British Columbia.* Vancouver, British Columbia: B.C. Research, 1975. 192 pages. (ED 115 324)

Please see no. 398 for the full annotation.

205 Edwards, Sandra J. *Science Education in Two-Year Colleges: Biology.* Los Angeles: Center for the Study of Community Colleges and ERIC Clearinghouse for Junior Colleges, 1980. 116 pages. (ED 188 709)

Please see no. 885 for the full annotation.

206 Edwards, Sandra J. *Science Education in Two-Year Colleges: Earth and Space.* Los Angeles: Center for the Study of Community Colleges and ERIC Clearinghouse for Junior Colleges, 1980. 87 pages. (ED 180 535)

Please see no. 886 for the full annotation.

207 Edwards, Sandra J. *Science Education in Two-Year Colleges: Environmental Sciences.* Los Angeles: Center for the Study of Community Colleges and ERIC Clearinghouse for Junior Colleges, 1980. 82 pages. (ED 180 558)

Please see no. 887 for the full annotation.

208 Fiedler, Fred E., and Gillo, Martin W. "Correlates of Performance in Community Colleges." *Journal of Higher Education,* 1974, *45* (9), 672–681.

This article describes a study undertaken to examine the relationship between the teaching effectiveness of college departments and related departmental characteristics. It correlates administrator ratings of individual departments at eighteen Washington State community colleges with the responses of 1,404 faculty members to a survey soliciting information on teaching styles used, job satisfaction, instructor participation in decision making, and faculty perceptions of the priority of different institutional goals. It reports separate correlations by department area (social science, humanities, math/science, business, and vocational) and uses findings to conclude that individual departments "exert an important influence on faculty attitudes and behavior" (p. 680).

209 Friedlander, Jack. *Science Education in Two-Year Colleges: Economics.* Los Angeles: Center for the Study of Community Colleges and ERIC Clearinghouse for Junior Colleges, 1980. 86 pages. (ED 188 719)

Please see no. 889 for the full annotation.

210 Friedlander, Jack, and Edwards, Sandra J. *Science Education in Two-Year Colleges: Engineering.* Los Angeles: Center for the Study of Community Colleges and ERIC Clearinghouse for Junior Colleges, 1980. 80 pages. (ED 191 538)

Please see no. 891 for the full annotation.

211 Godfrey, Eleanor P., and Holmstrom, Engin I. *Study of Community Colleges and Vocational-Technical Centers: Phase I.* Washington, D.C.: Bureau of Social Science Research, 1970. 357 pages. (ED 053 718)

Please see no. 19 for the full annotation.

212 Hill, Andrew. *Science Education in Two-Year Colleges: Psychology.* Los Angeles: Center for the Study of Community Colleges and ERIC Clearinghouse for Junior Colleges, 1980. 74 pages. (ED 181 972)

Please see no. 894 for the full annotation.

213 Hill, Andrew. *Science Education in Two-Year Colleges: Sociology.* Los Angeles: Center for the Study of Community Colleges and ERIC Clearinghouse for Junior Colleges, 1980. 57 pages. (ED 180 572)

Please see no. 895 for the full annotation.

214 Hill, Malcolm, and Morrison, James L. "The Relationship of Selected Community College Faculty Attitudes, Socialization Experiences and Reference Group Identities." *Community/Junior College Research Quarterly,* 1976, *1* (1), 25–50.

The authors surveyed faculty members in Pennsylvania community colleges to determine how instructor socialization experiences affect attitudes toward the community college philosophy and toward traditionalism and progressivism in education. They correlate respondents' attitudes with four sets of independent variables: (1) occupational experiences, including years of teaching experience at various institutions; (2) formal educational experiences; (3) socioeconomic characteristics, such as age and sex; and (4) reference-group identity; that is, where the respondents would prefer to teach (community college, four-year college, and so on). They conclude that faculty generally accept the community college philosophy, that those who accept that philosophy tend to have a progressive orientation, and that acceptance of the community college philosophy is more closely associated with group identity than with any other indicator of socialization experience.

215 Hines, Edward R. "Policy Making for More Effective Academic Advisement In Two-Year Colleges." *Research in Higher Education,* 1981, *14* (2), 119–134.

Please see no. 626 for the full annotation.

216 Kurth, Edwin L., and Mills, Eric R. *Analysis of Degree of Faculty Satisfactions in Florida Community Junior Colleges: Final Report.* Gainesville: Institute of Higher Education, University of Florida, 1968. 135 pages. (ED 027 902)

This publication details findings of a study conducted in 1968 to (1) assess the satisfaction of Florida community college faculty with institutional activities, programs, policies, organization, and working conditions and (2) identify the opinions, characteristics, and attitudes of those most satisfied and of those least dissatisfied. It draws upon responses from 2,756 individuals, representing approximately 64 percent of all part-time and full-time teachers, administrators, and counselors employed in Florida community colleges that had been in operation for more than one year. It compares satisfied and dissatisfied groups in terms of personal background, educational preparation, present status and position, and attitudes toward the importance of junior college functions. The work serves as an in-depth descriptive analysis of Florida's junior college faculty in the late 1960s.

217 London, Howard B. "In Between: The Community College Teachers." *Annals of the American Academy of Political and Social Science,* 1980, (448), 62–73.

The author views community college faculty as a subculture within higher education that is "demoralized and uncomfortably isolated from the larger academic culture" (p. 62). He notes that most two-year college instructors are products of the secondary schools or of the university and that, as a result, the faculty are ambivalent toward the mission of the community college and toward its poorly prepared students. He also points out the isolation of community college faculty from the mainstream of their academic disciplines and discusses the dilemma of occupying a second-class ranking within academe's professional hierarchy. He concludes that as long as the role of community colleges within higher education remains undefined, two-year college instructors will feel alienated and unfulfilled.

218 McCormick, Albert E., Jr. "Two-Year College Instructors and the Sociology Profession: An Exploratory Investigation." *Teaching Sociology,* 1982, *9* (2), 111–126.

This article draws upon survey responses from 100 sociology instructors at seventy-two community colleges to examine the gap "between the profession of sociology and its practitioners in the two-year college" (p. 123). The author notes the several problems that inhibit full faculty involvement in the mainstream of the sociology discipline, including (1) the low percentage of Ph.D. sociologists among the community college instructors; (2) the fact that many sociology instructors have graduate training in other disciplines and do not teach sociology courses exclusively; (3) their inability to attend sociological conferences and participate in professional networks; and (4) the perception among faculty that the mainstream sociology associations do not care about the needs of colleagues at two-year colleges. He urges the sociology profession to become more sympathetic to the special needs of two-year college faculty.

219 Michaels, Dennis F., and Boggs, David L. "Community Services: Community College Faculty Perceptions and Participation." *Community/Junior College Research Quarterly,* 1980, *4* (2), 137–149.

Please see no. 855 for the full annotation.

220 Monroe, Charles R. "Chapter Thirteen: Faculty." In Charles R. Monroe, *Profile of the Community College: A Handbook.* San Francisco: Jossey-Bass, 1972, pp. 245–271.

For an annotation of the work in its entirety, please see no. 27.

221 Mooney, William T., Jr. *Science Education in Two-Year Colleges: Chemistry.* Los Angeles: Center for the Study of Community Colleges and ERIC Clearinghouse for Junior Colleges, 1980. 109 pages. (ED 187 397)

Please see no. 900 for the full annotation.

222 Mooney, William T., Jr. *Science Education in Two-Year Colleges: Physics.* Los Angeles: Center for the Study of Community Colleges and ERIC Clearinghouse for Junior Colleges, 1980. 106 pages. (ED 191 534)

Please see no. 901 for the full annotation.

223 Morrison, James L. "Socialization Experience, Role Orientation and Faculty Acceptance of the Comprehensive Community Junior College Concept." *Review of Educational Research,* 1972, *42* (4), 573–588.

This article describes a study undertaken in 1968 to assess the correlation between the socialization experiences of two-year college faculty and the degree to which those faculty accept the student-centered orientation of the two-year college. It draws upon a survey of 628 junior college faculty in Florida who were asked to fill out a questionnaire that included items measuring the acceptance of the student-centered philosophy (such as degree of agreement with the open-door policy). It correlates those acceptance measures with other survey items, eliciting information on socialization experiences that might affect this acceptance, such as whether the respondents had taken courses in junior college education or whether they aspired to become university professors rather than junior college instructors. The author utilizes the findings to question the hypothesis that subject-oriented instructors are not generally student oriented.

224 National Science Foundation. *Junior College Teachers of Science, Engineering, and Technology, 1967: Experience and Employment Characteristics.* NSF-69-3. Washington, D.C.: National Science Foundation, 1968. 98 pages. (ED 028 768; available in microfiche only)

This publication reports findings of a nationwide survey of junior college faculty who teach the natural and social sciences, engineering, and technology, drawing upon responses from 2,540 instructors to assess their demographic characteristics, educational and teaching backgrounds, professional affiliations, administrative and research duties, outside employment and current work on higher degrees, salaries, and career aims and degree of job satisfaction. It notes, among other findings, that 85 percent of the respondents were men, 91 percent taught full time, and 20 percent of the part-timers were women. The work provides a comprehensive picture of junior college science faculty in the mid 1960s.

225 Ogilvie, William K., and Raines, Max R. (eds.). "Part Eight: Teaching Staff." In William K. Ogilvie and Max R. Raines (eds.), *Perspectives on the Community Junior College.* New York: Appleton-Century-Crofts, 1971, pp. 436–490.

For an annotation of the work in its entirety, please see no. 29.

226 Palinchak, Robert. "Chapter Five: The Community College Faculty." In Robert Palinchak, *The Evolution of the Community College.* Metuchen, N.J.: Scarecrow Press, 1973, pp. 210–248.

For an annotation of the work in its entirety, please see no. 30.

227 Park, Young. *Junior College Faculty: Their Values and Perceptions.* Horizons Monograph Series. Los Angeles: ERIC Clearinghouse for Junior Colleges; Washington, D.C.: American Association of Junior Colleges, 1971. 75 pages. (ED 050 725)

Drawing upon a survey of 242 faculty at three community colleges to assess the value systems of junior college instructors, the author details their responses to two survey instruments: (1) the Rokeach Value Survey, which asked the respondents to rank order values related to "desired states of existence" and "desired modes of conduct," and (2) a "staff survey" that solicited information on the views, values, and personalities of people who work at junior colleges. He concludes that the respondents do not fit the stereotype of the idealistic, dedicated teacher and that "they are engaged in a profession of which they seemingly know little and take little time to enlighten themselves" (p. 49). He emphasizes that the study is only a pilot investigation but suggests that institutional personalities of junior colleges are created by the value orientations of their staff and that the perceptions and values of staff can determine whether an institution succeeds or fails in achieving its objectives.

228 Patterson, Robert A. *Pennsylvania Community College Faculty: Career Patterns and Educational Issues.* University Park: Center for the Study of Higher Education, Pennsylvania State University, 1971. 89 pages. (ED 051 800)

This publication examines the prior career experiences of junior college faculty in Pennsylvania junior colleges to investigate the relationship between prior career experience and the degree to which faculty hold progressive (that is, student-oriented) attitudes toward education rather than traditional (subject-oriented) attitudes. The author draws upon survey responses from 547 instructors (58 percent) to conclude that faculty who came to the colleges directly from graduate study or from another teaching position at four-year institutions had the most progressive educational attitudes and thus were more sympathetic to the goals of the community college. He notes, on the other hand, that faculty with prior experience in public schools or in private business had the most traditional attitudes and suggests that the latter should be avoided when hiring new faculty.

229 Purdy, Leslie. "Community College Instructors and the Use of New Media: Why Some Do and Others Don't." *Educational Technology*, 1975, *15* (3), 9–12.

This article explores reasons why faculty become interested in or resist instructional technology, drawing upon a study conducted at a California community college in 1972–73. It reveals that attitudes toward instructional technology are closely related to the degree to which faculty believe that teaching is a solo activity and that the instructor must have total control over the learning environment and relates these attitudes to instructors' perceptions of media as a help or a hindrance to the teacher-student relationship. It also considers problems encountered by teachers who like to dabble in new technology and notes how administrative involvement may cause resentment. The author suggests that administrators should allow faculty to take the lead in introducing media and allow them enough time for the adoption process.

230 Schmeltekopf, Donald D. "Professional Status and Community College Faculty: The Role of the Associations." In Stanley F. Turesky (ed.), *Advancing the Liberal Arts*. New Directions for Community Colleges, no. 42. San Francisco: Jossey-Bass, 1983, pp. 77–89.

The author addresses issues related to the professional activities of community college faculty, including the relatively low level of participation in professional organizations, the efforts of professional associations to address the problems of community college faculty, the consequences of inadequate professional status, and the roles of professional associations in enhancing this status. He argues that low faculty participation in professional associations is due, among other factors, to a lack of professional identity and to the absence of a sense of obligation to participate in activities outside the classroom. He concludes that there is a need to establish professional associations for community college teachers in order to boost morale and to give instructors a chance to exercise their influence and voice their concerns.

231 State University of New York. *Disabled Student Project Faculty Survey. Beyond Access: Meeting the Instructional Needs of Handicapped Students in Postsecondary Occupational Education. Phase II. Final Report.* Albany: Two-Year College Student Development Center, State University of New York, 1982. 30 pages. (ED 235 331)

This report details the findings of a statewide survey conducted in 1982 to (1) determine whether two-year college occupational faculty are aware of and utilize instructional accommodations designed to meet the needs of disabled students and (2) assess faculty perceptions of the instructional problems created by disabled students in their classes. It reviews the responses of 817 occupational faculty in regard to their awareness of each of thirty-six special accommodations that can be made for disabled students. It examines how the respondents had learned about available services for the disabled and how to rate the relative importance of each of twenty activities or teaching competencies that may be used in teaching disabled students. The report provides insights into faculty awareness about the disabled and into staff-development needs.

232 Stecklein, John E., and Willie, Reynold. "Minnesota Community College Faculty Activities and Attitudes, 1956-1980." *Community/Junior College Quarterly of Research and Practice,* 1982, *6* (3), 217-237.

This article compares the findings of a 1980 survey of faculty at Minnesota institutions of higher education with similar faculty surveys conducted in 1956 and 1968. It examines trends over the years in faculty demographic characteristics, educational backgrounds, factors that influence the choice of college teaching as a career, professional activities, attitudes toward collective bargaining, and sources of job satisfaction and dissatisfaction, breaking down findings by type of institution (two-year or four-year).

Among the conclusions are that community college faculty in 1980 were not as satisfied with their work as they had been in previous years and that "gains in positive attitude about salaries made between 1956 and 1968 appear to have been lost . . ." (p. 237).

233 Thornton, James W. "Chapter Ten: Instructors for Community Junior Colleges." In James W. Thornton, *The Community Junior College.* New York: Wiley, 1972, pp. 132–144.

For an annotation of the work in its entirety, please see no. 34.

234 Winter, Gene M., and Fadale, LaVerna M. *A Profile of Instructional Personnel in New York State Postsecondary Occupational Education.* Albany: Two-Year College Development Center, State University of New York, 1983. 101 pages. (ED 252 261)

Please see no. 774 for the full annotation.

235 Wood, Olin R. "Measuring Job Satisfaction of the Community College Staff." *Community College Review,* 1976, *3* (3), 56–64.

This article describes an instrument that can be used to measure the job satisfaction and dissatisfaction of community college instructors. The instrument is based on the Herzberg motivation-hygiene theory, which holds that factors that are intrinsic to a person's actual work are motivators while extrinsic factors (such as supervisor demands) lead to dissatisfaction. The article includes a copy of the instrument itself, which asks respondents to rate their satisfaction with each of sixty-seven factors arranged under ten categories: achievement, growth, interpersonal relations, policy and administration, recognition, responsibility, salary, supervision, the work itself, and working conditions. It is useful for studying staff morale.

The Faculty as Professionals

236 Adams, Frank G. "A Personnel Model: Hiring, Developing and Promoting Community and Technical College Employees." *Journal of Studies in Technical Careers,* 1983, 5 (2), 100–110.

The author draws upon policies in business and industry to describe a staff-development model that allows colleges to develop talent from within the institution instead of seeking talent from without. He details the components of the alternative model: hiring (screening, selection, and classification of employees); developing (orienting staff to the institution); and promoting (increasing the variety of on-the-job experiences that might prepare employees to move more easily to other positions within the institution as they open). The article is useful for administrators who are faced with the task of maintaining staff morale at a time of decreased job mobility.

237 Albers, Donald J.; Rodi, Stephen B.; and Watkins, Ann E. (eds.). *New Directions in Two-Year College Mathematics.* New York: Springer-Verlag, 1985. 491 pages.

Please see no. 867 for the full annotation.

238 Arnold, George F. "In-Service Needs of Community College Instructors." *Community College Social Science Journal,* 1980–81, 3 (2), 39–43.

The author urges the establishment of faculty in-service programs that help perfect teaching skills and thus serve as a counterbalance to traditional preservice graduate programs that include no course work in education. He cites a 1974 survey of social science instructors and department heads to note the resistance of community college instructors to the inclusion of education course work in preservice graduate programs or to the promotion of nontraditional graduate degrees, such as the doctor of arts, and argues that in-service programs are thus the most promising approach to the development of faculty teaching skills.

239 Atwell, Charles, and Smith, Margaret L. "Competencies Needed by Teachers of Developmental English in Two-Year Colleges." *Journal of Developmental and Remedial Education,* 1979, *3* (2), 9–11.

This article details findings of a study conducted to determine what competencies are needed by developmental English instructors and how those competencies are generally attained. The study rank orders forty-two rhetorical, pedagogical, and human relations skills that were identified as important teacher attributes by 100 community college developmental English instructors who were judged by their supervisors to be "effective" teachers. Among other findings is that over half of the instructors believed that they had attained thirty-five of the forty-five competencies primarily through on-the-job teaching experience rather than through formal preservice instruction. The article provides a rare insight into how developmental instructors view their work.

240 Beamish, Eric, and Beuke, Vernon. *Staff Development Services. Final Report, 1979.* Ithaca: College of Agriculture and Life Sciences at Cornell University, State University of New York, 1979. 118 pages. (ED 178 716)

The authors examine staff development practices at two-year colleges so as to highlight issues and problems, outline possible solutions, and offer alternative models. They include a comprehensive review of the literature as well as case studies of staff development programs at a sample of five two-year institutions representing different sizes, locations, and maturity. They conclude with a discussion of two popular conceptualizations of staff development programming and with outlines of preliminary designs for new models. The work serves as a highly theoretical analysis of the organization and purposes of staff development efforts and is thus more useful to university students of the two-year college than to campus-level practitioners.

241 Blank, William E. "Analysis of Professional Competencies Important to Community College Technical Instructors: Implications for CBTE." *Journal of Industrial Teacher Education,* 1979, *16* (2), 56–69.

Please see no. 744 for the full annotation.

242 Bloom, Thomas K. "Current Professional Development Practices of Occupational Instructors." *Journal of Industrial Teacher Education,* 1976, *14* (1), 11–19.

The author surveyed a sample of 290 occupational instructors in the Illinois community colleges to determine the frequency with which they engage in each of forty-six professional development activities. He concludes that "high instructor utilization of a particular in-service activity is inversely related to the amount of preparation and planning required of that in-service activity" (p. 17). He also notes that in-service activities conducted away from the college were utilized less frequently than activities conducted on campus and that the respondents were more likely to participate in in-service programs dealing with subject content area than in programs dealing with educational practices. He warns that the study findings are useful only in describing staff development practices and should not be used to determine what activities should or should not be included in professional development programs.

243 Caffey, David L. "Full-Time Faculty on Faculty Development: Their Perceptions of What Is and What Should Be." *Community/Junior College Research Quarterly,* 1979, *3* (4), 311–323.

This article reports results of a survey of 300 full-time instructors in eight Texas community colleges, 204 of whom responded to questions about faculty development goals and activities. Among other findings are that (1) preferred goals of faculty development were improvement of teaching skills, additional knowledge in subject field, and motivating instructors to strive for excellence; (2) preferred activities were travel to professional meetings, released time, and developmental leave; and (3) activities considered unimportant were staff retreats, observation of teaching by colleagues, and videotaping of practice teaching sessions. The author concludes that activities relating to teaching importance were favored, while those related to personal development, performance evaluation, and group interaction were less favored.

244 Case, Chester H. "Chapter Four: Supporting Faculty Leadership for Change." In William L. Deegan, Dale Tillery, and Associates, *Renewing the American Community College: Priorities and Strategies for Effective Leadership.* San Francisco: Jossey-Bass, 1985, pp. 80–102.

For an annotation of the work in its entirety, please see no. 14.

245 Cohen, Arthur M. *Focus on Learning: Preparing Teachers for the Two-Year College.* Occasional Report no. 11. Los Angeles: Junior College Leadership Program, School of Education, University of California, 1968. 68 pages.

This report describes the development of a junior college teacher internship program established in the early 1960s at the University of California at Los Angeles. The author discusses the rationale for the program, the characteristics of program participants, and their placement rates and outlines the program curriculum, which included components on educational goals and objectives, tests and assessments, use of instructional media, course development, and instructor evaluation. The report provides an example of one university's response to demands for a teaching-oriented junior college faculty in the 1960s.

246 Cohen, Arthur M. "Credentials for Junior College Teachers?" *Improving College and University Teaching,* 1969, *17* (2), 97–100.

The author notes that junior college teacher certification and faculty evaluation procedures do not require instructors to submit evidence of student learning. He argues that quality instruction may be the key to junior college institutional identity and that faculty should plan courses by specifying behavioral objectives, plotting learning sequences, and collecting evidence of student learning gains. He suggests that these curriculum development tasks should be carried out by faculty teams and that these teams should be evaluated by assessing whether or not students stay in their classes and learn under their direction. He concludes that graduate programs preparing junior college teachers must produce subject-matter experts who are also learning specialists.

247 Cohen, Arthur M. "Evaluation of Faculty." *Community College Review,* 1974, *2* (2), 12–21.

This article reviews faculty evaluation procedures, showing how they tend to focus on inappropriate criteria for retaining or dismissing instructors. The author argues for evaluation practices that lead to the personal and professional growth of the instructor and that enhance student learning by focusing on criteria that reward good teaching. He emphasizes that evaluation should be based on demonstrated effects on students, not on the instructor's personality, and stresses that no one evaluation process can enhance the professional life of the instructor if at the same time it is used to gather evidence for possible dismissal. The article provides insights into why common faculty evaluation practices often have no positive effect on instruction.

248 Connolly, John J. "Will the Community College Survive the Ph.D. Surplus?" *Educational Record,* 1971, *52* (3), 267–272.

This article assesses implications of the influx of Ph.D. holders in community college faculties, stressing the fact that Ph.D.s are research-oriented scholars with values and training that set them apart from most community college teachers. The author warns that the philosophy of the two-year college could easily be altered by adding faculty who are not committed to existing goals and policies, such as open-door admissions policies. The article provides a forceful argument against those who believe that community colleges can and should absorb the oversupply of Ph.D. graduates.

249 Doty, Charles R. "Major Characteristics in the Development and Implementation of a Professional Staff Development Program for Technical Teachers." *Canadian Vocational Journal,* 1977, *13* (1), 5–11.

This article outlines major considerations in the development and implementation of staff development programs for postsecondary vocational instructors in programs of less than baccalaureate-degree level. It examines the rationale for staff development, the short- and long-term improvements that can be expected, methods of increasing staff participation, budget requirements, legal aspects affecting teacher evaluation, and staff development objectives at federal, state, and local levels. It serves as a useful checklist of factors to be considered in establishing staff development policies.

250 Doty, Charles R., and Cappelle, Frank. "Technical Updating in Community Colleges." *Journal of Studies in Technical Careers,* 1982, *4* (4), 361–372.

This article draws on a thirty-two-item bibliography to examine practices and research in in-service technical upgrading for community college vocational faculty. It summarizes research and development efforts, the activities of consortia and associations, and guidelines pertaining to funding, industry involvement, institutional commitment, and program structure and participants. It serves as a useful summary of state-of-the-art information for vocational education administrators.

251 Eells, Walter Crosby. "Chapter Fifteen: The Instructional Staff." In Walter Crosby Eells, *The Junior College.* Boston: Houghton Mifflin, 1931, pp. 388–426.

For an annotation of the work in its entirety, please see no. 15.

252 Fitzgerald, Maurice J., and Grafton, Clive L. "Comparisons and Implications of Peer and Student Evaluation for a Community College Faculty." *Community/Junior College Research Quarterly*, 1981, *5* (4), 331–337.

This article compares peer and student evaluations of fifty-two faculty members at a California community college. The authors note that peer ratings were somewhat higher than student ratings but that the differences were not significant. The article reveals greater faculty confidence in student evaluations than in peer evaluations and notes that faculty were more likely to change their teaching practices in response to student assessments. It provides a rare comparative analysis of the effectiveness of peer and student evaluations at the community college level.

253 Garrison, Roger H. *Junior College Faculty: Issues and Problems. A Preliminary National Appraisal.* Washington, D.C.: American Association of Junior Colleges, 1967. 99 pages. (ED 012 177)

This publication draws from informal interviews with approximately 700 junior college faculty from twenty institutions to describe the professional lives of those instructors and to examine their concerns. It summarizes, in an anecdotal fashion, faculty concerns related to the junior college and its role, the pressure of heavy teaching work loads, the need for professional development and upgrading, orientation for new faculty, faculty participation in governance, professional affiliations, and other job-related issues. The author concludes that more research is needed on preservice and in-service faculty development. The work helps in understanding the concerns of faculty during the growth era of the 1960s.

254 Hammons, James O., and Wallace, Terry H. Smith. "Planning for Staff Development." *Community College Frontiers*, 1974, *3* (1), 38–43.

The authors briefly discuss thirteen factors that should be considered in planning community college staff development programs. Included are short analyses of justifying the staff development program to college personnel, determining who will be responsible for planning the program, determining how staff development needs will be identified, striking a balance between institutional priorities and individual needs, determining who should participate, motivating staff to take part, choosing instructional and evaluation techniques, and solving scheduling and funding problems. The article serves as a planning guide for persons charged with the responsibility of establishing a staff development program.

★**255** Hammons, James O.; Wallace, Terry H. Smith; and Watts, Gordon. *Staff Development in the Community College: A Handbook.* Topical Paper no. 66. Los Angeles: ERIC Clearinghouse for Junior Colleges, 1978. 74 pages. (ED 154 887)

This paper provides practical information on how to establish, manage, and evaluate in-service faculty development programs. It includes separate chapters on (1) the definitions, purposes, and rationale of staff development; (2) steps in program planning and implementation; (3) methods of determining staff development needs; (4) the unique needs of part-time faculty; and (5) program evaluation. It also provides a bibliography of further resources and samples of a variety of needs assessment surveys.

256 Hekimian, Shirley. *Criteria for the Institutional Evaluation of Community College Staff Development Programs.* Gainesville: Institute of Higher Education, University of Florida, 1984. 68 pages. (ED 246 961)

This work provides a literature review on the evaluation of community college staff development programs, details a study conducted to identify and validate program evaluation criteria, and suggests a process for the use of these criteria in program evaluation, basing this evaluation process on the Stufflebeam Context-Input-Process-Product model and enumerating evaluative criteria for each of four decision-making areas: planning (context), procedural design (input), program implementation (process), and outcomes (product). It serves as an analytical framework to be used by administrators in increasing the accountability of institutional staff development programs.

257 Mark, Sandra F. "Faculty Evaluation in Community Colleges." *Community/Junior College Quarterly of Research and Practice,* 1982, *6* (2), 167–178.

This article notes the incompatible purposes of faculty evaluation (that is, judgment versus assistance) and reports findings of a study undertaken to identify the evaluation practices at four New York community colleges. The author concludes that management decision making is the primary purpose of evaluation at the four colleges and that the objectives of self-improvement, growth, and development are only secondary. She also discusses the types of evaluation measures utilized, noting that outcome (rather than performance) measures were preferred but that many study subjects doubted that outcome-oriented evaluation procedures could be agreed upon. The article provides a rank ordering of evaluation components that subjects would like to include in evaluation systems and offers fifteen suggestions for minimizing negative consequences of evaluation.

258 Martorana, S. V.; Toombs, William; and Breneman, David W. (eds.). *Graduate Education and Community Colleges: Cooperative Approaches to Community College Staff Development.* Technical Report no. 5. Washington, D.C.: National Board on Graduate Education, 1975. 149 pages. (ED 111 479)

This work presents fourteen essays by community college and university representatives on the special professional development requirements of two-year college faculty, discussing the implications of expanded programs and teaching practices at two-year colleges, the growing number of nontraditional students, and the projected decline in demand for new doctorate teachers at two-year colleges through 1990. The work reviews nontraditional forms of graduate education for two-year college teachers (including the Nova University program), examines the response of traditional

universities to community college staffing needs, and discusses the
university role in continuing professional development. It provides
faculty development professionals with cogent analyses of community college/university cooperation in educating a teaching-
oriented staff.

★259 O'Banion, Terry. *Teachers for Tomorrow: Staff Development in the Community-Junior Colleges.* Tucson: University of Arizona, 1972. 185 pages.

The author reviews the backgrounds of community college
instructors, showing that most have prior secondary school or
university experience and that few have been prepared particularly
to teach in two-year institutions. The work pleads for humanisti-
cally oriented instructors with a commitment to the community
college and its students and outlines an ideal preservice preparation program that would include a teaching internship and
provide information on the community college philosophy and on
the nature of two-year college students. The author recommends
that every college organize in-service programs offering institutes,
short-term workshops, staff retreats, continuing seminars, encoun-
ter groups, travel to professional meetings, and the opportunity for
professional reading. Appendixes present data on institutions
offering graduate degree programs for community college faculty
and overviews of various types of recommended preservice and in-
service preparation programs.

260 Padgett, Suzanne, and Thompson, Larry C. *A Survey of
Professional Development in Arizona Community Col-
leges.* Tucson: Center for the Study of Higher Education,
University of Arizona, 1979. 19 pages. (ED 188 681)

The authors survey the professional development activities
provided for faculty at the Arizona community colleges, noting
that the average community college offers nine separate professional development experiences and that the most commonly
offered activities are workshops, professional leaves, orientation,
seminars, consultant programs, and funding for travel. They also
note that most activities are conducted on a strictly voluntary basis.

The work is useful as a brief summary of actual faculty development practices.

261 Schultz, Raymond E., and Roed, William J. *Report on Inservice Needs of Community College Part-Time Occupational Instructors.* Tucson: College of Education, University of Arizona, 1978. 29 pages. (ED 156 290)

This publication describes a study undertaken to identify the training needs of part-time occupational instructors in the Arizona community colleges and to formulate recommendations for improved in-service delivery. It includes results from a survey of 192 part-time occupational instructors eliciting information on the kinds of assistance and training they have had or would like to receive at the community colleges where they teach. It also provides (1) a description of a part-time faculty development program at one of the colleges, (2) a list of possible rewards and incentives for part-time instructors, (3) performance-based teacher education modules, and (4) a self-assessment instrument that can be used by administrators to determine the types of assistance that should be provided to part-time instructors in occupational programs. It concludes with recommendations for the delivery of in-service programs.

262 Schultz, Raymond E., and Terrell, Roland. "International Education: A Vehicle for Staff Revitalization." In Maxwell C. King and Robert L. Breuder (eds.), *Advancing International Education.* New Directions for Community Colleges, no. 26. San Francisco: Jossey-Bass, 1979, pp. 37–47.

The authors argue that international education is an excellent vehicle for staff revitalization and offer administrative guidelines for institutions that may wish to incorporate international education in staff development efforts. Included are descriptions of seven international experiences that can make a significant contribution to staff development: faculty exchange programs; study-abroad experiences; the involvement of faculty from foreign countries in curriculum development efforts; the involvement of faculty and staff in hosting foreign students; workshops and conferences in international education; institutes; and teaching assignments abroad.

★**263** Seidman, Earl. *In the Words of the Faculty: Perspectives on Improving Teaching and Educational Quality in Community Colleges.* San Francisco: Jossey-Bass, 1985. 292 pages.

Using in-depth phenomenological interviewing with instructors and counselors at community colleges in Massachusetts, New York, and California, the author explores the nature and meaning of the work of community college faculty. He profiles the personal and career experiences of instructors who teach English, humanities, mathematics, science, social science, business, nursing, and various occupational curricula and also includes profiles of counselors and minority faculty. The work provides useful insights into how community college faculty decide to enter the teaching profession and how instructors are affected by issues related to the curriculum, diminished collegial relations, instructional improvement, and the need to balance commitment to students with other professional responsibilities.

264 Smith, Albert B. *Staff Development Practices in U.S. Community Colleges.* Washington, D.C.: American Association of Community and Junior Colleges, 1980. 90 pages. (ED 200 285)

This work reviews findings of a nationwide survey conducted in 1979 to draw a profile of staff development practices at two-year colleges, utilizing responses from 687 colleges to examine (1) the goals of staff development programs, (2) the estimated effectiveness of instructional methods used in these programs, (3) the estimated effectiveness of staff development practices such as sabbatical leaves and travel grants, (4) the participation rates of various faculty and staff groups, (5) the sources of program funding, (6) the organizational structure of staff development programs, and (7) the criteria used to evaluate these programs and the degree to which these criteria are met. It serves as a descriptive analysis of staff development programs in the late 1970s and of their perceived effectiveness.

265 Smith, Albert B. (ed.). *Evaluating Faculty and Staff.* New Directions for Community Colleges, no. 41. San Francisco: Jossey-Bass, 1983. 123 pages. (ED 225 633)

This sourcebook presents eleven essays that focus on evaluation processes and highlight successful and unsuccessful staff evaluation practices. It includes discussions of (1) the evaluation of full-time faculty, part-time faculty, and administrators, (2) the special problems posed by student evaluations of faculty, (3) the role of faculty development in the evaluation process, and (4) legal considerations, concluding with a review of relevant ERIC documents and journal articles. It provides practitioners and students of higher education with a good introduction to the controversies surrounding staff evaluation at the community college.

266 Smith, Milton L. "The Two-Year College and the Ph.D. Surplus." *Academe: Bulletin of the AAUP,* 1979, *65* (7), 429–433.

This article reports findings of a national survey conducted in 1978 to assess the extent to which Ph.D. holders are employed in teaching and administrative positions at two-year colleges. The author summarizes data (based on responses from 786 college presidents) relating to the percentage of full-time faculty and administrators hired in 1977–78 who held the doctorate and examines responses to questions soliciting information about the prospects of hiring more doctoral-degree holders in the future. He notes that less than 10 percent of the newly hired faculty in 1977–78 held the doctorate and that responding presidents were disinclined to hire more Ph.D. holders in the future. He concludes that two-year colleges will not become a major market for the surplus of Ph.D. holders.

267 Wallace, Terry H. Smith (ed.). *Community College Staff Development: An Annotated Bibliography.* N.p.: National Council for Staff, Program and Organizational Development, 1979. 48 pages. (ED 203 927; available in microfiche only)

This work provides an annotated bibliography of approximately 225 monographs, journal articles, dissertations, and unpublished documents dealing with in-service education programs for two-year college faculty. It is useful as a listing of relevant literature appearing in the 1970s, although some items from the 1960s are also noted.

268 Wallin, Desna L. *Faculty Development Activities in the Illinois Community College System.* Springfield, Ill.: Lincoln Land Community College; 1982. 25 pages. (ED 252 269)

This publication surveys the faculty development activities undertaken at the Illinois community colleges, examining (1) the type of activities being conducted, (2) whether chief academic officers feel that those activities actually improve instruction, (3) the comparative effectiveness of on-campus and off-campus activities, (4) the usefulness of group versus individual activities, and (5) methods used to evaluate faculty development activities. Among other findings are that most faculty development programs utilize a workshop or seminar approach and that such generalized approaches meet the needs of few instructors. The author urges the development of more individualized, one-on-one faculty development interventions.

269 Welch, Frederick G., and Yung, Kirby. "Inservice Training Needs of Postsecondary Occupational Teachers in Pennsylvania." *Journal of Industrial Teacher Education,* 1980, *17* (2), 41–45.

This article surveys postsecondary occupational teachers and administrators in Pennsylvania to determine their needs for in-service teacher education. It summarizes data on respondents' educational backgrounds, employment histories, and current educational pursuits and examines perceived needs for in-service education, preferred methods and location for in-service programs, and opinions concerning who should bear the cost. It reveals that most teachers are interested in participating in some form of in-service training and that sabbaticals with pay, scholarships, and fellowships are the most favored means of financing such training.

270 Wortham, Mary. "The Case for a Doctor of Arts Degree: A View from Junior College Faculty." *AAUP Bulletin*, 1967, *53*, 372-377.

The author questions whether traditional Ph.D. programs contribute to the pedagogical skills of future undergraduate teachers and urges the development of doctor of arts (D.A.) programs for junior college faculty. She argues that there are marked contrasts between the conditions of instruction in junior colleges and graduate schools and notes that junior college faculty need a greater range of teaching competencies. She outlines a proposed D.A. program that is less specialized than most Ph.D. programs, orients students toward a teaching career, expects completion within a definite time, and balances scholarship, research, and teaching competencies. She concludes that faculty with the D.A. degree will improve instructional quality at junior colleges and enhance the university equivalency of junior college transfer courses.

Faculty Relations with the College

271 Aussieker, Bill. "Community Colleges Without Community." In Joseph W. Garbarino and Bill Aussieker, *Faculty Bargaining: Change and Conflict*. Carnegie Commission on Higher Education Series. New York: McGraw-Hill, 1975, pp. 179-211.

Drawing upon a variety of sources to examine the causes and effects of faculty collective bargaining at community colleges, the author assesses the relationship between the tendency to unionize and (1) the presence of state collective bargaining laws, (2) fiscal difficulties, and (3) the changing character of the community college in terms of organizational structure, administration, and mission. He also examines available data on the impact of collective bargaining on faculty salaries and college governance. He determines that rapid organizational change in many community colleges destroyed the sense of collegial community and led faculty to organize and notes that unionism is not related to quality of instruction and that the alleged benefits of collective bargaining have yet to be proved.

272 Baker, H. Kent. "The Impact of Collective Bargaining on Faculty Compensation in Community Colleges." *Community/Junior College Quarterly of Research and Practice,* 1984, *6* (1-4), 193-204.

This article examines differences in faculty compensation at colleges with and without collective bargaining, utilizing thirty-one matched pairs of union and nonunion colleges. The author finds that (1) unionization does improve faculty compensation, but only in the very short run, and (2) there were no significant differences in the percentage of increase in compensation over the five-year period at the union and nonunion colleges. He concludes that unionized faculty do not experience significantly greater increases in compensation than their nonunionized colleagues.

273 Begin, James P.; Settle, Theodore C.; and Berke-Weiss, Laurie. *Community College Collective Bargaining in New Jersey: Study Report and Recommendations.* New Brunswick, N.J.: Institute of Management and Labor Relations, Rutgers, The State University of New Jersey, 1977. 345 pages. (ED 151 046)

This work analyzes collective bargaining systems in New Jersey's public two-year colleges and compares these systems with those in other states, profiling collective bargaining practices in New Jersey in terms of (1) the history and origins of bargaining, (2) employers' negotiating structures, (3) the issues covered in collective negotiations, impasse procedures, and job actions, (4) the effect of collective bargaining on traditional collegial governance patterns,

(5) the administration of grievance procedures, (6) the relationship of job satisfaction with selected bargaining outcomes, and (7) the representation of nonfaculty staff in bargaining units. The authors note the wide variation among the New Jersey two-year colleges in respect to processes and outcomes of collective bargaining, analyze the causes of these variations, and suggest policy recommendations.

274 Birmingham, Joseph C., and Borland, David T. "Collective Bargaining in the Future: A Study of Administrator Attitudes." *Community/Junior College Research Quarterly,* 1980, *4* (2), 169–183.

This article surveys administrator attitudes toward collective bargaining in Texas, a state that has not had a strong tradition of unionization. The authors find—predictably—that the administrators opposed collective bargaining and had especially negative attitudes toward the possibility of faculty strikes. They conclude that administrators in Texas—and in other states without collective bargaining—should educate themselves and plan for collective bargaining in order to avoid unnecessary dissension and discord in the future.

275 Blocker, Clyde E.; Plummer, Robert H.; and Richardson, Richard C., Jr. "Chapter Six: Faculty-College Relationships." In Clyde E. Blocker, Robert H. Plummer, and Richard C. Richardson, Jr., *The Two-Year College: A Social Synthesis.* Englewood Cliffs, N.J.: Prentice-Hall, 1965, pp. 135–168.

For an annotation of the work in its entirety, please see no. 7.

276 Cohen, Arthur M.; Brawer, Florence B.; and Lombardi, John. "Chapter Three: Characterizing the Faculty" and "Chapter Four: Faculty Preparation and Evaluation." In Arthur M. Cohen, Florence B. Brawer, and John Lombardi, *A Constant Variable*. San Francisco: Jossey-Bass, 1971, pp. 33-62.

For an annotation of the work in its entirety, please see no. 13.

277 Douglas, Joel M. (ed.). *Salary and Compensation Methodology in Academic Collective Bargaining*. New York: National Center for the Study of Collective Bargaining in Higher Education and the Professions, Bernard Baruch College, City University of New York, 1983. 10 pages. (ED 230 140)

This report examines salary and compensation provisions in academic collective bargaining agreements at 134 two-year colleges and 73 four-year colleges. It analyzes (1) provisions regarding salary increases, (2) cost-of-living clauses and/or wage reopener provisions, (3) faculty typologies used in bargaining agreements, (4) provisions for compensating chairpersons and adjunct faculty, and (5) compensation methodology for teaching during the summer. It also includes brief discussions of provisions for merit pay and overload compensation. It serves as a summary of current compensation practices and as useful background material for administrators engaged in collective bargaining.

★278 Ernst, Richard J. (ed.). *Adjusting to Collective Bargaining*. New Directions for Community Colleges, no. 11. San Francisco: Jossey-Bass, 1975. 110 pages. (ED 114 157)

This sourcebook identifies, in a series of twelve essays, the major issues that should be considered by faculty and staff in trying to decide whether to embrace collective bargaining. It presents different perspectives on academic unionization, including the viewpoints of faculty, college administrators, trustees, and legislators. It also includes discussions of the status and probable expansion of collective bargaining in the community college, the arguments for and against academic unionization, the role of administrators in the collective bargaining process, and the implications of collective bargaining for academic freedom, productivity, and tenure. It provides one of the most thorough analyses of the issues—both pro and con—that were attendant to the growth of college unionization during the 1960s and 1970s.

279 Ferguson, Tracy H., and Bergan, William L. "Grievance-Arbitration Procedures and Contract Administration." *Journal of College and University Law*, 1974, *1* (4), 371–389.

This article draws upon a review of the grievance procedures in college and university faculty contracts to examine provisions governing time limits in raising a grievance, the number of steps built into the grievance procedures, and the exclusion of personnel decisions that have been based on the academic judgment of peers. Among other observations, the authors conclude that contracts in academe provide for a much longer statute of limitations and allow twice as many steps in arbitration than do contracts negotiated in private industries. They note also that faculty do not yet have faith in the ability of arbitrators to handle cases arising in academe and suggest that there is a need to train more arbitrators in the field of higher education. The article provides a rare comparison of academic labor contracts with those found in business and industry.

280 Hansen, Glenn L., and Kramer, Robert E. "Iowa Postsecondary Vocational-Technical Teacher Retention Study." *Community/Junior College Research Quarterly*, 1978, *2* (3), 255–264.

Please see no. 760 for the full annotation.

281 Howe, Ray. *Community College Board of Trustees and Negotiations with Faculty*. Washington, D.C.: American Association of Community and Junior Colleges and Association of Community College Trustees, 1973. 48 pages. (ED 080 116)

Please see no. 355 for the full annotation.

282 Jaap, William M., and Baker, George A. "The Impact of Collective Bargaining on the Administrative Functions and Roles of Community College Presidents." *Community/Junior College Quarterly of Research and Practice*, 1982, *6* (2), 157–166.

This article reviews findings of a national survey conducted to determine the effect of collective bargaining on college presidents' perceptions of their administrative roles. Drawing upon responses from 100 randomly selected presidents at colleges with collective bargaining and 100 randomly selected presidents at colleges without collective bargaining, it compares the two respondent groups on the basis of their ratings of thirty-two administrative tasks. It suggests that there were no significant differences between the two groups in terms of the way presidents assigned these tasks priority or ordered them according to time requirements. The authors conclude that collective bargaining may not have had a pervasive effect on the role perceptions of community college presidents.

283 Kellett, Robert H. *Trends and Patterns of Change in Public Community College Collective Bargaining Contracts: Research Summary No. 1*. Washington, D.C.: Academic Collective Bargaining Information Service, 1975. 14 pages. (ED 115 356)

This paper analyzes initial and subsequent contracts negotiated at forty-one community colleges between September 1966 and September 1974 to determine whether collective bargaining has been effective in increasing faculty participation in governance and in increasing faculty salaries. The author notes that community college contracts are cumulative in nature and that contract provisions, once included in the bargaining agreement, are rarely deleted during subsequent contract negotiations. He also finds that contract provisions related to faculty remuneration and instructor involvement in decision making increased in frequency as new contracts were negotiated over time. The paper provides the reader with insights into the cumulative growth of contract provisions as new contracts are negotiated to replace older ones.

284 Lombardi, John. *Faculty Workload.* Topical Paper no. 46. Los Angeles: ERIC Clearinghouse for Junior Colleges, 1974. 23 pages. (ED 097 925)

This paper examines issues related to the definition of faculty work load and to the development of work-load formulas. It presents a historical picture of the status of faculty work load and elaborates on objections to its quantitative measurement. The author discusses the erosion of parietal regulations, the issue of quantity versus quality, and the effect of collective bargaining on work loads. He concludes that work loads will not likely increase by more than fifteen weekly contact hours, that class sizes will continue to fluctuate widely, that a large number of colleges will continue to eliminate parietal rules, and that the labor-intensive characteristics of education will probably not change.

285 Lombardi, John. *Reduction in Force: An Analysis of the Policies and Their Implementation.* Los Angeles: ERIC Clearinghouse for Junior Colleges, 1974. 30 pages. (ED 099 043)

Please see no. 486 for the full annotation.

286 Lovell, Ned. B.; Piland, William E.; and Bazik, Edna F. *Illinois Community College Grievance Procedure Analyzer.* Springfield: Illinois Community College Trustees Association; Normal: Center for the Study of Educational Finance, Illinois State University, and Office of the President, Illinois State University, 1983. 72 pages. (ED 234 834)

This publication analyzes the status of grievance procedures at the Illinois community colleges that engage in collective bargaining. It includes a review of collective bargaining contracts to determine definitions of "grievances," the extent of the issues that may be legitimately "grieved," steps and time limits in grievance procedures, no-reprisal clauses, sources of arbitrators, limitations of arbitrators' authority, and the conditions of arbitration. It also details the findings of a survey of administrators who were asked for information on the colleges' bargaining experience and grievance arbitration history, the impact of grievance procedures on governance, time expended in the grievance process, arbitration costs, involvement of the courts, and other factors. The authors conclude that grievance arbitration has "not fulfilled the objectives of its early advocates, who preferred arbitration to litigation" (p. 61).

287 Lovell, Ned B.; Piland, William E.; and Schack, Edna. *The Status of Collective Bargaining in Illinois Community Colleges, 1983–1984.* Springfield: Illinois Community College Trustees Association; Normal: Center for Higher Education, Illinois State University, and Office of the President, Illinois State University, 1984. 48 pages. (ED 251 148)

This publication analyzes the status of collective bargaining at the Illinois community colleges in 1983–1984, outlining the common characteristics of community college contracts, focusing on bargaining status, organizational affiliation, length of contract, reopener clauses, part-time faculty status, unit membership, academic-year calendar, class size limits, teaching-load provisions, and academic freedom. It also analyzes provisions for insurance, retirement, tuition waiver and reimbursement provisions, leaves, dues deduction, grievance definition and resolution, impasse procedures, management rights clauses, and strikes. It includes analyses of the impact of the Illinois Labor Relations Act on faculty contracts, instructional quality, college finances, and faculty/administrator interaction. The authors conclude that collective bargaining has contributed to the bureaucratization of community colleges.

288 Mannix, Thomas. "Community College Grievance Procedures: A Review of Contract Content in Ninety-Four Colleges." *Journal of the College and University Personnel Association*, 1974, *25* (2), 23–40.

This article reviews grievance procedures in ninety-four community college contracts, noting the varied definitions of *grievance*, the time limitations for filing grievances, provisions for informal settlement, the powers and duties of arbitrators, and the impact of collective bargaining on the governance structure. The author suggests that faculty perceptions about the fairness of different aspects of college governance will influence grievance machinery and that "if the faculty feels that matters excluded from grievance arbitration are being properly handled by a traditional governance structure . . . then there will be no pressure for change" (p. 30). The article serves as a succinct overview of negotiated grievance procedures at community colleges in the early 1970s.

289 Marshall, Joan L. "The Effects of Collective Bargaining on Faculty Salaries in Higher Education." *Journal of Higher Education*, 1979, *50* (3), 310–322.

This article reports findings of a study conducted to determine whether faculties at colleges and universities with collective bargaining enjoy greater salary increases than faculties at comparable institutions without collective bargaining. It details study methodology, in which faculty pay increases over a period of five years were traced at (1) thirty colleges and universities that entered into collective bargaining in 1971–72 or 1972–73 and (2) a control group of thirty nonunion institutions that were matched to the experimental group on the basis of institutional type, mean salary at the base year, size of faculty, and geographical location. The author concludes that unionization had little effect on salaries at four-year institutions but that faculty at nonunion two-year colleges experienced greater salary increases than faculty at two-year colleges with collective bargaining. The article serves as a challenge to the hypothesis that collective bargaining increases faculty salaries.

290 Medsker, Leland L. "Chapter Seven: Faculty Attitudes on the Role of the Two-Year College." In Leland L. Medsker, *The Junior College: Progress and Prospect.* New York: McGraw-Hill, 1960, pp. 169–206.

For an annotation of the work in its entirety, please see no. 25.

291 Metzler, John H. *Collective Bargaining for Community Colleges.* Washington, D.C.: Association of Community College Trustees, 1979. 110 pages.

This publication provides a comprehensive description of the collective bargaining process in community colleges. It includes a brief legal history of public employment bargaining, specific guidelines for selecting a negotiating team, recommendations for developing an effective negotiation strategy, and suggestions for effective communications. It also discusses issues related to negotiability, grievance procedures, mediation, fact finding, strikes, arbitration, and the arbitration award and concludes with do's and don't's in collective bargaining and a brief glossary of terms. It serves as a useful introduction to collective bargaining processes for college administrators.

292 Monroe, Charles R. "Chapter Sixteen: Faculty Participation in Governance." In Charles R. Monroe, *Profile of the Community College: A Handbook.* San Francisco: Jossey-Bass, 1972, pp. 321–349.

For an annotation of the work in its entirety, please see no. 27.

293 Moore, John W. *Pennsylvania Community College Faculty: Attitudes Toward Collective Negotiations.* University Park: Center for the Study of Higher Education, Pennsylvania State University, 1971. 60 pages. (ED 051 801)

This work reports findings of a survey conducted to assess attitudes of Pennsylvania community college faculty toward collective bargaining. It explores faculty dispositions toward collective negotiation, the relationships between attitude and sense of power and mobility, and the relationships between attitude and personal characteristics. It reveals that faculty are apparently willing to organize and utilize collective action, that there is a positive relationship between a sense of powerlessness and favorable attitudes toward collective negotiation, and that faculty who feel that they have high career mobility tend to show more favorable attitudes to collective bargaining. It suggests that faculty are no longer satisfied with a secondary role in governance and that faculty unions exemplify a growing sense of professionalism.

294 Mortimer, Kenneth P. (ed.). *Faculty Bargaining, State Government, and Campus Autonomy: The Experience in Eight States.* Report no. 87. University Park: Pennsylvania State University; Denver, Colo.: Education Commission of the States, 1976. 115 pages. (ED 124 224)

This publication presents seven essays that explore the scope of collective bargaining in higher education in Michigan, New Jersey, New York, Pennsylvania, Hawaii, Massachusetts, Alaska, and Montana. It focuses particularly on the impact of collective bargaining on the centralization of state authority in higher education but provides detailed information on the scope of bargaining legislation, the level at which bargaining is conducted, and the origins of bargaining in each state. It covers collective bargaining as it relates to all of higher education and makes several references to issues affecting community colleges in particular. The work provides the reader with succinct analyses of how collective bargaining originated in several states, how it has been administered, and what its likely effects are.

295 Poole, Larry H., and Wattenbarger, James L. "Has Collective Bargaining Influenced Administrative Policies?" *Community College Review*, 1977, *4* (3), 8–11.

This article compares the governance policies of community colleges without collective bargaining with the governance policies of colleges that have at least five years' experience in collective negotiation. It groups twenty governance policies into four categories: those on which collective bargaining has had no influence; those on which collective bargaining has had some influence; those on which collective bargaining has had substantial influence; and those that did not change as a result of collective bargaining but in which faculty gained greater influence. It concludes that policies undergoing the greatest change are grievance procedures and administrator selection and warns of the threat of collective bargaining to the collegial governance model.

296 "Retrenchment at Two-Year Colleges and Institutes." *Journal of the College and University Personnel Association*, 1980, *31* (3–4), 190–203.

Please see no. 489 for the full annotation.

297 Richardson, Richard C., Jr. "Governance and Change in the Community-Junior College." *Journal of Higher Education*, 1973, *44* (4), 299–308.

Please see no. 384 for the full annotation.

298 Richardson, Richard C., Jr., and Riccio, Elaine. "Collective Bargaining and Faculty Involvement in Governance." *Community College Review*, 1980, 7 (3), 60–65.

This article details the findings of a study conducted to assess perceptions of how collective bargaining has affected the faculty role in college decision making. It draws upon a survey of faculty union leaders and administrators at 107 community colleges to estimate the level of faculty involvement in twenty-eight decision areas both prior to and following collective bargaining. The authors note that for all decision areas (including issues related to personnel, academic, and administrative policies), administrator estimates of faculty involvement before collective bargaining were higher than the estimates made by union leaders. They also find that faculty involvement has become more formalized but that there are still some areas (including the development of academic policy) in which faculty do not play a major role.

299 Romoser, Richard C.; Randolf, Nancy L.; and Jonas, Jan H. *Faculty Workload: Full-Time Faculty Lecture Hour Workload in the Contiguous Forty-Eight States.* Management Report Series, no. 24. Cleveland, Ohio: Cuyahoga Community College, 1981. 7 pages. (ED 200 291)

This paper draws upon a survey of state administrators for community colleges, chief academic officers at individual institutions, and other knowledgeable individuals to determine the number of lecture hours assigned per week as a normal full-time faculty work load at 767 community colleges. It details work-load information for all but four exceptional instructional situations: writing classes or other courses in which faculty are allowed exceptional amounts of time to evaluate students' work; large classes for which special work-load arrangements are made; classes utilizing nontraditional instructional strategies (for example, computer-assisted instruction); and classes using a team-teaching approach. The authors explain the rationale for choosing lecture hours, as opposed to other measurements, for use as a frame of reference in quantifying faculty productivity. The paper is useful for understanding work-load norms at community colleges.

300 Smart, John C., and Rodgers, Samuel A. "Community Colleges with Collective Bargaining Agreements: Are They Different?" *Research in Higher Education,* 1973, *1* (1), 35–42.

This article describes a study undertaken to determine (1) differences between community colleges with and without collective bargaining and (2) differences between community colleges represented by the American Federation of Teachers (AFT) and those represented by the National Education Association (NEA).

The authors determine that, in comparison to NEA colleges or those with no bargaining agent, AFT institutions are more exclusive in that they charge higher tuition, have more faculty with doctorates, are more selective in admissions, and have larger library holdings. They note implications and question the assumed unity of the collective bargaining movement.

301 Smith, Milton L. *A Study of the Status of Tenure in the Nation's Public Two-Year Colleges.* San Marcos: Southwest Texas State University, 1984. 9 pages. (ED 250 029)

This paper surveys state administrators of two-year college education to assess tenure policies in community colleges. It examines the provision of statutory or customary tenure, the number of years of consecutive employment needed to become eligible for tenure, reasons for the dismissal of tenured faculty, the power of local boards to establish tenure policy, and the effect of collective bargaining on tenure. The author finds that only a minority of the states have formal tenure policies and that "public two-year college faculty members are not served well by the concept of tenure" (p. 5).

302 "Tenure at Two-Year Colleges and Institutes." *Journal of the College and University Personnel Association,* 1980, *31* (3-4), 109-135.

This article surveys tenure policies at 371 public and private two-year colleges and institutes, examining how colleges define an award of tenure, whether policies are established in writing, methods used to notify instructors of tenure eligibility, the departmental locus of tenure, and the college staff who make tenure decisions. It also reports data on (1) the relationship of tenure to funding sources, (2) faculty ranks applied to tenured and nontenured faculty, (3) the correlation of criteria used to make tenure and promotion decisions, and (4) tenure for noninstructional staff. It concludes with information on tenure eligibility for part-time faculty, time/service requirements for tenure, and faculty dismissal policies. The article provides useful background information for administrators developing faculty tenure policies.

303 "The Virginia Community College System: A Report on
Tenure and Due Process." *AAUP Bulletin*, 1975, *61* (1),
30–38.

This article recounts events leading up to and immediately
following the 1972 decision of the Virginia State Board for
Community Colleges to remove faculty tenure except for those
instructors who already possessed or had been recommended for
tenure. It concludes that the State Board of Community Colleges
and the chancellor acted furtively, without faculty consultation
and contrary to faculty will. It demonstrates the strong support of
the American Association of University Professors for faculty
tenure at community colleges.

304 Wallace, Terry H. Smith. "Provision for Community
College Faculty Development in Collective Bargaining
Agreements." *Research in Higher Education*, 1976, *4* (4),
381–392.

This article examines fifty-eight community college collective
bargaining agreements, focusing on the nature and value of
provisions negotiated for staff development programs. It reports
the frequency of specific provisions related to sabbaticals, tuition
reimbursement, educational travel, attendance at professional
meetings, released time, and stipends for developing experimental
instructional programs. The author concludes that few colleges
negotiate comprehensive staff development packages, that there is
only piecemeal agreement on faculty development policies, and
that the most common provisions are those that have low costs or
that are norms in academe (such as sabbaticals and leaves without
pay).

Part-Time Faculty

305 Bauer, William K. "Adjunct Faculty: Collective Bargaining and Affirmative Action Personnel Policies and Procedures." *Journal of the College and University Personnel Association*, 1982, *33* (4), 1–7.

The author analyzes the effect of collective bargaining and affirmative action on personnel policies regarding adjunct faculty at the Pennsylvania community colleges. He compares the policies of colleges that extend collective bargaining to adjunct faculty with the policies of colleges that do not extend collective bargaining to part-timers. He also compares the policies of colleges that utilize affirmative action in the selection of adjunct faculty with the policies of colleges that do not apply affirmative action in part-time hiring. He concludes that adherence or nonadherence to collective bargaining or affirmative action does not fully explain variances in personnel policies applied to adjunct instructors and notes that other financial factors weigh heavily in the institution and maintenance of personnel practices.

306 Bender, Louis W., and Breuder, Robert. "Part-time Teachers—'Step-Children' of the Community College." *Community College Review*, 1973, *1* (1), 29–37.

This article describes a national survey conducted in 1972 to assess community college policies toward adjunct, part-time faculty. The authors conclude that recruitment, training, and evaluation policies concerning adjunct faculty are weak or nonexistent and that the employment of part-time faculty is not used by colleges or prospective faculty members as a trial period before making a full-time employment commitment. They note implications in light of the increased use of part-timers to expand college services.

307 Fryer, Thomas W., Jr. "Designing New Personnel Policies: The Permanent Part-Time Faculty Member." *Journal of the College and University Personnel Association*, 1977, *28* (2), 14–21.

The author discusses emerging issues related to the growing number of permanent part-time faculty—those instructors who are hired year after year on a part-time basis. He notes the large proportion of instructional work load taught by part-timers, the difficulty of determining equitable compensation rates for part-timers, judicial rulings granting due process and tenure rights to part-time faculty who have continuity of service, and the organization of part-timers in faculty unions. He points out the righteous indignation of growing numbers of part-timers who see themsclves as victims of an unjust system that assigns them second-class status and concludes with eight suggested policies governing the use of part-time faculty and their relation to the college.

308 Guthrie-Morse, Barbara. "The Utilization of Part-Time Faculty." *Community College Frontiers*, 1979, 7 (3), 8–17.

This article examines the use of part-time instructors through a review of the literature and an analysis of national data on the numbers of part-timers employed. It uses data provided by the American Association of Community and Junior Colleges to point out that in the four years between 1973 and 1977, the part-time cohort had grown from 40 to 56 percent of the total faculty employed. The author discusses resulting benefits enjoyed by colleges, including lower wages, single-term contracts, reduced fringe benefits, job protection for full-time faculty, up-to-date expertise in some teaching areas, and increased contact with the community. She concludes with a discussion of the drive to institute pro rata salary scales for part-timers, arguing that pro rata salaries are possible only with a reduction in the number of instructors employed.

309 Hammons, James. "Adjunct Faculty: Another Look." *Community College Frontiers,* 1981, *9* (2), 46–53.

The author discusses growth in the use of part-time or adjunct faculty and the necessity for more careful training, supervision, and evaluation of these instructors. He notes that reasons for growth in part-time faculty include lower costs, staff flexibility and availability, and community relations. He cites the paucity of research on the performance of part-time instructors and recommends better training of supervisors and evaluators of part-timers and more direct methods for involving them in college processes.

310 Hoffman, John R. "The Use and Abuse of Part-Time Instructors." *Community Services Catalyst,* 1980, *10* (1), 12–18.

This article surveys the extended-day directors at community colleges in seven southwestern states to identify discrepancies between actual and ideal personnel policies governing the employment of part-time faculty. It draws upon an extensive literature review—as well as the survey findings—to note needed improvements in each of five areas: recruitment, selection, orientation, supervision, and evaluation. The author finds that the smaller the institution, the less well defined and systematic are the personnel practices directed toward part-timers. He also notes that recruiting is most often accomplished through contacts with full-time faculty members and that orientation and supervision activities are typically minimal. He recommends more systematic procedures, including evaluation of part-timers and deliberate steps to integrate them into the college environment.

311 Lombardi, John. *Part-Time Faculty in Community Colleges.* Topical Paper no. 54. Los Angeles: ERIC Clearinghouse for Junior Colleges, 1975. 62 pages. (ED 115 316)

The author utilizes a variety of data sources to provide an exhaustive analysis of the status of part-time faculty in community colleges as of 1975. He provides background information on the growing numbers of part-time instructors, the sources of part-time faculty, and their academic backgrounds and qualifications. He also discusses policy-related issues, including the definition of part-time work loads, provisions to control the number of part-timers teaching day courses, and wage patterns. He concludes that pro rata pay (computed as a fraction of the current salary paid to full-time instructors) can be expected for part-time teachers during the next ten years. The work includes a seventy-four-item bibliography.

312 Parsons, Michael H. (ed.). *Using Part-Time Faculty Effectively.* New Directions for Community Colleges, no. 30. San Francisco: Jossey-Bass, 1980. 115 pages. (ED 188 717)

This sourcebook presents thirteen essays examining the characteristics and support of part-time faculty at two-year colleges. It examines staff development opportunities for part-time faculty, the integration of part-time faculty into college life, support and training for vocational-technical adjunct faculty, legal issues, and the special problems of being a part-time instructor. It also suggests eight steps to be followed in achieving parity for adjunct faculty and concludes with a sixty-one-item bibliography. The book provides staff development officers with an introduction to the problems posed by the increased employment of part-time faculty and to the approaches that might be used in solving those problems.

313 Tuckman, Barbara H., and Tuckman, Howard P. "Part-Timers, Sex Discrimination, and Career Choice at Two-Year Institutions: Further Findings from the AAUP Survey." *Academic: Bulletin of the AAUP,* 1980, *66* (2), 71–76.

The authors utilize data from a national survey of adjunct faculty to discuss sex discrimination in wages, hiring practices, and employment conditions among part-time instructors, dividing respondents ($N = 1,980$) into four groups: "hopeful part-time" (those seeking full-time jobs), "full-mooners" (those with another full-time job), "part-mooners" (those with another part-time job), and "home-workers" (those attending to children or relatives at home). They discover that there is relatively little difference in the credentials of male and female part-timers but that men are more highly paid, hold more of the available permanent positions, are outside of the labor market for shorter periods of time, and are more mobile. They conclude that there is definite discrimination against women in all respondent groups and that part-time positions for women rarely lead to full-time academic posts.

314 Tuckman, Howard P., and Caldwell, Jaime. "The Reward Structure for Part-Timers in Academe." *Journal of Higher Education,* 1979, *50* (6), 745–760.

The authors utilize data collected in a national survey of part-time faculty at 128 colleges and universities to develop regression equations explaining variances in part-timers' salaries at two-year colleges, four-year colleges, and universities. They come to the general conclusion that salaries for adjunct instructors (unlike those for full-time staff) are more influenced by institutional policies (such as length of contract) than by professional skills (such as experience, educational attainment, and so on). They note, however, that two-year colleges are an exception, because salaries for adjunct faculty at those institutions are highly influenced by years of part-time teaching experience. They suggest, therefore, that part-timers are more accepted at two-year colleges than at four-year institutions or universities.

5

Governance, Administration, and Planning

The extraordinary growth in the numbers of two-year colleges during the 1950s and 1960s was matched with a growing concern for their efficient operation and administration. Numerous scholars turned their attention to administrative issues, with the result that a large body of the two-year college literature focuses on governance, administration, and planning. This chapter organizes a selection of that literature under five headings: administrators and administrative leadership (nos. 315–348); boards of trustees (nos. 349–361); institutional governance and administrative organization (nos. 362–391); the state role in administration and governance (nos. 392–422); and institutional research and planning (nos. 423–450). Writings dealing with finance and financial management are presented in Chapter Six.

Administrators and Administrative Leadership

The items cited in the first section of this chapter (nos. 315–348) deal with the characteristics and roles of two-year college administrators. Major themes covered in this literature include:

- the contradictory nature of the president's role as both administrator and educational leader (no. 321);

- the attitudes of college presidents toward their jobs (nos. 324, 338, 340);
- the characteristics and responsibilities of department chairpersons and deans (nos. 325, 326, 327, 331, 342, 344);
- the characteristics and responsibilities of miscellaneous college administrators, including student personnel administrators (nos. 317, 345), community service and continuing education directors (no. 335), financial aid officers (no. 343), and library administrators (nos. 333, 334); and
- the characteristics and perceptions of women and minority administrators (nos. 322, 330, 332).

Because the literature on college administrators is relatively small (especially in comparison to the large number of works dealing with faculty and students), it is difficult to draw generalizations about the state of administrative leadership at two-year colleges. A review of the available writings, however, indicates that administrators face considerable obstacles. Some authors, including Moore (no. 337), argue that the educational and professional backgrounds of administrators do not prepare them to deal with the special problems of the two-year college. Writers focusing on the department chairperson, including Pierce (no. 342), Lombardi (no. 331), Shawl (no. 344), and Hammons and Hunter (no. 326), emphasize the erosion of the chairperson's authority as the bureaucratic organization of the college grows larger. As for the president, Vaughan (no. 346) examines stress-related burnout among chief executive officers, noting that most presidents who started their careers in the growth era of the 1960s found themselves in a more stressful environment, characterized by diminished career mobility, reduced funding, and collective bargaining, in the 1980s.

Boards of Trustees

Although trustees are the chief architects of institutional policy, relatively few works examine their characteristics or responsibilities. Those authors who have examined trusteeship provide information on:

- board relations with the president (nos. 352, 354, 356, 357);
- the board's role in collective bargaining (nos. 355, 356);
- trustee characteristics and attitudes (nos. 349, 351, 359);
- responsibilities and requisite trustee competencies (nos. 350, 352, 358, 360, 361); and
- methods of trustee selection (nos. 350, 353).

One of the most controversial and long-standing debates about trusteeship centers on the alleged conservatism of trustees and the effect of that conservatism on the expansion of educational opportunities to the entire community. Moore (no. 360) posits that trustees are often ignorant of the special role of the community college and are unrepresentative of college constituencies in terms of race and social class. Bers (no. 349) notes that conservative boards are especially characteristic of rural areas, where the average trustee is more likely to be a male conservative Republican with no prior affiliation with a community college. But the effect of this conservatism is unclear. Mills (no. 359) found in 1972 that the average trustee was indeed politically conservative but that he at the same time was supportive of open admissions and the comprehensive curriculum.

Institutional Governance and Administrative Organization

As the colleges expanded and grew in numbers during the 1960s and 1970s, considerable attention was paid to the administrative organization of the colleges and to the participation of various college constituencies in the administrative decision-making process. At least two comprehensive texts on organization and governance in the two-year college have appeared: *Governance for the Two-Year College,* by Richardson, Blocker, and Bender (no. 387), and *Power and Politics in the Community College,* by Zoglin (no. 391). The former pays particular attention to participatory processes that involve all college groups in governance, while the latter illustrates the complex interactions of internal politics, collective bargaining, trustees, and governmental agencies in the governance process.

The major themes emerging in the remaining literature include the following:

- the growth and organization of multicampus and multicollege institutions (nos. 370, 375, 376, 377, 385);
- the bureaucratization of colleges as they grow older (no. 373);
- the department structure of the colleges (nos. 379, 380) and alternative "cluster" models of college organization (nos. 367, 372, 378); and
- participatory management within the college and the distribution of decision making among faculty and administrators (nos. 363, 371, 374, 376, 384, 387).

The last item mentioned—participatory management—has been a particularly troublesome and elusive goal for the two-year college. Prominent authors, such as Richardson (no. 384), have repeatedly called for a democratization of the traditional, hierarchical administrative structure of two-year colleges. Democratization has also been a major impetus behind proposed "cluster" models of college organization. Yet recent evidence advanced by Baldridge, Curtis, Ecker, and Riley (no. 363) indicates that community college governance is still characterized by weak faculty influence and greater administrator domination.

The State Role in Administration and Governance

Growing state authority is an important theme in the community college literature of the 1970s and early 1980s. Authors focusing on the state role in college governance have examined, among other topics, the following:

- statewide master plans (no. 402);
- patterns of state financial support (nos. 393, 394, 398, 406, 418);
- the characteristics and activities of state boards governing two-year colleges (no. 399, 411, 419);
- patterns and practices of statewide coordination and policy making (nos. 392, 396, 397, 400, 403, 407, 409, 412, 413, 417, 420, 421); and

- causes of increased state control and its impact on local autonomy (nos. 395, 416, 421).

Of these themes, the impact of state control on local autonomy has been the most controversial. Many authors, including Bender (no. 395) and Tillery and Wattenbarger (no. 416), focus on the potential damage to local autonomy and the ability of the colleges to respond to local, community needs. Authors contributing to the New Directions volume on *Balancing State and Local Control* (no. 396) also point to the negative consequences of increased state control (such as increased bureaucratization and diminished authority in curriculum development) but concede that there are benefits to be gained in terms of more stable funding. The story of community college governance in the past twenty years, then, has largely been one of a trade-off of some local autonomy for state funds.

Institutional Research and Planning

A good deal of the administrative literature is devoted to institutional research and planning. Authors focusing on the research function have covered a wide variety of related issues, including:

- economic approaches to college planning (no. 430);
- the planning involved in starting a new college (no. 423);
- problems in defining and measuring institutional accountability and productivity (nos. 434, 440, 446).
- the status of community college institutional research offices (nos. 432, 437, 438, 444);
- identifying research priorities and needs (nos. 433, 441);
- methods of conducting community impact studies (nos. 424, 442);
- comprehensive institutional planning (nos. 425, 435, 443, 445);
- utilization of student information systems (no. 431); and
- the statewide coordination of community college research efforts (no. 439).

In addition, two comprehensive works on the institutional research function have appeared: *Junior College Institutional Research: The State of the Art,* by Roueche and Boggs (no. 447), and *Community College Research: Methods, Trends, and Prospects,* a collection of essays compiled by the Educational Testing Service (no. 428). Both are by now somewhat dated.

Sources of Further Information

The items cited in this chapter of the bibliography by no means exhaust the literature on two-year college governance and administration. The ERIC data base (discussed in Chapter Thirteen) provides hundreds of additional relevant documents, including:

- state and national compilations of statistical data on the number and demographic characteristics of community college administrators;
- descriptions of governance structures at individual colleges;
- institutional and statewide master plans;
- institutional research reports from individual colleges;
- research reports emanating from the central offices of state community college systems; and
- annual summaries of state legislation affecting community colleges (compiled by S. V. Martorana and his associates at the Pennsylvania State University).

Besides these primary sources in the ERIC data base, the researcher should also consult the general works (nos. 7–39) listed in Chapter Two of this bibliography. Most of these works appearing after World War II include a chapter or two on administration and governance and thus provide an excellent starting point for those wishing an introduction to related issues and problems. Of particular note are the analyses provided by Bogue (no. 8), Medsker (no. 25), Blocker, Plummer, and Richardson (no. 7), Medsker and Tillery (no. 26), Ogilvie and Raines (no. 29), Monroe (no. 27), Thornton (no. 34), Bushnell (no. 10), and Cohen and Brawer (no. 12).

Administrators and Administrative Leadership

315 Alfred, Richard; Elsner, Paul; and LeCroy, Jan (eds.). *Emerging Roles for Community College Leaders.* New Directions for Community Colleges, no. 46. San Francisco: Jossey-Bass, 1984. 129 pages. (ED 245 773)

This sourcebook presents eleven essays that focus on changes in the environment of leadership for community colleges and consider methods for identifying and developing future leaders. In three sections, it addresses (1) the current context for leadership, touching upon institutional responsiveness, management challenges, and leadership development programs; (2) the provision of effective leadership in an area of transition, including new relationships with government, business and industry, and technological innovations; and (3) developing community college leaders for tomorrow through graduate education, on-the-job experience, and other means. It also provides a literature review on the community college presidency.

316 Birmingham, Joseph C., and Borland, David T. "Collective Bargaining in the Future: A Study of Administrator Attitudes." *Community/Junior College Research Quarterly*, 1980, *4* (2), 169–183.

Please see no. 274 for the full annotation.

317 Brooks, Gary D., and Avila, Jose F. "A Profile of Student Personnel Workers in Junior and Community Colleges." *Journal of College Student Personnel.* 1973, *14* (6), 532–536.

This article details the findings of a survey conducted in spring 1972 to develop a demographic and professional profile of the chief student personnel officers at the nation's two-year colleges. It draws upon the responses of 252 student personnel administrators (representing 53 percent of the national sample included in the survey) to assess their characteristics in terms of age, sex, ethnicity, educational background, titles, salaries, primary responsibilities, years of experience, and publications contributed to professional journals. The authors conclude that the profession suffers from a lack of representation of women and minorities and from a high mortality rate.

318 Brooks, Gary D., and Avila, Jose F. "A Descriptive Profile of Junior College Presidents." *Research in Higher Education.* 1974, *2* (2), 145–150.

This article profiles the community college president on the basis of data collected in a survey of chief executive officers at 556 randomly selected two-year institutions. It examines data related to sex, ethnicity, educational background, salary, age, length of service, professional affiliations, and prior publications and also summarizes major areas of concern, including the small number of women and minorities among college presidents and the high turnover rate of chief executive officers. The article serves as a concise summary of the demographic and background characteristics of community college presidents as of the mid 1970s.

319 Campbell, Dale F. (ed.). *Strengthening Financial Management.* New Directions for Community Colleges, no. 50. San Francisco: Jossey-Bass, 1985. 135 pages. (ED 258 654)

Please see no. 456 for the full annotation.

320 Cohen, Arthur M. "Chapter Eight: Leading the Educational Program." In George B. Vaughan and Associates, *Issues for Community College Leaders in a New Era.* San Francisco: Jossey-Bass, 1983, pp. 159–185.

For an annotation of the work in its entirety, please see no. 37.

321 Cohen, Arthur M., and Roueche, John E. *Institutional Administrator or Educational Leader? The Junior College President*. Washington, D.C.: American Association of Junior Colleges; Los Angeles: ERIC Clearinghouse for Junior Colleges; Rougemont, N.C.: Regional Education Laboratory for the Carolinas and Virginia, 1969. 55 pages. (ED 031 186)

The authors argue that community college presidents should be educational leaders rather than institutional administrators. They discuss the differences between the two job orientations, noting that the administrator is concerned with the maintenance and survival of the institution, while the educational leader changes the organizational structure of the college as needed to maximize student learning. They draw upon a survey of institutional documents (including presidential job descriptions) to demonstrate that, in reality, the junior college president is neither assigned responsibility nor held accountable for educational leadership. The work concludes with ten steps that trustees can take to rectify this situation, stressing the desirability of board policies that allow the president to delegate the day-to-day chores of fiscal administration.

322 Eaton, Judith S. (ed.). *Women in Community Colleges*. New Directions for Community Colleges, no. 34. San Francisco: Jossey-Bass, 1981. 110 pages. (ED 203 929)

This sourcebook presents seven articles analyzing the impact of the changing role of women on community colleges, including discussions of the backgrounds and experiences of women community college presidents, the struggle of women faculty for equal professional status, the contributions that women can make to strengthen humanities programs, programs targeted to serve special groups of women, ways community colleges can improve women's educational and occupational mobility, and the role of women trustees. It concludes with a review of those researching the role of women in two-year colleges.

323 Foresi, Joseph, Jr. *Administrative Leadership in the Community College.* Jericho, N.Y.: Exposition Press, 1974. 105 pages.

This guidebook for prospective and newly appointed administrators defines administrative responsibilities in general terms and sketches the concept of management by objectives. It considers the roles of the various administrators in a typical community college organization, presenting data from a survey of ninety-three California community college presidents asking about their prior experience and administrative emphasis. The book concludes with a statement of duties carried out by the governing board, administration, faculty, and citizen advisory groups.

324 Gillie, Angelo C., Sr. "Occupational Perceptions of Two-Year College Presidents." *Community College Frontiers,* 1978, 7 (1), 38–43.

The author examines factors that affect the community college presidency and analyzes the opinions of current presidents, former presidents, and current state directors about the duties and influence of the president. He notes that, while most agree that the president's main job is to maintain an optimal environment for learning, there is often disagreement as to the relative importance of the numerous other functions assigned to the president. He briefly compares the responses of current presidents and former presidents to survey questions concerning the most important function of the chief executive, preferred college governance models, the extent of the president's influence, and his or her decision-making authority. The article provides insights into how presidents view their jobs.

325 Groner, Norman E. "Leadership Situations in Academic Departments: Relations Among Measures of Situational Favorableness and Control." *Research in Higher Education,* 1978, 8 (2), 125–143.

The author utilizes data from a statewide survey of community college faculty and department chairpersons in Washington to test hypotheses about environmental factors that affect the ability of chairpersons to exert leadership. He examines the correlation between measures of chairperson control and "situational favorableness" measures related to the quality of relations between faculty and chairpersons, the degree to which the chairperson's job is clearly defined, and the clarity of criteria used to assess faculty performance. He compares his findings with a similar study undertaken at a university and concludes that good faculty-chairperson relations are significantly correlated with clarity in faculty assessment criteria. The article underscores the importance of clear, objective staff evaluation policies to organizational effectiveness.

326 Hammons, James O., and Hunter, Walter. "The Perceived Problems of Community College Department/Division Chairpersons as Revealed by the Nominal Group Process." *Community/Junior College Research Quarterly*, 1977, *1* (2), 163–170.

This article examines findings and implications of a workshop at which sixty-three community college chairpersons were asked to determine the five most prevalent factors that prevent them from exercising leadership, noting that the top-ranked obstacle to effective functioning was the lack of a clearly defined role for the chairperson. Other obstacles included weak support and direction from top administrators, faculty-related problems (such as lack of faculty motivation to improve or the lack of effective faculty evaluation criteria), and organizational problems within the college. The authors conclude that the majority of chairpersons felt powerless in facing and correcting these obstacles and that the middle-management structure of community colleges may be eroding.

327 Hammons, James, and Thomas, Wanda. "Performance Appraisal of Community College Department/Division Chairpersons." *Community College Review*, 1980, 7 (3), 41–49.

The authors draw upon a survey of 472 institutions to study the appraisal systems used to evaluate community college department and division chairpersons, analyzing (1) the percentage of colleges that have such systems; the purposes, procedures, criteria, and standards used to appraise the administrative performance of chairpersons; the perceptions of chairpersons regarding these systems; the standards and criteria that chairpersons would like to see in evaluation systems; and the degree to which current appraisal systems improve the chairperson's administrative performance. Among their findings are that 82 percent of the responding colleges had evaluation systems, that only 9 percent of the chairpersons felt that evaluation was based solely on objective criteria, and that the perceptions of chairpersons did not vary by academic discipline. They conclude with recommendations for strengthening the evaluation process.

328 Hammons, James O., and Wallace, Terry H. Smith. "Staff Development Needs of Public Community College Department/Division Chairpersons." *Community/Junior College Research Quarterly*, 1977, 2 (1), 55–76.

The authors study the staff development needs of 1,100 two-year college chairpersons who were surveyed to obtain information on (1) descriptive data about the colleges at which they work, such as region, size, presence of collective bargaining, and so on; (2) information on preservice and in-service training currently received by chairpersons; (3) chairperson opinions regarding areas that should be covered in professional development activities; and (4) chairperson opinions on the timing and duration of in-service activities. They indicate that preservice preparation, in-service training, and self-improvement activities of chairpersons are at best nominal and at worst nonexistent and suggest that this results in a loss of efficiency and in a hesitancy to make decisions. They conclude with seven recommendations to increase the availability of training for two-year college chairpersons.

329 Jaap, William M., and Baker, George A. "The Impact of Collective Bargaining on the Administrative Functions and Roles of Community College Presidents." *Community/Junior College Quarterly of Research and Practice,* 1982, *6* (2), 157–166.

Please see no. 282 for the full annotation.

330 Kimmons, Willie J. *Black Administrators in Public Community Colleges: Self-Perceived Role and Status.* New York: Carlton Press, 1977, 202 pages.

This publication examines the background of black community college administrators and assesses their perceptions about their roles and status, utilizing data from a survey of 189 black administrators who were categorized on three levels: (1) presidents, chancellors, or chief administrators; (2) vice-presidents, provosts, deans, associate deans, or assistant deans; and (3) department or division chairpersons, program coordinators, or department heads. It summarizes findings concerning the line positions that black administrators occupy, their self-perceived role function, and differences—if any—in the responses of administrators at predominantly black, predominantly white, and integrated institutions. Among the implications is that black administrators at predominantly black institutions experience a higher degree of role conflict than their colleagues at predominantly white institutions.

331 Lombardi, John. *The Duties and Responsibilities of the Department/Division Chairman in Community Colleges.* Topical Paper no. 39. Los Angeles: ERIC Clearinghouse for Junior Colleges, 1974. 21 pages. (ED 089 811)

This paper contrasts formally established duty lists of community college department chairpersons with research findings on what chairpersons actually do, noting that formal duty lists are grossly exaggerated and provide no indication of the authority exercised by chairpersons. The author argues that the chairperson's authority has, in fact, been eroded by the movement toward participatory democracy, collective bargaining, and administrators' efforts to gain control over the teaching-learning unit and concludes that the chairperson will become a "ministerial officer who acts as the 'servant' of the faculty performing duties . . . in accordance with directions established in policy manuals, state laws, and collective bargaining agreements" (p. 16).

332 Lopez, Alberta F., and Schultz, Raymond E. "Role Conflict of Chicano Administrators in Community Colleges." *Community College Review*, 1980, 7 (3), 50–55.

This article examines the role perceptions of Chicano administrators at public community colleges in five southwestern states, drawing upon a survey of 175 Chicano administrators who were asked for information on (1) how Chicano administrators perceive their professional roles, (2) whether the respondents feel that their role perceptions are at odds with what is expected of them by students, the community, and the institution, and (3) the specific experiences and beliefs that affect the role of Chicano administrators. The authors conclude that ethnicity is a significant factor in the way Chicano administrators perceive their roles and that Chicano administrators balance "allegiance to their institution, to their Chicano constituencies, and to their own Chicano value system" (p. 54).

333 Matthews, Elizabeth W. "Trends Affecting Community College Library Administrators." *College and Research Libraries*, 1977, *38* (3), 210–217.

Please see no. 669 for the full annotation.

334 Matthews, Elizabeth W. "Update in Education for Community College Library Administrators." *Journal of Education for Librarianship*, 1979, *19* (4), 304–311.

Please see no. 670 for the full annotation.

335 Miles, Leroy. "A Survey of Adult and Continuing Education Competencies Needed by Directors of Community Services and Continuing Education." *Community/Junior College Research Quarterly*, 1980, *4* (4), 319–330.

Please see no. 818 for the full annotation.

336 Moore, Kathryn M.; Twombly, Susan B., and Martorana, S. V. *Today's Academic Leaders: A National Study of Administrators in Community and Junior Colleges*. University Park: Center for the Study of Higher Education, Pennsylvania State University, 1985. 129 pages.

This publication details the findings of a national survey conducted in 1984 to provide descriptive information on the personal and professional characteristics of community college administrators. The authors examine data related to (1) demographic and socioeconomic characteristics, (2) participation in professional and community activities, (3) mentor relationships, (4) job-search activities leading to employment in administrative positions, (5) factors that attract administrators to their current positions, (6) reasons administrators have for remaining in their positions or for considering a job change, and (7) administrators' opinions concerning future issues. The work provides a cross-sectional picture of two-year college administrators at all levels, including presidents, campus executives, chief academic and business officers, student affairs officers, head librarians, financial aid directors, and directors of continuing education.

337 Moore, William, Jr. *Blind Man on a Freeway: The Community College Administrator*. San Francisco: Jossey-Bass, 1971. 173 pages.

The author points to inadequacies of graduate school programs that prepare community college administrators and examines the administrator's role in meeting the needs of new constituent groups. He presents anecdotes from community colleges concerning the function of the administrator and describes the new constituent groups that community college administrators interact

with, including student activists, women's rights advocates,
minority groups, and militant faculty members. He also examines
the responsibilities of the community college administrator in the
delivery of education to the disadvantaged. He urges the development of a national effort to train community college administrators and examines approaches to emerging campus problems, such
as racial bigotry and discrimination. The work serves as an
overview (albeit an anecdotal one) of the challenges to administrators that were posed by the social upheavals of the 1960s.

338 Morgan, Don A. *Perspectives of the Community College
Presidency.* Occasional Report no. 14. Los Angeles: Junior
College Leadership Program, Graduate School of Educa-
tion, University of California, 1970. 19 pages. (ED 038 955)

This report draws upon the findings of several surveys conducted
informally by the author to examine how community college
presidents—as well as their associates—view the community
college presidency. It summarizes survey findings as they relate to
the advice responding presidents have for newly appointed chief
executive officers, the reasons presidents have for eventually
leaving their jobs, and the characteristics of successful and
unsuccessful presidents. It also examines how the presidency is
viewed by "second-ranking" administrators (for example, vice-
presidents or assistants to the president), by the presidents' spouses,
and by the presidents' secretaries. It provides the reader with
insights into how community college presidents of the late 1960s
viewed their jobs.

339 Nicholson, R. Stephen. *Chief Executive Officers Contracts
and Compensation, 1981: A Study of the Contract Provisions. Language, Benefits, and Compensation of Chief
Executive Officers of Two-Year Colleges for the 1981 Year.*
Washington, D.C.: Presidents Academy, American Association of Community and Junior Colleges, 1981. 63 pages.
(ED 213 478)

This publication surveys the contract and compensation arrangements for chief executive officers of two-year colleges in the United

States and Canada. It includes a discussion of factors influencing compensation as well as excerpts from contracts covering areas of appointment, length of term, reappointment, duties, extent of services, housing and automobile allowances, liability, retirement, sabbaticals, disability, evaluation, termination, and other items. It is useful as a summary of the contract provisions governing college-president relations in 1981.

340 O'Connell, Thomas E. *Community Colleges: A President's View.* Urbana: University of Illinois Press, 1968, 172 pages.

Please see no. 28 for the full annotation.

341 Patten, W. G. *A Pilot Study: Priorities in Administrative Needs and Program Services for Community and Area Technical Colleges. Emphasis on Large Urban Areas.* Columbus: National Center for Research in Vocational Education, Ohio State University, 1979. 185 pages. (ED 186 703)

Please see no. 764 for the full annotation.

342 Pierce, Harmon B. "The Role of Science Division Chairmen in Regionally Accredited Two-Year Colleges: A National Survey." *Journal of Research in Science Teaching,* 1971, *8* (3), 251–254.

The author draws upon a survey of 285 community college science division heads to examine their characteristics and professional responsibilities. He summarizes survey data related to the educational backgrounds of the division heads, their years of professional experience, the roles and responsibilities of the division heads, and the factors that contribute to their job satisfaction, listing common duties performed by the respondents and obstacles to role fulfillment.

343 Puryear, James B. "Two-Year College Financial Aid Officers." *Journal of College Student Personnel,* 1974, *15* (1), 12–16.

This article details the findings of a study conducted in 1969 to compare the characteristics of financial aid directors at two-year colleges with those of financial aid directors at four-year institutions. It draws upon a survey of financial aid officers at 510 two-year colleges (60 percent of whom responded) to assess the demographic characteristics and professional backgrounds of the financial aid officers, the organization of the financial aid programs that they administer, and the factors that lead to satisfaction or dissatisfaction on the job. The author compares the resultant data with the findings of a survey of four-year college financial aid administrators conducted in 1967, noting, among other findings, that financial aid administrators at four-year and two-year colleges are similar in terms of characteristics and training.

344 Shawl, W. F. *The Role of the Academic Dean.* Topical Paper no. 42. Los Angeles: ERIC Clearinghouse for Junior Colleges, 1974. 22 pages. (ED 092 210)

This paper outlines the personal impressions and ideas of an academic dean on his role in the community college. It presents a brief historical view of the responsibilities of the academic dean and discusses the external forces impinging upon the dean in the role of curriculum developer. It also examines the dean's responsibilities in curriculum planning, staff selection, faculty evaluation, affirmative action, and collective bargaining. The author concludes that academic deans increasingly play middle-management roles, with growing numbers of administrators both above or below the dean on the college's organization chart.

345 Thurston, Alice J., and others. *The Chief Student Personnel Administrator in the Public Two-Year College.* Horizons Monograph Series. Washington, D.C.: American Association of Junior Colleges, 1972. 75 pages (ED 060 840)

This publication reviews findings of two studies, independently undertaken, that explore the roles and characteristics of chief student personnel administrators at junior colleges. One study, completed in 1968, surveyed a national stratified random sample of these administrators; the other study, conducted a year earlier, surveyed only those administrators in midwestern junior colleges. The authors summarize survey data as they relate to the personal characteristics of the administrators, their educational and employment backgrounds, and other job-related factors, such as salaries, job title, professional affiliations, aspirations, and the most pressing problems faced by the respondents. They conclude that student personnel administrators have only peripheral status within the college and that their departments are underfunded and understaffed, and they outline eight recommendations for improvement.

346 Vaughan, George B. "Burnout: Threat to Presidential Effectiveness." *Community and Junior College Journal,* 1982, *52* (5), 10–13.

This article discusses stress-related burnout and examines the factors contributing to the burnout of community college presidents, summarizing burnout symptoms and ways of preventing the malaise. The author notes that most community college presidents entered the profession at relatively young ages and now find themselves at the peak of their careers with no opportunity to advance. He also notes that most presidents who started their careers in the growth era of the 1960s now work in the more stressful environment of retrenchment, unionization, and enrollment stabilization. He urges sensitivity to burnout within the college community.

347 Wenrich, J. William. "Can the President Be All Things to All People." *Community and Junior College Journal,* 1980, *51* (2), 36–40.

This article lists five roles of the community college president: advocate and representative, manager of the institution as a whole, planner and visionary, negotiator and mediator, and legitimator. The author notes the many constraints placed on presidential prerogatives from both within and outside the community college, arguing that playing the above-mentioned roles requires a sense of timing and juggling. He concludes that, amidst the ever-increasing roles and demands made on community college presidents, ethical integrity must be the overriding principle of leadership, because it, in turn, promotes ethical integrity of all who interact with the college.

348 Wing, Dennis R. W. *The Professional President: A Decade of Community Junior College Chief Executives.* Topical Paper no. 28. Los Angeles: ERIC Clearinghouse for Junior Colleges, 1972. 23 pages. (ED 058 881)

This paper surveys community college presidents holding office in 1970 and compares the survey findings with data collected in similar presidential studies conducted in 1960 and 1964. It utilizes responses from 498 presidents (68 percent of those surveyed) to profile community college presidents in terms of age, employment experience, educational background, and future career aspirations. It also examines the presidents' opinions concerning why they were selected to become chief executive officers and the ideal preparatory sequence of positions that individuals should have before assuming the presidency. The author suggests that most presidents assuming office in the 1960s were steeped in the conservative traditions of standard collegiate education and that this conservatism may account for the fact that community colleges have not strayed far from traditional collegiate modes.

Boards of Trustees

349 Bers, Trudy H. "Trustee Characteristics and Decision Making Among Suburban and Rural Community College Trustees." *Community/Junior College Research Quarterly,* 1980, *4* (3), 249–262.

This article reports the results of a study comparing personal characteristics, decision making, and conflict among selected community college trustees in suburban and rural areas in Illinois, finding that rural trustees are more likely to be Republican, conservative, and male, more active in a variety of social organizations, and more likely to have had no prior affiliation with the community college than their suburban counterparts. The author maintains that trustees in rural and suburban districts have different notions about the programs that would most benefit their communities. She notes increased state control, however, and suggests that suburban/rural variations in trustee perspectives are "temporary and symbolic accommodations to the philosophy that community responsiveness is the special mission of community colleges" (p. 261).

350 Cosand, Joseph P. "The Community College in a New Period of Change." *AGB Reports,* 1975, *17* (8), 32–42.

This article provides an overview of the role and function of community college boards of trustees, examining (1) the ongoing evaluation and planning role of trustee boards, (2) the selection of board members, (3) the image, organization, size, and structure of the board, (4) the trustee role in selecting the college president, (5) the value of lay advisory committees, (6) guidelines for effective board meetings, (7) faculty input in board decisions, and (8) the trustee role in setting institutional goals. It also discusses emerging issues that board members should be aware of, including tenure and collective bargaining, affirmative action, interinstitutional cooperation, and nontraditional patterns of college attendance. The author concludes that trustee boards need to be dedicated, well informed, and willing to plan for changing community college needs.

351 Drake, Sandra L. *A Study of Community and Junior College Boards of Trustees.* Washington, D.C.: American Association of Community and Junior Colleges, Association of Community College Trustees, and Association of Governing Boards of Universities and Colleges, 1977. 59 pages.

This publication draws upon a national survey of community college presidents and governing board chairpersons to examine the characteristics, attitudes, and activities of two-year college trustees. It includes analyses of demographic, occupational, and other background characteristics, as well as analysis of the time spent by trustees on various functions. It serves as a descriptive profile of community college trustees in the mid 1970s.

352 Dziuba, Victoria, and Meardy, William (eds.). *Enhancing Trustee Effectiveness.* New Directions for Community Colleges, no. 15. San Francisco: Jossey-Bass, 1976. 109 pages. (ED 130 693)

This sourcebook presents sixteen articles on increasing the effectiveness of community college trustees. It identifies the numerous responsibilities and challenges trustees face, such as financial constraints, legal matters, increases in teacher militancy, collective bargaining, affirmative action, governance tasks, and other issues. It also examines a cost-benefit analysis of appointing trustees rather than electing them, ways to improve the board meeting's effectiveness, a self-evaluation instrument for trustee use, the relationship between the board and the president as management partners, the need for trustees to become politically involved at the local, state, and national levels, and guidelines for attaining financial stability. The volume concludes with projections of undergraduate education trends in the 1980s and a bibliography of relevant literature.

353 Goddard, Jeanne M., and Polk, Charles H. "Community College Trustees: Elect or Appoint?" *AGB Reports,* 1976, *18* (3), 37–40.

This article discusses the two principal methods of community college trustee selection: election and appointment. The authors argue that the selection of a trustee is a political act in which costs and benefits are weighed by each of the four actors involved in the process (the appointing authority, the voters, the trustee, and the college president). They note, for example, that trustee appointment by a governor may be used by the governor to mend political fences (a benefit to him or her) but may also alienate members of the public who are opposed to the appointee and that the elected trustee usually has more power or political independence than an appointed one, but only at the price of the financial and emotional rigors of a political campaign. They conclude that neither selection method is better, because each has counterbalancing pluses and minuses. The article serves as a reminder of the intricate political consequences of trustee selection.

354 Hall, Robert A. *Challenge and Opportunity: The Board of Trustees, the President, and Their Relationship in Community College Governance.* Annandale, Va.: Association of Community College Trustees, 1981. 29 pages. (ED 201 362)

This publication discusses the board-president relationship and its importance to community college governance. The author considers the political context within which this relationship operates, focusing on the external forces to which the president and board must jointly respond, and examines other aspects of governance, including (1) the state's role; (2) administrative areas determined partially by the state and partially by the board; (3) the nature of policy and its subdivisions—governing, executive, operating, and educational policy; (4) the roles of the board, president, deans, and students in policy making; and (5) how the subdivisions of policy blend together. He analyzes the respective roles of trustees and the president in the governance process and concludes with suggestions for strengthening the board-president relationship. The work serves as a useful introduction to governance for new community college trustees.

355 Howe, Ray. *Community College Board of Trustees and Negotiations with Faculty.* Washington, D.C.: American Association of Community and Junior Colleges and Association of Community College Trustees, 1973. 48 pages. (ED 080 116)

This publication provides board members with an introduction to collective bargaining and examines the role of the board in the bargaining process. It includes discussions of (1) what the reaction of the board should be when the prospect of collective bargaining first emerges on campus, (2) whether the faculty choice of a bargaining agent should be a serious concern of the board, (3) the board role in choosing a negotiator, (4) the relationship of the board to the negotiator, (5) the board's role in ratification, and (6) what the board should do immediately after ratification. The author emphasizes that hostile attitudes and reactions toward collective bargaining will lead to an uneasy relationship between administration and the bargaining unit.

356 Johnson, B. Lamar (ed.). *The Junior College Board of Trustees.* Occasional Report no. 16. Los Angeles: Junior College Leadership Program, University of California, 1971. 62 pages. (ED 078 817)

This publication presents nine papers delivered at the National Conference on the Junior College Board of Trustees in February 1971, including discussions of the role of the board in assuring accountability for student learning, managing college resources, and maintaining a good working relationship with the college president. It also presents analyses of the board's role in faculty negotiations and of the effects of student activism on trustees. The work serves as a review of trustee problems as they were perceived in the early 1970s.

357 King, Maxwell C., and Breuder, Robert L. *President-Trustee Relationships: Meeting the Challenge of Leadership: A Case Approach to Dysfunctional Assumptions and Techniques.* Washington, D.C.: American Association of Community and Junior Colleges, 1977. 72 pages. (ED 142 271; available in microfiche only)

This publication explores the issues involved in community college president-trustee relationships. It describes a hypothetical board meeting that portrays events representative of improper practices between boards of trustees and the chief executive officers. It also provides results of a comparative survey of presidents' and trustees' perceptions as to what the president should and should not do in working with his or her board. It concludes with a list of fundamental principles to which presidents and trustees should be sensitive in undertaking their educational responsibilities. The work serves as a representative example of the large number of works that have focused on the problems that can arise between presidents and trustees.

358 McLeod, Marshall W. *Patterns of Responsibility: Statutory Requirements of Community College Local Boards of Trustees.* Annandale, Va.: Association of Community College Trustees, 1979. 43 pages. (ED 201 363; available in microfiche only)

The author draws upon an examination of state statutes to examine the legal responsibilities of local community college governing boards. He examines the boards' legal status as corporations, the principal powers accorded to boards under state law, legal guidelines for meetings, trustee reimbursement, and statutes that define board liability. He also delineates the expressed, implied, mandatory, and permissive rights of governing boards. The work serves as a concise summary of the legally defined rights and duties of governing boards in 1979.

359 Mills, Peter K. "Community College Trustees: A Survey."
In *The Two-Year College Trustee: National Issues and
Perspectives.* Washington, D.C.: Association of Governing
Boards of Universities and Colleges, 1972, pp. 30–38. (ED
073 757)

The author draws upon a survey of 239 two-year college presidents
and 296 trustees to ascertain the characteristics of public community college trustees, describe the process by which institutional
change occurs at these colleges, and examine the interaction and
involvement of trustees with the process of change. Among the
findings are that (1) community college boards are smaller than
those at four-year institutions and usually operate as committees of
the whole, (2) the average trustee is politically conservative but
supportive of open admission and the comprehensive curriculum,
(3) trustees support the role of the president as educational change
agent, and (4) there is little faculty and student representation in
board deliberations. The work provides readers with a profile of
community college trustees in the early 1970s, noting that they
were conservative politically but progressive in terms of educational outlook.

360 Moore, William, Jr. "The Community College Board of
Trustees: A Question of Competency." *Journal of Higher
Education,* 1973, *44* (3), 171–190.

The author charges that boards of trustees are often uninformed
and incompetent, arguing that most trustees are ignorant of
educational matters and unrepresentative of the constituencies they
serve in terms of race and social class. He outlines fourteen criteria
for board competency, suggesting specific board responsibilities
related to policy formation, ethical standards, and requisite
knowledge of college affairs. This article presents one of the most
critical examinations of the community college trustee.

361 Potter, George E. *Trusteeship: Handbook for Community College and Technical Institute Trustees.* (2nd ed.) Annandale, Va.: Association of Community College Trustees, 1979. 180 pages. (ED 201 368; available in microfiche only)

This publication serves as a handbook providing basic informational aid for community college governing board members. It details (1) major trustee responsibilities, (2) the functions of board members, officers, and committees, (3) the selection and role of the board chairperson, (4) board-president relations and the evaluation of the college president, (5) legal issues, including litigation and criteria for selecting a college attorney, (6) the board's political role in state and local trustee associations, and (7) the board's role in collective bargaining. It includes several ancillary materials, such as a trustee code of ethics, sample bylaws for a trustee association, and a sample college labor agreement. The work is useful primarily as an introduction to the trustee's legal responsibilities.

Institutional Governance and Administrative Organization

362 Alfred, Richard L., and Smydra, David F. "Chapter Nine: Reforming Governance: Resolving Challenges to Institutional Authority." In William L. Deegan, Dale Tillery, and Associates, *Renewing the American Community College: Priorities and Strategies for Effective Leadership.* San Francisco: Jossey-Bass, 1985, pp. 199–228.

For an annotation of the work in its entirety, please see no. 14.

363 Baldridge, J. Victor; Curtis, David V.; Ecker, George; and Riley, Gary L. *Policy Making and Effective Leadership: A National Study of Academic Management.* San Francisco: Jossey-Bass, 1978. 290 pages.

This volume reports the findings of a national study of American college and university governance, discussing the organizational characteristics of colleges and universities and examining how these characteristics shape decision-making processes. It also

analyzes the diversity of institutional, management, and governance patterns; autonomy in academic work; faculty morale; the
effects of unionization; the role of women faculty in governance;
and governance patterns in the future. The authors compare
findings for community colleges with governance patterns at
"multiversities," liberal arts colleges, and other types of higher
education institutions. They conclude that community college
governance is characterized by relatively small faculty influence,
greater administrator domination, and increased tendency to
unionize.

364 Blocker, Clyde E.; Plummer, Robert H.; and Richardson,
Richard C., Jr. "Chapter Seven: Administrative Structure
and Functions." In Clyde E. Blocker, Robert H. Plummer,
and Richard C. Richardson, Jr., *The Two-Year College: A
Social Synthesis.* Englewood Cliffs, N.J.: Prentice-Hall,
1965, pp. 169–200.

For an annotation of the work in its entirety, please see no. 7.

365 Callahan, Daniel M., and Lake, Dale G. "Changing a
Community College." *Education and Urban Society,* 1973,
6 (1), 22–48.

The authors review a two-and-a-half-year organizational development effort conducted at a New York community college, focusing
on three conceptual models: entry, systems theory, and survey
feedback. They detail data-collection techniques, the survey
instrument package used, and data summaries. They report short-
term results of the workshops, as well as results one and two years
later, noting that, after two years of intervention efforts, the
administration experienced improvement in goal setting, program
planning, budgeting, task specification, and other areas. The
article provides an in-depth examination of an organization
development intervention in a two-year college.

366 Cohen, Arthur M., and Brawer, Florence B. "Chapter Four: Governance and Administration: Managing the Contemporary College." In Arthur M. Cohen and Florence B. Brawer, *The American Community College*. San Francisco: Jossey-Bass, 1982, pp. 93–126.

For an annotation of the work in its entirety, please see no. 12.

367 Collins, Charles C. *The Peoples' Community College: "A Cluster Model."* Pittsburg, Calif.: Community College Press, 1977. 140 pages. (ED 151 015)

This publication offers a model for building a community college dedicated to general education, replacing the traditional departmental organization of colleges with an arrangement that groups academic and vocational disciplines into clusters centered around the ideas of the physical world, the life process, economic and social institutions, human relations, and "man the creator," with, for example, engineering and computer sciences in the "physical world" cluster, health sciences and agriculture in the "life process" cluster, and business education in the "economic and social institutions" cluster. The author plots the costs of such a college and lists the specific staff positions that would be included.

368 Eells, Walter Crosby. "Chapter Thirteen: General Administrative Considerations" and Chapter Fourteen: The Administrative Staff." In Walter Crosby Eells, *The Junior College*. Boston: Houghton Mifflin, 1931, pp. 353–387.

For an annotation of the work in its entirety, please see no. 15.

369 Frankie, Richard J. "Legal Aspects of Authorization and Control in Junior Colleges: A Summary (1936-1979)." *College and University*, 1971, *46* (2), 148–154.

This article briefly sketches the role of the judiciary in defining the place of the junior college within the American educational system. It traces the role of the court in placing the early junior college in the same legal position as the high school and in upholding later legislative acts creating junior college districts outside of the common school system. It concludes with synopses of eleven court decisions affecting the authorization and control of junior colleges from 1936 to 1970.

370 Grede, John F. "Collective Comprehensiveness: A Proposal for a Big City Community College." *Journal of Higher Education*, 1970, *41* (3), 179–194.

The author argues that urban multicollege districts should be built around the principle of "collective comprehensiveness," which posits a district made up of specialized institutions rather than the development of a single mammoth college or a scattering of neighborhood comprehensive institutions. He cites two factors that have caused City Colleges of Chicago to consider this alternative: (1) the need to provide special services and operational structures for black communities and (2) the cost savings accrued by concentrating different vocational programs on a single campus. He argues further that the concentration of major occupational program groups (such as allied health or industrial and engineering technology) at single locations would improve the quality of vocational education and enhance faculty morale. The article provides one of the most forceful arguments against the belief that individual community colleges must necessarily provide a comprehensive curriculum.

371 Gunne, Manual G., and Mortimer, Kenneth P. *Distributions of Authority and Patterns of Governance*. Report no. 25. University Park: Center for the Study of Higher Education, Pennsylvania State University, 1975. 31 pages. (ED 116 757)

This report examines the distribution of decision-making authority among faculty and administrators at three community colleges and three public state colleges in Pennsylvania. The authors draw upon interviews with faculty and administrators to categorize governance conditions at each institution along a five-zone continuum: "administrative dominance," "administrative primacy," "shared authority," "faculty primacy," and "faculty dominance." They note that the community colleges were more dominance." They note that the community colleges were more likely to be characterized by administrative dominance but point out that no two institutions distributed their authority in exactly the same way and that such factors as history, tradition, and custom produce variations in governance even among colleges of a similar institutional type. The report is useful in understanding the inadequacy of research that focuses on the differences in governance between broad institutional categories (such as two-year and four-year colleges).

372 Heermann, Barry. *Organizational Breakthrough in the Community College.* Topical Paper no. 47. Los Angeles: ERIC Clearinghouse for Junior Colleges, 1974. 38 pages. (ED 100 441)

This paper challenges the traditional hierarchical and departmental structure of the community college, discussing alternatives based on (1) interdisciplinary clusters of academic and vocational departments, (2) the inclusion of faculty and students in a participative management scheme, and (3) a management-by-objectives approach to all levels of institutional planning. It provides brief case-study applications of each of these alternatives, citing strengths and weaknesses. The report serves as a description of the way in which some community colleges have departed from traditional organizational schemes.

373 Heron, R. P., and Friesen, D. "Growth and Development of College Administrative Structures." *Research in Higher Education,* 1973, *1,* 333–346.

This article examines the bureaucratization of publicly supported community colleges in Alberta, Canada, from the first operating year of each institution to December 31, 1971. The authors observe changes over the years in four groups of organizational variables: (1) methods of defining and regulating behavior, such as the degree to which procedures are written and formalized; (2) centralization of decision-making authority in the president; (3) autonomy, or the degree to which college decisions are made by college personnel rather than by outsiders, such as government agencies; and (4) measures of the configuration or shape of the organization, such as the average number of instructional personnel reporting to each immediate supervisor. They conclude that, as colleges get older, they adopt more authoritarian decision-making procedures and become less influenced by community wishes.

374 Jenkins, John A., and Rossmeier, Joseph G. *Relationships Between Centralization/Decentralization and Organizational Effectiveness in Urban Multi-Unit Community College Systems: A Summary Report.* Ann Arbor: Center for the Study of Higher Education, University of Michigan, 1974. 33 pages. (ED 110 103)

This work surveys 3,320 faculty members and administrators at twelve urban multicampus community college districts to assess perceptions of the distribution of decision-making authority and influence among six organizational levels: the board of trustees, the district administration, the unit/campus administration, deans, department chairpersons, and faculty members. It also examines the respondents' assessments of their districts' organizational effectiveness and compares those assessments with the perceived centralization of authority. Among the findings are that the twelve institutions were not highly centralized and that they differed primarily in the patterns of centralization/decentralization within their units rather than between units. The survey also indicates that there is an increase in effectiveness if participation in decision making is simultaneously increased for staff at all hierarchical levels. The work provides insights into how faculty viewed district administrative effectiveness in the early 1970s.

375 Kintzer, Frederick C. *Organization and Leadership of Two-Year Colleges: Preparing for the Eighties.* Gainesville: Institute of Higher Education, University of Florida, 1980. 35 pages. (ED 241 093)

The author examines the organization and administration of public and private American two-year colleges during the 1970s, describing changes in budgeting, the expansion of collective bargaining, and the pressure to provide increased opportunity for minority students. He also discusses developments in the administrative-management structure of two-year colleges, with a focus on the bureaucratic and participative governance models, and concludes with a comparative analysis of the organizational structures of two-year colleges, citing trends in public community colleges, single and multiunit districts, state university systems, branch colleges, state boards for community colleges, technical institutes/colleges, private institutions, and innovative institutions, such as noncampus and cluster colleges. The work serves as a brief overview of administrative trends shaping the college of the 1980s.

376 Kintzer, Frederick C. *Decision Making in Multi-Unit Institutions of Higher Education.* Gainesville: Institute of Higher Education, University of Florida, 1984. 56 pages. (ED 242 362)

This publication details the findings of a study conducted to determine the location of authority (that is, central office versus campus office) in multiunit two-year colleges. It draws upon responses from administrators at 108 campuses and 34 district offices to identify the loci of authority for eighty-four practices, categorized under eleven headings: accreditation, business, curriculum, instruction, administrative personnel, teaching personnel, nonteaching personnel, research, services, student development service, and relationships with other schools and organizations. Among the findings noted are that collective bargaining was the only activity seen by all groups as the prime responsibility of the district central office and that individual campus units controlled practices listed under curriculum, instruction, and student development services.

377 Kintzer, Frederick C.; Jensen, Arthur M.; and Hansen, John S. *The Multi-Institution Junior College District.* Horizons Monograph Series. Los Angeles: ERIC Clearinghouse for Junior Colleges; Washington, D.C.: American Association of Junior Colleges, 1969. 64 pages. (ED 030 415)

This publication provides a pioneering examination of the administration and administrative organization of urban, multicampus junior college districts, reviewing factors that have contributed to the growth of multicampus districts, guidelines for the formation and development of administrative patterns at these districts, and the pros and cons of centralized versus decentralized administrative structures. It includes case studies of multicampus districts that serve as a representative sample of common organizational patterns. The authors conclude with guidelines delineating the appropriate functions of the central office and the individual campuses. The work is useful in understanding the tensions that exist in multicampus districts between the central administration and campus personnel.

378 Koehnline, William A. "Learning Clusters: A Creative Alternative." *Community College Frontiers,* 1975, *4* (1), 26–31.

This article reports the interdisciplinary cluster pattern of organization instituted at Oakton Community College (Illinois), where each cluster is headed by a dean and has about thirty full-time faculty from the areas of business, communications, foreign languages, humanities, learning resources, mathematics and science, physical education, social science, student development, and vocational-technical programs. The author criticizes traditional department and division structures, arguing that the faculty in such groups tend to ignore the students who are not majors in their areas and that a logical coherence based on subject-matter analysis cannot be achieved. He concludes that the cluster approach is the most rational organization for community colleges, because it mitigates competition among departments and makes it more likely that students will receive a broader education.

379 Lombardi, John. *The Department/Division Structure in the Community College.* Topical Paper no. 38. Los Angeles: ERIC Clearinghouse for Junior Colleges, 1973. 25 pages. (ED 085 051)

This paper provides an overview of the composition and status of the department/division structure at community colleges, discussing the discipline orientation of the department, departmental governance, the role of nonfaculty members in the department, student demands affecting the department, and the grouping of departments in campus buildings. The author concludes that community college departments are moving toward the university model of self-governance and that college officials are trying to counteract this trend by creating a different teaching-learning unit and replacing the chairperson with an administrator. The paper provides a rare analysis of the role of the department in college governance.

380 Lombardi, John. "The Community College Departmental Structure: Directions for the Future." *Community College Review*, 1974, *2* (2), 33–40.

This article examines division and department structures in community colleges, noting (1) the history of the department structure, (2) modes of participation and governance in departments, and (3) administrative attempts to counteract the insularity of faculty and staff within traditional disciplinary units. The author points out that early junior colleges borrowed from traditional four-year institutions in establishing the department structure and that such structures have expanded in the modern age as colleges continue to adopt the university model of the autonomous academic department. He warns that increased academic departmentalization weakens institutional cohesiveness and the authority of college administrators.

381 Monroe, Charles R. "Chapter Fifteen: Governance and Decision-Making." In Charles R. Monroe, *Profile of the Community College: A Handbook.* San Francisco: Jossey-Bass, 1972, pp. 303–320.

For an annotation of the work in its entirety, please see no. 27.

382 Ogilvie, William K., and Raines, Max R. (eds.). "Part Nine: Structure and Control." In William K. Ogilvie and Max R. Raines (eds.), *Perspectives on the Community Junior College.* New York: Appleton-Century-Crofts, 1971, pp. 491–552.

For an annotation of the work in its entirety, please see no. 29.

383 Poole, Larry H., and Wattenbarger, James L. "Has Collective Bargaining Influenced Administrative Policies?" *Community College Review,* 1977, *4* (3), 8–11.

Please see no. 295 for the full annotation.

384 Richardson, Richard C., Jr. "Governance and Change in the Community-Junior College." *Journal of Higher Education,* 1973, *44* (4), 299–308.

The author argues that administrators must democratize community college governance structures or resign themselves to collective bargaining and the increased external interference of legislation and court decisions. He notes how the typical hierarchical administrative organization of the community college is dysfunctional for institutional problem solving and examines the pros and cons of two alternative mechanisms for involving faculty and staff in the governance process. He urges the adoption of an administrative philosophy based on a recognition of the interdependency of campus constituencies rather than on bureaucratic authority.

385 Richardson, Richard C., Jr. "Governing the Multiunit Community College System." *Educational Record*, 1973, *54* (2), 116–141.

The author argues that the multiunit college is best operated as a unified institution offering services in a variety of locations rather than as a multicollege district with autonomous campuses. He notes that (1) fiscal exigencies prohibit the duplication of staff, facilities, and programs that can result in a multicollege district; (2) collective bargaining is best carried out at the systemwide level; and (3) interinstitutional interdependencies mandate the system-wide coordination of campus activities. He describes a system governance model that incorporates a system governing board, a system chief executive, and campus service units, suggesting that the system chief executive and his or her staff be headquartered at a flagship campus and that governance procedures involving faculty and students in areas other than salaries, fringe benefits, and working conditions be left to individual campus initiatives.

386 Richardson, Richard C., Jr. (ed.). *Reforming College Governance*. New Directions for Community Colleges, no. 10. San Francisco: Jossey-Bass, 1975. 97 pages.

This sourcebook presents twelve essays dealing with governance structures, problems, and innovations at several community colleges in the United States and Canada, including discussions of (1) the structure and function of community college boards in Canada, (2) the organizational climate of Iowa's community colleges, (3) a "customized" system of governance that was developed to meet the special needs of a multicampus college in Florida, (4) an institutional self-study investigating how well various college constituencies participate in the decision-making process, (5) one college's attempt to improve communications and goodwill among various members of the college organization, and (6) the strengths and weaknesses of student participation in governance at a college in Quebec. It concludes with a literature review of relevant ERIC documents. The volume provides readers with an understanding of actual governance practices rather than mere theoretical discussions.

★**387** Richardson, Richard C., Jr.; Blocker, Clyde E.; and Bender, Louis W. *Governance for the Two-Year College.* Englewood Cliffs, N.J.: Prentice-Hall, 1972. 245 pages.

The authors promote the concept of administration as a participatory process involving all constituencies, advocating a college organization that is flatter than the typical hierarchical pyramid of the bureaucracy so that authority, responsibility, decision making, and communication are everyone's responsibility. They support coordination as a means of defining the role of the colleges, spelling out responsibilities of various administrators and outlining criteria for faculty evaluation. The work serves as excellent background reading for presidents and presidential aspirants who would move an institution toward participatory governance.

388 Richardson, Richard C., Jr., and Rhodes, William R. "Chapter Nine: Building Commitment to the Institution." In George B. Vaughan and Associates, *Issues for Community College Leaders in a New Era.* San Francisco: Jossey-Bass, 1983, pp. 186-204.

For an annotation of the work in its entirety, please see no. 37.

389 Richardson, Richard C., Jr., and Riccio, Elaine. "Collective Bargaining and Faculty Involvement in Governance." *Community College Review,* 1980, 7 (3), 60-65.

Please see no. 298 for the full annotation.

390 Thornton, James W. "Chapter Nine: Administration of the Community Junior Colleges." In James W. Thornton, *The Community Junior College.* New York: Wiley, 1972, pp. 115-130.

For an annotation of the work in its entirety, please see no. 34.

★**391** Zoglin, Mary L. *Power and Politics in the Community College*. Palm Springs, Calif.: ETC Publications, 1976. 170 pages.

This work considering community college governance focuses on how decisions are made and the interactions of all participating groups in the governance process. It includes analyses of the history of community college governance; local, state, and federal roles in the governance process; board of trustee membership and board relations with professional staff; internal college politics; the role of collective bargaining; and the future of community college governance. It presents hypothetical case studies to illustrate community college governance processes. The work provides a comprehensive description of the governance process that is particularly useful as an introductory text for new trustees and for other newcomers to the college decision-making arena.

The State Role in Administration and Governance

392 Alaska State Commission on Postsecondary Education. *National Survey of the Criteria Used by Each State in Determining the Establishment or Expansion of Community Colleges*. Juneau: Alaska State Commission on Postsecondary Education, 1978. 76 pages. (ED 195 291)

This publication surveys state agencies responsible for statewide community college planning to identify the criteria used by the agencies in determining the establishment, expansion, or termination of two-year colleges. It draws upon responses from forty-five states and the District of Columbia to note that only twelve states used specific criteria and that twenty-four used general criteria outlined in broad policy statements or in legislation. It also reveals that the most commonly used criteria were (1) population projections, (2) follow-up studies of high school graduates, (3) enrollment rates, (4) needs studies, (5) site-selection procedures, (6) funding availability, (7) evidence of community support and nonduplication of programs, (8) enrollment capacities of present institutions, and (9) the effect of a new campus on existing institutions. The work serves as a state-by-state analysis of how agencies expand or contract state community college systems.

393 Arney, Lawrence H. *State Patterns of Financial Support for Community Colleges.* Gainesville: Institute of Higher Education, University of Florida, 1970. 53 pages. (ED 038 129)

Please see no. 451 for the full annotation.

394 Augenblick, John. *Issues in Financing Community Colleges.* Denver, Colo.: Education Finance Center, Education Commission of the States, 1978. 70 pages. (ED 164 020)

Please see no. 452 for the full annotation.

395 Bender, Louis W. *The States, Communities, and Control of the Community College: Issues and Recommendations.* Washington, D.C.: American Association of Community and Junior Colleges, 1975. 63 pages. (ED 110 125)

The author discusses the causes and implications of the drift from local to state control of community colleges, arguing that increased state control is largely a consequence of the growing federal role in higher education, the subsequent establishment of state coordinating agencies, and the willingness of community college leaders to accept "the lure of federal dollars without regard to the concomitant administering machinery and requirements thereby created" (p. 37). He further maintains that some design or provision for local policy making is essential to the community-based mission of the two-year colleges, regardless of the source of funding. He concludes with recommendations for state and local action to preserve the community form of the college.

396 Charles, Searle (ed.). *Balancing State and Local Control.* New Directions for Community Colleges, no. 23. San Francisco: Jossey-Bass, 1978. 117 pages. (ED 158 822)

This sourcebook presents ten essays concerning the balance of local and state control in the governance of community colleges, including descriptions of the interactions between local and state authorities in Connecticut, California, Florida, Illinois, Washington, Pennsylvania, Mississippi, and Michigan. It emphasizes both the positive aspects of increased state control (such as more stable funding) and the negative aspects (such as increased bureaucratization and diminished autonomy in curriculum development). The volume serves as a balanced review of how increased state control has affected community college operations. It concludes with a review of relevant literature and an extensive bibliography.

397 Day, Robert W., and Bender, Louis W. *The State Role in Program Evaluation of Community Colleges: Emerging Concepts and Trends.* Tallahassee: State and Regional Higher Education Center, Florida State University, 1976. 42 pages. (ED 126 982)

This publication surveys personnel at fifty-one agencies in thirty-eight states to determine the role that state agencies play in evaluating or suspending extant community college programs, utilizing survey responses to list, for each state, the criteria used in program evaluation. It also presents six case studies demonstrating agency program evaluation criteria and procedures in Arkansas, California, Maryland, North Carolina, Oklahoma, and Virginia. The work provides the reader with insights into state-by-state variances in authority over institutional curriculum development during the mid 1970s.

398 Dennison, John D.; Tunner, Alex; Jones, Gordon; and Forrester, Glen C. *The Impact of Community Colleges: A Study of the College Concept in British Columbia.* Vancouver, British Columbia: B.C. Research, 1975. 192 pages. (ED 115 324)

This monograph describes a four-year comprehensive study of the British Columbia community colleges. It details study components, including achievement testing, analyses of enrollment and financial data, and surveys of high school seniors, community residents, faculty, and businesses. Findings are outlined as they relate to (1) student academic and socioeconomic backgrounds, (2) students' objectives, concerns, and opinions, (3) the characteristics of high school graduates in British Columbia, (4) the employment and academic experiences of community college graduates, (5) public opinion about the role of community colleges, (6) faculty characteristics and opinions, and (7) the financial status of the colleges. The study provides a comprehensive picture of the British Columbia community colleges as well as a rigorous research methodology that can be used by provincial and state planners to monitor future college developments.

399 Hall, George L. *State Boards for Community Colleges: An Analysis of Concepts and Practices.* Gainesville: Institute of Higher Education, University of Florida, 1974. 44 pages. (ED 089 804)

The author analyzes the problems of concern to state boards responsible for two-year colleges, detailing the topics covered at board meetings and board-member opinions concerning the most important problem areas faced by community colleges. He reveals that state boards devote most of their time to financial matters, facilities, curricula, personnel, policy matters, and students. He notes that, while board members are concerned with the issues of articulation and coordination, little time is devoted to these topics at board meetings, concluding that articulation problems are not in the province of state boards and not likely to be solved by board members. The work provides insights into the role of state boards as of the early 1970s.

400 Harris, Norman C. "State-Level Leadership for Occupational Education." In James L. Wattenbarger and Louis W. Bender (eds.), *Improving Statewide Planning.* New Directions for Higher Education, no. 8. San Francisco: Jossey-Bass, 1974, pp. 35–50.

Please see no. 716 for the full annotation.

401 Hoenack, Stephen A., and Roemer, Janet K. "Evaluating College Campus Closings for the 1980s: A Case Application of an Optimization Model." *Research in Higher Education,* 1981, *15* (1), 49–68.

This article describes a computerized model that assists state policy makers in analyzing the consequences of alternative campus closings and finding a case that minimizes the state's higher education costs. The authors note that the model examines two cost factors for each alternative: the costs of increased enrollments at other institutions that remain open and the costs of travel grants to students living closest to the closed campuses. They discuss the relationship of per-student costs to variations in enrollment and examine the problem of calculating how many students from a closed institution would enroll in surviving campuses. They describe the application of the model in analyzing two alternatives for closing a community college campus in Minnesota.

402 Hurlburt, Allan S. *State Master Plans for Community Colleges.* Horizons Monograph Series. Los Angeles: ERIC Clearinghouse for Junior Colleges; Washington, D.C.: American Association of Junior Colleges, 1969. 55 pages. (ED 032 887)

This paper describes and analyzes master plans under which junior colleges have been organized in nineteen states. It discusses a rationale for developing state master plans and lists their major purposes, elaborating on the need for statewide planning, the trend toward more state control, and the involvement of state planning groups in determining priorities. The author analyzes the content of master plans, including statements on institutional philosophy and objectives, curriculum, facilities, students, faculty, finance, and organization and coordination, and concludes that state planning must be continuous, flexible, and constantly reviewed and revised in light of changing conditions.

403 McKinney, T. Harry. *Section 1202 and Statewide Planning for Public Community and Junior Colleges: The New Reality.* Tallahassee: College of Education, Florida State University, 1974. 99 pages. (ED 093 405)

The author reviews developments related to the Education Amendments of 1972 to determine the impact of this legislation on statewide planning for public community and junior colleges. He provides a brief analysis of patterns and practices of statewide coordination before the legislation was enacted and summarizes major provisions of the act; describes efforts to develop rules and regulations concerning implementation of the act and discusses reactions throughout the nation; and presents information about the resulting "1202" commissions and about the nature of community college representation on these commissions. He concludes that there is growing support at the state level for comprehensive planning that involves all postsecondary institutions, regardless of the availability of federal funds.

404 Martorana, S. V., and Kuhns, Eileen. "Chapter Ten: Designing New Structures for State and Local Collaboration." In William L. Deegan, Dale Tillery, and Associates, *Renewing the American Community College: Priorities and Strategies for Effective Leadership.* San Francisco: Jossey-Bass, 1985, pp. 229–251.

For an annotation of the work in its entirety, please see no. 14.

405 Martorana, S. V., and Smutz, Wayne D. "Federal Programs Get Mixed Grades: Can Role Be Clarified?" *Community College Frontiers,* 1979, 7 (3), 40–44.

This article surveys state directors of community college education to assess their opinions about the influence of the federal government on two-year institutions. The authors note that some types of federal involvement were viewed positively, others neutrally, and still others negatively: positive involvement was seen in the provision of categorical grants, vocational education funds, and student aid; actions viewed as neutral included the creation of state postsecondary planning commissions, desegregation regulations, and federal involvement in vocational education; and actions viewed as negative included directly imposed costs, record-keeping requirements, and control over federal funds at the state level. The authors conclude that federal involvement in community colleges is a mixed blessing and that this is reflected in the ambivalent attitudes of state directors.

★**406** Martorana, S. V., and Wattenbarger, James L. *Principles, Practices, and Alternatives in State Methods of Financing Community Colleges and an Approach to Their Evaluation, with Pennsylvania a Case State.* Report no. 32. University Park: Center for the Study of Higher Education, Pennsylvania State University, 1978. 65 pages. (ED 158 807)

This report analyzes financial principles and practices in state funding, with a focus on state support for community colleges in Pennsylvania. It reviews methods of support in several states, examining their strengths and weaknesses in terms of consistency with community college goals, preservation of local college control, objectivity of formula data, protection of minimum quality levels, budget flexibility, equity and equalization, and accountability. It also compares Pennsylvania's funding approach with that of other states and discusses alternatives. It provides policy makers with a methodology for assessing the effects of state funding patterns on community college processes and outcomes.

407 Morsch, William. *State Community College Systems: Their Role and Operation in Seven States.* New York: Praeger, 1971. 149 pages.

This publication reports the results of an influential study of the role and operation of the state community college systems in California, Florida, Illinois, Michigan, New York, Texas, and Washington. It profiles each system in terms of history and development, administrative organization, allocation of state funds, admissions and transfer policies, and the degree of statewide planning and coordination. Summary chapters note differences among the systems and analyze the issues that state systems will have to confront in the future. The work serves as a textbook overview of the state role in community college education as of 1970.

408 Morse, Ed. *Student Services Planning Model (SSPM).* Richmond: Virginia State Department of Community Colleges, 1982. 57 pages. (ED 219 106)

Please see no. 636 for the full annotation.

409 Mortimer, Kenneth P. (ed.). *Faculty Bargaining, State Government, and Campus Autonomy: The Experience in Eight States.* Report no. 87. University Park: Pennsylvania State University; Denver, Colo.: Education Commission of the States, 1976. 115 pages. (ED 124 224)

Please see no. 294 for the full annotation.

410 National Council of State Directors of Community-Junior Colleges. *Status of Open Door Admissions: Issues, Trends and Projects.* Committee Report no. 1. N.p.: National Council of State Directors of Community-Junior Colleges, 1983. 35 pages. (ED 230 214)

Please see no. 971 for the full annotation.

411 Owen, Harold J., Jr. *Self-Study Manual for State Governing and Coordinating Boards for Community/Junior Colleges.* (2nd ed.) N.p.: National Council of State Directors of Community-Junior Colleges, 1977. 41 pages. (ED 151 035; available in microfiche only)

This manual is designed to assist state community college coordinating boards in assessing their role in the state's higher education system and identifying areas where change or improvement is necessary. It outlines several items to be considered in the board self-study procedure, including (1) board goals, scope, and legal responsibility, (2) organization and administration, (3) planning, research, and evaluation, (4) finance, (5) external influences, (6) the board role in such areas as instruction, student services, state rules and regulations, and public services and continuing education, and (7) management information systems. It also presents a 142-item bibliography of government documents, monographs, and journal articles pertaining to the state governance of community colleges and to state governing boards. The work serves as a concise review of state board responsibilities.

412 Parcells, Frank E. "Curriculum Approval in Illinois Community Colleges: Local and State Processes." *Community/Junior College Quarterly of Research and Practice,* 1983, 7 (4), 287–302.

Please see no. 531 for the full annotation.

413 Parrish, Richard M. "Statewide Program Approval Mechanisms for Community Colleges: A National Survey and a Case Analysis." *Community/Junior College Research Quarterly,* 1979, *4* (1), 21–45.

This article details a study undertaken in 1978 to (1) analyze statewide mechanisms for the approval of community college degree programs, (2) assess the opinions of community college academic administrators in New Jersey about the regionalization of high-cost, specialized programs, and (3) suggest appropriate courses of action concerning program approval procedures and regionalization. It provides a chart summarizing program approval mechanisms in the fifty states and concludes that only eight states have no review or approval authority. Among the findings noted are that few states have detailed plans for the regionalization of programs and that academic leaders are willing to live with program decisions made on a regional basis as long as regulations are adopted requiring equal access and differentiated funding.

414 Piland, William E. *Remedial Education in the States.* Normal: Department of Curriculum and Instruction, Illinois State University, 1983. 68 pages. (ED 251 160)

Please see no. 786 for the full annotation.

415 Steward, David W. "The Politics of Credit: What the State of California Discovered." *Educational Record,* 1982, *63* (4), 48–52.

Please see no. 538 for the full annotation.

416 Tillery, Dale, and Wattenbarger, James L. "State Power in a New Era: Threats to Local Authority." In William L. Deegan and James F. Gollattscheck (eds.), *Ensuring Effective Governance.* New Directions for Community Colleges, no. 49. San Francisco: Jossey-Bass, 1985, pp. 5–23. (ED 255 276)

The authors review the growth of state power and authority in community college governance by examining developments in governance in Florida and California. They trace the incremental transfer of final decision making to the state level and suggest options and likely outcomes for governance, providing descriptions of current statewide governance structures in both Florida and California. They conclude that mediocrity and fewer educational services may result if more power flows to the state.

417 Wattenbarger, James L., and Christofoli, Luther B. *State Level Coordination of Community Colleges: Academic Affairs.* Gainesville: Institute of Higher Education, University of Florida, 1971. 29 pages. (ED 050 719)

The authors draw upon a survey of the state agencies responsible for community colleges to examine the nature and extent of state coordination of academic affairs related to curriculum, faculty, degree requirements, and instruction. On the basis of responses from forty-four states, they describe three categories of statewide coordination: (1) statewide councils made up of administrators, faculty, and/or state agencies, (2) the "multiple approach," under which coordination is achieved through separate channels, including advisory committees and faculty councils, and (3) "other approaches," including state superboards or the periodic establishment of ad hoc committees. The work clearly delineates the various administrative structures used to effect statewide coordination in 1970 but does not examine the impacts of those varying systems on the colleges themselves.

418 Wattenbarger, James L., and Heck, James. *Financing Community Colleges, 1983*. Gainesville: Institute of Higher Education, University of Florida, 1983. 68 pages. (ED 232 751)

Please see no. 475 for the full annotation.

419 Wattenbarger, James L., and Sakaguchi, Melvyn. *State Level Boards for Community Junior Colleges: Patterns of Control and Coordination*. Gainesville: Institute of Higher Education, University of Florida, 1971. 77 pages. (ED 054 770)

This publication details the findings of a study conducted in 1970 to examine the characteristics and major activities of state boards for public junior colleges, revealing four patterns of state board coordination: (1) the establishment of independent boards for the coordination of junior colleges, (2) the coordination of junior colleges through a university board, (3) the utilization of state departments of education as the loci of responsibility, and (4) the assignment of responsibility for junior colleges to the same boards that are responsible for all of higher education. The authors review various board functions, noting that "all state boards exercising authority over junior colleges have specific activities in common, despite divergencies in overall functions or operational posture" (p. 28). The work is useful as a brief overview of the various methods used to facilitate statewide coordination in 1970.

420 Young, Raymond J., and Jones, Helen M. "State Governance Structures for Community Education." *Community Services Catalyst*, 1982, *12* (4), 15–20.

This article details the findings of a study conducted in 1980–81 to analyze the state-level coordination of community education, drawing upon surveys of and interviews with state agency officials from forty-six states to examine the extent to which the states have

governance plans, interagency agreements among agencies responsible for community education, state-level advisory groups, and
legislative appropriations for community education. It also
examines the placement of responsibility for community education
within the organizational hierarchy of the state agency and
outlines the perceived strengths and weaknesses of community
education plans.

421 Zoglin, Mary L. *Understanding and Influencing the State
Role in Postsecondary Education.* Management Report
77/7. Cupertino: Association of California Community
College Administrators, 1977. 37 pages. (ED 140 896)

This report explores the pros and cons of state involvement in
higher education governance, discussing the legal and philosophical basis of state control, as well as the causes of increased state
control and concomitant advantages and disadvantages. It also
examines the current role of different agencies and units of state
government in higher education governance, including the roles of
the legislature, the executive branch, and the coordinating agencies
themselves. The author concludes that the trend toward state
control shows no sign of abating and that attempts to bring about
change will require accurate identification of the role of each
agency of state government in the governance process, agreement
of essential elements of local autonomy, simplification of state
control mechanisms, and promotion of institutional autonomy
within multiunit systems.

422 Zusman, Ami. "State Policy Making for Community
College Adult Education." *Journal of Higher Education,*
1978, *49* (4), 337–357.

This article describes the political negotiations and compromises
leading to the passage of state legislation restricting the expansion
of adult education in the California community colleges. The
author notes that the legislation did not set policy regulations
concerning what courses should be funded and who should be
served, because legislators and other interested parties held
conflicting values and objectives about adult education, and

concludes that support for adult education is cyclical, for, while adult education is valued in the abstract, it is often seen as a marginal, not fully legitimate part of publicly supported education. The article provides insights into the complex politics of state funding for community colleges in general and for adult education in particular.

Institutional Research and Planning

423 Alfred, Richard L., and Ivens, Stephen H. *A Conceptual Framework for Institutional Research in Community Colleges.* New York: College Entrance Examination Board, 1978. 24 pages. (ED 154 865)

This publication details a conceptual model for conducting institutional research, describing four model components: (1) setting goals, (2) identifying programs and policies that meet these goals, (3) evaluating programs to find out whether they are useful to the institution, and (4) tracing the flow of resources to assess the cost effectiveness of college programs. It identifies, for each of these components, the data that need to be collected and resource materials that can be used by administrators to develop alternative plans of action. It provides institutional researchers with an easily understood framework for the research process.

424 Armijo, J. Frank; Micek, Sidney S.; and Cooper, Edward M. *Conducting Community-Impact Studies: A Handbook for Community Colleges.* Boulder, Colo.: National Center for Higher Education Management Systems, 1978. 223 pages. (ED 160 137; available in microfiche only)

This volume provides basic guidelines that can be followed by community college administrators in organizing and conducting community impact studies. It includes introductory material touching on the broad range of economic, educational, social, and technological impacts that community colleges have on their service areas, subsequently analyzing the steps in planning and managing an impact study, including choosing a project leader; designing the study with respect to data-collection tools, sampling, personnel considerations, and scheduling; and tabulating and analyzing data. It also examines questionnaire design and provides several examples of survey instruments and follow-up letters. It serves as a thorough introduction to the research methodology employed in college-impact studies.

425 California Community Colleges. *Models of Strategic Planning in Community Colleges.* Sacramento: Office of the Chancellor, California Community Colleges; Aptos, Calif.: Accrediting Commission for Community and Junior Colleges, Western Association of Schools and Colleges, 1983. 70 pages. (ED 242 360)

This publication describes the strategic planning processes utilized at four California community colleges: (1) the educational master plan project at the San Francisco Community College District, (2) the planning and budgeting process at Long Beach City College, (3) the planning process at Riverside City College, and (4) the annual review and planning process of the Yosemite Community College District. For each case report, it presents a brief characterization of the planning project, information on organizational structures and planning procedures, a history and projections, and a general commentary. It concludes with a discussion of the common characteristics of the four strategic planning models. The work is useful as an example of how strategic planning is actually operationalized at the institutional level.

426 Cohen, Arthur M.; Brawer, Florence B.; and Lombardi, John. "Chapter Two: Institutional Research." In Arthur M. Cohen, Florence B. Brawer, and John Lombardi, *A Constant Variable.* San Francisco: Jossey-Bass, 1971, pp. 23–32.

For an annotation of the work in its entirety, please see no. 13.

427 Cross, K. Patricia. "The State of the Art in Needs Assessments." *Community/Junior College Quarterly of Research and Practice*, 1983, 7 (3), 195–206.

This article examines the state of the art of educational needs assessments, pointing out common errors in their design and interpretation. The author notes that researchers often construct survey instruments that solicit information on respondent demographics without considering how such data are useful in determining the respondents' subject-matter interests, educational goals, scheduling needs, or preferred instructional formats. She also emphasizes that many needs assessments merely confirm what is already known, such as the axiom that the more education people have, the more likely they are to participate in available educational opportunities, and that needs assessments reveal the respondents' perceptions of what education is rather than what education might be. She concludes with a brief discussion of common errors made in interpreting needs assessment data.

428 Educational Testing Service. *Community College Research: Methods, Trends, and Prospects. Proceedings of the National Conference on Institutional Research in Community Colleges.* Princeton, N.J.: Educational Testing Service, 1976. 205 pages. (ED 187 363)

This publication presents fifteen papers analyzing a variety of issues related to institutional research, planning, and evaluation, including discussions of the nature of institutional research; the collection, organization, and analysis of research data; research methodology; and the development and dissemination of research reports. It also examines management aspects of community college research, research coordination at the national and state levels, user-oriented approaches to program evaluation, and the identification of institutional research needs. It serves as a useful introductory text for new institutional researchers and for students of higher education.

429 Evans, N. Dean, and Neagley, Ross L. *Planning and Developing Innovative Community Colleges.* Englewood Cliffs, N.J.: Prentice-Hall, 1973. 372 pages.

This volume provides how-to information for board members, administrators, and planners who are involved in starting a new community college, including chapters on state regulations, conducting local needs studies, selecting staff, organizing administrative services, planning facilities, developing special activities for students and the community, and gaining accreditation. It offers checklists for curriculum committees and for instructional leaders to ensure that their activities remain directed toward educational change. It also provides copies of a variety of materials drawn from existing community colleges, such as community survey instruments, organization charts, and sets of institutional philosophies and goals.

430 Fearn, Robert M., and Ihnen, Loren A. "An Economist's View of Planning Problems in Community College Systems." In Paul W. Hamelman (ed.), *Managing the University: A Systems Approach.* New York: Praeger, 1972, pp. 107–121.

The authors describe community colleges within the framework of human capital investment, explaining that the economist views the student as a demander of educational services and as a supplier of labor and accrued human capital in the employment market. They note further that education is viewed as investment in human capital and that the objective of any educational system is to maximize the monetary and nonmonetary benefits flowing to society through such investment, given the constraints imposed by scarce resources. They conclude with a review of three common methods used to plan college programs (the needs approach, the social demand approach, and the cost-benefit approach) and urge college planners to assess the benefits as well as the costs of new college programs. The work is useful in understanding how human capital theorists view the institutional planning process.

431 Hall, Toni M., and Reed, Jim F. "Utilization of Student Information Systems." In Mantha Mehallis (ed.), *Improving Decision Making*. New Directions for Community Colleges, no. 35. San Francisco: Jossey-Bass, 1981, pp. 63–81.

This work outlines procedures and suggestions that provide a framework for the development of an institutional approach to student follow-up analysis, describing (1) techniques for involving users in the process of choosing the information to be collected; (2) categories of students to be surveyed, including entering, withdrawing, nonreturning, and graduating students; (3) appropriate design characteristics and survey methods; and (4) data-processing procedures. It also outlines strategies for promoting data utilization by educational decision makers and concludes that successful student information systems must involve potential users in the development, implementation, and ongoing operation of the system. The work is useful as background reading for new institutional researchers.

432 Hazard, Francis E. *Status Survey of Institutional Research—Ohio's Two-Year Campuses*. Columbus: Ohio Board of Regents, 1977. 37 pages. (ED 135 444)

The author examines the status of the institutional research function at Ohio's two-year colleges in 1977, reviewing survey responses from 84 percent of the colleges to examine the number of colleges that have autonomous institutional research offices, the titles of persons responsible for institutional research, the educational backgrounds of those persons, the immediate supervisors to whom institutional research directors report, and the percentage of time those directors devote to institutional research tasks. He also details responses concerning the number and types of institutional research studies completed during 1975 and 1976 and the relative importance of eleven institutional research functions. The work provides a useful descriptive analysis of the status of institutional research but provides no insights into the impacts of institutional research on the colleges themselves.

433 Illinois Community College Board. *Research Needs and Priorities as Perceived by Community College Administrators in Illinois.* Springfield: Illinois Community College Board, 1979. 56 pages. (ED 168 648)

This publication summarizes the findings of a survey conducted in 1978 to assess the perceived research needs for which (1) statewide studies would be most desirable, (2) interinstitutional research efforts would be most desirable, and (3) locally conducted research studies would be most desirable. It utilizes responses from decision makers at thirty-nine public community college districts in Illinois to note, among other findings, that statewide research was needed in the areas of systemwide college impact, system management and resource allocation, and curriculum and program priorities. It notes also that perceived needs for local, campus-based research focus on the areas of college impact on the community; community, staff, and student characteristics; and campus management and resource allocation. The work serves as an illustration of how one state addressed the problem of defining the state and local roles in community college research.

434 Kastner, Harold H., Jr. "Instructional Accountability and the Systems Approach." *Community College Review,* 1974, *2* (1), 35–41.

The author examines the meaning of accountability, noting that it has implications for the community college in terms of management, instruction, and social responsibility. He points out that institutional accountability is measured in three ways: (1) the degree to which administrators derive maximum outcomes from available institutional resources, (2) the degree to which colleges provide instructional programs that are relevant to the needs of society and students, and (3) the rate of return (both in the long run and in the short run) that society can expect from its investment in community colleges. He discusses problems encountered in measuring accountability at each of these levels. The article serves as a brief summary of the ways in which community colleges are accountable to the public.

435 Knoell, Dorothy M., and McIntyre, Charles. *Planning Colleges for the Community.* San Francisco: Jossey-Bass, 1974. 142 pages.

The authors argue that traditional higher education planning modes are inappropriate in the community college setting. They discuss community college planning on the basis of six themes: (1) planning should not be focused on new facilities; (2) plans should make provision for alternative, off-campus modes of instruction; (3) planning should include a consideration of the leisure, recreational, and general education needs of constituents and not focus solely on job-training needs; (4) planners should accommodate nontraditional students as well as recent high school graduates; (5) barriers to access should be eliminated; and (6) planning should be comprehensive, incorporating academic, fiscal, and physical plant considerations. The work provides institutional planners with an in-depth discussion of how these goals can be implemented.

436 Koehnline, William A., and Brubaker, C. William. "Trends in Community College Planning and Design." *Community College Frontiers,* 1978, *6* (4), 28–35.

The authors relate institutional changes to physical facilities, indicating that, if the college is to be perceived as a place of learning for the entire community, it must be designed for that purpose. They argue that, if the college is to serve as a cultural and recreational center offering services to anyone at any time, the single-campus configuration will have to give way to satellite campuses and other means of extending the college into the community. They illustrate several alternative configurations, advocating the use of temporary facilities, leased space, shared facilities, and movable structures, and conclude that college planners must also design their facilities to reflect social concerns with energy efficiency.

437 Kohl, Peggy L.; Lach, Ivan J; Howard, James M.; and Wellman, Fred L. *Survey of the Institutional Research Function in Illinois Public Community Colleges: 1980.* Springfield: Illinois Community College Board, 1980. 26 pages. (ED 191 520)

This publication details findings of a survey conducted to assess the status of institutional research at the Illinois community colleges and to determine how that status had changed since the completion of similar surveys in 1973 and 1976. It provides data on the number of colleges with an established research office, the percentage of time devoted to institutional research by the person in charge of that function, the administrative status of the person responsible for institutional research, the number of staff members assigned to the function, and the educational and work-experience backgrounds of research directors. It also examines the interest of institutional researchers in staff development and the types of activities in which researchers are engaged. The work provides insights into the organization and functions of college research offices but not into the impact of research efforts on the colleges themselves.

438 Lach, Ivan F. "The Need for Institutional Research in the Community Colleges." *Community College Frontiers,* 1975, *3* (2), 42–45.

This article examines the status of institutional research in community colleges, emphasizing the state of Illinois. It indicates the importance of institutional research that provides information for administrative decision making, increases program accountability, and assists in understanding the characteristics of nontraditional students and instructional methods. The author notes that only a minority of community colleges have well-established offices of institutional research with qualified staff and adequate resources and recommends the strengthening of the institutional research office in community colleges and the involvement of professional researchers who will maintain their currency through participation in professional conferences, seminars, and workshops conducted by professional associations and area universities.

439 Lach, Ivan J. "Research for Policy Formulation at the State Level." In Mantha Mehallis (ed.), *Improving Decision Making. New Directions for Community Colleges*, no. 35. San Francisco: Jossey-Bass, 1981, pp. 5–15.

The author examines problems in the collection of state-level data on two-year colleges and notes the features of successful statewide community college research. He argues that increased demands for state data are being answered with misleading and invalid information, attributing this problem to (1) the tendency to measure community colleges against outcomes (such as graduation rates) that are more appropriate for universities, (2) the great diversity among two-year colleges, and (3) inadequate cooperation between state agencies and college personnel. He cites exemplary statewide research efforts in California, Texas, and Illinois and concludes with guidelines for statewide research efforts: involve local college personnel; conduct needs assessments of critical research efforts; coordinate data-collection efforts; and provide local colleges with research assistance.

440 McAninch, Harold D., and Connellan, Thomas. "Accountability Through Management by Objectives." *Community College Frontiers*, 1978, *6* (3), 45–50.

This article describes the application of management by objectives in the community colleges, using the classic input-activities-output paradigm, with students, faculty, and resources as inputs, instruction, counseling, and planning as activities, and classes offered, students graduated, and services rendered as outputs. The authors argue that people failing to perform their jobs satisfactorily typically do so because they are unclear about overall organizational goals and about how their jobs tie into those goals. They recommend that top-level administrators first define their own roles and then receive the training necessary to bring their subordinates into the management-by-objectives process. They suggest that the management-by-objectives technique assists people in attending to the important aspects of their work and in establishing criteria for evaluation.

441 McLaughlin, Gerald W., and Montgomery, James R. "Asserting the Demand and Needs for Research as Indicated by Various Groups in Community Colleges." *Research in Higher Education,* 1975, *3* (2), 177–186.

This article illustrates the application of the delphi procedure, used in conjunction with a panel of experts, to determine priorities for community college research and planning in a southeastern state. It notes that those on the panel included community college presidents, deans, department heads, state-level administrators, and professors of higher education and describes how surveys and statistical procedures were used to identify the top research concerns. It provides administrators with a technique that, though mathematically complicated, can help determine priorities for state and institutional research offices.

442 Micek, Sidney S., and Cooper, Edward M. "Community Impact: Does It Really Make a Difference?" In Ervin L. Harlacher and James F. Gollattscheck (eds.), *Implementing Community-Based Education.* New Directions for Community Colleges, no. 21. San Francisco: Jossey-Bass, 1978, pp. 79–90.

Please see no. 854 for the full annotation.

443 Myran, Gunder A. (ed.). *Strategic Management in the Community College.* New Directions for Community Colleges, no. 44. San Francisco: Jossey-Bass, 1983. 129 pages. (ED 238 477)

This sourcebook presents seven essays on strategic planning and management in the community colleges, including discussions of (1) the definition of strategic management, (2) external forces that shape college policy, (3) administration/faculty alliance in a shared governance model, (4) goal setting, internal audit, and external assessment, (5) financial planning, including sources and allocation of funds, (6) program and service development, including the assessment of goals, student needs, and community priorities, and (7) conversion of plans to actualities. It concludes with a bibliography of relevant ERIC materials. The volume provides an overview of the necessary elements of successful community college planning as well as a description of the pitfalls to be avoided.

444 Platt, Chester C. "Institutional Research: A National Survey." *Community and Junior College Journal*, 1975, *45* (7), 30, 35.

This article reports findings of a national survey of two-year colleges conducted in 1973–74 to assess the budgets and priorities of institutional research offices, revealing, among other findings, that only 15 percent of the colleges routinely used research findings to make important decisions. The author contrasts the findings with those of a similar study conducted in 1968, noting that research on curricula and instruction dropped from second-place priority in 1968 to fifth place in 1973.

445 Richardson, Richard C., Jr., and Rhodes, William R. "Chapter Twelve: Effective Strategic Planning: Balancing Demands for Quality and Fiscal Realities." In William L. Deegan, Dale Tillery, and Associates, *Renewing the American Community College: Priorities and Strategies for Effective Leadership*. San Francisco: Jossey-Bass, 1985, pp. 284–302.

For an annotation of the work in its entirety, please see no. 14.

446 Romney, Leonard C. "On Community College Productivity: Perceptions from the Inside." *Community/Junior College Research Quarterly*, 1979, *3* (3), 215–230.

This article draws upon a national survey of administrators, faculty, and trustees at forty-five colleges and universities (including ten community colleges) to examine opinions concerning the goals against which higher education productivity should be measured. The author notes that the respondents from community colleges registered stronger preferences than their colleagues at four-year institutions for the goals of "vocational preparation," "meeting local needs," "social egalitarianism," "innovative climate," and "accountability/efficiency." He also reveals that the community college respondents expressed weaker preferences for academically oriented goals, such as "intellectual orientation" and "cultural/aesthetic awareness." The article provides useful insights into the professional values of community college leaders.

447 Roueche, John E., and Boggs, John R. *Junior College Institutional Research: The State of the Art.* Horizons Monograph Series. Los Angeles: ERIC Clearinghouse for Junior Colleges; Washington, D.C.: American Association of Junior Colleges, 1968. 76 pages. (ED 021 557)

This publication provides one of the first large-scale examinations of institutional research in American junior colleges, presenting examples of research produced and recommendations for the support of the research function. The authors discuss the concept of institutional research, resistance to research, and purposes of such research, detail four common research methodologies found in junior college research reports, and review studies on students, teachers, programs and instruction, and student services. They summarize results of a national survey designed to determine junior college involvement with and commitment to programs of institutional research, concluding that a strong institutional research program is the most logical way for junior colleges to find solutions to their own peculiar problems.

448 Scigliano, John A. "Strategic Marketing Planning: Creative Strategies for Developing Unique Income Sources." Paper presented at the annual conference of the National Council on Community Services and Continuing Education, Danvers, Mass., Oct. 20–22, 1980. 22 pages. (ED 196 474)

Please see no. 491 for the full annotation.

449 Van Ausdle, Steven L. *Comprehensive Institutional Planning in Two-Year Colleges: A Planning Process and Case Study.* Columbus: National Center for Research in Vocational Education, Ohio State University, 1979. 140 pages. (ED 186 682)

This publication provides college administrators with theoretical and practical information on how to implement an institutional planning process that defines the direction in which the college is going (that is, its goals), how the college will achieve its goals, and what resources will be required to meet these goals. It describes the prerequisites to effective planning in terms of leadership, staffing, scheduling, board participation, and integration with state-level planning activities. It also details the steps in a comprehensive institutional planning model and discusses special considerations in planning the vocational education program. It concludes with a case study describing the planning process at Walla Walla Community College (Washington) and with appendixes that provide goal statements, an enrollment and planning worksheet, a budget analysis form, and other useful materials.

450 Van Ausdle, Steven L. *Comprehensive Institutional Planning in Two-Year Colleges: An Overview and Conceptual Framework.* Columbus: National Center for Research in Vocational Education, Ohio State University, 1979. 109 pages. (ED 186 683)

This publication examines the theoretical underpinnings of comprehensive institutional planning and presents a conceptual framework to facilitate an understanding of the role, function, and operation of planning within the college. It begins with a discussion of the societal forces that make comprehensive planning imperative and then reviews literature on planning theory, as well as the literature that has specific application and reference to planning in the two-year college. The author synthesizes premises found in the literature as they relate to the essential characteristics of the planning process, essential prerequisite conditions, and essential requirements of the process. He also conceptualizes the planning process through a review of the planning-management-evaluation model and discusses the inadequacy of closed organizational models that do not consider the impact of the environment. The work serves as theoretical background reading for college planners.

6

Financing and Budgeting

Funding mechanisms have always been a major concern of college administrators, but never more so than in today's era of stabilized growth and diminished budgets. The literature of the last twenty years chronicles the transformation from a period of growth to one of retrenchment. This financial literature can be subdivided under three headings: funding and fiscal management (nos. 451-477), retrenchment, fund raising, and institutional development (nos. 478-494), and tuition and student financial aid (nos. 495-506).

Funding, Budgeting, and Fiscal Management

The plurality of works listed in this chapter examine how colleges are funded and how institutional funds are managed. Among these works are general texts: *Managing Finances in Community Colleges,* by Lombardi (no. 465); *More Money for More Opportunity: Financial Support of Community College Systems,* by Wattenbarger and Cage (no. 473); *Financing Community Colleges,* by Garms (no. 460); and *Financing Community Colleges: An Economic Perspective,* by Breneman and Nelson (no. 455). Lombardi, a former college president, analyzes finances from an administrator's point of view, discussing causes of fiscal crisis, including voter rejection of bond issues and increasing demands for special programs geared toward nontraditional students. Wattenbarger and Cage trace support patterns for community colleges by pointing out the differences in state, federal, private, and local funding. Garms writes from the point of view of a theoretical economist, discussing the pros and cons of community college funding as it would be approached in a free-market economy, in a centrally planned economy, and in a mixed economy. Breneman and Nelson also bring the economist's perspective to the funding issue, but in a more applied manner. They marshal several data sources to examine the efficiency and equity of various funding mechanisms and fiscal policy decisions (such as a decision to raise tuition). A variety of topics are addressed in the remaining works, including:

- differing patterns of financial support (nos. 451, 452, 475, 476);
- the differing costs of instructional programs (nos. 453, 454, 471, 474);
- fund allocations within multiunit districts or colleges (no. 458);
- institutional productivity (nos. 454, 469); and
- sources of financial support (nos. 461, 464).

The works emanating from the University of Florida's Institute of Higher Education (nos. 474, 475, 476) are particularly useful in analyzing the different approaches that have been taken to the allocation of state funds for community colleges.

Retrenchment, Fund Raising, and Institutional Development

Fiscal exigencies of the 1970s and 1980s have forced community college administrators to face the issues of retrenchment and fund raising. Tax limitation measures, for example, have taken a noticeable toll. Kintzer (no. 483) discusses the changes in educational mission, college programming, governance, staffing, and funding that are attributable to tax revolts in seventeen states. In light of these and other cuts, several works focus on faculty reduction in force; these works include those authored by Lombardi (no. 486), Schultz (no. 490), and the College and University Personnel Association (no. 489). Two other works (Kastner, no. 482, and Long and others, no. 487) examine the problem of cutting whole programs. The New Directions monograph edited by Alfred (no. 478) provides several essays on the general theme of coping with reduced resources.

Recent attention has also been focused on methods of fund raising, including:

- the management of college real estate (no. 479);
- the establishment of college foundations (nos. 480, 481, 484, 488, 494);
- the establishment of college alumni associations (nos. 480, 485, 488);
- institutional marketing (no. 491); and
- increased public relations (no. 493).

A comprehensive, how-to text on fund-raising techniques for two-year colleges is provided by Ottley (no. 488).

Tuition and Student Financial Aid

Two major themes emerge in the literature on tuition and student financial aid: (1) the desirability of low or no tuition and (2) the question of whether two-year college students receive their fair share of financial aid made available through such mechanisms as the Basic Educational Opportunity Grants program. The tuition question is taken up by Simonsen (no. 505), Richardson (no. 503), Lombardi (no. 500), Howard and Gardiner (no. 497), and Zucker and Nazari-Robati (no. 506). The financial aid debate is examined by Gladieux (no. 496), James Nelson (no. 501), Russo (no. 504), and Susan Nelson (no. 502). One can generalize from the literature that tuition is an unavoidable fact of life at two-year colleges but that the colleges have been less than successful in securing sufficient financial aid for the students. On this latter point, however, Susan Nelson (no. 502) warns that available data are insufficient to properly judge whether students are receiving their fair share of financial support.

It should be pointed out that the most comprehensive analysis of tuition and student financial aid is provided by Breneman and Nelson (no. 455) in their *Financing Community Colleges: An Economic Perspective*. The authors examine—from the perspectives of efficiency and equity—the question of how much the individual student should contribute toward his or her education and how much should be publicly subsidized. They conclude that tuition is not necessarily inequitable, as long as financial aid is available.

Other Sources of Information

College fiscal management has always commanded the attention of those who write about two-year institutions. Indeed, most of the general works (nos. 7–39) listed in Chapter Two of this bibliography devote considerable space to the problems of institutional funding. Of particular note are the analyses by Henry (no. 20), Medsker (no. 25), Blocker, Plummer, and Richardson (no. 7), Medsker and Tillery (no. 26), and Cohen and Brawer (no. 12). Other sources of information include the ERIC data base and the *Statistical Reference Index (SRI)*. The researcher turning to ERIC will find:

- state and national statistical compilations of financial data such as revenues and expenditures;
- descriptions of efforts undertaken at individual colleges to improve productivity, raise funds, or manage retrenchment; and
- conference papers and speeches on topics related to institutional finance.

SRI includes state documents (many of which are not in the ERIC data base) that provide aggregated statistical data on the revenues and expenditures of two-year colleges. Chapter Thirteen provides additional information on ERIC, *SRI,* and other relevant sources of information.

Funding and Fiscal Management

451 Arney, Lawrence H. *State Patterns of Financial Support for Community Colleges.* Gainesville: Institute of Higher Education, University of Florida, 1970. 53 pages. (ED 038 129)

This publication examines mechanisms and sources of community college funding in each of forty-two states during 1967–68, detailing (1) the number of colleges in each state that were controlled locally and the number of colleges that were controlled by a state-level agency, (2) the methods used to distribute state funds to junior colleges, and (3) the percentage of funds received by the colleges from federal sources, state sources, local districts, local charge-backs, and student fees and tuitions. It provides only a limited analysis of the implications of the study findings but serves as a concise picture of the state role in community college funding as of 1968.

452 Augenblick, John. *Issues in Financing Community Colleges.* Denver, Colo.: Education Finance Center, Education Commission of the States, 1978. 70 pages. (ED 164 020)

The author draws upon a variety of data sources "to discuss the problems associated with state systems of financing community colleges and to examine the relationships that arise between states, local community college districts and students when each is an important contributor to institutional revenues" (p. vi). The work includes a chart delineating the state-by-state characteristics of state support for community colleges in 1976 as well as detailed descriptions of the finance systems in Mississippi, New Jersey, California, and Illinois. It focuses primarily on the problems associated with interdistrict equalization and provides insights into the distribution of wealth and the distribution of students and revenues.

453 Balinsky, Warren, and Burns, John. "Program Costing in a Community College." *Socio-Economic Planning Sciences*, 1975, *9* (3-4), 105-109.

This article describes a crossover accounting procedure by which line-item budget data are converted into cost and revenue data for individual community college programs. It explains the methods used in the procedure to calculate direct charges and overhead, the per-student costs of individual courses, and the average cost of elective credit. The authors note that cost-revenue analyses of individual courses can help administrators identify "the relative positions of the programs in their use of institutional resources" (p. 107). They also emphasize that such analyses can be used to evaluate the line-item financial budget ex ante by comparing the budgeted costs of different progams with projected enrollments and revenues. They conclude, therefore, that accurate program costing will have great benefits for institutional long-range planning.

454 Berchin, Arthur. *Toward Increased Efficiency in Community Junior College Courses: An Exploratory Study.* Los Angeles: League for Innovation in the Community College, 1972. 236 pages. (ED 063 915)

This publication identifies and describes community college courses that are considered highly efficient; that is, "those that save their respective colleges some instructional costs and are at the same time effective in terms of learning outcomes" (p. 2). The author devises a formula to compute the per-pupil direct costs of instruction for college courses and draws on data collected from member institutions of the League for Innovation in the Community College to compare the per-pupil costs of traditional classroom instruction with those of three nontraditional modes: large groups, individualized programmed instruction, and audiotutorial instruction. He concludes with a series of calculations detailing instructional costs for courses that take a variety of approaches to instruction in English, mathematics, data processing, economics, history, home economics, and other subject areas.

455 Breneman, David W., and Nelson, Susan C. *Financing Community Colleges: An Economic Perspective.* Washington, D.C.: Brookings Institution, 1981. 222 pages.

This publication addresses questions of community college financing in the broader context of educational purpose, priorities, and equity. It includes analyses of (1) the modes and levels of financing community colleges, (2) the efficiency of community college education in terms of finance, economic theory, and outcomes, (3) the implications of tuition and student financial aid for equity, (4) intersectoral equity in the distribution of state and local support for postsecondary education, and (5) interdistrict equity in the provision of local support for community colleges. It also discusses federal and state aid within the framework of the efficiency and equity of the total educational system. The work provides the reader with a thorough analysis of the numerous variables that come into play when assessing the impact of policy decisions (such as a raise in tuition) on educational efficiency and equity.

456 Campbell, Dale F. (ed.). *Strengthening Financial Management.* New Directions for Community Colleges, no. 50. San Francisco: Jossey-Bass, 1985. 135 pages. (ED 258 654)

This sourcebook presents eleven essays that examine financial management in the community colleges from the perspective of college finance and administrative support officers. Part One reviews selected role functions that college business officers perform, including planning and budgeting, cost accounting, purchasing and maintenance, and student financial aid. Part Two focuses on the shift toward entrepreneurial management, with essays on institutional research, auxiliary services, generating new financial resources, and investing college funds. The volume concludes with an examination of emerging issues and implications for strengthening financial management in the areas of public policy and future issues.

457 Cohen, Arthur M., and Brawer, Florence B. "Chapter Five: Finances: Maintaining Fiscal Support." In Arthur M. Cohen and Florence B. Brawer, *The American Community College*. San Francisco: Jossey-Bass, 1982, pp. 127–146.

For an annotation of the work in its entirety, please see no. 12.

458 Dunn, John W. "Financially Autonomous College in a Multi-College System." *Community and Junior College Journal*, 1975, *45* (7), 10–11.

This article describes a method of fund allocation for multicollege districts, under which allocations for individual colleges are determined on an impartial formula basis and college-level personnel are free to develop their own budget plans within the allocated amounts. The author notes that, under this plan, district-level budgetary officials fulfill a service function rather than a controlling function. He argues that benefits of the plan include decreased competition between district campuses and improved budget administration at the campus level. He concludes that the plan offers a viable alternative to standard budgeting procedures, under which colleges fight among themselves for district allocations.

459 Eells, Walter Crosby. "Chapter Nineteen: Problems of Finance." In Walter Crosby Eells, *The Junior College*. Boston: Houghton Mifflin, 1931, pp. 506–548.

For an annotation of the work in its entirety, please see no. 15.

460 Garms, Walter I. *Financing Community Colleges*. New York: Teachers College Press, 1977. 120 pages.

This publication analyzes the financing of community colleges from an economist's point of view, considering the economic rationale for funding community colleges and outlining nine criteria for evaluating community college finance plans. It also examines the effects of tuition and three types of funding models: (1) market-economy models, which posit systems of private colleges competing in the free market; (2) planned-economy models, which envision a system of state-financed and -controlled public institutions; and (3) mixed models, combining features of the above two. It provides a highly theoretical discussion of the applications of economic analysis to the development and evaluation of college funding systems and is useful more for theorists than for educational practitioners.

461 Gillie, Angelo C., Sr. "Public Two-Year College Funding and Program Patterns." *Community/Junior College Quarterly of Research and Practice,* 1982, *6* (3), 203–216.

The author utilizes data from a variety of sources to calculate (1) the percentage of community college funds derived from national, state, local, and student sources in the period between 1974 and 1978; (2) the average cost per public two-year college student; and (3) the percentage of students who were in terminal vocational programs in fall 1979. He details findings by state, noting that the percentage of revenues derived from state appropriations varied from 21 to 100 percent and that the same range applied to state-by-state variations in the proportion of students enrolled in occupational curricula. The article is useful as an illustration of how state community college systems vary in terms of both funding and curricular emphasis.

462 Kintzer, Frederick C. *Organization and Leadership of Two-Year Colleges: Preparing for the Eighties.* Gainesville: Institute of Higher Education, University of Florida, 1980. 35 pages. (ED 241 093).

Please see no. 375 for the full annotation.

463 Listou, Robert E. *Financial Management in Higher Education: An Approach to Improvement.* Advanced Institutional Development Program (AIDP) Two-Year College Consortium, vol. 2, no. 3. Washington, D.C.: McManis Associates, 1976. 32 pages. (ED 133 022)

This publication presents a series of cost sheets that allow for the calculation of instructional costs at differing institutional levels, including (1) an instructor cost sheet, which facilitates the calculation of cost per student contact hour, (2) a course cost sheet for the calculation of average per-student costs in individual classes, (3) a discipline cost sheet for the calculation of total cost and average costs per student contact hour in related clusters of courses, (4) a division cost sheet, which aggregates these data for individual departments, and (5) a curriculum program cost sheet, which aggregates the above data for the entire college. The author presents examples of the use of the forms and notes that changes in existing accounting systems are not required. The work provides colleges with a costing methodology that allows people besides financial managers to collect, aggregate, and rearrange financial data and then apply them to the problems of concern to decision makers.

464 Loftus, Virginia L.; Hines, Edward R.; and Hickrod, G. Alan. *Financial Characteristics of U.S. Community College Systems During Fiscal Years 1977 and 1980.* Normal: Center for the Study of Educational Finance, Illinois State University, 1982. 41 pages. (ED 226 791)

The authors examine community college funding data from 1977 through 1980, concluding that during this time period (1) local revenues decreased by 6.9 percent, tuition and fees by 0.8 percent, and federal funding by 0.2 percent; (2) nine states experienced an increase in tuition and fees as a percentage of total revenues while thirty-seven states experienced a decrease; (3) average revenues per full-time equivalent student increased 28 percent; and (4) the largest shift in funding occurred in California, where state revenues increased from 40 to 65 percent, while local revenues decreased from 46 to 19 percent. The work provides a succinct overview of shifting trends in the sources of community college funds.

★465 Lombardi, John. *Managing Finances in Community Colleges.* San Francisco: Jossey-Bass, 1973. 145 pages.

The author discusses the external and internal causes of fiscal crisis in community colleges, including voter rejection of bond issues and tax referendums, and shows how it is difficult to control costs in a labor-intensive enterprise and how increasing demands for special programs geared toward special groups of students place a constant burden on fiscal managers. He examines the variety of funding sources and the variations in state support patterns and offers several recommendations for controlling expenditures through financial planning and more efficient use of physical facilities.

466 Marks, Joseph L. "Understanding the Dynamics of Change: The Case of the Humanities." *Community College Review*, 1981, *9* (1), 6–11.

Please see no. 899 for the full annotation.

467 Medsker, Leland L. "Part One: Financing Public Junior College Operation." In Nelson B. Henry (ed.), *The Public Junior College*. Fifty-fifth yearbook of the National Society for the Study of Education. Part I. Chicago: National Society for the Study of Education, 1956, pp. 247–266.

For an annotation of the work in its entirety, please see no. 20.

468 Palola, Ernest G., and Oswald, Arthur R. *Urban Multi-Unit Community Colleges: Adaptation for the '70s.* Berkeley: Center for Research and Development in Higher Education, University of California, 1972. 129 pages. (ED 068 096)

Please see no. 163 for the full annotation.

469 Priest, Bill J., and Pickelman, John E. *Increasing Productivity in the Community College: An Action-Oriented Approach.* Washington, D.C.: American Association of Community and Junior Colleges, 1976. 40 pages. (ED 125 721)

This publication describes efforts undertaken by the Dallas (Texas) Community College District to obtain an optimal return on the investment of educational dollars. It introduces the concept of productivity in general, examines its relevance to education, and identifies community college outputs that can and cannot be quantified. It details the eight contiguous phases used by the district to increase productivity: increasing staff awareness of the need for enhanced productivity; establishing a group to lead the productivity project; reviewing current productivity of operations and work stations; generating recommendations for improvement; evaluating the recommendations; implementing the recommendations; monitoring productivity gains; and rewarding staff and departments for demonstrated gain. The authors conclude that top administrative commitment to the project, the positive response of college staff, and the timeliness of responses to suggestions all contributed to the success of the program.

470 Thornton, James W. "Chapter Seven: Legal Controls of Community Junior Colleges." In James W. Thornton, *The Community Junior College*. New York: Wiley, 1972, pp. 89–99.

For an annotation of the work in its entirety, please see no. 34.

471 Warren, John T.; Anderson, Ernest F.; and Hardin, Thomas L. "Differential Costs of Curricula in Illinois Public Junior Colleges: Some Implications for the Future." *Research in Higher Education*, 1976, *4* (1), 59–67.

This article identifies and compares the per-student costs oɪ baccalaureate and vocational curricula at a stratified random sample of eight public community colleges in Illinois. It details the type of data collected in the study and notes that the majority of occupational curricula examined cost more per student than the transfer curricula. The authors conclude that cost studies should be refined to include capital expenditures for instructional equipment and that approximation techniques can be used when complete data are not available. They also note study implications for differential funding and cost-benefit calculations.

472 Wattenbarger, James L. "Chapter Eleven: Dealing with New Competition for Public Funds: Guidelines for Financing Community Colleges." In William L. Deegan, Dale Tillery, and Associates, *Renewing the American Community College: Priorities and Strategies for Effective Leadership.* San Francisco: Jossey-Bass, 1985, pp. 252–283.

For an annotation of the work in its entirety, please see no. 14.

★473 Wattenbarger, James L., and Cage, Bob N. *More Money for More Opportunity: Financial Support of Community College Systems.* San Francisco: Jossey-Bass, 1974. 109 pages.

The authors trace support patterns for community colleges by pointing out the differences in state, federal, private, and local funding. They chronicle the trend toward greater funding of community colleges by states and reduced emphasis on local support, describe the variety of state funding formulas, and conclude with a plea for maintaining local control. The work provides a clear, thorough analysis of the varied funding patterns among the states.

474 Wattenbarger, James L.; Cage, Bob N.; and Arney, L. H. *The Community Junior College: Target Population, Program Costs and Cost Differentials.* Gainesville: Institute of Higher Education, University of Florida, and National Educational Finance Project, 1970. 163 pages. (ED 045 068)

This work utilizes enrollment and financial data from fifteen community colleges—considered exemplary institutions by the researchers—to examine differences in the costs of various instructional programs, explore how funds are allocated, and investigate student characteristics and projected enrollment growth. It details, among other findings, (1) cost differentials for fifty-six programs in the fifteen community colleges, (2) 1980 community college enrollment projections based on the proportions of the surrounding populations served by the fifteen colleges, and (3) the distribution within each of ten program areas of budget allocations made to administration, physical plant maintenance, instructional resources, student services, supportive instructional costs, auxiliary services, and instructional salaries. It provides a fairly accurate prediction of the growth in community college enrollments during the 1970s and represents one of the earliest attempts to identify program cost differentials.

475 Wattenbarger, James L., and Heck, James. *Financing Community Colleges, 1983*. Gainesville: Institute of Higher Education, University of Florida, 1983. 68 pages. (ED 232 751)

The authors utilize data collected from forty-four state directors of community college education to review various state approaches to community college funding. They describe financing patterns in each reporting state, including information on community college structure, enrollments, funding formulas and procedures, and major problems facing community colleges within the state. They also provide statistical data on sources of community college support, changes in state expenditures from 1980 to 1983, and changes in operating funds between 1967 and 1982. The work serves as a brief, state-by-state overview of funding mechanisms and problems in 1982.

476 Wattenbarger, James L., and Mercer, Sherry L. *Financing Community Colleges, 1985*. Gainesville: Institute of Higher Education, University of Florida, 1985. 68 pages. (ED 259 797)

This publication reviews state approaches to community college financing in the mid 1980s, including statistical data reflecting general trends and changes in sources of funds, expenditures per full-time-equivalent student, operating funds by source, capital outlay fund sources, and student fees. This is the most recent of a series of publications on state-level finance that have been compiled over the years by Florida's Institute of Higher Education and made available in the ERIC data base.

477 Young, John E. *Conditions and Factors Associated with Successful Federal Funding.* Resource Paper no. 15. Washington, D.C.: National Council for Resource Development, 1978. 9 pages. (ED 162 693)

This paper analyzes conditions and factors that may affect the success of two-year colleges in securing federal categorical aid funds. The author determines that highly funded institutions have a well-planned federal relations development program that is given top priority by the chief executive officer. He notes that other important factors are clearly defined institutional objectives, institutional credibility, well-prepared project proposals, close contact with federal agencies, and a high level of agreement between the president and resource development personnel and contrasts these conditions with those characteristic of low-funded institutions. The paper is useful as a brief summary of organizational factors that contribute to the success of college development efforts.

Retrenchment, Fund Raising, and Institutional Development

478 Alfred, Richard L. (ed). *Coping With Reduced Resources.* New Directions for Community Colleges, no. 22. San Francisco: Jossey-Bass, 1978. 112 pages. (ED 154 888)

This sourcebook presents nine essays on topics related to the theme of reduced resources for community colleges in the current period of decelerating growth. It includes discussions of (1) the loss of institutional autonomy resulting from increased state support; (2) the effects of budget cuts on curriculum, instruction, and student personnel services; and (3) administrative approaches to resource reduction. It also provides two retrenchment models and concludes with "heretical concepts" that administrators can adopt in order to maintain the growth that characterized earlier years. The work presents the reader with insights on the retrenchment problem from well-known community college experts, such as S. V. Martorana, Dorothy Knoell, and Richard C. Richardson.

479 Bender, Louis W. *Land-Use: A Financial Resource for Community Colleges? A Report of a National Survey of Land-Use Practices of Community Colleges.* Tallahassee: Center for State and Regional Leadership, Florida State University, 1978. 51 pages. (ED 162 715)

The author considers how community colleges use institutionally owned land for fund raising, public service, or other noninstructional purposes. He reports findings of a national survey of community colleges that was conducted in 1978 to (1) determine the various uses of excess land and estimate the various costs of maintenance and improvement; (2) identify the ways colleges use income generated by land use; and (3) assess problems or barriers encountered by institutions in using land for income purposes. He concludes that there are three major types of noneducational land use: commitment of surplus land to esthetic or land-bank purposes, dedication of some excess land to public use, and dedication of available portions of land to income purposes. He notes, however, that few institutions have a comprehensive land-use plan. The work serves as background information for administrators considering the use of excess land as an income source.

480 Council for Advancement and Support of Education. *Building Voluntary Support for the Two-Year College.* Washington, D.C.: Council for Advancement and Support of Education, 1979. 141 pages.

This publication presents strategies for attracting voluntary support for community colleges through foundations, community donations, and alumni organizations. It outlines steps in establishing a college foundation and examines sample bylaws and methods of fund raising; describes the value of public relations, volunteer programs, speakers' bureaus, and the use of college facilities by public groups as a means of enhancing community support; and details the activities of an alumni office. It provides useful how-to information for college development officers.

481 Duffy, E. F. *Characteristics and Conditions of a Successful Community College Foundation.* Resource Paper no. 23. Washington, D.C.: National Council for Resource Development, 1980. 13 pages. (ED 203 918)

The author draws upon a review of the literature and the opinions of a panel of experts to identify the characteristics of a successful community college foundation. He notes that success criteria include strong public relations, involvement of community leaders and potential donors as members of the foundation, and the use of the foundation as a vehicle for community involvement in the college. He also notes the importance of organized and defined planning efforts, a governing board that is aware of its roles and responsibilities, and a clear statement of purpose for the foundation. The paper serves as a useful resource for people charged with the responsibility of establishing a community college foundation.

482 Kastner, Harold H., Jr. "Modifying the Open-Door Policy." *Community College Review,* 1979, *6* (4), 28–33.

The author argues that reduced financial resources require college planners to limit the number of courses that are offered free or at a low cost. He outlines criteria that can be used to identify those classes of students most deserving of subsidized educational offerings and determine the types of programs that should be made available on a low- or no-cost basis. He maintains that every citizen should have an opportunity to obtain two years of education beyond high school and that first-time, in-state students should have a higher access priority to low-cost programs than out-of-state students, nonresident military personnel, or those who have already completed at least two years of postsecondary education. The article provides a framework for further discussion on limiting the scope of subsidized college services.

★**483** Kintzer, Frederick C. *Proposition 13: Implications for Community Colleges.* Topical Paper no. 72. Los Angeles: ERIC Clearinghouse for Junior Colleges, 1980. 39 pages. (ED 188 711)

This paper reviews tax limitation legislation, its impact on the community college, and strategies for dealing with cutbacks, examining historical precedents of such legislation and discussing the changes in educational mission, college programming, governance, staffing, and funding that are attributable to tax-rate limitation legislation in seventeen states (Arizona, California, Colorado, Connecticut, Hawaii, Idaho, Illinois, Iowa, Maryland, Michigan, Nebraska, New Jersey, New York, Pennsylvania, Texas, Virginia, and Washington). It provides suggestions for dealing with cutbacks, including tactical changes in institutional operation, new approaches to teaching, program budgeting, resource development programs, alliances with community agencies and industry, experiential learning programs, and volunteerism. It concludes with a seventy-item bibliography.

484 Kopecek, Robert J. "An Idea Whose Time Is Come: Not-for-Profit Foundations for Public Community Colleges." *Community College Review*, 1982–83, *10* (3), 12–17.

This article urges the development of nonprofit college foundations as a means of securing additional funding for two-year institutions. The author notes the benefits of such foundations, including improved institutional quality resulting from the addition of programs and services that could not otherwise be funded with limited public appropriations. He warns, however, that monies raised by the foundation should be used at the discretion of the college governing board and that the foundation itself should not be involved in institutional policy making. The article is useful as background information for development officers charged with the responsibility of establishing a community college foundation.

485 Kopecek, Robert J., and Kubik, Susan. "Untapped Reservoir of Support." *Community and Junior College Journal,* 1979, *50* (1), 18–21.

The authors argue for the organization of community college alumni associations, noting that such associations assist the college intangibly through goodwill and tangibly through financial contributions, assistance in the placement of graduates, and guidance to college officials. They suggest that membership be open to all who have completed one semester of full-time study but point out that a yearly fee may be useful in keeping only interested individuals on the rolls (though the costs of collection may be problematical). They maintain that the college should appoint an alumni officer and bear the organizational and administrative costs of the association. The article draws upon experiences of an alumni association at Northampton County (Pennsylvania) Area Community College to illustrate how alumni can be organized to support the college. It serves as useful background reading for college development officers.

486 Lombardi, John. *Reduction in Force: An Analysis of the Policies and Their Implementation.* Los Angeles: ERIC Clearinghouse for Junior Colleges, 1974. 36 pages. (ED 099 043)

This publication reviews reduction in force (RIF) guidelines in twenty-four faculty collective bargaining agreements, examining how these guidelines address issues related to faculty participation in the RIF process, conditions that must exist to initiate RIF procedures, the role of seniority in faculty dismissal, the rights of dismissed instructors, RIF and affirmative action, RIF-related litigation, and administrator liability for damages. The author emphasizes that damage to morale can be mitigated if administrators involve faculty in the development of RIF procedures and if the criteria for activating reductions in force are objective and easily identified.

487 Long, James P., and others. *How to Phase Out a Program.*
Special Publication Series, no. 42. Columbus: National
Center for Research in Vocational Education, Ohio State
University, 1983. 46 pages. (ED 231 984)

This paper provides two-year college administrators with suggested guidelines for program phase-out, including a discussion of
the three typical situations that render a program phase-out
necessary (insufficient enrollment, insufficient funding, and
unsatisfactory job placement of graduates). It also examines
possible alternatives to phase-out, the development of a phase-out
plan, and factors involved in obtaining approval and support from
trustees, state associations, students, faculty, and other constituencies. It concludes with a consideration of the phase-out implementation stage, along with procedures to ease the phase-out for
students, faculty, and staff. It serves as an outline of factors that
should be considered in planning and implementing the phase-out
of college programs.

488 Ottley, Alford H. *Funding Strategies for Community
Colleges.* Chicago: Central YMCA Community College;
Washington, D.C.: McManis Associates; N.p.: Advanced
Institutional Development Program Two-Year College
Consortium, 1978. 88 pages. (ED 162 708)

This publication describes approaches to fund raising for public
two-year colleges, including individual chapters on the college
development office, grantsmanship, alumni activities, the annual
fund campaign, the establishment of a college foundation, and
deferred giving. It also includes extensive appendixes that provide
a sample certificate of corporation and a sample bill of articles for
a community college foundation. It provides useful how-to advice
for college development officers, although many of the resources
listed in the monograph are by now out of date.

489 "Retrenchment at Two-Year Colleges and Institutes." *Journal of the College and University Personnel Association,* 1980, *31* (3–4), 190–203.

This article surveys faculty retrenchment policies in a national sample of 320 public and private two-year colleges. It examines the frequency of retrenchment actions at those colleges between 1974 and 1978, the reasons retrenchment became necessary, methods used to select specific faculty for retrenchment, and the impact of retrenchment on employment rights and benefits. It includes analyses of how faculty rank and length of service figure into the retrenchment process and also discusses provisions for appeal, reappointment rights, and retention of tenure. The article provides administrators with a brief summary of how retrenchment is carried out at other institutions.

490 Schultz, Raymond E. "A Sane Approach to Staff Reduction." *Community College Review,* 1976, *3* (3), 6–13.

This article discusses the need for periodic reductions in staff and outlines procedures for making decisions about terminating the employment of individual staff members. The author rejects seniority as the basis for staff retention, because it provides the least financial relief, prevents the introduction of new ideas, and results in terminating the employment of newly employed minority-group staff members. He suggests that most staff reductions are undertaken by simply not filling vacancies and by terminating the employment of part-time and nontenured instructors. He recommends (1) maintaining accurate records on course and program enrollment so that staff in undersubscribed programs can be reduced, (2) using clearly formulated due-process procedures, and (3) assisting faculty to obtain other positions.

491 Scigliano, John A. "Strategic Marketing Planning: Creative Strategies for Developing Unique Income Sources."
Paper presented at the annual conference of the National
Council on Community Services and Continuing Education, Danvers, Mass., Oct. 20–22, 1980. 22 pages. (ED 196
474)

This paper discusses current community college financial problems and examines the acquisition of alternative funding through
the application of strategic marketing planning. It begins with a
definition of marketing and a description of the ability of a
marketing program to attract new consumers and to provide early
identification of potential threats to the college, such as community apathy or reductions in state funding. It subsequently examines
the use of the marketing process in identifying alternative funding
and the ways in which the college bookstore and other college
operations may legitimately serve as profit-making enterprises and
thus reduce dependence upon legislative funding. It includes a
marketing audit instrument and a form for use in identifying and
evaluating marketing issues.

492 Stevenson, Mike R., and Walleri, R. Dan. "Financial
Decision Making in a Period of Retrenchment." In
Mantha Mehallis (ed.), *Improving Decision Making*. New
Directions for Community Colleges, no. 35. San Francisco:
Jossey-Bass, 1981, pp. 83–93.

The authors draw upon a literature review to discuss guidelines for
managing retrenchment, urging administrators to (1) anticipate
and plan for coming fiscal exigencies, (2) decentralize the
budgeting process so as to involve all parties that have a vested
interest in the retrenchment problem, (3) reassess college missions
and priorities in light of changing fiscal restraints, (4) base fiscal
projections on accurate data that allow for comparisons of all
budget units, and (5) utilize program outcome measures in the
decision-making process. They also recommend that the budgeting
and planning processes be merged and that all data items collected
in these processes be accurately defined and weighted as to relative
importance. The work serves as a clear summary of the factors that

need to be considered by administrators facing the process of reduced funding.

493 Trent, Richard L. (ed.). *Public Relations in the Community College: How to Start Up an Operation, Determine the Program, and Master the Skills of Community College Public Relations.* Washington, D.C.: Council for Advancement and Support of Education, 1981. 68 pages. (ED 207 633; available in microfiche only)

This publication serves as a practical guide to community college public relations (PR) efforts. Individual chapters explore (1) the philosophy of community college PR, the role of the PR director, and potential problem areas; (2) guidelines for establishing PR programs; (3) the establishment and maintenance of alumni relations; (4) the resource materials and equipment needs of PR offices; (5) the printing and large-scale distribution options available to the PR officer; (6) the place of the PR office within the college administration; and (7) ways of gauging the effectiveness of PR programs. The work provides useful background reading for new PR or college development officers.

494 Woodbury, Kenneth B., Jr. "Establishing a Foundation: A Public Institution, Including the Two-Year College, May Find That Having a Foundation Aids Fund Raising." *CASE Currents,* 1980, *6* (4), 18–21.

The author notes how a foundation can increase the college's base of financial support and provides practical advice on how a foundation should be established and administered, including information on the types of foundations that may be established, who should be included on the foundation board, the duties of foundation officers, and the number of board meetings that should be held annually. The article is useful as a brief introduction to the operation of community college foundations.

Tuition and Student Financial Aid

495 Eckert, Miles A., and Murphy, Harold D. "A Functional Model for a Community-Junior College Financial Aid Office." *Journal of Student Financial Aid,* 1976, *6* (3), 5–12.

The authors draw upon the opinions of a panel of experts to outline ninety-nine functions of the community college financial aid office, including tasks related to ten broad areas: counseling, application processing and determination of awards, public relations, recruitment, office management, placement, cooperative functions with other college divisions, research and evaluation, professional development, and "other functions" related to federal, state, and local aid programs. The article provides the reader with insights into the wide range of skills required by student aid professionals.

496 Gladieux, Lawrence E. *Distribution of Federal Student Assistance: The Enigma of the Two-Year Colleges.* New York: College Entrance Examination Board, 1975. 30 pages. (ED 110 128)

This work examines the participation of two-year colleges in three federal student assistance programs: Supplemental Educational Opportunity Grants, the College Work-Study Program, and National Direct Student Loans. The author concludes that application, allotment, and allocation procedures do not inherently militate against participation by two-year colleges but that many community colleges simply do not apply for funds. He also concludes that participating colleges probably are not requesting enough funds to meet actual student needs. He suggests that many two-year colleges "are penalizing themselves and their students by not devoting more systematic attention and greater staff resources to the management of student assistance" (p. 18).

497 Howard, James E., and Gardiner, Peter C. "Computer-Assisted Policy Analysis in Higher Education: Assessing the Impacts of Charging Tuition in Community Colleges." *Community/Junior College Research Quarterly,* 1979, *3* (4), 341–362.

This article describes the application of a computer simulation modeling technique to the analysis of alternative policy decisions that are made by community college administrators. It shows how the simulation model can be developed by stating the problem or issues that it is intended to answer, determining the key factors involved, drawing a causal loop diagram, programming the simulation, making initial runs, and applying sensitivity testing. It demonstrates the use of the model in assessing the probable effects of tuition on institutional costs, total revenue, and student attendance and recommends using such simulation models in individual institutions.

498 Johnson, Jane L. "An Analysis of the Relationship Between Instructional Costs and Differential Tuition Levels." *Journal of Higher Education,* 1979, *50* (3), 280–288.

The author utilizes fiscal data collected from Washington colleges and universities in 1974–75 to determine whether differing tuition charges at two-year and four-year institutions are the result of actual cost differences between the two types of colleges. She determines that cost-based tuition differentials between community colleges and four-year institutions may result if the four-year institutions' *total* average undergraduate costs are used in calculating tuition rates but notes that if the calculations are based on *lower-division* costs alone, the tuition rates charged to community college students in transfer programs and to freshmen and sophomores at four-year institutions should be approximately equal. The article serves as a useful analysis for state planners charged with the task of setting tuition rates for students in different segments of the state's higher education system.

499 Johnson, Richard. "Strengthening the Student Aid System in the Community Colleges." In Martin Kramer (ed.), *Meeting Student Aid Needs in a Period of Retrenchment.* New Directions for Higher Education, no. 40. San Francisco: Jossey-Bass, 1982, pp. 49–55.

The author examines barriers to the development of successful student aid programs at community colleges and makes suggestions for improvement. He argues that the image of the community college as a low-cost institution has resulted in a general tendency to ignore the nontuition costs of attending college and to avoid the responsibility of hiring knowledgeable financial aid administrators. He also notes that the colleges have done little to seek private donor funds for student aid purposes and that two-year colleges have not organized effective lobbying campaigns to secure adequate public funding. He calls on college aid administrators to place a high priority on informing other college personnel of the importance of student financial aid and securing institutionwide support for a well-planned aid program.

★500 Lombardi, John. *No- or Low-Tuition: A Lost Cause.* Topical Paper no. 58. Los Angeles: ERIC Clearinghouse for Junior Colleges, 1976. 46 pages. (ED 129 353)

This paper reviews the issues surrounding the debate about community college tuition charges, concluding that arguments for no or low tuition are a lost cause. The author draws from an extensive review of the literature to point out the large gap between the rhetoric of low tuition and actual practice, emphasizing that at no time in the history of public two-year colleges has there been widespread acceptance of low- or no-tuition policies. He also discusses the different rates at which tuition is charged, the types of fees charged to students, the impact of tuition and fees on access, the increase in tuition and fees from 1961 through 1975, and the anomalous tuition debate in California. The paper helps in understanding historical trends in tuition charges at community colleges, as well as the forces counteracting any push for a no-tuition policy.

501 Nelson, James E. "Student Aid at the Two Year College: Who Gets the Money?" *Community and Junior College Journal,* 1976, *47* (2), 12–13, 15, 17.

This article examines the provision of financial aid to community college students, noting that they receive less than 16 percent of available aid, although they account for over 25 percent of all full-time students in higher education and over 53 percent of all first-time, full-time freshmen from low-income families. It also notes that significantly lower proportions of eligible students apply for available aid and blames this underparticipation on the misperceptions that community college education is inexpensive, that funds are not available for part-time students, and that community colleges do not have sufficient financial aid staff. The author recounts the need for skilled staff to administer aid programs and recommends that financial aid staff need to be increased if the colleges are to continue to attract low-income students.

502 Nelson, Susan C. *Community Colleges and Their Share of Student Financial Assistance.* Washington, D.C.: College Entrance Examination Board, 1980. 70 pages. (ED 188 718)

The author draws from a variety of data sources to examine two conflicting contentions: (1) that community colleges receive a smaller amount from state and federal student assistance programs than they should and (2) that there is, on the other hand, a prevalence of individual overawarding at these colleges. She emphasizes the conceptual issues of the aid utilization debate (for example, conflicting opinions about how to define student need) and the lack of data necessary for an adequate analysis. She draws only tentative conclusions, noting that charges of overawarding arise from disputed definitions of need and that a pattern of underutilization does seem to exist for campus-based award programs. The work serves as a comprehensive analysis of the statistical and conceptual problems that cloud the debate concerning the community college share of federal student assistance.

503 Richardson, Richard C., Jr. "Tuition in Community
Colleges: Another View." *Community and Junior College
Journal,* 1974, *44* (9), 21, 24–25.

The author argues that there are sound reasons for community
colleges to charge tuition, as long as there is enough financial aid
to ensure that no student is denied access because of a lack of
funds. He maintains that (1) tuition already accounts for a large
proportion of college revenues and is a "fact of life" that cannot be
ignored, (2) public tuition subsidies have not effectively removed
financial barriers to college attendance, and (3) students in states
that provide tuition subsidies have difficulty obtaining grants-in-
aid that help cover living expenses and other costs incurred while
attending college. He also warns that if community colleges
continue to charge no or very low tuition, they will be hard
pressed to compete for federal subsidies that are administered
through individual students.

504 Russo, Joseph A. "Community College Student Aid: A
Hard Look from Within." *Journal of Student Financial
Aid,* 1976, *6* (1), 20–27.

This article traces the disproportionately low utilization of
financial aid by community college students to inadequate
staffing, funding, and administrative support for community
college financial aid offices. The author maintains that underpaid
and overworked financial aid officers simply do not have the time
or resources available to make sure that all students receive the aid
for which they are eligible. He argues against the statewide
consolidation of community college requests for federal student
financial aid and suggests instead that colleges provide adequate
staff for the student aid operation and encourage financial aid
administrators to keep up with new developments in the field.

505 Simonsen, Edward. "The Case Against Tuition in the Community College." *Community and Junior College Journal,* 1974, *44* (9), 20, 22–23.

The author argues that community colleges—like public libraries and public schools—should not charge tuition or any other type of user fee. He bases this argument on ethical rather than economic grounds, maintaining that tuition will result in education for the elite, while a policy of no tuition will ensure the education of the masses. The article serves as an example of the strong—almost emotional—commitment that many community college practitioners have to the no-tuition philosophy.

506 Zucker, Jacob D., and Nazari-Robati, Ali. "Tuition and the Open-Door: A Relative Perspective." *Community/ Junior College Research Quarterly,* 1982, *6,* (2), 145–155.

This article utilizes state-by-state enrollment and tuition data to study the relationship between tuition charged by community colleges and the number of students who enroll. The authors determine that there was a negative correlation between tuition and enrollment at two-year colleges and argue that, while this correlation was small, *any* drop in enrollment attributed to higher tuition threatens the survival of two-year colleges in that prospective students will seek out other alternatives for education and training. They recommend high levels of government subsidization of two-year colleges so that tuition increases can be avoided.

7

Instruction, Instructional
Support, and Student
Services

The importance of good teaching has been emphasized
since the earliest days of the community colleges. College planners
never envisioned these institutions as homes of research scholars.
The community colleges could not reasonably expect to influence
total student development, because few of them built residence
halls and because commuter institutions have minimal environmental impact on students. Nor did custodial care of the young, a
major feature of the lower schools, become significant in the
community colleges, because attendance was not required.
Classroom teaching was the hallmark.

This chapter cites those works dealing with instruction
and instructional support. The large body of literature in this area
can be subdivided under four headings: curriculum planning and
development (nos. 507–542), instructional practices, innovations,
and media (nos. 543–608), student personnel and support services
(nos. 609–648), and libraries and learning resource centers (nos. 649–
685).

Curriculum Planning and Development

Two comprehensive works on the two-year college curriculum have been published: Colvert's 1939 *The Public Junior*

College Curriculum: An Analysis (no. 516) and Reynolds's 1969 *The Comprehensive Junior College Curriculum* (no. 535). Both works are enumerative, rather than evaluative; the authors outline and describe the various curricular offerings of the colleges without extensive elaboration on curriculum development problems and without analyzing how well the colleges perform their various curricular functions.

Other writings on the curriculum focus on an array of more specific themes, including:

- the role of faculty in curriculum development (no. 513);
- procedures involved in the curriculum development process and the responsibility of persons who are involved in curriculum planning (nos. 512, 515, 517, 531, 532, 542);
- the incorporation of mastery learning in curriculum and instructional development (no. 509);
- the development of special types of curricula, including cooperative education (no. 523), occupational programs (no. 522), bilingual education (no. 534), and programs for small-business development (nos. 525, 529);
- management approaches to curriculum development (nos. 508, 509, 510, 521, 540); and
- the involvement of lay citizens in curriculum planning (nos. 526, 537, 524).

Perusal of these works underscores the fact that curriculum development is a complicated process involving much more than the collective decisions of a campus faculty. Zoglin (no. 542) notes that the expansion of the community college mission into occupational and other nonacademic areas is largely the result of layperson and community influences in the curriculum planning process. Other works, including those by Stewart (no. 538) and Parcells (no. 531), illustrate the growing state influence in curriculum development and approval.

Instructional Practices, Innovations, and Media

Instructional innovation is a hallmark theme of the community college literature. Because the colleges reach out to "nontraditional" students who had previously been unserved by American higher education, college leaders have stressed the need for new approaches to instruction that meet the varying needs and abilities of a diverse student body. The most comprehensive text on instructional innovation in the community college is Johnson's 1969 *Islands of Innovation Expanding: Changes in the Community College* (no. 582). Johnson's work describes innovative practices in such areas as cooperative work-study, programmed instruction, audiotutorial teaching, instructional television, games and simulations, and remedial instruction. Since then, other authors contributing to the literature of instructional innovation have focused on several themes, including:

- the employment of mastery-learning systems based on behavioral objectives and variable-length terms (nos. 548, 580, 583, 601, 602, 603);
- experimental curricula for high-risk students (no. 572);
- team-taught courses (no. 564);
- instructional television and other nonprint media (nos. 544, 545, 546, 558, 574, 584, 586, 588, 595, 597, 599, 606, 607);
- experiential education (nos. 576, 608);
- credit for prior learning and life experience (nos. 568, 604, 605);
- individualized instruction (nos. 552, 573);
- the integration of the humanities into occupational curricula (nos. 549, 585);
- international education (nos. 543, 577); and
- honors programs (nos. 553, 596, 598).

Although instructional innovation receives much attention in the literature, available research on community college instructional practices provides evidence that the traditional lecture mode is still the norm. (See the studies on science education conducted by the Center for the Study of Community Colleges during the late 1970s, nos. 550, 551, 565, 566, 567, 570, 578, 579, 591, 592.)

Student Personnel and Support Services

Since the mid 1960s, at least five monographs have appeared on the subject of two-year college counseling and guidance programs: *Community College Student Personnel Work,* edited by MacLean and Washington (no. 630); *Student Development Programs in the Community Junior College,* edited by O'Banion and Thurston (no. 639); *Career Counseling in the Community College,* by Healy (no. 624); *Counseling in the Community Colleges: Models and Approaches,* by Paradise and Long (no. 642); and *Counseling: A Crucial Function for the 1980s,* edited by Thurston and Robbins (no. 647). These works are invaluable in describing the scope of student personnel services provided by the colleges, problems in the management of student personnel service programs, and the characteristics and responsibilities of counselors and other student personnel workers. In addition, the reader should be aware of the few state and regional surveys that have been undertaken to describe and assess the status of community college student services programs (nos. 621, 622, 625, 626, 645).

Of the remaining works in the student services literature, several more specific themes are addressed. These include:

- special services for minority, female, and foreign students (nos. 616, 617, 618, 620, 637, 644);
- the characteristics and responsibilities of chief student personnel officers (no. 706);
- the problems involved in providing adequate counseling and other services for evening and part-time students (no. 611); and
- academic advisement practices and innovations (no. 623).

The last item mentioned—academic advisement—has become increasingly important during the 1980s in light of growing demand for more rigid academic standards. Although O'Banion (no. 638) argued for the abolition of testing programs, grades, and academic probation in the early 1970s, more recent authors— including McCabe (nos. 628, 629)—have called for a return to such practices as a means of combating mounting attrition rates. Future researchers will need to examine the effectiveness of this return to enforced academic standards.

Libraries and Learning Resource Centers

The community college library has long been recognized as an integral part of the college's instructional program. In 1939, Johnson (no. 666) called it the heart of the college and recommended numerous ways it might become central to the instructional process. By the end of the 1970s, many libraries had become learning resource centers (LRCs). In some colleges, this meant only that the library remained intact, with facilities added for the provision of self-instructional programs. But in many, totally new LRCs were built to encompass a library, audiovisual materials, learning assistance centers, and media production units. Wallace (no. 684) traces the history of this development and shows how the LRC is different from other types of libraries. The range of services provided by modern-day LRCs is extensively analyzed by Bender (no. 657).

Veit (no. 682) presents us with the only contemporary textbook on two-year college library and LRC services. Other, less comprehensive works in the community college library literature focus on several themes, including:

- library personnel needs (nos. 668, 671);
- reference services (no. 678);
- student and faculty attitudes toward and usage of the library (nos. 650, 651);
- library services for specific types of students (nos. 656, 658, 674, 681);
- surveys of management practices and services (nos. 660, 663, 672, 673, 675, 676, 680);
- the characteristics and responsibilities of library administrators (nos. 669, 670);
- bibliographical instruction (nos. 658, 659, 681);
- two-year college library buildings (no. 662); and
- library and LRC standards and guidelines (nos. 652, 653, 654, 655, 679, 683, 685).

It should be stressed that most of this literature is descriptive rather than evaluative. The relationship between library services and student learning and academic success is an area open to further investigation.

Further Sources of Information on Instruction and Instructional Support

A variety of sources can be used to find additional information on instruction and instructional support. The ERIC data base includes hundreds of relevant documents that describe curriculum development and instructional practices at individual community colleges. In addition, ERIC provides numerous instructional modules and course outlines that can be used or adapted by community college faculty. Among these instructional materials, for example, are over 100 individualized instructional modules designed by a professional nursing association for use in teaching allied health students a variety of job-related tasks.

The researcher looking for further information on two-year college libraries should consult two additional journals: *College and Research Libraries* and *College and Research Libraries News*. The former includes substantive and scholarly articles, many of which have been cited in this bibliography. The latter serves primarily as a newsletter for the Association of College and Research Libraries (ACRL) and provides, along with other information, synopses of the activities of the ACRL Community and Junior Colleges Section. Further information on how to obtain ERIC documents and journal articles is provided in Chapter Thirteen.

The general texts listed in Chapter Two of this bibliography are also invaluable sources of information on curriculum and instruction (albeit *not* on library services). Practically every one of these works includes extensive sections on the curriculum or on individual curricular functions. Read sequentially, these works provide the historian of the two-year college with insights into how the curriculum expanded from one dealing primarily with baccalaureate studies to one encompassing career, compensatory, and community service components. The literature of these individual components is detailed in the following three chapters.

Curriculum Planning and Development

507 Albers, Donald J.; Rodi, Stephen B.; and Watkins, Ann E. (eds.). *New Directions in Two-Year College Mathematics.* New York: Springer-Verlag, 1985. 491 pages.

Please see no. 867 for the full annotation.

508 Balinsky, Warren, and Burns, John. "Program Costing in a Community College." *Socio-Economic Planning Sciences,* 1975, *9* (3–4), 105–109.

Please see no. 453 for the full annotation.

509 Barbee, David. *A Systems Approach to Community College Education.* Princeton, N.J.: Auerbach, 1972. 184 pages.

This publication advocates a systems approach for the integration of instruction, curriculum, and student guidance, referring to theories of instruction stemming from behaviorists in educational psychology and weaving those ideas into a mastery-learning approach to curriculum and instructional development based on specific objectives, feedback, separation of subject matter into small units of learning, and variable time. It offers examples of instructional systems models used at Colorado Mountain College and criticizes a model at Oakland (Michigan) Community College, noting that it is fixed on a single instructional system. The work presents guidelines for employing a systems approach, along with model flow charts that tie the management and guidance areas of the college to curriculum and instruction.

510 Beaulieu, Reo A., and Dubois, Eugene E. "Systems Simulation for the Community College: Implications for Curriculum Development." *International Journal of Instructional Media,* 1974, *1* (4), 377–387.

This article urges community college leaders to take a systems approach to curriculum development by identifying and assessing the relations between numerous factors concerning (1) the characteristics, motives, and decision-making processes of students; (2) indicators of curricular effectiveness; (3) linkages between the college and area universities, industries, and agencies; (4) alternative curriculum policies and programs that might be selected; and (5) administrative decision making in such areas as budgeting, admissions, and faculty hiring rates. The authors utilize charts to illustrate how the systems approach assesses the factors influencing graduate employment opportunities, student entrance rates, and student transfer rates. They argue that the systems approach is better than traditional ad hoc planning efforts that do not fully accommodate changes in demographic, technological, and other factors.

511 Beilby, Albert E., and Corwin, Luene. *Curricular Decision Making in Occupational Education: A Procedural Checklist and Guide.* Research Publication 76-5. Ithaca: Cornell Institute for Research and Development in Occupational Education, State University of New York, 1976. 115 pages. (ED 130 728)

Please see no. 708 for the full annotation.

512 Borgen, Joseph A., and Davis, Dwight E. *An Investigation of Decision-Making Practices in Illinois Junior Colleges with Implications Toward a Systems Approach to Curriculum Development and Evaluation in Occupational Education as Part of the Phase II Report.* Joliet, Ill.: Joliet Junior College, 1971. 178 pages. (ED 060 199)

The authors draw upon interviews with deans, department heads, and other personnel of twenty-nine Illinois junior colleges to examine the decision-making process undertaken at the college level in vocational curriculum development. They focus on the specific activities completed and the resources utilized during the program identification phase, the program development phase, and the program evaluation phase. They conclude, among other findings, that most decisions during each of these phases were made by the occupational dean and that most of these decision makers looked at programs at other institutions and relied on advisory committees to assist them in program development. The work provides readers with insights into how college-level personnel in Illinois approached vocational program development and evaluation in the early 1970s.

513 Cohen, Arthur M. "Credentials for Junior College Teachers?" *Improving College and University Teaching,* 1969, *17* (2), 97–100.

Please see no. 246 for the full annotation.

514 Cohen, Arthur M. "Academic Planning in Community Colleges." *Planning for Higher Education,* 1979, 7 (5), 28–32.

This article examines internal and external forces that shape the community college curriculum and discusses principles on which program planning should operate. The author notes that, while transfer and vocational curricula are influenced by university course requirements and labor-market conditions, community college programs are often shaped by the initiative of faculty members and administrators within the institution. He argues that curricular planning cannot be based on assumptions of unlimited growth and posits that all college programs should be socially utilitarian, verifiably educative, and not readily available elsewhere. The article presents program planners and curriculum developers with a planning philosophy that eschews college expansion into unlimited community services on the basis of an infinite growth agenda.

515 Cohen, Arthur M. (ed.). *Shaping the Curriculum.* New Directions for Community Colleges, no. 25. San Francisco: Jossey-Bass, 1979. 125 pages. (ED 171 334)

Eleven articles provide a comprehensive overview of the curriculum of the community college, with discussions of curricular revision, the process of change, and a program evaluation model; the importance of state agencies in planning instructional programs; the need for career education and how to prepare career programs in association with employers; appropriate goal statements and the need for competency-based general education; ways faculty can integrate values education into the curriculum; and administrative strategies to shape the curriculum. The book concludes with a review of relevant literature. It serves as an overview of the processes of and participants in curriculum development.

★516 Colvert, Clyde C. *The Public Junior College Curriculum: An Analysis.* Louisiana State University Studies, no. 38. University: Louisiana State University Press, 1939. 177 pages.

This publication surveys the college catalogues of 195 public junior colleges to analyze the components of the junior college curriculum. It details the types of courses offered by the colleges for each of forty-three disciplines under five broad headings: (1) English and foreign languages, (2) social sciences, (3) biological and physical sciences, (4) fine arts, and (5) vocational, semiprofessional fields. For each discipline, it charts the number and types of courses offered, the percentage of colleges offering those course types, and the range of semester hours offered per course. The work provides a detailed picture of the junior college curriculum in the mid 1930s.

517 Day, Robert W., and Bender, Louis W. *The State Role in Program Evaluation of Community Colleges: Emerging Concepts and Trends.* Tallahassee: State and Regional Higher Education Center, Florida State University, 1976. 42 pages. (ED 126 982)

Please see no. 397 for the full annotation.

518 Eells, Walter Crosby. "Chapter Eighteen: The Curriculum." In Walter Crosby Eells, *The Junior College.* Boston: Houghton Mifflin, 1931, pp. 473–505.

For an annotation of the work in its entirety, please see no. 15.

519 Elovson, Allana. *Women's Studies in the Community College.* Women's Studies Monograph Series. Washington, D.C.: National Institute of Education, 1980. 54 pages. (ED 187 398)

This paper examines the development of women's studies programs at the community college level and provides suggestions to increase their effectiveness. It includes (1) a discussion of the potential role of women's studies in developing the self-confidence and economic status of the large numbers of older, part-time female students at community colleges; (2) a review of relevant literature; and (3) an examination of the status of women's studies programs as determined by a survey of fifteen community colleges and eight women's studies program directors. It serves as a cursory overview of the status of women's studies programs in community colleges and of the factors that have led to the establishment of those programs.

520 Evans, N. Dean, and Neagley, Ross L. *Planning and Developing Innovative Community Colleges.* Englewood Cliffs, N.J.: Prentice-Hall, 1973. 372 pages.

Please see no. 429 for the full annotation.

521 Greenaway, John. "A Block-Matrix Method for Course Development." *Canadian Vocational Journal,* 1977, *12* (4), 33–38.

This article describes the use of a grid matrix as an organizing tool by course planners and advising committee members who are charged with the task of developing new courses. Noting that the columns in the matrix represent specific subjects or course units while the blocks within each column represent specific competencies, it details information to be provided in each competency block: estimated time required for mastery, prerequisites, behavioral objectives, and evaluation methods. The author discusses actual applications of the technique and provides illustrations.

522 Harris, Norman C., and Grede, John F. *Career Education in Colleges: A Guide for Planning Two- and Four-Year Occupational Programs.* San Francisco: Jossey-Bass, 1977. 419 pages.

Please see no. 717 for the full annotation.

★523 Heermann, Barry. *Cooperative Education in Community Colleges: A Sourcebook for Occupational and General Educators.* San Francisco: Jossey-Bass, 1973. 219 pages.

The author presents a rationale for cooperative education and details model programs, taking the position that cooperative education should be integrated throughout the community college curriculum and not provided just for vocational students. He proposes model programs organized around clusters for students who have defined career objectives, who have semiprofessional or technological goals but no particular occupation in mind, who are preparing for further professional training, who want career upgrading, who are interested in further university work, who are undecided on their goals, or who need basic skills remediation. He outlines defined outcomes for each program and provides a description of how cooperative arrangements with area employers can enhance the college's standing in the community and help promote student retention. He also describes work-experience

programs at several colleges and presents sample student and
community survey forms, letters to potential employers, visitation
reports, and expense account records for cooperative education
coordinators.

524 Howard, William R. "Community Transactions and the
Marketing Process." In John A. Lucas (ed.), *Developing a
Total Marketing Plan.* New Directions for Institutional
Research, no. 21. San Francisco: Jossey-Bass, 1979, pp. 69–
86.

Please see no. 844 for the full annotation.

525 Jellison, Holly M. (ed.). *Small Business Training: A Guide
for Program Building.* Washington, D.C.: National Small
Business Training Network, American Association of
Community and Junior Colleges, 1983. 68 pages. (ED 229
072; available in microfiche only)

This publication provides college practitioners with guidance on
how to organize and deliver educational programs that meet the
needs of small businesses. It includes an outline of steps to be
followed in starting a small-business training program: creating a
community-based advisory committee, marketing and financing
the program, making timetables and developing strategies, and
securing the cosponsorship of the small-business association. It
also describes the types of small-business programs offered by two-
year colleges and examines the development and functions of the
Small Business Training Network, an affiliate organization of the
American Association of Community and Junior Colleges. The
work serves primarily as a resource for those charged with the
responsibility of extending college services to the small-business
community.

526 Light, John J. *A Practitioner's Guide to Using and Meeting with Advisory Groups.* Columbus, Ohio: National Postsecondary Alliance, 1982. 68 pages. (ED 237 140)

This publication presents strategies, suggestions, and a rationale for the use of advisory committees as a means of securing input from business and industry. It examines the state of the art of advisory groups, noting examples of state-level mandates, common problems associated with advisory committees, and the innovative ways that such committees have been put to use. It also surveys the different types of advisory committees in use and suggests operating procedures covering membership, staff training, meetings, and attendance. It concludes with case studies illustrating institutional experiences with advisory committees and provides a sample manual for committee members. The work serves as useful background reading for college practitioners who are charged with the responsibility of establishing and overseeing lay advisory committees for vocational programs.

527 Lukenbill, Jeffrey D., and McCabe, Robert H. "Getting Started: Straightforward Advice." In B. Lamar Johnson (ed.), *General Education in Two-Year Colleges.* New Directions for Community Colleges, no. 40. San Francisco: Jossey-Bass, 1982. 124 pages. (ED 222 236)

For an annotation of the work in its entirety, please see no. 956.

528 Monroe, Charles R. "Chapter Three: Curriculum Development." In Charles R. Monroe, *Profile of the Community College: A Handbook.* San Francisco: Jossey-Bass, 1972, pp. 46–58.

For an annotation of the work in its entirety, please see no. 27.

529 Nelson, Robert E., and Piland, William E. *Organizing Small Business Programs in Community Colleges.* Urbana: Department of Vocational and Technical Education, University of Illinois, 1982. 74 pages. (ED 219 517)

This publication provides guidelines and resource materials for organizing small-business programs in community colleges. It includes individual chapters on student needs, program content, the use of advisory committees in establishing the program, needs assessment strategies, and methods of promoting and evaluating the program. It also provides a bibliography of curriculum guides and textbooks, as well as appendixes that include such items as a small-business survey, a timetable for organizing management courses, a small-business management seminar, and sample evaluation forms. The work serves as a brief guide to the factors that should be considered in starting programs to assist persons who want to initiate or maintain a small-business operation.

530 Ogilvie, William K., and Raines, Max R. (eds.). "Part Five: Curricular Programs and Instruction." In William K. Ogilvie and Max R. Raines (eds.), *Perspectives on the Community Junior College.* New York: Appleton-Century-Crofts, 1971, pp. 222–340.

For an annotation of the work in its entirety, please see no. 29.

531 Parcells, Frank E. "Curriculum Approval in Illinois Community Colleges: Local and State Processes." *Community/Junior College Quarterly of Research and Practice,* 1983, 7 (4), 287–302.

This article presents a step-by-step review of the process of course and program approval in the Illinois community colleges, focusing on the respective roles of the local college and the Illinois Community College Board. The author concludes that most of the responsibility for course and program approval in Illinois rests with college administrators and trustees, who must develop procedures to ascertain employer demands, student interest, and available resources. He reports that the Illinois Community

College Board is responsible for coordinating course and program changes, guaranteeing need, ensuring consistency, categorizing courses for funding purposes, and discouraging needless duplication of effort. The article provides the reader with insights into how state-level coordination affects the community college curriculum.

532 Parrish, Richard M. "Statewide Program Approval Mechanisms for Community Colleges: A National Survey and a Case Analysis." *Community/Junior College Research Quarterly,* 1979, *4* (1), 21–45.

Please see no. 413 for the full annotation.

533 Posnes, George, and others. *Program Planning in Two-Year Colleges: A Handbook.* Ithaca: Cornell Institute for Research and Development in Occupational Education, State University of New York, and College of Agriculture and Life Sciences at Cornell University, 1975. 160 pages. (ED 112 957)

Please see no. 723 for the full annotation.

534 Regan, Timothy F. (ed.). *Bilingual/Bicultural Education in the Community College.* Advanced Institutional Development Program (AIDP) Two-Year College Consortium, vol. 2, no. 2. Washington, D.C.: McManis Associates, 1976. 32 pages. (ED 133 021)

This publication presents three brief essays on bilingual/bicultural education in the community college. It includes discussions of the application of linguistic theory to the bilingual/bicultural education programs that are available in two-year colleges and the value of bilingual/bicultural education. It also provides descriptions of program implementation at El Paso (Texas) Community College. It is useful in gaining a rudimentary understanding of the goals and components of bilingual education at the community college level.

535 Reynolds, James W. *The Comprehensive Junior College Curriculum.* Berkeley, Calif.: McCutchan, 1969. 227 pages.

This work serves as a comprehensive (albeit dated) textbook to be used by students of the two-year college curriculum. It presents a detailed classification of the curriculum, citing common course titles in the general education, transfer education, and vocational education curricula. It also examines the types of community services provided by the colleges and the factors inhibiting the development of community services programs; the relationship of student services and the library to the instructional program; curriculum organization; and the problems involved in curriculum development. It concludes with a discussion of seventeen theoretical issues affecting the curriculum, including the place of the two-year college in the hierarchy of formal schooling.

536 Schroder, Ralph J. "Independence for the Junior College Transfer Curriculum." *Journal of Higher Education,* 1969, *40* (4), 286-296.

Please see no. 906 for the full annotation.

537 Schussele, Michael. "Systematic Curriculum Planning." *Community College Frontiers,* 1974, *2* (3), 12-16.

This article outlines the process of involving lay citizens in curriculum planning, noting that citizen involvement is justified because of the community college's commitment to serving local needs. It explains how college staff can involve citizens in several stages of the curriculum planning process: identifying objectives, developing a statement of purpose, arranging objectives into priorities, analyzing available resources and the programs of other institutions in the area, converting objectives into desired behaviors, preparing evaluation methods, and developing programs to achieve stated goals. It provides useful information for curriculum planners who are concerned with relating their programs to the perceptions of key community groups.

538 Stewart, David W. "The Politics of Credit: What the State of California Discovered." *Educational Record,* 1982, *63* (4), 48-52.

This article discusses factors involved in the decision to offer courses on a credit or noncredit basis in the California community colleges. It details the effect of Proposition 13 (a state ballot measure reducing property taxes) on the credit issue and lists standards and criteria for credit, noncredit, and community service courses resulting from state legislative intervention. The author examines such issues as who makes credit decisions, whether students should earn credit for developmental courses, and the effects of increased state control on the credit issue. He also discusses the fiscal value and the prestige of credit, as well as the effects of declining enrollment, student financial aid, and student interest in transfer on course credit designations, stressing the importance of recognizing potential hazards to credit integrity resulting from political pressures.

539 Thornton, James W. "Chapter Twelve: Developing the Curriculum." In James W. Thornton, *The Community Junior College.* New York: Wiley, 1972, pp. 159-174.

For an annotation of the work in its entirety, please see no. 34.

540 Valentine, Ivan E., and Larson, Milton E. "A Systems Approach to Curriculum Development." *Community College Review,* 1974, *2* (2), 48-57.

The authors present a thirty-three-cell flow chart demonstrating the process of curriculum development, beginning with input from state agencies, students, staff members, and local constituents, and then carrying the process through institutional committees and intramural organizations, with review and approval stations along the way. They explain how the process accounts for resource availability, evaluation mechanisms, and extramural agency approval and include a Performance and Evaluation Review Technique (PERT) chart showing the steps that must be taken in planning a curriculum, implementing it, and evaluating the program. They note that curriculum development in most community colleges is a haphazard process and that the steps outlined in the flow charts can be used by college practitioners in utilizing a systems approach to program planning.

541 Walsh, Patricia Ann (ed.). *Serving New Populations.* New Directions for Community Colleges, no. 27. San Francisco: Jossey-Bass, 1979. 114 pages. (ED 175 520)

Please see no. 188 for the full annotation.

542 Zoglin, Mary L. "Community College Responsiveness: Myth or Reality?" *Journal of Higher Education,* 1981, *52* (4), 415–426.

The author analyzes the course additions and deletions made at three California community colleges during 1975–76 and 1977–78 in four curricular areas: transfer education, vocational education, remedial studies, and community services. Using data gathered from personnel at the colleges to determine where the impetus leading to these curricular changes emerged, she concludes that changes in the transfer and remedial curricula resulted primarily from professional influences (that is, those emanating from faculty, administrative, and other academic spheres), while changes in the vocational and community service curricula emanated from community influences, such as lay advisory committees. She notes that governmental influences were small and observes that the expansion of the community college mission into vocational and other nonacademic areas is largely the result of a willingness to permit lay influences in the curricular decision-making process.

Instructional Practices, Innovations, and Media

543 Adams, A. Hugh, and Earwood, Glenda. *Internationalizing the Community College*. ISHE Fellows Program Research Report no. 2. Tallahassee: Institute for Studies in Higher Education, Florida State University, 1982. 54 pages. (ED 225 638)

The authors note that North American Students have a low level of awareness of international affairs and examine the role of the community college in the furtherance of international education. They present a chronology of developments in internationalizing the community college and highlight efforts undertaken in the areas of faculty development and exchange programs, student study-abroad programs, the enrollment of international students in community colleges, the development of international education consortia, and the sharing of expertise with foreign countries developing their own systems of two-year college education. The work also includes a bibliography of related materials and a formal statement on the role of international/intercultural education in community colleges.

544 Agler, Linda S., and Pohrte, Theodore W. "College-Credit Courses by Open-Circuit Television." *Educational Technology*, 1976, *16* (10), 39–43.

The authors review the development of credit courses offered by the Dallas (Texas) Community College District over open-circuit television, finding that this instructional method—which is accompanied by a telephone hot line, telephone conferences with instructors, and supplementary study materials—is well geared to adult students. They analyze the steps in a systematic approach to telecourse development, noting that records of hot-line calls, surveys, and instructor comments are used to assess course success. The article provides a thorough evaluation of a well-organized alternative method of adult education that appears to have a good rate of learner success.

545 Alderman, Donald L. *Evaluation of the TICCIT Computer-Assisted Instructional System in the Community College: Final Report*. Vol. 1: *Appendices*. Princeton, N.J.: Educational Testing Service, 1978. 544 pages. (ED 167 606)

This publication details findings of a study conducted to evaluate the impact of Time-Shared Interactive, Computer-Controlled, Information Television (TICCIT) on community college students in introductory algebra and English composition courses. It contrasts the performance of students in classes taught primarily with TICCIT (a computer-assisted instructional program) with the performance of similar students in lecture-discussion sections of the same courses. It details study data gathered from 5,000 students at two community colleges on course completion rates, student achievement, student attitudes, and student activities and examines faculty acceptance of the TICCIT program and the role teachers played in courses where the primary instructional resource was the computer. The work provides useful insights into the problems and outcomes of computer-assisted instruction.

546 Alderman, Donald L., and Mahler, William A. "Faculty Acceptance of Instructional Technology: Attitudes Toward Educational Practices and Computer-Assisted Instruction at Community Colleges." *Programmed Learning and Educational Technology*, 1977, *14* (1), 77–91.

Please see no. 189 for the full annotation.

547 Appel, Victor H., and Roueche, John E. *Installation and Assimilation of Educational Innovations in Vocational/ Technical Programs in Post-Secondary Institutions: Final Report*. Austin: Department of Educational Psychology, University of Texas, 1978. 217 pages. (ED 162 711)

This publication details methodology and findings of a two-part study undertaken in the mid 1970s to examine the factors that contribute to the successful installation and assimilation of instructional innovations in vocational/technical programs. It reviews the responses of 555 instructors, administrators, and nonteaching professional staff who were surveyed regarding the degree to which they use individualized instruction instead of more traditional methods. It also evaluates the intervention of an action research team that was convened at a two-year college to establish, plan, and implement institutional change. Among the findings is that the characteristics and qualities of the instructors, rather than the characteristics of the institutional setting, are more likely to account for variances in the degree to which faculty undertake innovative activities.

548 Barshis, Donald. "The Art of Teaching Versus Teaching the Arts." In Stanley F. Turesky (ed.), *Advancing the Liberal Arts*. New Directions for Community Colleges, no. 42. San Francisco: Jossey-Bass, 1983, pp. 55–62.

The author addresses the question of whether mastery learning is an appropriate mode of teaching the humanities, arguing that there are no basic contradictions between the pedagogical goals of mastery learning and the assumptions underlying humanities instruction and suggesting that the resistance of humanities faculty to mastery learning stems from another set of reasons, including (1) lack of experience with and professional devaluation of teacher education and (2) distrust of pedagogical innovations embraced by administrators. The work provides the reader with a balanced discussion of faculty resistance to mastery learning and of the efforts that can be undertaken to overcome this resistance.

549 Beckwith, Miriam M. *Integrating the Humanities and Occupational Programs: An Inventory of Current Approaches*. Project Report no. 12. Los Angeles: Center for the Study of Community Colleges, 1980. 8 pages. (ED 196 489)

Please see no. 743 for the full annotation.

550 Beckwith, Miriam M. *Science Education in Two-Year Colleges: Interdisciplinary Social Sciences.* Los Angeles: Center for the Study of Community Colleges and ERIC Clearinghouse for Junior Colleges, 1980. 69 pages. (ED 181 955)

Please see no. 871 for the full annotation.

551 Beckwith, Miriam M. *Science Education in Two-Year Colleges: Mathematics.* Los Angeles: Center for the Study of Community Colleges and ERIC Clearinghouse for Junior Colleges, 1980. 80 pages. (ED 176 386)

Please see no. 872 for the full annotation.

552 Belmore, William E., and Sellers, Martha. "Individualized Instruction: Rationale and Factors for Success." *Community College Frontiers*, 1977, *5* (2), 13–17.

The authors argue in favor of individualized instruction techniques, such as the personalized system of instruction, audiotutorial instruction, open classroom, and mastery learning, noting that these techniques allow learners to proceed at their own pace in accordance with their own learning styles. They maintain that successful development of such programs requires full support at all levels of the institution, with the understanding that program initiation takes time and that program success cannot be evaluated on the basis of one term's experience. They argue further that instructional support services such as test- and media-construction facilities must be made available to students. They outline ten factors that are requisite to the success of individualized programs and provide instructional development personnel with suggestions for effective program implementation.

553 Bentley-Baker, Kandell, and others. *Honors in the Two-Year College.* Washington, D.C.: National Council of Instructional Administrators, American Association of Community and Junior Colleges; Cranford, N.J.: Community College Humanities Association; Cranford, N.J.: National Collegiate Honors Council, 1983. 58 pages. (ED 246 933)

This work serves as a handbook addressing issues related to the development, implementation, and management of special programs for talented and gifted students in the community college. It includes a rationale for such honors programs and highlights their role in (1) attracting, retaining, and meeting the special needs of superior students; (2) improving the overall image of the college; (3) increasing faculty job satisfaction; and (4) promoting innovative programs, services, and courses. It also examines the unique characteristics of two-year colleges that are likely to influence the philosophy and development of honors programs, the methods used to combine honors program components, and the factors to be considered in implementing and managing honors programs. The work provides insights into how these programs can be developed to meet the special needs of the two-year college.

554 Blocker, Clyde E.; Plummer, Robert H.; and Richardson, Richard C., Jr. "Chapter Eight: Curriculum and Instruction." In Clyde E. Blocker, Robert H. Plummer, and Richard C. Richardson, Jr., *The Two-Year College: A Social Synthesis.* Englewood Cliffs, N.J.: Prentice-Hall, 1965, pp. 201–238.

For an annotation of the work in its entirety, please see no. 7.

555 Brawer, Florence B. (ed.). *The Humanities in Two-Year Colleges: Trends in Curriculum.* Los Angeles: ERIC Clearinghouse for Junior Colleges and Center for the Study of Community Colleges, 1978. 162 pages. (ED 156 285)

Please see no. 875 for the full annotation.

556 Brawer, Florence B. (ed.). *Teaching the Sciences.* New Directions for Community Colleges, no. 31. San Francisco: Jossey-Bass, 1980. 69 pages. (ED 191 543)

Please see no. 876 for the full annotation.

557 Brawer, Florence B., and Friedlander, Jack. *Science and Social Science in the Two-Year College.* Topical Paper no. 69. Los Angeles: ERIC Clearinghouse for Junior Colleges and Center for the Study of Community Colleges, 1979. 37 pages. (ED 172 854)

Please see no. 877 for the full annotation.

558 Coder, Ann. "Why Do Community College Faculty Resist Media as an Instructional Delivery System?" *Educational Technology,* 1983, *23* (5), 7–11.

Please see no. 199 for the full annotation.

559 Cohen, Arthur M. (ed.). *The Humanities in Two-Year Colleges: Reviewing Curriculum and Instruction.* Los Angeles: ERIC Clearinghouse for Junior Colleges and Center for the Study of Community Colleges, 1975. 101 pages. (ED 110 119)

Please see no. 879 for the full annotation.

560 Cohen, Arthur M., and Brawer, Florence B. "Chapter Six: Instruction: Old Methods and New Media." In Arthur M. Cohen and Florence B. Brawer, *The American Community College.* San Francisco: Jossey-Bass, 1982, pages 147–168.

For an annotation of the work in its entirety, please see no. 12.

561 Cohen, Arthur M.; Brawer, Florence B.; and Lombardi, John. "Chapter Seven: What Is Good Teaching?" and "Chapter Eight: Challenging Traditional Concepts in Curriculum." In Arthur M. Cohen, Florence B. Brawer, and John Lombardi, *A Constant Variable.* San Francisco: Jossey-Bass, 1971, pages 99–136.

For an annotation of the work in its entirety, please see no. 13.

562 Cosner, Thurston L.; Chandler, Theodore A.; and Spies, Carl. "Theories and Instruments for Student Assessment." *Community College Review*, 1980, 7 (4), 51–57.

This article briefly describes the application to student assessment of four psychological constructs: cognitive style, anxiety theory, attribution theory, and conceptual level theory. For each of the four constructs, it presents a synopsis of what the theory entails, a brief description of the instruments used to measure students against the construct, and implications of the construct for teaching. It serves as a useful synopsis for educators interested in entry-level testing that matches individual students with modes of instruction on the basis of individual psychological profiles.

563 Cross, K. Patricia. *Accent on Learning: Improving Instruction and Reshaping the Curriculum.* San Francisco: Jossey-Bass, 1976. 291 pages.

The author urges instructional and curricular reform at the postsecondary level in light of the need to replace the current emphasis on "educational opportunity for all" with an emphasis on "education for each." She suggests the utilization of nontraditional, individualized approaches to instruction, as well as increased attention to the effective development of students and to the development of nonacademic abilities such as interpersonal skills. She reviews research relevant to the application of these reforms, focusing particularly on mastery learning, self-paced modules, cognitive style, individualized learning techniques, such as computer-assisted instruction, and structured and unstructured approaches to curriculum development. The work serves primarily as an easily understood synthesis of what researchers have determined about the success and failures of these educational innovations.

564 Dickinson, Gary. "Planning for Team Instruction in the Community College." *Continuous Learning*, 1971, *10*, 230–235.

This article presents guidelines for organizing and planning team teaching in community colleges, identifying major problems and noting structural considerations, such as size, composition, and hierarchy of the team; the representation of various departments on the team; and the physical classroom setting. It reviews functional, or process, considerations, such as the determination of course goals, objectives and priorities; the identification and arrangement of learning tasks; the development and utilization of teaching techniques; and the evaluation of the team-teaching effort. It provides instructors with a concise outline of the factors that need to be considered in organizing a team-taught course.

565 Edwards, Sandra J. *Science Education in Two-Year Colleges: Biology.* Los Angeles: Center for the Study of Community Colleges and ERIC Clearinghouse for Junior Colleges, 1980. 116 pages. (ED 188 709)

Please see no. 885 for the full annotation.

566 Edwards, Sandra J. *Science Education in Two-Year Colleges: Earth and Space.* Los Angeles: Center for the Study of Community Colleges and ERIC Clearinghouse for Junior Colleges, 1980. 87 pages. (ED 180 535)

Please see no. 886 for the full annotation.

567 Edwards, Sandra J. *Science Education in Two-Year Colleges: Environmental Sciences.* Los Angeles: Center for the Study of Community Colleges and ERIC Clearinghouse for Junior Colleges, 1980. 82 pages. (ED 180 558)

Please see no. 887 for the full annotation.

568 Feasley, Charles E. "Actual Costs of Assessing Prior Learning: Institutions Report." *Community/Junior College Research Quarterly,* 1978, *3* (1), 25–35.

The author utilizes data from thirty-one four-year institutions and thirty-four two-year institutions to investigate the costs incurred in evaluating students' prior learning experiences. He finds that colleges have different ways of assessing prior learning for credit purposes and that most do not have a way of comparing the costs of nontraditional methods of prior-learning assessment with the costs of conventional classroom-related testing methods. He argues that this diversity points to a general state of disarray when it comes to prior-learning assessment.

569 Friedlander, Jack. *Innovative Approaches to Delivering Academic Assistance to Students.* Los Angeles: Center for the Study of Community Colleges, 1982. 20 pages. (ED 220 172)

Please see no. 797 for the full annotation.

570 Friedlander, Jack, and Edwards, Sandra J. *Science Education in Two-Year Colleges: Engineering.* Los Angeles: Center for the Study of Community Colleges and ERIC Clearinghouse for Junior Colleges, 1980. 80 pages. (ED 191 538)

Please see no. 891 for the full annotation.

571 Gibbs, O. B., and Lee, Herman C. "Colleges Without Walls: The Status of Nontraditional Learning in California Community Colleges." *College and University*, 1974, *49* (3), 267–274.

This article reviews findings of a survey conducted to assess the extent to which the California community colleges utilize nontraditional institutional systems that are characteristic of college-without-walls programs. It reveals that, of the seventy-three responding institutions, 94 percent allowed students to challenge courses and earn credit through examination, 86 percent had pass-fail options, 84 percent utilized off-campus community facilities, 55 percent had a learning resource center, 49 percent utilized noncredentialed instructors, 45 percent offered weekend classes, 43 percent utilized the College Level Examination Program, 14 percent permitted self-directed studies, and 5 percent allowed students to earn degrees through independent study. It provides insights into the degree to which nontraditional instructional innovations were utilized by community colleges in the early 1970s.

572 Gibson, Walker (ed.). *New Students in Two-Year Colleges: Twelve Essays.* Urbana, Ill.: National Council of Teachers of English, 1979. 130 pages.

Please see no. 892 for the full annotation.

573 Greathouse, Lillian, and Bedient, Douglas. "An Examination of the Difficulties Attributed to Individualized Instruction." *Journal of Studies in Technical Careers*, 1980, *2* (4), 724–732.

This article reports findings of a survey conducted to examine the extent to which individualized instruction is used in community college typing classes and to identify problems in the use of the individualized technique. It details the responses of the heads of secretarial science programs at thirty-two Illinois two-year colleges who were asked whether ten problems commonly associated with individualized instruction were present, drawing conclusions as to the effects of individualized instruction on course standards and student effort and whether there were sufficient instructional materials and resources to meet the needs of students in the individualized classes. It outlines suggested solutions to problems encountered and thus provides the reader with practical information on how to go about the individualized approach to instruction.

574 Gross, Ronald. "The Other Open University, Part 2." *Planning for Higher Education,* 1978, 7 (1), 25–36.

The author informally discusses the efforts of community colleges to produce, buy, and use telecourses, examining (1) the development and operation of the Bay Area Community College Television Consortium and the Southern California Consortium for Community College Television; (2) the organization and benefits of less structured, ad hoc consortia; (3) the different ways telecourses have been used; (4) the controversy over the impact of telecourses on faculty employment; (5) the cost of a typical telecourse program; and (6) the need for more interaction and support among institutions using telecourses. He concludes with an outline of common mistakes made by colleges using telecourses for the first time.

575 Heath, Paul R., and Peterson, Susan L. *The Common Market Concept: Contracting for Community-Based Educational Services.* Monograph no. 2. Stockton, Calif.: Cooperative for the Advancement of Community-Based and Performance-Oriented Postsecondary Education, 1980. 12 pages. (ED 190 186)

This paper describes the common-market system at John Wood Community College (Illinois), whereby the college contracts with other area educational institutions to provide instruction for its students. It discusses the legal basis for the common-market system and describes the efforts of the college to provide student services. The authors outline the advantages of the educational common-market system to the students, taxpayers, and contracting organizations and conclude with a discussion of the application of the contractual model at other colleges and a checklist of factors to consider in forming a community-based contractual education system. The paper is useful for administrators who are seeking methods of eliminating duplication of effort among area educational agencies.

576 Heermann, Barry. *Experiential Learning in the Community College.* Topical Paper no. 63. Los Angeles: ERIC Clearinghouse for Junior Colleges, 1977. 84 pages. (ED 140 909)

This paper introduces the concept of experiential learning and explores means of implementing experiential learning programs at community colleges, focusing on two broad categories of experiential learning: learning through life experience or nonsponsored prior learning and sponsored learning that is incorporated into institutional programs to give students off-campus experience in integrating and applying knowledge. It includes several examples illustrating the essential components of sponsored programs and discusses methods used to assess and recognize nonsponsored prior learning through student portfolios. It closes with a description of the college-without-walls concept and how such colleges operate. The paper provides information of use to persons planning experiential learning curricula.

577 Hess, Gerhard. *Freshmen and Sophomores Abroad: Community Colleges and Overseas Academic Programs.* New York: Teachers College Press, 1982. 194 pages.

This publication examines the mechanics of establishing and maintaining overseas academic programs for community college students. It provides a history of internationalism in higher learning and presents a rationale for the involvement of community colleges in international programs. The author reviews Rockland (New York) Community College's involvement in overseas programming, noting cooperative efforts between the college and other educational institutions, and subsequently discusses national cooperative efforts to develop overseas programs, the College Consortium for International Studies (a national umbrella organization encompassing overseas academic

programs of all member colleges), and administrative support
services essential to international programs. He concludes with an
examination of the impact of international programs on faculty
and students. The work serves as a guidebook for administrators
wishing to involve their colleges in overseas programming.

578 Hill, Andrew. *Science Education in Two-Year Colleges:
Psychology.* Los Angeles: Center for the Study of Com-
munity Colleges and ERIC Clearinghouse for Junior
Colleges, 1980. 74 pages. (ED 181 972)

Please see no. 894 for the full annotation.

579 Hill, Andrew. *Science Education in Two-Year Colleges:
Sociology.* Los Angeles: Center for the Study of Community Colleges and ERIC Clearinghouse for Junior Colleges,
1980. 57 pages. (ED 180 572)

Please see no. 895 for the full annotation.

580 Huther, John. "Behavioral Objectives and Guaranteed
Learning: Equality Carried to Its Final Extreme." *Community College Review,* 1973, *1* (2), 30–36.

The author criticizes the use of behavioral objectives, arguing that
(1) the best objectives may be difficult to identify, (2) the
elimination of time as a factor in learning may simply replace one
screening technique with another, (3) the community college that
seeks to stop screening students for the university or for employers
is out of harmony with a society that thrives on inequality of
rewards, and (4) society does not want students who have achieved
only minimum competency. He maintains further that instruction
with behavioral objectives may not lead people to become
independent learners and suggests external audits to convince
community college leaders of the limitations of the objectives
specified.

581 Jarvie, L. L. "Making Teaching More Effective." In Nelson B. Henry (ed.), *The Public Junior College*. Fifty-fifth Yearbook of the National Society for the Study of Education. Part 1. Chicago: National Society for the Study of Education, 1956, pp. 213–231.

For an annotation of the work in its entirety, please see no. 20.

582 Johnson, B. Lamar. *Islands of Innovation Expanding: Changes in the Community College*. Beverly Hills, Calif.: Glencoe Press, 1969. 352 pages.

This publication provides examples of instructional innovation based on visits to or conferences with the representatives of 159 community colleges. It reports innovative practices in the areas of cooperative work-study, programmed instruction, audiotutorial teaching, instructional television, games and simulation, remedial instruction, student tutors, group instruction, and independent study. It also discusses the relationship between social change and educational innovation, aids and obstacles to instructional innovation, and trends and projections. The author notes the dearth of evidence regarding the success of instructional innovation and calls for increased evaluation of instructional methods.

583 Jones, Emmett L.; Gordon, Howard A.; and Schechtman, Gilbert L. *Mastery Learning: A Strategy for Academic Success in a Community College*. Topical Paper no. 53. Los Angeles: ERIC Clearinghouse for Junior Colleges, 1975. 54 pages. (ED 115 315)

This paper describes the implementation of a mastery-learning approach to instruction at Olive-Harvey Community College (Illinois), discussing the history of experimentation and innovation at the college and examining the tasks involved in developing courses within the mastery-learning framework: specifying the objectives and content of instruction; preparing final exams; establishing achievement criteria; defining course learning units; identifying the learning elements within units; and constructing formative tests. It also details operating procedures, including the establishment of control and experimental groups to test the effectiveness of mastery learning against traditional instruction, and presents outcomes in terms of student achievement, attrition, and affective characteristics. It concludes that a mastery-learning strategy, when implemented with precise care, produces superior results in all academic areas.

584 Julian, Augusta A. *Utilizing Telecommunications for Non-Traditional Instruction in the North Carolina Community College System: Project Final Report.* Durham: Durham Technical Institute and North Carolina Consortium for Instructional Telecommunications, 1982. 148 pages. (ED 224 957)

This publication describes, among other components of a state-wide project on instructional television, a survey of 648 students enrolled in telecourses sponsored by a consortium of North Carolina community colleges and technical institutes. It summarizes survey data on (1) the factors influencing students to enroll in telecourses, (2) their demographic characteristics, and (3) the delivery, operational, and support services that are useful and helpful to telecourse students. The author notes that telecourse students are similar demographically to those in on-campus programs and that the major reason for telecourse enrollments is time/place convenience coupled with interest in course content. The work provides useful insights into the characteristics and objectives of telecourse students.

585 Koltai, Leslie (ed.). *Merging the Humanities.* New Directions for Community Colleges, no. 12. San Francisco: Jossey-Bass, 1975. 105 pages. (ED 115 334)

Please see no. 896 for the full annotation.

586 Kressel, Marilyn (ed.). *Adult Learning and Public Broad-casting.* Washington, D.C.: American Association of Community and Junior Colleges, 1980. 69 pages. (ED 181 985; available in microfiche only)

This publication summarizes the activities and findings of each phase of the Adult Learning and Public Broadcasting Project, a study conducted by the American Association of Community and Junior Colleges to examine television usage in adult education. It includes a review of the findings of a national survey of community colleges conducted in 1978 to assess the extent of television utilization for instruction and examines case studies of station-college cooperation, legal issues affecting instructional television, and recommendations made by the National Assembly of Community College/Broadcast Cooperation in September 1979. It is useful as a national summary of the use of broadcast media by community colleges in the late 1970s.

587 League for Innovation in the Community College. *Orientation to Instruction in the Community College: A Series of Ten Self-Instructional Units for Part-Time Faculty Members, and Other Instructors New to the Community College.* Los Angeles: League for Innovation in the Community College, 1979. 157 pages. (ED 196 480)

This publication provides a series of self-instructional units that are designed to acquaint new instructors with the special mission of the community college and with teaching and evaluation strategies that enhance instructor effectiveness. Included are ten units covering (1) the curricular and governance characteristics of the community college, (2) the academic and demographic characteristics of students, (3) student personnel programs, (4) the writing of performance objectives, (5) ways of enhancing learning and motivation, (6) guidelines for large-group instruction, (7) individualized instruction, (8) the selection and use of instructional media, (9) test construction, and (10) criterion-referenced grading. For each unit, it provides objectives, reinforcement exercises, and suggestions for further reading that are useful in acquainting new community college instructors with effective teaching techniques.

588 Lester, Glenda R., and Cox, David W. *Utilization of Educational Television for Instruction in Mississippi Public Junior Colleges: A Technical Report.* Jackson: Mississippi Authority for Educational Television, 1984. 98 pages. (ED 244 716)

The authors investigate the use of instructional television in the Mississippi community colleges, utilizing information provided by media specialists at each college to detail the types of institutional support provided for instructional television, the amount of hardware and software available on campus, the ways television has been put to use by the colleges, and perceived needs for more effective utilization. They also review the responses of a random sample of 450 instructors to a survey soliciting information on faculty use of instructional television and media centers, factors influencing faculty usage, and perceived needs for instructional television. They note, among other findings, that 90 percent of the faculty felt that television was a valuable instructional tool but that only 53 percent actually made use of the medium. The work serves as a comprehensive description of television usage within the state.

589 Maxwell, Martha. *Improving Student Learning Skills: A Comprehensive Guide to Successful Practices and Programs for Increasing the Performance of Underprepared Students.* San Francisco: Jossey-Bass, 1979. 518 pages.

Please see no. 782 for the full annotation.

590 Monroe, Charles R. "Chapter Fourteen: Improvement of Teaching." In Charles R. Monroe, *Profile of the Community College: A Handbook.* San Francisco: Jossey-Bass, 1972, pp. 272–302.

For an annotation of the work in its entirety, please see no. 27.

591 Mooney, William T., Jr. *Science Education in Two-Year Colleges: Chemistry.* Los Angeles: Center for the Study of Community Colleges and ERIC Clearinghouse for Junior Colleges, 1980. 109 pages. (ED 183 397)

Please see no. 900 for the full annotation.

592 Mooney, William T., Jr. *Science Education in Two-Year Colleges: Physics.* Los Angeles: Center for the Study of Community Colleges and ERIC Clearinghouse for Junior Colleges, 1980. 106 pages. (ED 191 534)

Please see no. 901 for the full annotation.

593 Moore, William, Jr. *Against the Odds: The High Risk Student in the Community College.* San Francisco: Jossey-Bass, 1970. 244 pages.

Please see no. 783 for the full annotation.

594 Morrison, James L.; Watson, Eugene R.; and Goldstein, Jerry. *Compensatory Education in the Community College: An Interactionist Approach.* Topical Paper no. 52. Los Angeles: ERIC Clearinghouse for Junior Colleges, 1975. 60 pages. (ED 111 455)

Please see no. 785 for the full annotation.

595 Murphy, Richard T., and Appel, Lola R. *Evaluation of the PLATO IV Computer-Based Education System in the Community College: Final Report.* Princeton, N.J.: Educational Testing Service, 1977. 446 pages. (ED 146 235)

This publication describes and evaluates a demonstration project conducted in the early 1970s to assess the impact of PLATO (an interactive computer-assisted instruction program) on community college students and faculty. It details the hardware and software components of PLATO, the steps involved in the implementation of the demonstration project at five community colleges, and the methodology employed to evaluate the project. It utilizes data collected from experimental and control groups to assess the effects of PLATO on the attrition rates, knowledge gains, and attitudes of students in accounting, business, biology, chemistry, English, and mathematics courses. It also examines faculty attitudes toward the PLATO system and the impact of the system on the community colleges themselves. The work provides useful insights into the outcomes of a large-scale effort to introduce computer-assisted instruction to the community colleges.

596 Olivas, Michael A. "A Statistical Portrait of Honors Programs in Two-Year Colleges." Unpublished paper, 1975. 16 pages. (ED 136 890)

This paper details findings of a national survey conducted in 1975 to examine the extent to which the nation's two-year colleges make honors programs available to students of exceptional ability. The author notes that, of the 644 institutions responding, only 47 had honors programs with formalized academic and administrative structures. He points out, however, that the bulk of the institutions at least had "honors elements," such as honors classes, honor societies, colloquia, independent-study provisions, or financial aid based at least partly on achievement. He concludes that the development of honors opportunities for gifted students in two-year colleges is a relatively new phenomenon and a "fledgling attempt to educate one constituency in an extremely heterogeneous student population" (p. 12).

597 Oxford, Jacqulinn F., and Moore, David M. "Media Use and Instructional Methods in Community College Science Courses and Related Areas." *Community/Junior College Quarterly of Research and Practice,* 1982, *6* (3), 261–270.

The authors utilize data collected in a national survey of two-year institutions to examine the use of instructional media in community college science courses, comparing media usage in two types of classes: those in which media usage accounts for less than 25 percent of the available class time and those in which it accounts for more than 25 percent. Among their findings are that media usage does not decrease attrition and that the availability of media facilities and assistance does not increase the frequency of media use.

598 Piland, William E., and Gould, Kathy. "Community Colleges and Honors Programs: Are They Mutually Exclusive?" *College Board Review*, 1982, (123), 25–27, 36.

This article surveys forty-eight Illinois community colleges to ascertain the frequency, characteristics, and features of honors programs. It summarizes results from thirty-six responding institutions, noting: (1) only seven of the respondents had honors programs enrolling between 10 and 100 students; (2) entrance criteria usually include ACT score, grade-point average, and recommendations; (3) specific features of honors programs include social activities, recognition banquets, special class sections, independent study, and recognition at graduation; and (4) most programs are guided by a faculty advisory committee. The authors conclude that honors programs are in keeping with the comprehensive community college mission and the goal to provide a quality education to all who desire it.

599 Purdy, Leslie. "Community College Instructors and the Use of New Media: Why Some Do and Others Don't." *Educational Technology*, 1975, *15* (3), 9–12.

Please see no. 229 for the full annotation.

600 Romine, Stephen. "Perceptions of an Effective Community College Instructional Climate." *Journal of Higher Education*, 1974, *45* (6), 415–449.

This article reports findings of a survey conducted at twenty-nine colleges in fifteen states to determine student and faculty opinions about the attributes of an effective instructional climate. It details the responses of 2,058 students and 325 faculty members who were asked to rate the relative contributions of seventy items to instructional effectiveness. The author notes that both faculty and students placed greater significance on items related to instructor behavior than on items related to student involvement and responsibility for learning. He proposes a series of nine statements that can be used in describing an effective institutional climate and in developing faculty assessment instruments, arguing that such statements can be developed and used by individual colleges in establishing instructional and institutional evaluation criteria.

601 Roueche, John E., and McFarlane, William H. "Improved Instruction in the Junior College: Key to Equal Opportunity." *Journal of Higher Education*, 1970, *41* (9), 713–722.

The authors argue that "equal opportunity in the community college is more a slogan than a fact" (p. 714), because the colleges have yet to adapt teaching strategies to the special needs of students with academic skills deficiencies. They note the large proportion of remedial students who fail to complete their courses satisfactorily and attribute this attrition largely to negative faculty attitudes toward disadvantaged students and to teacher training programs that do not provide community college instructors with requisite pedagogical skills. They urge colleges to employ mastery-learning instructional systems based on behavioral objectives and variable-length terms. The article constitutes one of the strongest challenges in the literature to the presupposition that community colleges are superior teaching institutions.

602 Roueche, John E., and Pitman, John C. *A Modest Proposal: Students Can Learn*. San Francisco: Jossey-Bass, 1972. 142 pages.

This publication provides junior college instructors with an introduction to mastery-learning technologies and their application in developing instructional programs for nontraditional students. The authors argue that most students can master college material given sufficient time and proper instruction, but they warn that traditional modes of normative evaluation do not enable colleges to meet the varied learning needs of a diverse student body. They define teaching as "the deliberate attempt to cause change in learners by means of predetermined behavioral objectives" (p. 63) and discuss organizational changes required to build college instructional programs around Bloom's concept of mastery learning. They conclude with examples of affective and cognitive learning objectives.

603 Shearon, Ron W., and Templin, Robert G., Jr. "The Debate over Behavioral Objectives: A Call for Bringing the Learner into the Matter of Learning." *Community College Review*, 1973, *1* (3), 23–30.

The authors recount the pros and cons of behavioral objectives, noting the arguments of both proponents, who believe that behavioral objectives increase instructional efficiency and facilitate learning, and opponents, who maintain that there is little evidence to indicate the value of stated objectives in increasing student learning and that complex human behavior cannot be reduced to mechanistic measurements without dehumanizing the teaching-learning process. They suggest that the perceptions of learners are not sufficiently taken into account when behavioral objectives are specified and that the relationship between specifying behavioral objectives and measuring actual learning thus falls short of expectations.

604 Shisler, Clifford L., and Eveslage, Sonja A. "Awarding Credit for Noncollegiate Learning in Illinois Colleges and Universities." *Community/Junior College Research Quarterly*, 1980, *4* (4), 309–318.

This article examines the extent to which Illinois colleges and universities award academic credit for noncollegiate learning experiences, detailing (1) the percentage of institutions that award credit for training received in the military and in training programs conducted by industries and labor unions; (2) the percentage of institutions that award credit through formal testing programs or through individual assessments of life and employment experience; and (3) the methods used by the colleges and universities to assess noncollegiate-sponsored instruction offered by industries and the military. The authors compare findings by type of institution (community college, four-year college, and graduate university), noting that public community colleges are the most receptive to crediting external learning experience.

605 Young, James, and Healy, Therman. *Survey of Practices of Community Colleges in Granting Credit for Non-Traditional Learning Experiences.* Douglas, Ariz.: Cochise College, 1975. 43 pages. (ED 156 289)

This publication details findings of a national survey conducted in 1975 to identify college practices in granting credit for nontraditional learning experiences. It draws upon responses from ninety-six colleges in six regional accrediting associations to determine (1) whether there were differences in practices among colleges belonging to different accrediting associations; (2) whether the date of institutional establishment altered credit-granting practices; and (3) whether there were differences in practices between public and private institutions. Among the findings is that colleges in all six districts awarded varying degrees of credit for College Level Examination Program (CLEP) exams, for work experiences, for military experiences, for United States Armed Forces Institute participation, for courses taken in nonaccredited institutions, and for in-service professional training. The work is useful as a review of common prior-learning assessment practices in the mid 1970s.

606 Zigerell, James J., and Chausow, Hymen M. *Chicago's TV College: A Fifth Report.* Chicago: Learning Resources Lab, City Colleges of Chicago, 1974. 38 pages. (ED 089 806)

This report reviews progress made in the first eighteen years of the "TV College," an effort begun by the City Colleges of Chicago in 1956 to use broadcast television for instruction. It examines the place of the TV College within the administrative structure of the city colleges, the variety of course offerings provided by the TV College, the characteristics of students enrolled in telecourses, and the costs involved in producing TV College courses. It also summarizes the findings of a study undertaken during the early years of the TV College to compare the achievement of at-home telecourse students with the achievement of students in traditionally taught classrooms. It is useful as a brief overview of one of the earliest and longest efforts undertaken to incorporate instructional television in community college education.

★**607** Zigerell, James J.; O'Rourke, James S.; and Pohrte, Theodore W. *Television in Community and Junior Colleges: An Overview and Guidelines.* Los Angeles: ERIC Clearinghouse for Junior Colleges; Syracuse, N.Y.: ERIC Clearinghouse on Information Resources, 1980. 46 pages. (ED 206 329)

This paper provides, in question-and-answer format, introductory information on the use of educational television in the community college. It includes three sections, covering (1) current developments in telecommunications use at two-year postsecondary institutions in the United States; (2) what the research says about the use of telecommunications by adult learners; and (3) how to get started in using the new media to provide cost-effective instruction. It serves as an excellent introductory guide for college practitioners who need to know how television has been applied in the community college and what resources are needed to start up an instructional television program.

608 Zwerling, L. Steven. "Experiential Education at a Community College." In John Duley (ed.), *Implementing Field Experience Education.* New Directions for Higher Education, no. 6. San Francisco: Jossey-Bass, 1974, pp. 1–12.

For an annotation of the work in its entirety, please see no. 990.

Student Personnel and Support Services

609 Ames, W. Clark, and Elsner, Paul A. "Chapter Seven: Redirecting Student Services." In George B. Vaughan and Associates, *Issues for Community College Leaders in a New Era.* San Francisco: Jossey-Bass, 1983, pp. 139–158.

For an annotation of the work in its entirety, please see no. 37.

610 Barbee, David. *A Systems Approach to Community College Education.* Princeton, N.J.: Auerbach, 1972. 184 pages.

Please see no. 509 for the full annotation.

611 Bimstein, Donald. "How Good Are the Community College Adult Programs?" *Adult Leadership,* 1975, *23* (7), 199–202.

The author argues that students in evening programs "do not receive the same consideration and services accorded those of the daytime division" (p. 199), noting that many evening students frequently do not receive adequate counseling, convenient registration services, evening library or cafeteria services, or the attention of fully qualified instructors. He discusses the administrative and financial problems that lead to this situation, citing the pressure to focus on popular, high-enrollment courses at the expense of courses that may actually be more vital.

612 Blocker, Clyde E.; Plummer, Robert H.; and Richardson, Richard C., Jr. "Chapter Nine: The Student-Personnel Program." In Clyde E. Blocker, Robert H. Plummer, and Richard C. Richardson, Jr., *The Two-Year College: A Social Synthesis.* Englewood Cliffs, N.J.: Prentice-Hall, 1965, pp. 239–268.

For an annotation of the work in its entirety, please see no. 7.

613 Brooks, Gary D., and Avila, Jose F. "A Profile of Student Personnel Workers in Junior and Community Colleges." *Journal of College Student Personnel,* 1973, *14* (6), 532–536.

Please see no. 317 for the full annotation.

614 Clarke, Johnnie R. *Commitment to the Nontraditional Student.* Topical Paper no. 51. Los Angeles: ERIC Clearinghouse for Junior Colleges, 1975. 18 pages. (ED 107 327)

Please see no. 171 for the full annotation.

615 Cohen, Arthur M., and Brawer, Florence B. "Chapter Seven: Student Services: Providing Adequate Assistance." In Arthur M. Cohen and Florence B. Brawer, *The American Community College*. San Francisco: Jossey-Bass, 1982, pp. 169–190.

For an annotation of the work in its entirety, please see no. 12.

616 College Entrance Examination Board. *The Foreign Student in United States Community and Junior Colleges: A Colloquium Held at Wingspread, Racine, Wisconsin, October 18–20, 1977*. New York: College Entrance Examination Board, 1978. 86 pages.

Please see no. 172 for the full annotation.

617 Davis, James M. "Foreign Students in the 2-Year College." *International Educational and Cultural Exchange*, 1971, 7 (2), 25–32.

Please see no. 176 for the full annotation.

618 Diener, Thomas. "Foreign Students and U.S. Community Colleges." *Community College Review*, 1980, 7 (4), 58–65.

The author notes the influx of large numbers of foreign students in community and junior colleges since the early 1970s and reviews the literature on this phenomenon, highlighting the concerns revealed in the literature as they relate to admissions, finances, language problems, advisement procedures, and cultural differences. He also notes the implications for two-year colleges and summarizes appropriate institutional responses, such as providing adequate preadmissions counseling and information to foreign students and ensuring adequate financial resources.

619 Eells, Walter Crosby. "Chapter Eleven: The Guidance Function." In Walter Crosby Eells, *The Junior College*. Boston: Houghton Mifflin, 1931, pp. 315–333.

For an annotation of the work in its entirety, please see no. 15.

620 Eliason, Carol. *Equity Counseling for Community College Women*. Washington, D.C.: American Association of Community and Junior Colleges, 1979. 291 pages. (ED 187 369)

Please see no. 756 for the full annotation.

621 Galant, Richard L. "Priority for Future Role Activities of Counselors in Michigan Community Colleges." *Community/Junior College Research Quarterly*, 1978, *3* (1), 61–73.

This article describes a study conducted to determine whether there is a need to reorganize the counseling programs offered at the Michigan community colleges. It surveys three groups (counselor educators, administrators, and counselors) to investigate whether they think that the future role of the counselor will remain as traditionally established (consisting of remedial, administrative, and therapeutic tasks) or whether the counselor will become engaged in emerging roles that stress activities aimed at preventative and developmental tasks. The author finds that the established role will still be given higher priority in the next few years and that, despite changes in educational philosophy and student body clientele, the counselor's role will change only through a slow, evolutionary process.

622 Goodman, Leonard H.; Beard, Richard L.; and Martin, Carol L. "Counseling Services in the Two-Year College: A Southeastern Survey." *NASPA Journal*, 1975, *12* (4), 241–248.

This article describes the counseling services available at 140 two-year colleges that responded to a survey conducted in the early 1970s. It summarizes survey findings on the types of organized counseling services available, student-counselor ratios, methods of publicizing available counseling services, the types of tests and interest inventories that are available to students, the frequency with which follow-up studies of students are conducted, and the titles, salaries, and educational backgrounds of student personnel directors. It also examines responses concerning counseling areas

that should be emphasized to more adequately meet students'
needs. It serves as a concise review of counseling activities in
southeastern community colleges during the early 1970s.

623 Harper, Harold; Hervig, Joanna; Kelly, J. Terence; and
Schinoff, Richard B. *Advisement and Graduation Information System.* Miami, Fla.: Miami-Dade Community College, 1981. 34 pages. (ED 197 776)

This publication describes the Miami-Dade Community College
Advisement and Graduation Information System (AGIS), an on-
line computer aid for academic advisement that is designed to inform students about the progress they are making in completing
program requirements. It discusses the need for AGIS, the
information function and advantages of the AGIS system, the
system's hardware, its on-line and batch capabilities, the three
phases involved in implementing the system, and the potential use
of AGIS as a graduation application file. Appendixes include an
Associate in Arts Student Flow Model, a sample AGIS transcript
report, and a sample AGIS report of suggested courses. The work
serves as an example of how computer technology can aid the
academic advisement process.

624 Healy, Charles. *Career Counseling in the Community
College.* Springfield, Ill.: Thomas, 1974. 140 pages.

This publication presents counseling procedures developed by the
author from information gained in a survey of 200 community
colleges. It describes counseling procedures that can aid in career
choice, including a method developed by the author in which the
client learns career planning and problem-solving skills and then
applies them to his or her own plans. It presents other model
counseling procedures, tying them to psychological theory.
Appendixes offer career counseling plans and excerpts from group
counseling sessions held in community colleges.

625 Higgins, Earl B. "Community College Counseling Centers: Structure and Focus." *Community College Review,* 1981, *9* (1), 18–23.

This article reports findings of a national survey of 180 two-year colleges conducted to assess the practices and services offered by student counseling programs. It examines (1) characteristics of counseling staff, (2) the location of counseling services on campus and methods of student contact, and (3) the types of counseling and outreach services provided, concluding that the colleges are providing traditional counseling services to increasing numbers of nontraditional students and calling for new, innovative practices.

626 Hines, Edward R. "Policy Making for More Effective Academic Advisement in Two-Year Colleges." *Research in Higher Education,* 1981, *14* (2), 119–134.

This article reports the findings of a statewide survey conducted to assess the status of academic advising in New York two-year colleges. It examines responses as they relate to (1) which staff are involved in academic advising, (2) preservice and in-service training for academic advisers, (3) the evaluation of advisers and the advising process itself, and (4) the impact of collective bargaining on academic advising. It also reviews respondents' degree of agreement with ten statements about academic advising that were gleaned from the literature. Among the findings are that faculty are the primary academic advisers at New York two-year colleges and that fewer than half of the responding colleges engaged in activities relating to preservice training, in-service training, or evaluation of advising. The article provides a useful overview of how advising is carried out at the community college.

627 Kintzer, Frederick C. (ed.). *Improving Articulation and Transfer Relationships.* New Directions for Community Colleges, no. 39. San Francisco: Jossey-Bass, 1982. 117 pages. (ED 220 146)

Please see no. 931 for the full annotation.

★**628** McCabe, Robert H. "Now Is the Time to Reform the American Community College." *Community and Junior College Journal,* 1981, *51* (8), 6–10.

The author reviews factors contributing to the development of the community college and suggests changes to permit continuance of the open-door policy while at the same time strengthening academic standards. He discusses the societal origins of the open-door policy and the dilemma of maintaining both open access and educational excellence. He calls for a systematic reformation of the community college educational program, including such policies as raising expectations of students, controlling student flow, providing more feedback information to students, utilizing variable-time and variable-service programs, maintaining high standards, and enforcing student suspension. The article provides one of the most influential calls for reform in contemporary community college education.

629 McCabe, Robert H. *Why Miami-Dade Community College Is Reforming the Educational Program.* Miami, Fla.: Miami-Dade Community College, 1981. 7 pages. (ED 211 145)

This publication explains reform efforts undertaken at Miami-Dade Community College (Florida) to retain the open-door policy while strengthening academic standards. The author argues that increases in the number of unprepared students and concurrent demands for higher academic standards have "set up the community colleges for failure" (p. 2) and calls for policies that maintain the open door but at the same time (1) increase expectations of students, (2) provide more feedback, (3) direct students through sequential programs based on ability, (4) implement variable-time and variable-service programs, (5) maintain a commitment to high standards, (6) and enforce student academic suspension. An appendix summarizes evidence of improved student performance seen one year after these reforms were implemented at Miami-Dade.

630 MacLean, L. S., and Washington, R. O. (eds.). *Community College Student Personnel Work*. Columbia: University of Missouri, 1968. 386 pages. (ED 025 265)

This publication provides thirteen essays examining problems and projects related to student personnel services at junior colleges. It includes discussions of the underlying philosophy of student personnel services, the special needs of community college students, and problems and innovations in the areas of admissions and records, student orientation, remedial services, counseling and guidance, student activities, and student financial aid and job placement services. It also includes essays on faculty advising and student personnel services in vocational-technical institutes. The work provides the reader with insights into the student personnel function as of the mid 1960s, with a thorough analysis of the relevant literature to date.

631 Matson, Jane E., and Deegan, William L. "Chapter Six: Revitalizing Student Services." In William L. Deegan, Dale Tillery, and Associates, *Renewing the American Community College: Priorities and Strategies for Effective Leadership*. San Francisco: Jossey-Bass, 1985, pp. 131-149.

For an annotation of the work in its entirety, please see no. 14.

632 Medsker, Leland L. "Chapter Six: Student Personnel Services in Two-Year Institutions." In Leland L. Medsker, *The Junior College: Progress and Prospect*. New York: McGraw-Hill, 1960, pp. 141-168.

For an annotation of the work in its entirety, please see no. 25.

633 Meyer, A. M., and Hannelly, Robert J. "The Student Personnel Program." In Nelson B. Henry (ed.), *The Public Junior College*. Fifty-fifth yearbook of the National Society for the Study of Education. Part 1. Chicago: National Society for the Study of Education, 1956, pp. 191-212.

For an annotation of the work in its entirety, please see no. 20.

634 Monroe, Charles R. "Chapter Nine: Student Personnel Services." In Charles R. Monroe, *Profile of the Community College: A Handbook*. San Francisco: Jossey-Bass, 1972, pp. 144–180.

For an annotation of the work in its entirety, please see no. 27.

635 Morrison, James L., and Ferrante, Reynolds. *Compensatory Education in Two-Year Colleges*. Report no. 21. University Park: Center for the Study of Higher Education, Pennsylvania State University, 1973. 60 pages. (ED 078 818)

Please see no. 784 for the full annotation.

636 Morse, Ed. *Student Services Planning Model (SSPM)*. Richmond: Virginia State Department of Community Colleges, 1982. 57 pages. (ED 219 106)

This publication describes the Virginia community colleges' strategic and operational planning methodology for student services programs, noting that the model operates within a framework created by the state's social, political, and technological environment. The author outlines five model components: (1) preplanning, which includes the establishment of the basis for the plan; (2) strategic planning, which includes a review of mission and services, an assessment of needs, and the specification of planning assumptions and goals; (3) operational planning, which encompasses the specification of activities, resource requirements, and budget; (4) operation and management of the student services themselves; and (5) evaluation of outcomes. The publication includes worksheets, forms, and survey instruments used in the planning process. It serves as a framework for planning and developing student services programs.

637 Nichols, Donald D. "Women's Programs at Public Community Colleges." *Community and Junior College Journal*, 1976, *46* (4), 7–8.

Please see no. 187 for the full annotation.

638 O'Banion, Terry. "Humanizing Education in the Community College." *Journal of Higher Education,* 1971, *42* (8), 657–668.

This article places the community college within the context of student criticism of higher education in the 1960s, arguing that two-year institutions, like the large multiversity, operate on a dehumanizing production principle that ignores individuality and molds students to fit the requirements of employers or upper-division institutions. The author calls for a humanization of the learning process through courses in self-development; the abolition of testing programs, grades, and academic probation; the involvement of students in setting course objectives; and the reconceptualization of faculty as "human development facilitators." The article demonstrates how the upheaval of the 1960s challenged the self-proclaimed reputation of the community college as "the people's college."

639 O'Banion, Terry, and Thurston, Alice (eds.). *Student Development Programs in the Community Junior College.* Englewood Cliffs, N.J.: Prentice-Hall, 1972. 235 pages.

This publication presents nineteen papers authored by community college presidents, deans of student personnel services, and university professors specializing in community colleges covering the role of student development programs, problems in organizing student development services, and the future of student development in community colleges. The work argues that student personnel services should be an integral part of the community college mission and shows how student counseling can be organized and evaluated. It points to internal and external influences on the development of student personnel programs and recommends that student personnel workers be especially trained to staff community colleges.

640 Ogilvie, William K., and Raines, Max R. (eds.). "Part Six: Student Services." In William K. Ogilvie and Max R. Raines (eds.), *Perspectives on the Community Junior College.* New York: Appleton-Century-Crofts, 1971, pp. 341–392.

For an annotation of the work in its entirety, please see no. 29.

641 Palola, Ernest G., and Oswald, Arthur R. *Urban Multi-Unit Community Colleges: Adaptation for the '70s.* Berkeley: Center for Research and Development in Higher Education, University of California, 1972. 129 pages. (ED 068 096)

Please see no. 163 for the full annotation.

642 Paradise, Louis, and Long, Thomas J. *Counseling in the Community Colleges: Models and Approaches.* New York: Praeger, 1981. 220 pages.

This publication provides a comprehensive introduction to the organization and functions of community college counseling programs, describing the need and rationale for counseling, the major tasks of the counselor, and the diverse student subpopulations served by community colleges. It includes further discussions of the organization and administration of counseling services, ways to facilitate individual and group counseling, the use of tests in counseling, and outreach programs. It serves as a useful state-of-the-art textbook for counselors and students of community college education.

643 Rippey, Donald. *What Is Student Development?* Horizons Monograph Series. Washington, D.C.: Council of Universities and Colleges, American Association of Community and Junior Colleges; Los Angeles: ERIC Clearinghouse for Junior Colleges, 1981. 109 pages. (ED 207 619)

This publication advocates a theory of education that focuses on total student development rather than on the transmission of content knowledge within academic disciplines. It delineates a student development model that assigns administrators, instructors, and counselors specific professional roles in meeting student developmental needs, classified under three headings: (1) the development of knowledge, skills, and attitudes; (2) the development of self-determination; and (3) the development of an ability to control one's environment. It illustrates the application of the model in community college settings.

644 Southern Regional Education Board. *The Black Community and the Community College: Action Programs for Expanding Opportunity, A Project Report*. Atlanta, Ga.: Institute for Higher Educational Opportunity, Southern Regional Education Board, 1970. 60 pages. (ED 046 380)

Please see no. 165 for the full annotation.

645 *Status Survey of Guidance and Counseling Services in Michigan Community Colleges*. Berkley, Mich.: Instructional Development and Evaluation Association, 1981. 127 pages. (ED 215 714)

This publication outlines findings of a study conducted to assess the status of counseling and guidance services in Michigan's twenty-nine community colleges. It details (1) the types of services provided, (2) the use and staffing of job-placement offices, (3) the different college staff who have counseling or advisement responsibilities, (4) the sources of career information used by students, (5) professional development activities of guidance personnel, (6) methodologies used to conduct occupational skills needs assessments, (7) efforts undertaken to inform students about available career education and guidance services, (8) opinions concerning the areas in which the state could provide technical assistance, (9) features considered beneficial to community colleges, and (10) exemplary programs. It recommends the establishment of a state technical bureau to disseminate information and render technical assistance.

646 Thornton, James W. "Chapter Seventeen: Student Personnel Services." In James W. Thornton, *The Community Junior College*. New York: Wiley, 1972, pp. 262–283.

For an annotation of the work in its entirety, please see no. 34.

647 Thurston, Alice S., and Robbins, William A. (eds.). *Counseling: A Crucial Function for the 1980s*. New Directions for Community Colleges, no. 43. San Francisco: Jossey-Bass, 1983. 144 pages. (ED 235 865)

This sourcebook presents ten essays dealing with the status and future of counseling in the community college, including discussions of (1) counseling services that fluctuate in effectiveness according to the approach used; (2) the counselor's expanded, highly professional role; (3) academic counseling for nontraditional and disadvantaged students; (4) the role of noncounseling personnel; (5) advisement and counseling innovations at Miami-Dade Community College (Florida); (6) the organization of counseling services in multiunit systems; (7) preservice training for counselors; (8) student development programs; and (9) problems that must be solved in the 1980s if the viability of community college counseling services is to be preserved. It concludes with a bibliography of relevant literature.

648 Thurston, Alice S.; Zook, Fredric B.; Neher, Timothy; and Ingraham, Joseph. *The Chief Student Personnel Administrator in the Public Two-Year College*. Horizons Monograph Series. Los Angeles: ERIC Clearinghouse for Junior Colleges; Washington, D.C.: American Association of Junior Colleges, 1972. 75 pages. (ED 060 840)

This publication reports findings of two studies exploring the role and characteristics of chief student personnel administrators (CSPAs), describing procedures for each study, one surveying a national random sample and the other surveying CSPAs in midwestern institutions. It provides data on background characteristics, academic preparation, and career goals; program functions, administration, and staffing; and perceived administrative problems. Major problems noted include apparent inadequate preparation for the position, disparities between job duties and perceived program goals, a tendency toward crisis management, noninvolvement in preparing own budget or hiring own staff, and problems due to understaffing and lack of funds. The authors conclude that top administrators perceive student personnel programs as only peripherally important to the junior college program and offer eight recommendations to strengthen student personnel services.

Libraries and Learning Resource Centers

649 Adams, Harlen Martin. *The Junior College Library Program: A Study of Services in Relation to Instructional Procedures.* Chicago: American Library Association; Stanford, Calif.: Stanford University Press, 1940. 92 pages.

This publication reviews practices used to correlate junior college library services with curriculum and instruction, utilizing responses from administrators at 136 colleges to examine standards and functions of the junior college library, methods used to plan library services "in conformity with the philosophy of the curriculum" (p. 18), library services to students, and administration of the library. It concludes with a description of efforts to improve library service at Menlo (California) Junior College during the 1930s and an outline of selected principles for junior college library programming. It provides the reader with insights into the role of the junior college library just prior to World War II.

650 Allen, Kenneth. "Student and Faculty Attitudes." *Library College Journal*, 1970, *3* (4), 28–36.

This article describes a study conducted at three Illinois community colleges to assess student and faculty attitudes toward the community college library and to determine how students and faculty actually use the library. It draws upon data collected in a survey of students in randomly selected course sections, a survey of faculty, and a survey of students and faculty while in the library. The author examines opinions concerning the relationship of library usage to academic success and responses concerning the reasons for coming to the library. He compares the responses of freshmen and sophomores, full-time students and part-time students, vocational and nonvocational students, and humanities instructors versus instructors in other divisions. The article is useful as an example of how researchers can investigate attitude and usage patterns among the various library constituencies.

651 Allen, Kenneth W. *Use of Community College Libraries.* Hamden, Conn.: Shoe String Press, 1971. 159 pages.

This publication reports findings of a study conducted at three Illinois community colleges to assess student and faculty utilization of and attitudes toward library resources. It details study methodology, which involved student surveys, faculty surveys, and surveys of students and faculty while in the library, and explores such questions as (1) whether students and faculty feel that library utilization is necessary for academic success, (2) whether library resources meet educational needs, (3) how often students use the library, (4) how often faculty expect students to use the library, (5) whether students consult librarians, and (6) which library materials are used by students. It compares findings for students by curriculum major, enrollment status (full-time/part-time), and educational level (freshman/sophomore).

652 American Library Association, American Association of Community and Junior Colleges, and Association for Educational Communications and Technology. "Guidelines for Two-Year College Learning Resources Programs." *College and Research Libraries News,* 1972, *33* (11), 305–315.

This article outlines guidelines that supersede the 1960 "Standards for Junior College Libraries" (no. 655). It includes qualitative guidelines dealing with the objectives and purposes of the learning resources program, organization and administration, budgeting, staff qualifications and duties, facilities, materials, services, and interagency cooperation. It recognizes the expansion of the two-year college library into learning resource services and notes that the learning resource program can be scattered among several campus sites, not located just within the library. (Note: for information on the controversies surrounding these guidelines— especially their lack of quantitative standards—see Wallace, no. 685.)

653 American Library Association, Association of College and Research Libraries, and Association for Educational Communications and Technology. "Guidelines for Two-Year College Learning Resources Programs (Revised), Part I." *College and Research Libraries News,* 1982, *43* (1), 5-10.

This article outlines suggested guidelines that supersede the 1972 "Guidelines for Two-Year College Learning Resources Programs" (no. 652). It enumerates diagnostic and descriptive guidelines in the areas of (1) the objectives and purposes for a learning resource program, (2) the organization and administration of such programs, and (3) budgeting. (Note: Part II of the guidelines is presented in no. 654.)

654 American Library Association, Association of College and Research Libraries, and Association for Educational Communications and Technology. "Guidelines for Two-Year College Learning Resources Programs (Revised), Part II." *College and Research Libraries News,* 1982, *43* (2), 45-49.

This article outlines suggested guidelines that supersede the 1972 "Guidelines for Two-Year College Learning Resources Programs" (no. 652). It includes diagnostic and descriptive guidelines for the instructional system components of learning resource programs (staff, facilities, and instructional equipment and materials) and provides guidelines for user services and interagency cooperation activities.

655 Association of College and Research Libraries, Committee on Standards. "Standards for Junior College Libraries." *College and Research Libraries,* 1960, *21* (3), 200–206.

This article provides, according to Wallace (no. 683), the first national definition of library services for junior colleges. It includes qualitative and quantitative standards and guidelines dealing with (1) functions of the junior college library, (2) structure and governance, (3) budget, (4) staffing, (5) collection size and development, (6) library buildings, (7) library service and its evaluation, and (8) interlibrary cooperation.

656 Association of College and Research Libraries. *Needs Assessment Package for Learning Resource Services to Handicapped and Other Disadvantaged Students.* Chicago: Junior College Libraries Section, Association of College and Research Libraries, 1978. 44 pages. (ED 164 035)

This publication contains assessment packages designed to identify and appraise learning resource services provided for disadvantaged students at two-year colleges. It identifies eight student populations for whom services may be evaluated: sight-handicapped students; hearing-impaired students; students in wheelchairs; the ambulatory handicapped; educationally disadvantaged students; students whose native language is not English; foreign students; and students with mental or psychological disorders. Each assessment section requires the evaluator to record information about total number enrolled, numbers in component groups, whether enrollments have increased or decreased or are expected to do so, and the names of staff members providing assistance to the students. It then provides checklists of learning resources and services already available, forms to record results of interviews with students, and a plan to effect change. It is useful for colleges evaluating their services in terms of the Education for All Handicapped Children Act.

657 Bender, David R. *Learning Resources and the Instructional Program in Community Colleges.* Hamden, Conn.: Library Professional Publications, 1980. 294 pages.

This publication reports findings of a national study undertaken to assess the learning resource services at community colleges. It details methodology, which involved a survey of 322 institutions as well as site visits and interviews with learning resource personnel, and examines (1) the interrelationship of print and nonprint materials, (2) the use of media to provide portions of the instructional program to individual learners, (3) the scope of learning resource services provided, (4) the type and size of learning resource facilities, (5) the types of services that directly facilitate instruction, (6) the responsibilities of staff, (7) the administrative organization of learning resource services, and (8) patterns of program development. It draws on the study findings to provide guidelines for the development of learning resource programs and thus serves as a basic reference for program planners and learning resource directors.

658 Breivik, Patricia Senn. "Resources: The Fourth R." *Community College Frontiers,* 1977, *5* (2), 46–50.

This article recounts successes and failures in offering library instruction to educationally disadvantaged students. The author argues that successful library-based instruction must be directly related to the work that students are doing in their classes and that sufficient time must be secured from the students' programs to ensure the successful transference of the skills learned in the library. She outlines six principles of library instruction and calls for a re-evaluation of the relationship between library use and school achievement.

659 Cammack, Floyd M.; DeCosin, Marri; and Roberts, Norman. *Community College Library Instruction: Training for Self-Reliance in Basic Library Use.* Hamden, Conn.: Linnet Books, 1979. 283 pages.

This publication constitutes a manual for the development of undergraduate library instruction programs that are especially geared toward institutions with an open-door policy. It discusses the rationale for bibliographical instruction and outlines activities necessary to develop, maintain, and evaluate such programs. It provides samples of teaching and testing materials, including items that are designed to acquaint students with the library and its collections, the use of the card catalogue, proper use of library subject headings, and the use of periodical indexes. It also provides course outlines, sample workbooks, and tests. It concludes with an extensive bibliography on college library instruction covering the years 1965 to 1978.

660 Carter, Eleanor M. "Chapter Eight: Application of Micros in Libraries and LRCs." In Donald A. Dellow and Lawrence H. Poole (eds.), *Microcomputer Applications in Administration and Instruction.* New Directions for Community Colleges, no. 47. San Francisco: Jossey-Bass, 1984. 122 pages. (ED 247 990)

The author examines the utilization of microcomputers in libraries and learning resource centers, citing examples from practice at the learning resource center at the State University of New York's Cobleskill campus. She discusses microcomputer-related user services, including equipment and software access and the provision of professional consulting, and elaborates on user control systems based on the organization of the facility, the availability of staff, and the adequacy of microcomputer resources. She also details administrative applications, such as data gathering and analysis, word processing, inventory control, time management, data-base management, and electronic filing. She concludes that microcomputers will play a significant role in library automation by providing a low-cost approach to automation.

661 Dale, Doris C. "The Community College Library in the Mid-1970s." *College and Research Libraries,* 1977, *38* (5), 404–411.

This article provides a composite picture of the community college library, drawing upon visits to thirty-one libraries between 1975 and 1976. The author describes the various terms and phrases used to label the library and examines trends in physical facilities, administrative organization, book-selection procedures, cataloguing and classification schemes utilized, and services offered to students and faculty. She concludes with a depiction of the typical community college library of the mid 1970s.

662 Dale, Doris C. *Two-Year Community and Junior College Library Buildings: A Bibliography of Books, Articles, and Research Studies.* Vance Bibliographies Architecture Series, no. A747. Monticello, Ill.: Vance Bibliographies, 1982. 27 pages.

This 130-item bibliography (with brief annotations) on two-year college library buildings covers books, periodical articles, dissertations, and other research studies produced from the 1960s through 1980. It lists items dealing with architecture, interior planning, and the planning of a new library building. It also includes journal articles that describe the library buildings on various two-year college campuses. It is an invaluable resource for those who are charged with the task of designing a new library.

663 Dennison, Lynn C. "The Organization of Library and Media Services in Community Colleges." *College and Research Libraries,* 1978, *39* (2), 123–129.

This article studies community college learning resource centers to determine whether differences in their organizational structures are associated with differences in the levels of services provided. It describes the differing organizational patterns of twenty learning resource centers in terms of the physical integration of print and nonprint materials, the integration of those materials in the catalogue, and the way in which staff positions are differentiated.

It examines these patterns in relation to three indicators of service quality: the promotion of the center in the college's general catalogue, restrictions (if any) on the use of materials, and efforts at self-evaluation. It draws only tentative conclusions about the relationship of center organization to service quality but provides the reader with insights into the differing ways that learning resource centers organize their materials and staff.

664 Edsall, Shirley. "The Community College Librarian: A Profile." *Community and Junior College Journal*, 1976, *46* (4), 32–33.

This article details findings of a national survey of 1,662 full-time librarians employed at 508 community colleges, profiling the respondents in terms of sex, age at which they entered the profession, educational background, prior work experience, participation in professional activities, job satisfaction, and academic status on the college staff. The author concludes that community college librarians are committed to their profession, even though the majority were unoriented to the special mission of the community college at the time they were first employed.

665 Eells, Walter Crosby. "Chapter Seventeen: The Library." In Walter Crosby Eells, *The Junior College*. Boston: Houghton Mifflin, 1931, pp. 443–472.

For an annotation of the work in its entirety, please see no. 15.

★**666** Johnson, B. Lamar. *Vitalizing a College Library*. Chicago: American Library Association, 1939. 122 pages.

This publication describes a program at Stephens College (Missouri) that placed the library at the center of the college's educational effort. It outlines three program objectives: (1) to assure that the library contributes to the instructional program, (2) to teach students how to use books effectively, and (3) to lead students to read for pleasure. It provides details on how each of these objectives was met and describes the breadth of library materials essential to a successful program, including art, music, and films. It also discusses the administration of the program, including record keeping and the budget. The work provides an early and classic example of the central role played by junior college libraries in the instructional program; the author was, at the time, both head librarian and dean of instruction.

667 Johnson, B. Lamar (ed.). *The Junior College Library.* Occasional Report from UCLA Junior College Leadership Program, no. 8. Los Angeles: University of California, 1965. 96 pages. (ED 012 606)

This publication presents sixteen papers delivered at the 1965 Conference on the Junior College Library, including discussions of the role of the library as an agency of instructional improvement, library operations at Stephens College (Missouri) under the leadership of B. Lamar Johnson, barriers encountered by librarians in their attempt to become part of the college's educational program, the history of junior college library standards established by the American Library Association, and the institutional accreditation process as a means of strengthening the junior college library. It also profiles the libraries at eight individual institutions. It serves as insightful background reading on the educational role of junior college libraries as of the mid 1960s.

668 Martin, Elizabeth, and others. *Junior College Library Personnel Needs: Report of a Survey 1966-67.* Chicago: American College and Research Libraries, 1967. 7 pages. (ED 014 983)

Utilizing data from a survey of 201 junior colleges to assess junior college library personnel needs in 1966-67, the authors define four levels of personnel: professionals, semiprofessionals, technicians, and untrained staff. For each category, they determine (1) the number of staff currently employed, (2) the optimum number of employees, (3) the number of positions for which funding is available, and (4) the number of applicants. They also examine requisite skills and knowledge for staff at each level and whether these skills are learned through course work or through job experience. The findings reveal that there was significant understaffing in the late 1960s but that this probably resulted more from a lack of funds than from a lack of applicants. The work serves as a brief overview of junior college library staffing problems in the growth era of the 1960s.

669 Matthews, Elizabeth W. "Trends Affecting Community College Library Administrators." *College and Research Libraries,* 1977, *38* (3), 210-217.

This article details findings of a national survey of the directors of libraries and learning resource centers at public comprehensive community colleges, utilizing responses from 465 directors to examine (1) their administrative titles, (2) their professional backgrounds and demographic characteristics, (3) their duties and responsibilities, and (4) their positions within college administrative hierarchies. The author concludes that the directors have had to take on roles beyond that of the traditional librarian to become "analyst(s) and designer(s) of instructional systems with a concern for planning a learning environment" (p. 216).

670 Matthews, Elizabeth W. "Update in Education for Community College Library Administrators." *Journal of Education for Librarianship,* 1979, *19* (4), 304-311.

This article surveys chief administrators of community college learning resource centers to solicit their opinions concerning their educational preparation. It investigates (1) the respondents' preparation in media techniques, (2) whether their academic preparation adequately prepared them for their careers, (3) preparation in specific subject areas, such as reference or cataloguing, (4) academic courses and training that the respondents would recommend for future directors, and (5) the highest degree attained. Among the findings is that chief administrators are highly educated and generally well prepared, although lack of preparation is indicated in certain areas, such as audiovisual materials.

671 Means, Robert P. "Comprehensive Statewide Needs Assessment of Community College Library Personnel." In Floyd C. Pennington (ed.), *Assessing Educational Needs of Adults.* New Directions for Continuing Education, no. 7. San Francisco: Jossey-Bass, 1980, pp. 25–35.

The author summarizes findings of a statewide survey conducted to identify the continuing education needs and preferences of professional and nonprofessional staff at the libraries of the Illinois community colleges. He reviews data related to (1) the extent to which staff keep abreast of changes in the field, (2) the incentives and obstacles to participation in continuing education, (3) the job-related tasks in which staff see a need for continuing education, and (4) staff preferences for methods and types of continuing education. He also provides an in-depth discussion of the survey methodology employed and thus presents useful how-to information for college practitioners charged with the task of conducting continuing education needs assessments.

672 Mosley, Madison, Jr. "A Profile of the Library Learning Resources Center in Small Community/Junior Colleges." *College and Research Libraries,* 1984, *45* (5), 392–395.

This article surveys twenty-eight library learning resource centers at small, rural two-year colleges to identify selected administrative practices. It summarizes data pertaining to the division of functional units, the title of the director and his or her place in the college's administrative organization, staffing patterns, duties of nonprofessionals, classification systems used, the type of catalogue used, participation in computer networks, circulation systems, on-line services in effect, and instructional assistance provided to faculty. He sees limited staff and lack of automation as deleterious to the quality of library service.

673 Orban, Deborah. "The Learning Resources Center at the Community College: Its Function and Future." *Community College Frontiers,* 1980, *8* (3), 29–34.

This article serves as a general introduction to the functions and organization of community college learning resource centers (LRCs). It outlines the many services provided by LRCs in the areas of instructional support and materials, discusses the steps an LRC director can take to implement the learning resource concept, and examines the LRC organizational structure. It concludes with a discussion of the new technologies that will affect LRC operations in the future. The article provides a rudimentary knowledge of what the LRC is, how it is organized, and how it differs from the traditional library.

674 Peskind, Ira J. "The Junior College Library." *Library Trends,* 1975, *23* (3), 383–390.

The author considers the unique characteristics of junior college library service for students in music and fine arts programs, briefly describing the objectives of junior college education and noting the diversity among students and the emphasis on instructional innovation. He contrasts approaches to music and fine arts curricula at two- and four-year institutions, emphasizing the role and type of instructional materials used. He illustrates how a junior college library integrates its services with instruction by describing library services in music and fine arts at Loop College (Illinois). He proposes that junior college libraries continue the trend toward innovation, despite limitations of space, facilities, staff, and budget.

675 Platte, James I. (ed.). *The Status and Prospects of Library/Learning Resource Centers at Michigan Community Colleges.* Lansing: Michigan Community and Junior College Library Administrators and the Michigan Community College Association, 1979. 96 pages. (ED 181 954)

This publication reports the results of a 1979 survey of twenty-nine Michigan community college libraries and learning resource centers, providing background information on the responding colleges and examining (1) types of services offered, including library orientation, reference, and audiovisual services; (2) the size and variety of the collection, its use, and its circulation; (3) staffing patterns and task allocation; and (4) budgets. It compares data, where applicable, to those reported in a similar study concluded in 1971. Among the conclusions noted are that the percentage of staff time devoted to acquisitions activities has been reduced since 1969–70 and that this shift suggests that librarians are spending less time on collection development and more time in instruction and promotional roles.

676 Reeves, Pamela. "Junior College Libraries Enter the Seventies." *College and Research Libraries,* 1973, *34* (1), 7–15.

This article reports findings of a study involving a national survey of 250 junior college libraries and visits to an additional 53 college libraries in twenty-one states (including the "pacesetter" states of California, Florida, Illinois, Michigan, New York, Texas, and Washington). It briefly describes common practices in library instruction, cooperation with the libraries, collection development, and automation and examines data related to volumes per full-time-equivalent student, library staff per full-time-equivalent student, the ratio of professional to nonprofessional staff, and hours of operation, making some comparisons with university libraries. The author attempts to shift the focus of junior college library literature from the definition of standards to the description of actual practices.

677 Rolland, Joanne. "A Look at Ontario LRCs." *Canadian Library Journal,* 1983, *40* (3), 157–161.

This article provides an introduction to the learning resource centers of the Ontario Colleges of Applied Arts and Technology (CAATs). It briefly describes the mission and structure of Ontario's community college system and defines the learning resource center concept, under which all formats of learning materials (including books and audiovisual materials) are housed, administered, and organized by a single college unit. The author traces the historical evolution of this concept and cites various Canadian government documents describing how Ontario adopted much of the structure of the American community college and committed itself to the development of learning resource centers at its two-year colleges.

678 Tanis, Norman E. (ed.). "Reference Service in Junior Colleges: Growing Challenge." *RQ,* 1969, *9,* 105–123.

Eight articles on library reference services in junior colleges include discussions of the role of reference librarians in the community college, the case for considering nonbook materials as an integral part of a reference collection, and new techniques to increase student access to reference sources. They also examine the function of media counseling in reference services and special reference services for technology programs. They serve the reader as an overview of reference policies and practice in junior colleges during the late 1960s.

679 Tanis, Norman E., and Powers, Milton. "Profiles of Practice in the Public Junior College Library." *College and Research Libraries,* 1967, *28,* 331–336.

The authors propose a "minimum quantitative threshold standard for adequacy in public junior college libraries throughout the United States" (p. 333), defining this threshold in terms of median annual budget, staffing, and collection-size data gathered for accredited public two-year colleges that have enrollments of at least 1,000 full-time-equivalent students and that have been in operation for at least seven years. They suggest that junior colleges falling below these benchmarks may be providing inferior service to students and demonstrate how the benchmark data may be charted and used by librarians to compare the progress of their own libraries. The article provides an example of one attempt to define library standards during the growth era of the 1960s.

680 Thomson, Sarah K. *Learning Resource Centers in Community Colleges: A Study of Budgets and Services.* Chicago: American Library Association, 1975. 146 pages.

This publication examines the interrelationship between expenditures and service programs in twenty-seven community college library learning resource centers in California, Florida, Illinois, New Jersey, Missouri, Ohio, Texas, Virginia, and Maryland. It draws upon interviews with and surveys of key personnel at these learning resource centers to gather information on features of the learning resource program; budgets, purchasing policies, and grants; student utilization of media hardware and software; and the production of audiovisual materials. It is useful in understanding variances in budgeting and service patterns.

681 Truett, Carol. "Services to Developmental Education Students in the Community College: Does the Library Have a Role?" *College and Research Libraries*, 1983, *44* (1), 20–28.

This article draws upon a survey of fifty-two community college libraries in Texas to identify library services performed for developmental students and to assess the relationship between these services and student persistence. The author notes, among other findings, that, while the vast majority of the responding colleges had developmental education programs, 63 percent did not offer special library instruction for remedial students, and that there was no correlation between the number of special library services offered and student persistence. She confirms earlier research revealing low levels of library service to the developmental program and warns that library services may be growing less relevant to student needs as ever-larger proportions of the community college curricula are devoted to remedial instruction.

★**682** Veit, Fritz. *The Community College Library.* Contributions in Librarianship and Information Science, no. 14. Westport, Conn.: Greenwood Press, 1975. 221 pages. (ED 112 858)

This publication provides a comprehensive overview of the state of the community college library, reviewing its history and discussing issues related to personnel, administrative organization, technical services, types of learning materials and equipment housed, microforms, types of services offered, and cooperative arrangements and extension of services to other institutions and organizations. It also examines library standards and guidelines, problems in planning the library building, and educational movements and developments that affect the library. It draws from a variety of sources, including the junior college literature, institutional publications, questionnaire replies, the author's correspondence, meetings at conferences, and on-site visits. The work serves as a comprehensive, though dated, textbook on the community college library.

683 Wallace, James O. "Two-Year College Library Standards." *Library Trends,* 1972, *21* (2), 219–232.

This article provides a brief history of the efforts undertaken to develop standards and guidelines for two-year college libraries. It examines the development and landmark nature of the 1960 "Standards for Junior College Libraries" (no. 655), the controversies surrounding those standards, and the steps leading to the 1972 "Guidelines for Two-Year College Learning Resources Programs" (no. 652). It serves as useful background reading for those interested in knowing more about the parties involved in the development of two-year college library standards.

684 Wallace, James O. "Newcomer to the Academic Scene: The Two-Year College Library/Learning Center." *College and Research Libraries,* 1976, *37,* 503–513.

This article reviews the development of the two-year college library in light of junior college history. It discusses the early years of the junior college, the junior college movement of 1945–1960, developing professional support for the junior college library, and the broadening of library services to meet the expanding community college mission. The author argues that today's community college library can be differentiated from other types of libraries by its (1) commitment to involvement in instruction, (2) utilization of a variety of media, (3) inclusion of both librarians and educational-technology specialists on its professional staff, and (4) development of a support staff that includes media technicians as well as traditional library assistants.

685 Wallace, James O. "Two-Year College Learning Resources Standards." *Library Trends,* 1982, *31* (1), 21–31.

This article chronicles the efforts undertaken by community college librarians to utilize and revise the 1972 "Guidelines for Two-Year College Learning Resources Programs" (no. 652). The author reviews research studies that have been undertaken to assess learning resource programs against the qualitative criteria outlined in the guidelines and details the problems encountered in supplementing the guidelines with quantitative standards. He examines the use of these quantitative standards in subsequent research, noting the pros and cons of applying Higher Education General Information Survey (HEGIS) data to determine the percentage of colleges that meet minimum standards. The article serves as a summary of the work on community college library standards during the 1970s.

8

─••─

Occupational Education

Although two-year institutions started in the early twentieth century as junior colleges providing prebaccalaureate instruction at the 13th- and 14th-grade levels, vocational programming has become a mainstay of the modern two-year college curriculum. Since the mid 1970s, the rise in occupational enrollment has more than kept pace with the large increase in total enrollments and in most states has in fact outstripped the rise in transfer enrollment. This chapter lists those works that deal with the vocational curriculum. The literature is subdivided under four headings: the developing two-year college role in occupational education (nos. 686–706), program and curriculum development (nos. 707–728), program evaluation and outcomes (nos. 729–742), and miscellaneous writings on occupational education (nos. 743–774).

The Developing Two-Year College Role in Occupational Education

The first twenty-one works cited in this chapter (nos. 686–706) trace the growth of vocational education in the two-year college from the 1920s through the early 1980s. Bennett's pioneering work on *Vocational Education of Junior College Grade* (no. 688) justified college participation in occupational curricula on the basis of the need to train people for a growing number of middle-status careers that require a level of education midway between the high school diploma and the baccalaureate degree. During the 1940s, Walter Crosby Eells (nos. 695, 696) emphasized the need for "terminal education" programs that would combine vocational and general studies in a capstone curriculum for the vast majority of students destined never to attain the baccalaureate degree. Later, advocates of the career education movement, including Grede (no. 701), espoused a "career ladder" concept whereby community college occupational programs would be articulated with high schools and four-year college programs in a multisegmental effort to promote student career development from grade 9 through the baccalaureate.

Lombardi's 1978 enrollment analysis (no. 703) clearly demonstrates that vocational programs now rival the transfer curriculum in terms of size. But the growth of the occupational curriculum does not continue unquestioned. Arns (no. 686) notes the difficulty of developing occupational curricula in light of increased job specialization and an unstable labor market. Grubb (no. 702) argues that community college leaders exaggerate the numbers of jobs available to graduates and make unrealistic claims about the role of occupational education in solving economic problems. Baron (no. 687) asserts that growth in the vocational curriculum has been achieved at the expense of the transfer function. More serious criticisms have been made by the social critics of the community college, whose works are listed in Chapter Twelve.

Program and Curriculum Development

Besides items dealing with the community college role in vocational education, the literature includes several works that examine occupational program and curriculum development. Harris and Grede (no. 717) provide one of the most comprehensive analyses of the program development process, examining trends in the curricular structures of certificate and associate degree programs in business, engineering, allied health, and public and human services. Another comprehensive work is provided by Mayer (no. 721), who presents an exhaustive review of the literature (as of 1971) on curriculum design and development in postsecondary vocational education. Other curriculum development themes examined in the literature include:

- statewide coordination of vocational education (nos. 714, 716);
- the differential costs of vocational and other curricula (no. 727);
- competition from other types of institutions that provide associate degree vocational programs (no. 719);
- the use of advisory committees (no. 720, 724);
- curriculum development in specific occupational fields (nos. 709, 710, 712, 718, 725, 726); and
- the adoption of instructional innovations in vocational curricula (no. 707).

In addition, manuals, checklists, and other aids have been developed for those who are charged with the responsibility of planning vocational curricula. These items include nos. 708, 715, 723.

Program Evaluation and Outcomes

Vocational programs are most often evaluated against two student outcome measures. One measure is the percentage of graduates who find employment in the areas for which they were trained. Researchers using this measure employ follow-up analyses, such as those presented in nos. 732, 733, 734, and 735. The second measure is the "rate of return" to investment in the vocational program. Studies utilizing this measure (nos. 729, 730, 731) analyze estimated lifetime earnings streams to determine the added income that graduates can expect to enjoy as a result of their investment of tuition and forgone earnings during the training program. Both follow-up and rate-of-return studies have considerable limitations. Williams and Snyder (no. 741) note that most follow-up studies suffer from low response rates and a host of other methodological flaws. As for rate-of-return analyses, they are based on questionable estimates of future lifetime earnings and do not consider nonpecuniary benefits that accrue to students. To date, studies examining the benefits accrued to vocational education students have served primarily to underscore the extreme difficulties involved in conducting such research. Whether the majority of students successfully find employment and whether students benefit in other, less tangible ways are questions that require more extensive examination.

Miscellaneous Writings on Occupational Education

The remaining literature on vocational education covers a wide variety of topics, including:

- program accreditation (no. 769);
- faculty development (no. 745, 754, 755, 765, 770);
- screening candidates for oversubscribed programs (no. 763);
- developmental studies programs for occupational students (no. 758);
- faculty job satisfaction (no. 760);
- the incorporation of liberal arts into vocational programs (nos. 743, 749);
- recruiting female students into technological fields (nos. 750, 756);
- articulation between secondary and postsecondary programs (nos. 762, 773);
- vocational programs in specific occupational areas (nos. 746, 748, 752, 761);
- handicapped students in vocational programs (no. 768);
- student and faculty characteristics (nos. 747, 753, 759, 760, 766, 767, 774);
- preservice education needs of occupational program administrators (no. 764);
- cooperative education programs (no. 751); and
- the similarities and dissimilarities between community colleges and proprietary institutes (no. 757).

The recent literature also includes discussions of what has been termed "contract education," or "customized job training." These phrases refer to special programs under which colleges or college systems contract with area businesses and industries to provide training needed by employees. Such training usually focuses on job-related skills and is often conducted at the workplace. Though vocational in nature, these programs are often part of the college's community service and development efforts; thus, works dealing with job training on a contractual basis and with other efforts to serve area industries are cited in Chapter Ten.

Sources of Further Information on Occupational Education

Since the 1940s, practically all of the major comprehensive works on the two-year colleges have included analyses of the vocational education function. The researcher looking for further information on vocational education should consult the appropriate chapters in Bogue (no. 8); Medsker (no. 27); Gleazer (no. 18); O'Connell (no. 28)); Cohen, Brawer, and Lombardi (no. 13); Monroe (no. 27); Thornton (no. 34); Palinchak (no. 30); and Cohen and Brawer (no. 12).

Another valuable source of information is the ERIC data base, which includes hundreds of documents describing occupational programs and curricula at individual institutions. Vocational faculty who are charged with the responsibility of developing a course or program in welding, for example, could consult the data base to find a series of course guides describing four welding courses developed at Allegheny County Community College in Pennsylvania. Further information on the use of the ERIC data base is provided in Chapter Thirteen.

The Developing Two-Year College Role in Occupational Education

686 Arns, Kathleen F. (ed.). *Occupational Education Today.* New Directions for Community Colleges, no. 33. San Francisco: Jossey-Bass, 1981. 124 pages. (ED 200 286)

This sourcebook presents ten articles on the role of occupational education in community colleges, examining the history of occupational education at the community colleges and the implications of its growth, problems that occupational education will face in the 1980s, college roles in government-funded manpower programs, and college involvement in job development and training for the unemployed. It also discusses comprehensive occupational program reassessment, the implications of societal trends for occupational education, and methods of integrating the humanities into the vocational curriculum. It concludes that the four central issues in occupational education are uncertain enrollment patterns, unclear future employment markets, an uneasy economic climate, and the trend toward increased specialization.

687 Baron, Robert F. "The Change from Transfer to Career Education at Community Colleges in the 1970s." *Community/Junior College Quarterly of Research and Practice,* 1982, 7 (1), 71–87.

This article documents and examines the implications of the dramatic rise in vocational enrollments during the 1970s and the concomitant decline in the proportion of students in transfer curricula. The author argues that the shift in enrollment patterns has not only affected the curriculum of two-year colleges but has also affected the community college as a whole, in such areas as funding, organizational structure, instruction, faculty hiring, and student advising and counseling. He points out that this process of change has put into question the traditional proclaimed mission of the two-year colleges. He concludes by suggesting ways in which the overall organization of the college curriculum could be rearranged in order to strengthen the faltering transfer programs.

688 Bennett, G. Vernon. *Vocational Education of Junior College Grade.* University Research Monographs, no. 6. Baltimore, Md.: Warwick and York, 1928. 244 pages.

This publication presents a pioneering analysis of the need for "junior college grade" vocational education to prepare students for occupations at skill levels above the high school diploma but below the baccalaureate degree. The author draws upon a variety of secondary data sources—as well as upon surveys of schools and vocational education leaders—to identify the specific occupations that fit this middle, semiprofessional mold and to predict the maintenance cost of a nationwide program providing training. The work includes an analysis of how each of six educational delivery systems would fit into such a system: (1) the federal rehabilitation program for disabled veterans, (2) land-grant colleges, (3) state universities, (4) normal schools, (5) public junior colleges, and (6) the vocational education systems operationalized under the Smith-Hughes Act. It provides insights into the genesis of junior college vocational education.

689 Bennett, Kenneth F., and Blackburn, Robert T. "Social Indicators of Institutional Commitment." *Journal of Industrial Teacher Education,* 1975, *13* (1), 48–52.

This article examines problems related to the development of measures that can be used to determine the commitment of individual community colleges to vocational education. It notes that such measures should be easy to calculate, that they should be based on publicly available, standardized data, and that they should not reflect factors outside of the institution's control, such as size and location (urban, rural). The authors describe a pilot study utilizing five indices to rank order community colleges in Michigan on the basis of commitment to vocational education: number of vocational students per full-time vocational faculty; ratio of full-time vocational faculty to total full-time faculty; number of vocational students per vocational program; number of full-time vocational faculty per program; and ratio of vocational courses to liberal arts courses. They provide, however, only scant justification for the proposed measures.

690 Bethel, Lawrence L. "Vocational Education." In Nelson B. Henry (ed.), *The Public Junior College.* Fifty-fifth yearbook of the National Society for the Study of Education. Part 1. Chicago: National Society for the Study of Education, 1956, pp. 94–117.

For an annotation of the work in its entirety, please see no. 20.

691 Bogue, Jesse Parker. "Chapter Eight: Technical Education in the Community College." In Jesse Parker Bogue, *The Community College.* New York: McGraw-Hill, 1950, pp. 179–206.

For an annotation of the work in its entirety, please see no. 8.

692 Cohen, Arthur M., and Brawer, Florence B. "Chapter Eight: Career Education: Preparing Students for Occupations." In Arthur M. Cohen and Florence B. Brawer, *The American Community College.* San Francisco: Jossey-Bass, 1982, pp. 191–222.

For an annotation of the work in its entirety, please see no. 12.

693 Cohen, Arthur M.; Brawer, Florence B.; and Lombardi, John. "Chapter Nine: Vocational Education." In Arthur M. Cohen, Florence B. Brawer, and John Lombardi, *A Constant Variable.* San Francisco: Jossey-Bass, 1971, pp. 137–156.

For an annotation of the work in its entirety, please see no. 13.

694 Eells, Walter Crosby. "Chapter Ten: The Terminal Function." In Walter Crosby Eells, *The Junior College.* Boston: Houghton Mifflin, 1931, pp. 283–314.

For an annotation of the work in its entirety, please see no. 15.

695 Eells, Walter Crosby. *Present Status of Junior College Terminal Education*. Washington, D.C.: American Association of Junior Colleges, 1941. 340 pages.

This publication presents a comprehensive analysis of the role of the junior college (as of 1940) in providing "terminal" education programs for students wishing to complete their formal schooling with two years of postsecondary study. The author stresses that such terminal programs prepare students for citizenship *and* careers, thus necessitating a curriculum that combines vocational studies with general education. He draws from a variety of sources to examine the legal status of terminal education, recognition by accrediting agencies, curricula and enrollments, major fields of study offered, instructional staff, library services, equipment available for instruction, and financial support. This work provides the historian of the community college with an important resource on the expansion of the junior college into areas other than the preparation of students for university study.

★696 Eells, Walter Crosby. *Why Junior College Terminal Education?* Terminal Education Monograph no. 3. Washington, D.C.: American Association of Junior Colleges, 1941. 365 pages.

The author presents evidence supporting the importance of "terminal" education that provides for the personal, social, and vocational development of students who end their formal schooling at the junior college. He examines the relative emphasis on vocational and general education in terminal curricula, as well as the social, economic, and educational trends affecting curriculum development. He also includes an analysis of the opinions of educational and business leaders gathered in a survey of 4,000 individuals conducted in 1940. He concludes with four essays on the principles of curriculum revision at the two-year college, the "philosophy of semiprofessional education," new roles for junior colleges, and the need for terminal education. The work provides historians of the two-year college with first-hand information on the factors that led to the expansion of the curriculum beyond traditional academic studies.

697 Engleman, Lois E., and Eells, Walter Crosby (ed.). *The Literature of Junior College Terminal Education.* Terminal Education Monograph no. 1. Washington, D.C.: American Association of Junior Colleges, 1941. 322 pages.

This classified and annotated bibliography of 1,400 books, journal articles, proceedings, and reports on junior college terminal education divides the literature—covering the years 1900 through 1940—into eleven chapters: the terminal education function; general discussions of terminal education; college organization and administration as they relate to terminal education; guidance and personnel services; the library; physical plant and equipment; faculty; cultural aspects of the curriculum; general occupational curricula; specific semiprofessional curricula; and items dealing with the American Association of Junior Colleges' study of terminal education. It provides access to the early literature chronicling the efforts of junior college leaders to develop a terminal curriculum for those students not planning to obtain a baccalaureate degree.

698 Gillie, Angelo C. *Essays on Occupational Education in the Two-Year College.* University Park: Department of Vocational Education, Pennsylvania State University, 1970. 169 pages. (ED 037 210)

These eight essays examine the historical roots of postsecondary vocational education, the ways that vocational curricula can be organized to meet the needs of school-alienated youth who are not academically inclined, and the future prospects of vocational programming. Included are a brief overview of the history of the community college and its role in providing vocational education, a description of a curriculum development technique based on the broad cognitive attributes of the technician rather than on specific job skills, a proposed experimental community college for urban youth, a general-technician curriculum for school-alienated youth, and an argument for a "six-four-four" configuration of American education, with six years in elementary school, four years in secondary school, and four years in junior college. The author provides little information on the actual status of the vocational education function but makes a considered case for the potential role of vocational education in meeting future employment needs as well as the personal development needs of alienated youth.

699 Gillie, Angelo C. "The Postsecondary Institution's Role in Career Education." In Joel H. Magisos (ed.), *Career Education*. Washington, D.C.: American Vocational Association, 1973, pp. 344–353.

The author describes a proposed alternative to postsecondary vocational education based on the principle that training for skills needed in specific occupations should be provided only after the student has secured employment. He argues for a two-year vocational education curriculum that (1) counsels students into broad occupational core curricula that include a common general education component, (2) provides job placement, and (3) provides specialized skills training after employment. He notes that this two-year program can be expanded to include the last two years of high school and argues that "the two-year institution should be converted into 'universal colleges' that encompass grades 11 through 14, with a large majority of students steered into occupational programs" (p. 353).

700 Gleazer, Edmund J., Jr. "Chapter Four: The Two-Thirds Who Will Not Transfer." In Edmund J. Gleazer, Jr., *This Is the Community College*. Boston: Houghton Mifflin, 1968, pp. 64–79.

For an annotation of the work in its entirety, please see no. 18.

701 Grede, John F. "The Role of Community Colleges in Career Education." In Larry McClure and Carolyn Buan (eds.), *Essays on Career Education*. Portland, Oreg.: Northwest Regional Educational Laboratory, 1973, pp. 117–126.

The author examines how community colleges provide an alternative to the traditional role of postsecondary education in preparing people for careers. He argues that, instead of the traditional insistence on broad exposure to the liberal arts as a prerequisite to specialized career courses, community college career programs are predicated on early specialization and a "career lattice" concept that allows the student, if he or she desires, to go on for further education. He notes, for example, that the student who has been prepared in high school to be a laboratory assistant should be able to go on to the community college to become a laboratory technician and then transfer to a four-year college to earn a baccalaureate degree. He urges the development of such lattice networks that would embrace all educational levels to provide a stepping-stone approach to career development.

702 Grubb, W. Norton. "The Bandwagon Once More: Vocational Preparation for High-Tech Occupations." *Harvard Educational Review*, 1984, *54* (4), 429–451.

The author notes the emphasis that community college leaders place on training students for middle-level positions in emerging high-tech industries and argues that the case for expanding community college vocational offerings in high-tech areas has been overstated. He draws upon a variety of data sources to make the point that contemporary community college leaders—like the proponents of vocational education at the turn of the century—exaggerate the number of jobs that will be available for graduates and make unrealistic claims about the role of vocational education in solving national economic problems and increasing educational opportunity. He warns that, while high-tech vocational programs may, in the short run, serve the interests of industry, they could ultimately weaken the educational mission of the community college.

★**703** Lombardi, John. *Resurgence of Occupational Education.* Topical Paper no. 65. Los Angeles: ERIC Clearinghouse for Junior Colleges, 1978. 41 pages. (ED 148 418)

This paper presents an overview of the history, current status, and probable future of the occupational education component of the community college curriculum. It provides a historical perspective on the growth of occupational education, utilizing institutional, state, and national data to document the rise in occupational enrollments, and examines the growth in the number of occupational instructors, the causes of the tremendous growth in occupational education, questions concerning the reliability of data regarding occupational courses and students, and the concerns of educators involving the role of occupational programs in higher education. It concludes that the dramatic enrollment increase in occupational programs is part of the cyclical nature of student enrollment patterns and that it does not spell the end of liberal arts in the community college.

704 Monroe, Charles R. "Chapter Six: Occupational Education." In Charles R. Monroe, *Profile of the Community College: A Handbook*. San Francisco: Jossey-Bass, 1972, pp. 78–102.

For an annotation of the work in its entirety, please see no. 27.

705 Thornton, James W. "Chapter Thirteen: The Curriculum: Occupational Education." In James W. Thornton, *The Community Junior College*. New York: Wiley, 1972, pp. 175–200.

For an annotation of the work in its entirety, please see no. 34.

706 Ward, Phebe. *Terminal Education in the Junior College*. New York: Harper & Row, 1947. 282 pages.

This publication draws upon a five-year study conducted by the American Association of Junior Colleges to present an overview of the principles of terminal education and to suggest procedures and practices for the development of junior college terminal education programs. It discusses the philosophy of terminal education, stressing that it provides for the personal and vocational development of students who wish to complete their formal schooling at a level between the high school diploma and the baccalaureate degree. It also examines needed student personnel services and provides how-to information on various facets of curriculum planning, implementation, and evaluation. The work helps historians of the junior college understand the forces behind the expansion of the curriculum into areas outside of traditional prebaccalaureate studies.

Program and Curriculum Development

707 Appel, Victor H., and Roueche, John E. *Installation and Assimilation of Educational Innovations in Vocational/ Technical Programs in Post-Secondary Institutions: Final Report.* Austin: Department of Educational Psychology, University of Texas, 1978. 217 pages. (ED 162 711)

Please see no. 547 for the full annotation.

708 Beilby, Albert E., and Corwin, Luene. *Curricular Decision Making in Occupational Education: A Procedural Checklist and Guide.* Research Publication 76-5. Ithaca: Cornell Institute for Research and Development in Occupational Education, State University of New York, 1976. 115 pages. (ED 130 728)

This publication provides college personnel—particularly those involved in occupational programs—with a checklist of questions to be answered in planning and evaluating curricula. It includes questions related to (1) purposes of the curriculum; (2) the prerequisites that entering students will have to meet; (3) intended learning outcomes; (4) the courses that will make up the curriculum, including required courses, remedial work, and electives; (5) the instructional strategies to be used; (6) external and internal planning considerations, such as state master plans and existing programs at the college; (7) required resources; (8) student characteristics and attendance patterns; (9) employment opportunities for graduates; (10) anticipated external support; and (11) evaluation criteria. It provides advice on how to go about answering these questions as well as references to additional resource materials.

709 Brawley, Edward A. *The New Human Service Worker: Community College Education and the Social Services.* New York: Praeger, 1975. 178 pages.

This work examines different conceptualizations of the role of human services workers (such as mental health workers, child-care workers, and corrections officers) and the implications of those conceptualizations for associate degree programs that prepare people for employment in human services careers. It focuses on two models of human services education and practice: (1) the "technician model," under which each worker possesses a high degree of competence in one specialized function, and (2) the "generalist model," under which the worker possesses knowledge and skills that can be utilized in a wide variety of settings. The author argues that both models present serious problems and proposes an alternative conceptual framework under which the human services worker is viewed as one of several specialists who operate with a team of colleagues to provide a wide range of services. The work provides readers with an example of one attempt to define the semiprofessional role of workers at the associate degree level.

710 Brawley, Edward A., and Schindler, Ruben (eds.). *Community and Social Service Education in the Community College: Issues and Characteristics.* New York: Council on Social Work Education, 1972. 70 pages. (ED 119 750)

This publication presents seven essays that are designed to assist community college faculty and administrators in the development of associate degree programs that prepare students for employment in community and social service roles. The essays discuss current issues related to the role of the Council on Social Work Education in associate degree education, the content of community and social service programs for students, and job development. They also draw upon the findings of a national survey of 144 associate degree programs to assess student and faculty characteristics and the degree to which field experiences are included in the curriculum, concluding that further study is needed of the place of liberal arts in such programs, faculty recruiting problems, and the amount of appropriate field experience. The work serves as a useful summary of the status of community and social service programs in the late 1960s.

711 Cohen, Arthur M. (ed.). *Shaping the Curriculum.* New Directions for Community Colleges, no. 25. San Francisco: Jossey-Bass, 1979. 125 pages. (ED 171 334)

Please see no. 515 for the full annotation.

712 Dopp, Joan, and Nicholson, Athyleen. *Guidelines for Cooperative Vocational Education in Community Colleges.* Olympia: Washington State Board for Community College Education and Washington State Coordinating Council for Occupational Education, 1972. 49 pages. (ED 061 440)

This is a manual of "how-to" information for community college administrators and teacher coordinators who are interested in implementing, evaluating, or developing cooperative vocational education programs. It includes individual sections on (1) the definition and benefits of cooperative vocational education, (2) steps to be taken in planning a cooperative education program, (3) the responsibilities of the instructor-coordinator, (4) the responsibilities of the employer, (5) general legal responsibilities, (6) the initiation and maintenance of good public relations, and (7) evaluation procedures. It also provides the reader with forms and survey instruments used in conducting feasibility studies, recording visits with participating businesses, outlining student training schedules, delineating college and industry responsibilities, and evaluating student progress. Despite its age, it is a useful introduction to program planning procedures in cooperative education.

713 Doty, Charles R. "Vertical Articulation of Occupational Education from Secondary Schools to Community Colleges." *Journal of Studies in Technical Careers,* 1985, 7 (2), 98–112.

This article outlines the principles of high school–community college articulation and presents a 122-item bibliography of resources to be consulted for further information on this topic. It includes citations to materials that provide articulation-related information on fifty-five vocational subject areas, such as electronics, automotive repair, criminal justice, office occupations, welding, and solar energy. It also lists references to general studies of articulation problems and practices. It is useful primarily as a bibliographical resource for those charged with the task of establishing competency-based vertical articulation programs between community colleges and surrounding high schools.

714 Florida Community Junior College Inter-institutional Research Council. *Post-Secondary Occupational Education in Florida: Planning, Implementation, Evaluation.* Gainesville: Florida Community Junior College Interinstitutional Research Council, 1972. 260 pages. (ED 077 504)

This publication details findings of a study conducted in the early 1970s to describe postsecondary occupational education in Florida in terms of state coordination, program planning and development, program implementation, program evaluation, and student characteristics. It draws upon a number of interviews and surveys to examine (1) the state-level administrative structure for postsecondary occupational education in Florida; (2) the perceptions of faculty and administrators on procedures used to plan, implement, and evaluate vocational programs; (3) the opinions of lay advisory committee members concerning the ways in which the committees should operate in the program development process; and (4) the abilities, interests, goals, and special needs of students in occupational programs. It provides a descriptive analysis of occupational programming in the early 1970s, although implications for future directions are not examined.

715 Greenaway, John. "A Block-Matrix Method for Course Development." *Canadian Vocational Journal*, 1977, *12* (4), 33–38.

Please see no. 521 for the full annotation.

716 Harris, Norman C. "State-Level Leadership for Occupational Education." In James L. Wattenbarger and Louis W. Bender (eds.), *Improving Statewide Planning*. New Directions for Higher Education, no. 8. San Francisco: Jossey-Bass, 1974, pp. 35–50.

The author notes the increased state control of community colleges and examines the status of the statewide coordination of occupational education at those institutions. He reviews responses of chief state community college officers to a survey soliciting information on their role in coordinating vocational education and allocating federal funds for occupational programs and describes exemplary approaches to state leadership in South Carolina, Colorado, California, Illinois, Massachusetts, and Florida. Among his conclusions is that effective statewide coordination is hindered by an administrative duality that divides responsibility for community colleges between state directors of vocational education and state directors of community college systems. He calls for stronger statewide coordination efforts, noting the inability of individual colleges to conduct manpower planning and other research projects needed to develop quality vocational programs.

★717 Harris, Norman C., and Grede, John F. *Career Education in Colleges: A Guide for Planning Two- and Four-Year Occupational Programs*. San Francisco: Jossey-Bass, 1977. 419 pages.

This publication provides vocational education administrators and students of higher education with a guide to the development of career programs that train students "for careers at paraprofessional, semiprofessional, technical, and very highly skilled level" (p. x). It introduces the reader to necessary background information, including the increased demand for vocationally oriented higher education in the 1970s, changes in the labor market, and the different types of institutions providing vocational education. It examines trends in program development at the certificate and associate degree levels for four career clusters: business, engineering and science, allied health, and public and human services. It notes career potential for liberal arts graduates and examines organization, evaluation, and planning in postsecondary career education.

718 Kiffer, Theodore E., and Burns, Martha A. *Human Services Occupations in the Two-Year College: A Handbook*. University Park: Center for the Study of Higher Education, Pennsylvania State University, 1972. 134 pages. (ED 071 651)

The authors draw upon a survey conducted by Burns (no. 748) to provide college administrators with a guide that can be used to establish human services curricula (that is, those vocational programs that prepare paraprofessionals in occupations that are designed to help people). Individual chapters discuss nine human services programs: child day care, library and teacher aides, fire prevention, government services, hotel and food services, allied health, parks and recreation, social work, and law enforcement. For each field, seven factors are examined that need to be considered in program development: steps in initiating the program, costs, faculty requirements, student admissions, curriculum design, accreditation, and placement procedures and employment opportunities. The work provides insights into the organization of human services curricula, although much of the information on costs and accreditation may be outdated.

719 Kuhns, Eileen, and Martorana, S. V. "Programming Occupational Education: An Old Problem in a New Setting." *Community College Review*, 1977, 5 (2), 29-42.

This article examines occupational programming at community colleges, noting that other types of institutions—as well as industry-based programs—are providing associate-level education.

The authors suggest that community colleges can reaffirm their leadership position in this area by (1) studying and addressing industry concerns about the deficiencies in general competencies exhibited by employees, (2) exploring alternatives to course and degree programming, (3) developing and using outcome measures, and (4) basing programming decisions on coordinated data and information rather than on ad hoc knowledge of educational needs. They conclude that community colleges will succeed in occupational education if students feel good about themselves and their programs and about the quality of their work.

720 Light, John J. *A Practitioner's Guide to Using and Meeting with Advisory Groups.* Columbus, Ohio: National Postsecondary Alliance, 1982. 68 pages. (ED 237 140)

Please see no. 526 for the full annotation.

721 Mayer, Lynne S. *Needed: A Compromise in Postsecondary Vocational-Technical Curricula.* Huntington: West Virginia Research Coordinating Unit for Vocational Education, 1971. 58 pages. (ED 059 369)

This publication reviews literature to date on curriculum design and development in postsecondary vocational education, examining writings related to (1) program identification through manpower needs analysis, (2) job analysis as a basis for curriculum design, (3) basic skills and general abilities required of the student, (4) student characteristics, (5) instructional programs and student services, and (6) the content and sequence of vocational-technical curricula. It includes an extensive chart delineating the percentage of course work devoted to general education courses, job-related courses, and skills courses in thirty-three programs within five curricular areas: business and office education, health education, occupational home economics, technical education, and trade and industrial education. It also examines the percentage of class time devoted to theory and laboratory in vocational skills courses. It serves as a thorough review of the literature produced during the 1960s.

722 Messersmith, Lloyd E., and Medsker, Leland L. *Problems and Issues in Accreditation by Specialized Agencies of Vocational-Technical Curricula in Postsecondary Institutions.* Berkeley: Center for Research and Development in Higher Education, University of California, 1969. 142 pages. (ED 030 750)

This publication details the methodology and findings of a study undertaken to analyze the scope and effects of agency accreditation of vocational-technical curricula in two-year institutions. It utilizes several data sources, including a study of materials and legislation relating to the scope and function of professional and regional accrediting agencies, interviews with key personnel at accrediting agencies, surveys of personnel at forty-three two-year institutions in eighteen states, and surveys of the professional associations that are most active in two-year college vocational programming. It examines the extent to which professional associations are approving community college curricula, the degree to which accreditation inhibits or promotes program development, the effects of accreditation on institutional autonomy, and the helpfulness of accreditation in institutional evaluation. The work provides a comprehensive picture of vocational program accreditation in the late 1960s.

723 Posnes, George, and others. *Program Planning in Two-Year Colleges: A Handbook.* Ithaca: Cornell Institute for Research and Development in Occupational Education, State University of New York, and College of Agriculture and Life Sciences at Cornell University, 1975. 160 pages. (ED 112 957)

This work describes an approach to planning occupational programs at two-year colleges, focusing planning methodology on the assessment of seven subquestions or systems: (1) identity—what should be the general content of the program?; (2) articulation—does the program fit college, local, regional, and state plans?; (3) resources—are there sufficient resources to administer the program?; (4) students—how many and what kinds of students will the program attract?; (5) employment—will graduates be able to obtain jobs?; (6) support—will the programs be supported by the college and the community?; and (7) evaluation—how will the program be evaluated? It outlines factors to be considered at each step of the planning process and provides a simulated program planning exercise. It is useful for occupational faculty and administrators as a framework for program development.

724 Rippey, Donald T., and Vickers, Mozell. "Advisory Committee: Dr. Jekyll or Mr. Hyde?" *Journal of Studies in Technical Careers*, 1978, *1* (1), 83–96.

This article reviews the literature on community college advisory committees, noting why such committees are often ineffective and how they might be better utilized. The authors conclude that advisory committees have not been adequately utilized, because (1) administrators fear community involvement, (2) there is a lack of consensus concerning the responsibilities of advisory committees, (3) committee activities are poorly organized and planned, (4) members receive neither enough recognition nor enough responsibilities to keep them interested, and (5) there is a lack of communication between administrators and committee members. They outline fifteen areas in college planning that committee members should be involved in.

725 Schmidt, Mildred S. *Factors Affecting the Establishment of Associate Degree Programs in Nursing in Community Junior Colleges.* League Exchange no. 77. New York: National League for Nursing, 1966. 136 pages. (ED 026 460)

This publication details findings of a national survey of community college administrators conducted in fall 1963 to assess the factors that lead to or inhibit the establishment of associate degree nursing programs. Among the findings noted are several barriers to program development: the comparatively high cost of nursing programs; difficulty in providing needed facilities; and the scarcity of qualified nurse administrators. The author recommends steps that can be taken to overcome these barriers and establish successful programs. The work is useful as an in-depth analysis of the problems faced by nurse educators at a time when the nation's junior colleges were viewed as the most promising avenue for the expansion of the nursing profession.

726 Southern Regional Education Board. *A Guidebook for Mental Health/Human Service Programs at the Associate Degree Level*. Atlanta, Ga.: Southern Regional Education Board, 1976. 182 pages. (ED 148 419)

This work provides program directors, college officials, faculty, advisory board members, and agency field instructors with information on program development in the area of mental health services. It includes background information on the mental health technology movement and provides separate discussions of (1) needs assessment approaches, program organization, and faculty and student recruitment; (2) curriculum objectives and instructional methods and activities; (3) the program's role in securing jobs for graduates; and (4) administrative responsibilities. It is a useful guide to those charged with the responsibility of establishing programs that train paraprofessionals, such as psychiatric aides and mental health technicians.

727 Warren, John T.; Anderson, Ernest F.; and Hardin, Thomas L. "Differential Costs of Curricula in Illinois Public Junior Colleges: Some Implications for the Future." *Research in Higher Education*, 1976, *4* (1), 59–67.

Please see no. 471 for the full annotation.

728 Zoglin, Mary L. "Community College Responsiveness: Myth or Reality?" *Journal of Higher Education*, 1981, *52* (4), 415–426.

Please see no. 542 for the full annotation.

Program Evaluation and Outcomes

729 Berlanger, C. H., and Lavallee, L. "Economic Returns to Schooling Decisions." *Research in Higher Education,* 1980, *12* (1), 23-35.

The authors employ rate-of-return analysis to compare the economic benefits accrued to associate degree holders and baccalaureate degree holders in each of four occupational areas: computer science, nursing, nutrition, and social work. For each of these four fields, they utilize cost-of-schooling data (collected by the province of Quebec) and estimated lifetime earnings streams to calculate average internal rates of return for investment in a bachelor's degree versus investment in a community college associate degree. They conclude that the benefits accrued to bachelor's degree holders outweighed the additional investment required to obtain the baccalaureate degree. The article provides insights into the varying economic benefits enjoyed by people in occupations (such as nursing) in which both the associate and bachelor's degrees serve as entrance credentials.

730 Blair, L. M.; Finn, M. G.; and Stevenson, W. "The Returns to the Associate Degree for Technicians." *Journal of Human Resources,* 1981, *16,* 449-451.

This article utilizes data from the 1972 Postcensal Manpower Survey (a data base compiled by the National Science Foundation) to compare the earnings enjoyed by technicians who have an associate degree with the earnings of technicians who attended one or two years of college but did not earn a degree. It concludes that the rate of return to an associate degree was twice as large as the rate of return enjoyed by nondegree holders with only one year of college and about 50 percent larger than the rate of return enjoyed by nondegree holders with two or more years of college. It provides evidence, therefore, that the associate degree has a "sheepskin" effect; that is, that technicians with an associate degree earn more than technicians who have an equal amount of education but no credential.

731 Bowlby, R. L., and Schriver, W. R. "Academic Ability and Rates of Return to Vocational Training." *Industrial and Labor Relations Review,* 1973, *26,* 980–990.

The authors employ rate-of-return analysis to calculate the economic benefits accrued to people who invest in postsecondary vocational education. They utilize matched pairs of subjects to compare the estimated lifetime earnings streams of (1) graduates of postsecondary area vocational-technical institutes in Tennessee and (2) high school graduates who did not continue their education but who were similar to the postsecondary students in terms of intelligence (IQ), educational background, demographic characteristics, and socioeconomic background. They conclude that rates of return for investment in additional schooling after high school were positive for low-IQ students but zero or negative for higher-IQ students and therefore suggest that funding for postsecondary vocational programs should focus on the training of students of low academic ability.

732 Dennison, John D.; Jones, Gordon; and Forrester, Glen C. *A Longitudinal Follow-Up Survey of Students from Career/Technical Programs in British Columbia Community Colleges and Institutions: Summary Report.* Vancouver, British Columbia: B.C. Research, 1983. 34 pages. (ED 238 473)

Please see no. 108 for the full annotation.

733 Francis, John B., and Jones, Griffith, III. *Education (—?—) Employment: Comprehensive Follow-Up Study of Two-Year College Graduates in New York State. Phase II.* Buffalo: Department of Higher Education, State University of New York, 1976. 101 pages. (ED 156 273)

Please see no. 111 for the full annotation.

734 Illinois Community College Board. *Illinois Public Community Colleges Statewide Occupational Student Follow-Up Study: Final Report of a Three Year Longitudinal Study of Fall 1974 New Students Enrolled in Occupational Programs.* Springfield: Illinois Community College Board, 1979. 72 pages. (ED 169 958)

Please see no. 114 for the full annotation.

735 Lach, Ivan J., and Kohl, Peggy L. *Follow-Up Study of FY 1979 Occupational Non-Graduate Completers.* Springfield: Illinois Community College Board, 1981. 28 pages. (ED 213 453)

Please see no. 118 for the full annotation.

736 Morgan, Mary Y., and Piland, William E. "Locally-Directed Evaluation of Vocational Education." *Journal of Vocational and Technical Education,* 1984, *1* (1), 22–31.

This article reports the results of a study conducted to identify the factors that facilitate self-evaluation of vocational programs in Illinois community colleges, secondary schools, area vocational centers, and state agencies. It examines (1) the types of personnel involved in self-evaluation and the incentives used to encourage involvement, (2) the institutional factors—such as top administrative support—that facilitate self-evaluation, (3) the strengths and weaknesses of evaluation materials used, (4) ways in which self-evaluation results are best utilized, and (5) the role of the state in the self-evaluation process. It provides a comprehensive summary of problems encountered by Illinois educators in evaluating their own vocational programs.

737 Noeth, Richard J., and Hanson, Gary. "Occupational Programs Do the Job." *Community and Junior College Journal,* 1976, *47* (3), 28–30.

Please see no. 125 for the full annotation.

738 Oregon State Department of Education. *Follow-Up of 1980 Community College Vocational Program Graduates and Early Leavers and Their Employers.* Salem: Division of Vocational Education, Oregon State Department of Education, 1982. 33 pages. (ED 216 749)

Please see no. 126 for the full annotation.

739 Pincus, Fred L. "The False Promises of Community Colleges: Class Conflict and Vocational Education." *Harvard Educational Review,* 1980, *50* (3), 332–361.

Please see no. 987 for the full annotation.

740 Vogler, Daniel E., and Asche, F. Marion. "Surveying Employer Satisfaction with Occupational Education: State of the Art." *Journal of Studies in Technical Careers,* 1981, *3* (2), 135–140.

This article examines research conducted to assess employer satisfaction with community college vocational education, noting problems in employer follow-up procedures established for the Vocational Education Data System (VEDS) and summarizing a brief review of follow-up studies in vocational education. It lists different approaches to follow-up research and cites the limited usefulness of data collected to date, concluding with four suggestions for improvement. The article provides a succinct synopsis of the problems that have heretofore plagued vocational follow-up efforts.

741 Williams, William G., and Snyder, Fred A. "The Status of Community College Follow-Up: Some Ideas for Improvement." *American Vocational Journal,* 1974, *49* (1), 40, 42–43.

This article notes common methodological flaws in community college vocational follow-up studies and outlines suggestions for improvement. The authors point out that (1) few institutional researchers make use of consultants or textbooks on survey research, (2) most study samples are not representative of the entire study population, (3) response rates are often low, (4) precollege employment experiences are rarely taken into account, (5) longitudinal data are lacking, and (6) employer assessments of employees' community college training are only infrequently considered. They also find that few researchers assess the nonpecuniary goals of vocational education (such as good citizenship) and that a large number of research reports fail to provide careful descriptions of procedures and subjects. The article provides the reader with a concise analysis of the methodological problems that plague follow-up research.

742 Wilms, Wellford W., and Hansell, Stephen. "The Dubious Promise of Postsecondary Vocational Education: Its Payoff to Dropouts and Graduates in the U.S.A." *International Journal of Educational Development*, 1982, 2, 42–59.

This article reports the results of a longitudinal study investigating the effects of postsecondary vocational training at community colleges and proprietary schools on students' subsequent employment and earnings. The authors conclude that minority and lower-class students were more likely to drop out, that dropout rates were higher at community colleges than at proprietary schools, that graduates of higher-status programs (for example, accounting or computer programming) were no more successful than dropouts in getting jobs for which they were trained, and that graduates from lower-status programs (for example, secretarial science) *were* more successful than dropouts in finding training-related employment. They hypothesize that postsecondary vocational education has little economic payoff for professional- and technical-level jobs.

Miscellaneous Writings on Occupational Education

743 Beckwith, Miriam M. *Integrating the Humanities and Occupational Programs: An Inventory of Current Approaches.* Project Report no. 12. Los Angeles: Center for the Study of Community Colleges, 1980. 8 pages. (ED 196 489)

This report describes twenty-one programs designed to integrate humanities instruction into community college occupational curricula, dividing the programs into four categories: interdisciplinary courses that introduce a variety of humanities disciplines to nontransfer students; specialized humanities courses for targeted occupational areas, such as ethics courses for allied health majors; modules that can be integrated into vocational courses; and faculty development workshops and guest-lecture programs that promote the inclusion of the humanities in vocational curricula. It outlines objectives for each program, names the sponsoring institutions, and identifies contact persons. It is useful for curriculum administrators seeking to develop integrated humanities/occupational programs.

744 Blank, William E. "Analysis of Professional Competencies Important to Community College Technical Instructors: Implications for CBTE." *Journal of Industrial Teacher Education,* 1979, *16* (2), 56–69.

This article describes a study undertaken in 1975–76 to identify the professional competencies required of instructors in community college vocational programs. It reports responses of a sample of two-year college vocational instructors in Florida who were asked to rank the importance of each of eighty-two competencies related to program and instructional planning, teaching, instructional management, and other areas, breaking down findings by full-time/part-time status of respondents, length of teaching experience, and area of expertise (engineering/industrial, health, sales/distributive, public service, and business/office). The author recommends that current certification requirements be examined to determine whether instructors are adequately prepared in requisite competencies.

745 Bloom, Thomas K. "Current Professional Development Practices of Occupational Instructors." *Journal of Industrial Teacher Education,* 1976, *14* (1), 11–19.

Please see no. 242 for the full annotation.

746 Brawley, Edward A. "Community College Programs for the Human Services: Results of a National Survey." *Journal of Education for Social Work,* 1981, *17* (1), 81–87.

This article reports the results of a nationwide survey of human services programs in community colleges, discussing the number and types of human services programs, curriculum design models, student and faculty characteristics, the employment success of graduates, and the transfer of students to four-year institutions. Among the findings noted are that the student population remains predominantly female and that surprisingly large proportions of students have been transferring into four-year institutions. The article serves to some degree as a follow-up of earlier studies conducted by Brawley and Schindler (no. 710), though a low response rate (24 percent) requires the reader to view the study findings with caution.

747 Brue, Eldon J.; Engen, Harold B.; and Maxey, E. James. *How Do Community College Transfer and Occupational Students Differ?* Iowa City, Iowa: Research and Development Division, American College Testing Program, 1971, 31 pages. (ED 049 723)

Please see no. 64 for the full annotation.

748 Burns, Martha A. *New Careers in Human Service: A Challenge to the Two-Year College. A Preliminary Report.* University Park: Center for the Study of Higher Education, Pennsylvania State University, 1971. 87 pages. (ED 049 732)

This publication surveys 194 two-year colleges in the United States and Canada to assess the educational programs offered by the colleges to prepare students for employment in human services occupations. The author finds that human services curricula at two-year colleges can be classified into four categories: those that have a general education emphasis; those that combine general education with specialized courses on a more or less even basis; those that have a specialized, technical emphasis; and those that have a laboratory-practicum emphasis. She also utilizes data from the responding colleges to develop a taxonomy of human services programs under twelve broad categories. The work helps in understanding the types of human services courses offered by two-year colleges in the early 1970s.

749 Carpenter, Don A. "Bridging the Gap Between Vocational Education and the Liberal Arts." *Community College Review*, 1979, *6* (3), 13–23.

This article reviews the history of separation between technical and liberal studies in higher education and argues for a merger of the two. It discusses the forces that have maintained separation of the practical and liberal arts, including funding channels, tradition, and inter- and intrainstitutional territoriality. The author cites reasons for bringing the practical and liberal arts together and urges the provision of career experiences for liberal arts students and the development of liberal arts offerings at the workplace for employed persons. He suggests that, as students become more sophisticated consumers of educational offerings, they will demand greater flexiblity in the curriculum.

750 Carvell, Fred; Carvell, Joan Barnes; Holzkamper, Charlot; and Vann, Lyn. *Options and Opportunities: A Community College Educator's Guidebook for Nontraditional Vocational Program Improvement.* Los Altos, Calif.: Carvell Education Management Planning, 1980. 119 pages. (ED 192 824)

This publication draws upon a survey of students and administrators at twelve California community colleges to provide background information and implementation strategies for the improved recruitment, retention, and placement of male and female students in vocational programs that are considered nontraditional for their gender. It includes a discussion of definitional and legal issues concerning sex equity and analyzes the characteristics of students in nontraditional courses, including the demographic profiles of the students, their reasons for enrolling in nontraditional programs, the support services they require, and the seriousness of their intentions to find employment in their fields of study. It concludes with strategies for gaining institutional commitment to sex equity, improving the recruitment of students into nontraditional programs, and increasing the chances of employment success.

751 Cornell University. *Cooperative Education in Two-Year Colleges: Final Report.* Ithaca, N.Y.: Institute for Research and Development in Occupational Education, Cornell University, 1980. 160 pages. (ED 193 513)

This publication describes a study undertaken to determine which two-year colleges in New York State operate cooperative education programs and to assess the perceived value of these programs. It delineates 102 cooperative education offerings in thirty-seven interest areas and describes the development of an assessment instrument used to identify benefits accrued to students. It also provides (1) a working definition of cooperative education; (2) a checklist to determine whether an experiential program is in fact a cooperative education program; (3) a listing of fifteen major issues and problems faced by cooperative education coordinators at New York two-year colleges; and (4) a chart delineating the benefits of cooperative education and the relative contributions of the classroom and work environment to those benefits. It provides useful insights into how cooperative education should be defined and assessed.

752 Defore, Jesse J. (ed.). *Technician Monographs: A Collection of Papers and Research Studies Related to Associate Degree Programs in Engineering Technology.* Washington, D.C.: American Society for Engineering Education, 1971. 247 pages. (ED 213 442)

This work provides a series of papers and research reports that were originally prepared as background information for a national study of engineering-technology education (ETE) in the United States. It includes chapters covering (1) the history of ETE, (2) ETE curricula and a classification system for content areas, (3) the types of ETE curriculum guides that appear in the catalogues of two-year institutions, (4) the math, chemistry, and physics components of ETE curricula, (5) accreditation, (6) faculty characteristics and attitudes, (7) student and graduate characteristics, (8) the certification of engineering technicians, and (9) the future of ETE programs. It also provides an extensive bibliography. The work serves as a general overview of engineering education at the associate degree level as of 1970.

753 Dennison, John D.; Forrester, Glen C.; and Jones, Gordon. "An Analysis of Students Enrolling in Career Technical Programs in the Colleges and Institutes of British Columbia." *Canadian Vocational Journal,* 1983, *18* (4), 24–27.

Please see no. 71 for the full annotation.

754 Doty, Charles R. "Major Characteristics in the Development and Implementation of a Professional Staff Development Program for Technical Teachers." *Canadian Vocational Journal,* 1977, *13* (1), 5–11.

Please see no. 249 for the full annotation.

755 Doty, Charles R., and Cappelle, Frank. "Technical Updating in Community Colleges." *Journal of Studies in Technical Careers*, 1982, *4* (4), 361–372.

Please see no. 250 for the full annotation.

756 Eliason, Carol. *Equity Counseling for Community College Women*. Washington, D.C.: American Association of Community and Junior Colleges, 1979. 291 pages. (ED 187 369)

This publication presents articles written by women educators and counselors on the need for and the implementation of sex-equity vocational counseling at community colleges. It examines the role of the counselor in meeting women's occupational needs as well as the institutional commitment needed for sex-equity advisement, outlines the needs of target populations (including multicultural groups, re-entry women, displaced homemakers, and welfare recipients), and describes methods of facilitating sex equity, including peer-group counseling, awareness training, life/work planning, workshops, community activities, and credit for prior life experiences. It concludes with a bibliography and with descriptions of six exemplary community college counseling programs. The work serves as useful background reading for vocational counselors and administrators charged with the task of establishing a sex-equity program in the occupational curriculum.

757 Erickson, Edward W., and others. *Proprietary Business Schools and Community Colleges: Resource Allocation, Student Needs, and Federal Policies*. Washington, D.C.: Inner City Fund, 1972. 64 pages. (ED 103 723)

This publication details the findings of a study conducted to (1) describe management techniques and incentives used to operate successful proprietary vocational schools, (2) compare these techniques and incentives with those existing at community colleges, and (3) review federal policies affecting the utilization of proprietary vocational schools. Utilizing data obtained from a survey of existing literature and from interviews with students, faculty, and administrators at twenty accredited proprietary schools and two community colleges, the authors compare the two types of institutions in terms of mission, students, student completion and job-placement rates, student costs and financial aid, and institutional revenues and costs. The work provides insights into how the community college differs from other providers of vocational education, although the reader should be cautioned that data sources used in the study are limited.

758 Fadale, LaVerna M., and others. *Post-Secondary Developmental Studies Programs for Occupational Students: An Impact Study.* Ithaca: Cornell Institute for Research and Development in Occupational Education, State University of New York, 1977. 88 pages. (ED 152 344)

Please see no. 794 for the full annotation.

759 Garbin, A. P., and Vaughn, Derrald. *Community-Junior College Students Enrolled in Occupational Programs: Selected Characteristics, Experiences, and Perceptions. Final Report.* Columbus: Center for Vocational and Technical Education, Ohio State University, 1971. 280 pages. (ED 057 196)

Please see no. 74 for the full annotation.

760 Hansen, Glenn L., and Kramer, Robert E. "Iowa Postsecondary Vocational-Technical Teacher Retention Study." *Community/Junior College Research Quarterly,* 1978, *2* (3), 255–264.

This article studies current and former postsecondary vocational teachers in Iowa to identify reasons for the high turnover rate among vocational instructors. It reviews background information from existing state data, revealing that the highest turnover rate is experienced by teachers who are younger, less experienced, and in the lowest pay categories. It also surveys both current and former teachers on preservice training experiences, job satisfaction, reasons why instructors left or would leave, and the most and least rewarding aspects of teaching. It details survey findings, concluding that there is not necessarily a causal relationship between turnover and job dissatisfaction. The article is useful as a descriptive analysis of teacher attitudes but provides only limited insights into the reasons for faculty turnover.

761 Hawthorne, Mary E., and Perry, J. Warren. *Community Colleges and Primary Health Care: Study of Allied Health Education (SAHE) Report.* Washington, D.C.: American Association of Community and Junior Colleges, 1974. 303 pages. (ED 099 047)

This publication describes the activities and outcomes of a project undertaken in the early 1970s to determine the role that community and junior colleges might play in increasing ambulatory health care in the United States. It draws upon workshops, survey findings, and a literature review to examine the status of allied health education in the United States and outline recommendations for improvement. Among the findings detailed are (1) the number of community college clinical instruction programs offered during 1972–73 in each of several allied health fields and (2) the number and titles of continuing education and consumer health courses offered by each of several hundred colleges during the same year. It concludes with an annotated 223-item bibliography of books, articles, and documents on allied health education. The work is useful as an overview of the allied health curriculum as of 1974.

762 Kraska, Marie. "Curriculum Articulation Between Secondary and Post-Secondary Vocational and Technical Education Programs." *Journal of Industrial Teacher Education,* 1980, *17* (2), 53–61.

The author presents vocational educators with a rationale for articulating secondary and postsecondary vocational curricula and provides guidelines for planning such articulation, arguing that diminished high school enrollments, recent social and economic trends affecting employment needs, and increased national concern make articulation a high priority. She suggests two essential elements in planning articulation projects: (1) gaining support of state officials and school personnel and (2) utilizing special committees to plan curricula and develop learning modules. She notes the importance of maintaining records and information concerning the articulation project and stresses that evaluation of articulation projects should be an ongoing process. She concludes by listing articulation benefits: efficient student transfer, improved instruction, well-defined programs, increased research into employment needs, and better service.

763 Morgan, Margaret K. "Selecting Candidates for Over-Subscribed Programs." *Community College Review*, 1977, 5 (2), 65–73.

This article analyzes the problem of screening candidates for oversubscribed programs in community colleges, with particular focus on health care programs. It discusses research on selecting applicants into educational programs, indicating that little or no relation has been found between cognitive measures and the ability to function as a professional, and reports the results of several studies that tried to develop a means of predicting job success in the health professions. The author suggests that any academic selection plan is inadequate if manpower needs are not being met. She concludes that possible approaches to oversubscribed programs should consider (1) educating students about alternative career options, (2) identification of characteristics of effective practitioners, (3) identification of appropriate competencies, and (4) exploration with differential testing.

764 Patten, W. G. *A Pilot Study: Priorities in Administrative Needs and Program Services for Community and Area Technical Colleges. Emphasis on Large Urban Areas.* Columbus: National Center for Research in Vocational Education, Ohio State University, 1979. 185 pages. (ED 186 703)

This publication draws upon a survey of 217 vocational education administrators at urban two-year colleges to assess (1) the desirable components of preservice graduate education for vocational education administrators and (2) the special efforts that should be undertaken by two-year colleges to expand vocational education to the structurally unemployed and to the undereducated. The author notes that the survey findings reveal administrator concern for additional preservice education in fiscal management and that the respondents endorse special counseling programs and recruiting efforts to reach target groups that need job-training assistance. The work is useful in understanding the professional concerns of vocational education administrators.

765 Schultz, Raymond E., and Roed, William J. *Report on Inservice Needs of Community College Part-Time Occupational Instructors.* Tucson: College of Education, Arizona University, 1978. 29 pages. (ED 156 290)

Please see no. 261 for the full annotation.

766 Seidman, Earl. *In the Words of the Faculty: Perspectives on Improving Teaching and Educational Quality in Community Colleges.* San Francisco: Jossey-Bass, 1985. 292 pages.

Please see no. 263 for the full annotation.

767 Sheldon, M. Stephen. "What Is a Vocational Student? Why Is VEDS Inadequate?" *VocEd*, 1983, *58* (6), 30–32.

The author notes the inadequacies of the Vocational Education Data System (VEDS) data base, arguing that it does not adequately identify the numerous types of students in secondary and postsecondary vocational programs. He utilizes data from the California Statewide Longitudinal Study (no. 93) to disaggregate community college vocational students by educational objective: (1) program completers—those who expect to earn an associate degree or certificate; (2) job seekers—those who attend only for the length of time required to obtain requisite employment skills; (3) job upgraders—those who attend a class or two to upgrade present job skills; (4) career changers—those who are employed but who wish to learn new job skills; and (5) license maintainers—those taking courses required to maintain a professional license. The article serves as a reminder that students enroll in vocational programs for a variety of reasons.

768 State University of New York. *Disabled Student Project Faculty Survey. Beyond Access: Meeting the Instructional Needs of Handicapped Students in Postsecondary Occupational Education. Phase II. Final Report.* Albany: Two-Year College Student Development Center, State University of New York, 1982. 30 pages. (ED 235 331)

Please see no. 231 for the full annotation.

769 Ward, Charles F. *The State of Accreditation and Evaluation of Postsecondary Occupational Education in the United States.* Raleigh: Center for Occupational Education, North Carolina State University, 1970. 243 pages. (ED 052 364)

This publication draws upon surveys, interviews, and an extensive literature review to assess the status of occupational program accreditation and evaluation. The author analyzes data from numerous regional and specialized accrediting agencies to assess (1) the extent of their activities in postsecondary vocational education, (2) the administration of accreditation, (3) the underlying philosophy of accreditation, (4) the clientele and membership of the agencies, and (5) the standards and evaluative criteria used to evaluate occupational programs. He also examines the role of federal, state, and local agencies in the accreditation process. The work provides the reader with a thorough analysis of the procedures and underlying philosophies of program accreditation during the growth era of the 1960s; it includes a 345-item bibliography.

770 Welch, Frederick G., and Yung, Kirby. "Inservice Training Needs of Postsecondary Occupational Teachers in Pennsylvania." *Journal of Industrial Teacher Education,* 1980, *17* (2), 41–45.

Please see no. 269 for the full annotation.

771 Wenrich, J. William. "Meeting the Occupational Needs of the Part-Time Student." *Community College Review.* 1977, *4* (3), 27–32.

The author argues that vocational programs at community colleges should not focus on preservice education that prepares students with no prior job experience for entry-level positions, maintaining that such preservice vocational education is best left to the high schools and that community colleges are in a better position to provide special, part-time programs for working adults. He discusses two categories of such part-time programming: (1) inservice education for people who need to upgrade skills on their present jobs and (2) interservice education for persons who want to learn skills for a new job while maintaining their employment in another occupation. He concludes that by focusing on these educational services, community colleges will avoid duplicating vocational programs that are offered at the secondary level.

772 West, Russell F., and Shearon, Ronald W. "Differences Between Black and White Students in Curriculum Program Status." *Community/Junior College Quarterly of Research and Practice,* 1982, *6* (3), 239–251.

Please see no. 168 for the full annotation.

773 Wilcox, Lynne M., and Pautler, Albert J., Jr. "Articulation in Occupational Education: Considerations for the Future." *Journal of Studies in Technical Careers,* 1983, *5* (2), 177–184.

The authors advocate the establishment of articulated vocational education programs that begin in the secondary school and continue in the community college. They discuss seven factors that need to be addressed in establishing such programs: admissions policies and procedures, curriculum development, student personnel services, faculty cooperation and development, facilities and equipment sharing, research and planning, and advisory committees. They note that articulated high school–community college programs prevent needless duplication of effort and provide students with an economical means of continuing their education.

774 Winter, Gene M., and Fadale, LaVerna M. *A Profile of Instructional Personnel in New York State Postsecondary Occupational Education*. Albany: Two-Year College Development Center, State University of New York, 1983. 101 pages. (ED 252 261)

This publication examines the characteristics and in-service education needs of faculty and administrators in New York State two-year college occupational programs, detailing responses of occupational faculty and administrators to surveys soliciting information on demographic characteristics, education and employment backgrounds, in-service needs, future career plans, and (in the case of the administrator survey) faculty recruitment needs and practices. Among the findings are that most faculty want in-service programs to focus on content-area problems rather than on teaching techniques and that local and regional workshops are the preferred method of in-service education.

9

•⊶•⊶•⊶•⊶•⊶•⊶•⊶• •⊶•⊶•⊶•⊶•⊶•⊶•⊶•⊶•⊶•⊶•⊶• •⊶•⊶•⊶•⊶•

Remedial and Developmental Education

Since the mid 1960s, the community college literature has been filled with references to the need for compensatory programs that address the skills deficiencies of growing numbers of poorly prepared students. Yet, in comparison to the writings on other two-year college curricular functions, relatively few authors have contributed substantive analyses of remedial education that go beyond exhortation or the simple description of programs at individual colleges. Those works that are available can be divided into two groups: general works on remedial education in the two-year college (nos. 775–790) and works on individual aspects of the remedial education function (nos. 791–811).

General Works on Remedial Education in the Two-Year College

Included in the works listed in this chapter are nine comprehensive studies or texts of the remedial education function at community colleges. Six of these works are descriptive in that they present national or state analyses of the status of remedial education and include information such as the characteristics of instructors teaching remedial programs, the types of programs and services offered, the numbers of students served, and the state role in remedial programs. The remaining three works are textbook analyses that take a prescriptive approach to the compensatory education problem. Moore (no. 783) and Morrison, Watson, and Goldstein (no. 785) stress the need to provide counseling and other services in the remedial program so that students will have avenues for communication and emotional support as well as instruction in cognitive skills. Roueche and Kirk (no. 788) pay less attention to the emotional needs of the student and focus more on the administrative steps and pedagogical techniques that will promote the achievement and persistence of students with academic skills deficiencies.

How effective are community college remedial programs? Do students in these programs successfully find their way into the regular college-level curriculum? With the signal exceptions of Roueche and Snow (no. 789) and Maxwell (no. 782), the published literature yields little evaluative information and few analyses of what works in remedial education and what does not.

Individual Aspects of the Remedial Education Function

The remaining items listed in this chapter focus on specific aspects of developmental education, including:

- the structure and operation of community college reading programs (no. 791, 803);
- the debate over whether to incorporate remedial instruction in regular college-level courses (nos. 793, 796, 808);
- the question of whether credit should be granted for remedial courses (no. 802);
- factors contributing to the success of developmental studies programs for vocational students (no. 794);
- the entry-level assessment of student basic skills competencies (nos. 804, 806, 807) and whether remediation should be mandatory for those with demonstrated skills deficiencies (no. 796);
- approaches to delivering academic support services to students in content courses (nos. 797, 799); and
- the role of the library in developmental education (no. 810).

One other aspect of remedial education—literacy development—deserves special mention. Richardson, Fisk, and Okun (no. 805) examine literacy development as a problem concerning the entire institution, not just those involved in the remedial courses. The authors stress that students in all classes need to practice in-depth literacy skills through extensive reading and writing. The implication of the study is that special remedial programs may be of little help if the remaining curricula do not reinforce literacy skills.

Further Information on Remedial Education

The ERIC data base includes numerous documents describing developmental studies programs at individual institutions. Included are descriptions of college entry assessment programs, special services provided for developmental students, and—in rare cases—efforts undertaken to evaluate compensatory education programs. Compensatory education has also been the subject of a good many dissertations. Information on how to find ERIC documents and dissertations is provided in Chapter Thirteen.

Of the general texts cited in Chapter Two, relatively few examine the remedial curriculum. Those providing extensive coverage of the topic include Ogilvie and Raines (no. 29), Cohen and Brawer (no. 12), Deegan and Tillery (no. 14), and Vaughan (no. 37).

General Works on Remedial Education in the Two-Year College

775 Barshis, Donald E., and Guskey, Thomas R. "Chapter Four: Providing Remedial Education." In George B. Vaughan and Associates, *Issues for Community College Leaders in a New Era.* San Francisco: Jossey-Bass, 1983, pp. 76–99.

For an annotation of the work in its entirety, please see no. 37.

776 California Postsecondary Education Commission. *Promises to Keep: Remedial Education in California's Public Colleges and Universities.* Sacramento: California Postsecondary Education Commission, 1983. 161 pages. (ED 230 087)

This publication reports on a survey of California postsecondary institutions conducted to gather information on remedial education activities in the state. It provides information on the types of remedial programs, courses, and support services; the use of diagnostic testing and assessment activities; the number of courses, sections, and enrollments in remedial reading, writing, mathematics, and English as a second language over three academic years; and the administration and costs of these remedial activities. It touches upon the problem of college underpreparedness and the history of remedial education in the United States. It considers policy implications of the survey and offers recommendations for each segment of postsecondary education, among which is that community colleges continue to be considered as the primary postsecondary providers of remedial courses and services.

777 Cohen, Arthur M., and Brawer, Florence B. "Chapter Nine: Compensatory Education: Enhancing Literacy Through Remedial Studies." In Arthur M. Cohen and Florence B. Brawer, *The American Community College.* San Francisco: Jossey-Bass, 1982, pp. 223–250.

For an annotation of the work in its entirety, please see no. 12.

778 Donovan, Richard A. "Chapter Five: Creating Effective Programs for Developmental Education." In William L. Deegan, Dale Tillery, and Associates, *Renewing the American Community College: Priorities and Strategies for Effective Leadership.* San Francisco: Jossey-Bass, 1985, pp. 103–128.

For an annotation of the work in its entirety, please see no. 14.

779 Ferrin, Richard I. *Developmental Programs in Midwestern Community Colleges.* Evanston, Ill: College Entrance Examination Board, 1971. 53 pages. (ED 048 848)

This publication briefly reviews the findings of a survey conducted in fall 1970 to examine the extent and nature of developmental education programs offered by community colleges in the Midwest. It utilizes data from 135 responding institutions (out of a possible 180) to summarize (1) the number of students served by remedial, developmental, and academic skills courses; (2) racial composition of those students; (3) the types of services provided, such as tutorial help in basic skills, academic counseling, or special courses; and (4) the percentage of colleges that award full or partial credit for remedial or developmental program courses. It also examines faculty characteristics, the percentage of developmental students who receive financial aid, and the proportion of developmental students' first-term course work that is taken within the developmental program itself. It provides a useful description of the developmental education curriculum but includes little information on the effectiveness of remedial studies.

780 Linthicum, Dorothy S. *Statewide Assessment of Developmental/Remedial Education at Maryland Community Colleges.* Annapolis: Maryland State Board for Community Colleges, 1979. 100 pages. (ED 175 514)

This publication summarizes the findings of a study conducted in 1979 to determine the scope and characteristics of developmental/remedial activities in Maryland's seventeen community colleges. It provides extensive information on (1) the objectives and goals of credit and noncredit remedial activities, (2) the types of courses and activities provided, (3) enrollments in credit and noncredit remedial courses, (4) costs and revenues, and (5) administration and organization. It also examines the impact of developmental English courses by comparing the academic achievement of students who completed a remedial English course with that of students who had not undergone remedial instruction. It concludes with a discussion of study implications for placement, open admissions, faculty development, organizational structure, evaluation, and funding.

781 Lombardi, John. "Developmental Education: A Rapidly Expanding Function." *Community College Review,* 1979, 7 (1), 65–72.

This article draws from a review of the literature to examine four subcomponents of the developmental curriculum: courses offered at the pretransfer level, handicapped services and education, adult basic education, and remedial education. It defines these curricular areas and then examines program costs in and faculty attitudes toward each. It also examines evidence of program effectiveness. The author concludes that these components of the developmental curriculum will accommodate 50 percent of total community college enrollment by the end of the 1980s. The article serves to illustrate the many functions of developmental studies and the large proportion of community college effort that is devoted to students with special needs.

★**782** Maxwell, Martha. *Improving Student Learning Skills: A Comprehensive Guide to Successful Practices and Programs for Increasing the Performance of Underprepared Students.* San Francisco: Jossey-Bass, 1979. 518 pages.

This book draws upon an extensive bibliography—as well as upon the author's extensive professional experience—to examine the learning problems of college students and the support services that have been designed to help them. It includes chapters on the history and extent of the remediation problem; the organization and evaluation of learning services, such as learning centers and tutorial programs; and problems in the areas of English as a second language, study-skills development, reading, science, and mathematics. It concludes with a thoughtful analysis of the successes and failures of efforts that have been undertaken to help unprepared students since the advent of open-admissions policies. The work provides the reader with one of the most thorough discussions of practice and theory in postsecondary remedial education.

783 Moore, William, Jr. *Against the Odds: The High Risk Student in the Community College.* San Francisco: Jossey-Bass, 1970. 244 pages.

The author criticizes programs for academically unprepared students in community colleges, maintaining that such students are shunted to remedial offerings taught by poor teachers. He contends that such students receive ineffective counseling and are forced to participate in curricula that are antagonistic to their needs and in which they have no hope of succeeding. He cites an experimental curriculum designed for marginal students at Forest Park Community College (Missouri), which combines basic skills study with sociology, science, humanities, guidance, and the use of a programmed materials learning laboratory. He argues against offerings for marginal or high-risk students that do not integrate counseling, reproducible media, sensitive instructors, and carefully paced learning sequences.

★**784** Morrison, James L., and Ferrante, Reynolds. *Compensatory Education in Two-Year Colleges.* Report no. 21. University Park: Center for the Study of Higher Education, Pennsylvania State University, 1973. 60 pages. (ED 078 818)

This publication reports methodology and findings of a national survey conducted to identify the special programs, courses, and services provided by two-year colleges for minority and academically disadvantaged students. Those surveyed included the chief executive officers of fifty-three randomly selected public and private institutions, of whom 90 percent responded. The authors summarize information on admissions policies, special efforts to recruit the academically disadvantaged, special guidance and counseling services, and efforts to educate faculty about the disadvantaged. They note that only 40 percent of the responding colleges have special programs for the academically disadvantaged and conclude that community colleges need to do more if they are to provide opportunity for upward mobility. The work includes a literature review and provides the survey instrument.

785 Morrison, James L.; Watson, Eugene R.; and Goldstein, Jerry. *Compensatory Education in the Community College: An Interactionist Approach.* Topical Paper no. 52. Los Angeles: ERIC Clearinghouse for Junior Colleges, 1975. 60 pages. (ED 111 455)

The authors argue that the affective domain has been largely ignored in developmental education programs and propose a small-group approach to remediation that provides students with avenues for communication and emotional support. They review literature on the affective components of academic achievement, noting that many nontraditional students need to reorient their attitudes concerning education, develop positive feelings about themselves, and experience some success. They discuss the implementation of a small-group approach, including initial faculty and student training, provide sample exercises that can be used in initiation group efforts, and conclude with a seventy-item bibliography.

786 Piland, William E. *Remedial Education in the States.* Normal: Department of Curriculum and Instruction, Illinois State University, 1983. 68 pages. (ED 251 160)

This publication reports findings of a study conducted to ascertain the status of remedial education in the United States as perceived by state directors of community college education. It examines (1) how the states define remedial education, (2) the states' mission in regard to remedial education, (3) the governmental agencies that have authority in this area, (4) methods of funding remedial programs, (5) the educational levels at which remedial education is conducted, and (6) the present condition of remedial education in each state. The author concludes that remedial education is of approximately equal importance to other community college missions and outlines recommendations for the state role in remediation.

787 Roueche, John E. *Salvage, Redirection or Custody? Remedial Education in the Community Junior College.* Horizons Monograph Series. Los Angeles: ERIC Clearinghouse for Junior Colleges; Washington, D.C.: American Association of Junior Colleges, 1968. 77 pages. (ED 019 077)

The author reviews research related to remedial students and programs at community colleges, discussing the history of open-door admissions, the implications of open-door policies for remedial education, changes in the composition of the college student body, and characteristics of instructors teaching remedial courses. He elaborates on the objectives of remedial courses, describes remedial programs at a variety of different colleges, and details research on program effectiveness. He urges better identification of students needing remediation and describes two techniques for evaluating remedial programs. The work concludes with a 147-item bibliography.

788 Roueche, John E., and Kirk, R. Wade. *Catching Up: Remedial Education.* San Francisco: Jossey-Bass, 1973. 106 pages.

This publication describes remedial education programs in five community colleges, noting that each program is characterized by a separate divisional structure and by the involvement of staff who have volunteered to teach basic academic skills to poorly prepared students. It offers information showing that students enrolled in these special programs achieve more and persist longer than students in the regular college program. It provides a prescription for successful remediation that calls for total institutional commitment, volunteer instructors, separately organized developmental divisions, graduation credit for developmental courses, nonpunitive grading practices, individualized instruction, identification and recruitment procedures for entering students, and counseling efforts to mitigate the transition from developmental studies to traditional curricula.

★**789** Roueche, John E., and Snow, Jerry J. *Overcoming Learning Problems: A Guide to Developmental Education in College*. San Francisco: Jossey-Bass, 1977. 188 pages.

This work draws upon a national survey of two-year and four-year colleges to describe the state of the art of developmental programming in higher education. It provides a synopsis of survey findings in terms of the context in which remedial education takes place, program philosophy and rationale, methods used to place students, the organizational structure of remedial programs, the curricular content of remedial courses, staffing patterns, methods of evaluating remedial programs, and support services, such as tutoring or peer counseling. It also presents descriptive case studies of twelve remedial programs and identifies factors that contribute to program success. The work serves as a useful resource for those charged with the responsibility of establishing and leading developmental education programs.

790 Texas College and University System. *Compensatory/ Developmental Programs in Texas Public Community Colleges: Report of a Survey*. Austin: Coordinating Board, Texas College and University System, 1975. 12 pages. (ED 110 133)

This publication details findings of a survey conducted in 1975 to assess the current status of developmental/compensatory programs in the Texas community colleges. It utilizes responses from forty-two of forty-seven colleges to examine program goals, student characteristics, student selection procedures, program organizational structures, funding, evaluation, and follow-up. It notes, among other findings, that programmatic goals fall into two categories: (1) the improvement of cognitive skills to the extent that students can progress into credit courses and (2) affective development to improve student self-concept, provide motivation, and reduce attrition. The work serves as a brief descriptive analysis of developmental programs in Texas during the mid 1970s.

Individual Aspects of the Remedial Education Function

791 Ahrendt, Kenneth M. *Community College Reading Programs.* Newark, Del.: International Reading Association, 1975. 71 pages. (ED 101 283)

The author summarizes research and practice in community college reading programs, reviewing the literature as of 1975 and examining (1) basic principles in the development and operation of a reading program, (2) the components of a suggested training program for community college reading teachers, (3) available instruments for diagnosis and testing, (4) informal group and individual reading inventories, (5) instructional materials, including kits, workbooks, and hardware, and (6) instructional methods. The work serves as a useful summary of the state of the art in reading instruction as of the mid 1970s. It includes a seventy-eight-item bibliography.

792 Atwell, Charles, and Smith, Margaret L. "Competencies Needed by Teachers of Developmental English in Two-Year Colleges." *Journal of Developmental and Remedial Education,* 1979, *3* (2), 9–11.

Please see no. 239 for the full annotation.

793 Cohen, Arthur M. "Shall We Segregate the Functionally Illiterate?" *Community and Junior College Journal,* 1979, *49* (7), 14–18.

The author argues against selective screening into transfer programs and calls instead for tutorial, counseling, and supplementary basic skills instruction to help poorly prepared students complete transfer courses. He maintains that tests used to restrict entrance into transfer courses are not sufficiently precise, because course requirements vary greatly—even among different sections of the same course. He identifies various stratagems for teaching functional literacy in the transfer program and pleads for further research on students who go through the programs and on the level of literacy that is needed to function in specific courses. He asserts that segregating students on the basis of inappropriate criteria is a violation of the community colleges' stated philosophy of open access to higher learning.

794 Fadale, LaVerna M., and others. *Post-Secondary Developmental Studies Programs for Occupational Students: An Impact Study.* Ithaca: Cornell Institute for Research and Development in Occupational Education, State University of New York, 1977. 88 pages. (ED 152 344)

This publication details methodology and findings of a study conducted to assess the factors that contribute to the success of occupational students in remedial programs. The authors define success as student eligibility to continue in a chosen program or the ability of the student to make a conscious, informed decision to leave the program or change career goals. They compare successful and unsuccessful developmental students on the basis of cognitive and affective variables (for example, attitudinal measures and grade-point average) and program environment variables and discuss the possible utilization of findings in assessing students at entrance or during the first semester of instruction.

795 Friedlander, Jack. *Why Don't Poorly Prepared Students Seek Help?* Los Angeles: Center for the Study of Community Colleges, 1981. 14 pages. (ED 203 901)

The author reports findings of a survey of 6,426 community college students who were asked to (1) indicate their degree of confidence in their reading, writing, arithmetic, algebra, science, and study skills, (2) identify which, if any, of the college's support services they had used, and (3) state their reasons for not using these services. Among his findings is that fewer than 30 percent of the students who did not feel confident in one or more skill areas took advantage of a remediating support program. He suggests that, in light of these findings, community colleges should take steps to ensure that students with skills deficiencies receive the remediation they need.

796 Friedlander, Jack. "An ERIC Review: Should Remediation Be Mandatory?" *Community College Review*, 1981–82, *9* (3), 56–64.

This article addresses the issue of whether compensatory programs should be mandatory for underprepared students. The author argues that voluntary enrollment has not been an effective strategy, because only a small percentage of students requiring help take advantage of available services; he points to research indicating, on the other hand, that mandatory developmental programs can be successful in increasing student achievement and retention if properly planned and presented. He also notes that basic skills instruction can be successfully integrated into regular college-level courses and that such integration can eliminate the stigma attached to students in separate remedial classes. He concludes that two-year college educators must ensure that all high-risk students receive the help they need.

797 Friedlander, Jack. *Innovative Approaches to Delivering Academic Assistance to Students*. Los Angeles: Center for the Study of Community Colleges, 1982. 20 pages. (ED 220 172).

This publication reports findings of a survey conducted to identify the academic assistance programs in operation at six large urban community college districts (Chicago, Dallas, Los Angeles, Maricopa, Miami-Dade, and St. Louis). It discusses exemplary approaches in outreach efforts, early and midterm interventions, use of faculty referral slips, coordination of support services with content courses, attrition reduction in high-risk courses, block programming, and funding. It also examines support services coordination, identification of high-risk courses, innovative funding support, and faculty participation. It serves as a brief state-of-the-art resource for administrators interested in improving their academic assistance programs.

798 Friedlander, Jack. "Delivering Academic Assistance: Exemplary Approaches." *Journal of Developmental and Remedial Education,* 1984, 7 (3), 13–15, 31.

This article discusses the importance of out-of-class academic assistance for students who need additional help. It reports studies showing that few students seek such help on their own and relates efforts made by several community colleges to overcome this problem, including supplemental lectures, additional classes, reading instruction, advising and counseling, the development of learning skills through adjunct courses, and special programs that provide assistance to all students in courses that have high failure and dropout rates. It serves as a useful review of state-of-the-art practices that are designed to provide supplementary academic assistance to those who need it.

799 Garner, Ambrose. "A Comprehensive Community College Model for Learning Assistance Centers." In Kurt V. Lauridsen (ed.), *Examining the Scope of Learning Centers.* New Directions for College Learning Assistance, no. 1. San Francisco: Jossey-Bass, 1980, pp. 19–31.

The author describes a comprehensive learning assistance program initiated at Miami-Dade Community College (Florida), emphasizing that the program is designed to meet the learning needs of all students—from the most academically able to those needing substantial remediation—and arguing that this arrangement eliminates the pejorative labeling of some students as "developmental" or "remedial." He details the three program components: (1) a basic skills center that provides individualized, self-paced instruction in reading, writing, and mathematics; (2) a program to help mainstream handicapped students and provide them with an array of services from initial educational diagnosis to job placement; and (3) a library of audiovisual learning materials. He points out that at most colleges these three components are operated independently but maintains that their coordination in one service unit is more beneficial.

800 Gibson, Walker (ed.). *New Students in Two-Year Colleges: Twelve Essays.* Urbana, Ill.: National Council of Teachers of English, 1979. 130 pages.

Please see no. 892 for the full annotation.

801 Gilbert, Fontelle (ed.). *Minorities and Community Colleges: Data and Discourse.* Washington, D.C.: American Association of Community and Junior Colleges, 1979. 29 pages. (ED 171 345)

Please see no. 155 for the full annotation.

802 Hertz, Sharon M.; Gold, Barbara K.; Kaufman, Lenore J.; and Wallach, Meralee G. "College Credit for Reading Courses?—Yes!" *Journal of Reading,* 1977, *20* (8), 688–692.

This article argues that community colleges should grant credit to students who complete remedial courses, noting that denial of credit confirms students' belief that remedial courses have no worth and maintaining that no-credit policies will deter large numbers of underprepared students from seeking the assistance they need. The authors conclude that credit will remove the stigma from remediation and help the community college fulfill its role in increasing access to higher education.

803 Lieberman, Janet E., and Cohen, Barbara. "Five Contemporary Fallacies: Remedial Reading at the Community College Level." *Adult Literacy and Basic Education,* 1982, *6* (2), 91–99.

This article examines remedial reading programs at the community college, noting common fallacies under which the majority of college remedial programs operate. The authors recommend steps to correct these fallacies, including (1) treating students as adults rather than using instructional materials designed for children; (2) providing diagnostic testing in addition to achievement tests; (3) utilizing a clinical approach that builds on individuals' strengths and weaknesses; (4) creating new approaches to teaching skills; and (5) initiating reforms at the classroom level, where the teacher has both responsibility and control. They conclude that providing a curriculum in thinking skills offers a new approach to solving some of the failures of remedial programs.

804 Ramey, Luellen. *Assessment Procedures for Students Entering Florida Community Colleges: Theory and Practice.* Gainesville: Florida Community Junior College Interinstitutional Research Council, 1981. 151 pages. (ED 231 474)

This publication surveys the coordinators of student assessment programs to describe procedures utilized by the Florida community colleges in assessing the academic skills of entering students. It provides information on the subject areas that are assessed at entrance, the ways assessment instruments are administered, entrance criteria, assessment costs, the types of assessment instruments utilized, factors determining cutoff scores for placement, and the types of students who are assessed. It also includes an extensive literature review, covering such topics as the history and philosophical foundations of community colleges, the development of student assessment in these institutions, competency-based education and testing, and student advising and counseling. It serves as an extensive state-of-the-art resource for those involved in community college student assessment programs.

★805 Richardson, Richard C., Jr.; Fisk, Elizabeth C.; and Okun, Morris A. *Literacy in the Open-Access College.* San Francisco: Jossey-Bass, 1983. 187 pages.

This publication details the findings of a three-year case study conducted at an open-access community college to examine the causes of and possible resolutions for the decline of literacy in community colleges, concluding that students at the college had little opportunity to practice in-depth literacy skills. The authors trace the roots of this problem to institutional policies in the past twenty years that have stressed institutional growth and an expanded mission at the expense of literacy development. They detail how institutional policies related to admissions, financial aid, curriculum development, course designations, remediation, standards of academic progress, and use of part-time faculty can either inhibit or promote student literacy. They urge open-access colleges to re-emphasize academic advisement and program coherence instead of strategies that are designed to enroll as many part-time students as possible in discrete, unrelated courses.

806 Roueche, John E., and Archer, Patricia F. "Entry Level Assessment in College." *Community College Review,* 1979, *6* (4), 15–27.

This article presents basic information regarding the assessment of entry-level students in community colleges. The authors argue that locally designed diagnostic tests, tailored to the individual needs of the college, are the most widely used and most successful instruments, but they provide information on how to assess and select a commercially available test. They also discuss necessary qualities of the examiner, the appropriate atmosphere of the testing site, and the manner in which test scores should be interpreted to students. They warn of the dangers inherent in any placement testing and emphasize the necessity of confidentiality in regard to test scores. They conclude that the open door will remain a viable policy only as long as the educational problems of students are diagnosed.

807 Rounds, Jeanine Crandall, and Anderson, Don. "Entrance Assessment and Student Success." *Community College Review,* 1984–85, *12* (3), 10–15.

The authors urge the establishment of mandatory assessment and placement procedures as a means of serving students who lack the skills that are requisite for academic success in college. They note that such procedures were dropped during the 1960s and 1970s in response to concerns for equal access but argue that public dissatisfaction with declining student skills, as well as high dropout rates, have rekindled college interest in assessment policies. The article draws upon a survey of assessment procedures in California to note the small percentage of colleges that have an assessment system in place. It concludes with ten recommendations for college administrators who want to establish effective assessment programs.

808 Schiavone, James. "Integrated Remediation for the Community College." *Improving College and University Teaching,* 1976, *24* (3), 183–185.

This article describes an integrated remediation program initiated at the Borough of Manhattan (New York) Community College, noting that, rather than operating a separate developmental studies program, the college incorporates remedial instruction into the regular associate degree curriculum. The author describes six components of the program: (1) remediation in the classroom, a process by which subject-area instructors work with students on basic skills; (2) individual tutoring by faculty during office hours; (3) programmed instruction and testing at the college media center; (4) the provision of reading laboratories; (5) a tutorial program involving student peer tutors, students at senior colleges, and college graduates; and (6) computer-assisted instruction. The article provides a good example of the involvement of the entire college community in meeting the remediation needs of an urban, disadvantaged student body.

809 Sternglass, Marilyn S. "How Useful Are Readability Formulas to Content-Area Teachers in Community Colleges?" *Community College Frontiers,* 1976, *4* (2), 24–28, 49.

The author estimates the value of three textbook readability formulas: Fry's Graph for Estimating Readability, the SMOG Grading Formula, and the Cloze Test. She notes that, regardless of the test applied, instructors can gain only a rough estimate of readability levels from the existing diagnostic measures. She cites problems of unreliability among the measures and questions the applicability of reading-level formulas to disparate community college populations. She recommends supplemental aids that instructors can use with students as an alternative to expecting students to find their own way through the textbooks.

810 Truett, Carol. "Services to Developmental Education Students in the Community College: Does the Library Have a Role?" *College and Research Libraries,* 1983, *44* (1), 20–28.

Please see no. 681 for the full annotation.

811 Zoglin, Mary L. "Community College Responsiveness: Myth or Reality?" *Journal of Higher Education,* 1981, *52* (4), 415–426.

Please see no. 542 for the full annotation.

10

Continuing Education
and Community Services

Since the mid 1940s, when the President's Commission on
Higher Education (no. 52) urged the development of community-
based colleges that would respond to local educational needs as
well as prepare students for the university, many two-year college
leaders have promoted community services as the primary institutional function. This commitment to the community service
function is nowhere more evident than in the writings of Edmund
Gleazer (no. 18), who, as president of the American Association of
Community and Junior Colleges, waged a long campaign to
promote the college as a nexus of community learning activities
rather than as a component of the traditional system of higher
education. While two-year colleges have not become the community learning centers that Gleazer envisioned, the community service
function has taken its place alongside the vocational and transfer
curricula as one of the primary college missions. According to the
1985 *Community, Junior, and Technical College Directory*,
3,723,629 students were enrolled in noncredit community service
programs during 1983–84, as compared to 4,836,819 students
enrolled during fall 1984 in credit courses. The literature on the
community service function can be classified under two subhead-
ings: continuing and adult education (nos. 812–824) and community services and community development (nos. 825–866). These
headings reflect the two primary goals of community services

efforts: (1) addressing educational needs that are not met by traditional degree or certificate programs and (2) promoting community welfare and quality of life.

Continuing and Adult Education

A small portion of the community college literature focuses on the educational needs of adults at various life stages and on the role of the community college in meeting those needs. These works include discussions of:

- the integration of adult, continuing education into the college's departmental structure (nos. 812, 820);
- college services to the elderly (no. 815);
- the state role in special college programming for adults (no. 824);
- the characteristics and competencies of adult education administrators (no. 818); and
- criticisms raised about the appropriateness of focusing college efforts on adult and continuing education (no. 823).

As is evident from the small number of citations under this heading, the literature on the college role in serving adults is relatively weak. While numerous authors present exhortations about the desirability of meeting educational needs emerging throughout the adult life cycle, there have been few substantive analyses. The concept of lifelong learning, as Richardson (no. 821) points out, has been a vague, catchall phrase attached to a variety of programs. In addition, it has become apparent that adult education cannot easily be defined as a distinct college function with its own niche in the institution's administrative organization. As the student surveys listed in Chapter Three make clear, adults take traditional transfer and vocational courses on a sporadic basis to fulfill personal interests and educational needs that have little to do with transfer or degree attainment. Although community colleges are commonly associated with the term *adult education*, the adult education component of the community college's total effort cannot be easily identified and examined except as it reflects differential funding awarded for credit and noncredit classes.

Community Services and Community Development

A larger body of work focuses on the role of the college as a community service and development agency. Three comprehensive monographs promote this community agency philosophy: *The Community Dimension of the Community College,* by Harlacher (no. 842); *Community Services in the Community College,* by Myran (no. 857); and *College Leadership for Community Renewal,* by Gollattscheck, Harlacher, Roberts, and Wygal (no. 838). All three stress the need for the college to provide adult education but also argue that the college should become the center for a variety of other community activities. Under this philosophy, the college works with other social agencies in the community to promote cultural and intellectual events, respond to local problems posed by urbanization, poverty, or other social ills, and otherwise promote the general welfare of the community.

Additional authors focusing on the community service function have examined a variety of themes, including:

- the types of services and activities provided under the community service rubric (nos. 829, 840, 849, 865, 866);
- college collaboration with labor unions (no. 825);
- the characteristics of community service students and the reasons they have for enrolling (no. 858);
- assessing college impact on the community (nos. 827, 854);
- conducting marketing surveys to assess community needs (no. 844);
- the types of cooperative agreements that colleges have entered into with local community agencies (nos. 834, 845);
- faculty perceptions of and participation in community service activities (no. 855);
- the state role in community service programming (no. 862);
- contracted educational services for business and industry (nos. 830, 846, 850, 852, 857); and

- other efforts to improve the local work force and the economy (no. 864).

The community agency philosophy, however, has not been without its critics. Some authors, including Frankel (no. 833) and Cohen (no. 831), question the ability of the college to deliver on all its promises to the community. Gottschalk (no. 838) contends that college community service efforts meet the needs of the community power structure but do not address the needs of the poor and uneducated. Lombardi (no. 851) notes the damage that the community service function might do to the college's identity as an institution of higher education, and Parnell (no. 860) asks whether frivolous courses, such as belly dancing, will be the college's nemesis. Finally, there is the problem of definition. Brawer (no. 829) notes the conflict and overlap in the various ways colleges define community services. This definitional theme is picked up by Atwell, Vaughan, and Sullins (no. 829), who argue that community college leaders have not clearly defined the role of the community service function in relation to other college missions and that, as a result, community service departments are not living up to their full potential.

Further Information on Continuing Education and Community Services

Continuing education and community services have been the focus of several dissertations and ERIC documents. Among the available ERIC documents are descriptions of (1) individual college efforts in the areas of adult basic education, (2) services to displaced homemakers, the handicapped, and other disadvantaged community residents, (3) local labor-force development efforts, and (4) services to business and industry. Other ERIC documents also provide information on the structure and administration of community service divisions of individual colleges. Information on how to locate dissertations and ERIC documents is provided in Chapter Thirteen.

The general texts cited in Chapter Two also provide a wealth of information, especially those published since World War

II. Bogue's 1950 text (no. 8) provides one of the first in-depth analyses of adult education programming. Subsequent works that can be consulted for information on adult education and community services include Henry (no. 20), Hillway (no. 21), Gleazer (no. 16), O'Connell (no. 28), Medsker and Tillery (no. 26), Ogilvie and Raines (no. 29), Monroe (no. 27), Thornton (no. 34), and Cohen and Brawer (no. 12). These works are especially valuable in tracing the growth of the adult education and community service functions. Future works will undoubtedly focus on how these functions have fared in the present period of stabilized growth and lowered funding.

Continuing and Adult Education

812 Adams, Frank G. "Financing the 'College in the Community': A Model." *Community Services Catalyst,* 1983, *13* (3), 20–25.

The author notes the dwindling financial support for off-campus programs that meet the needs of part-time adult students, suggesting that such programs should be funded through a single office within the college's administrative organization. He posits that this office—in charge of all off-campus programming—would maintain its own budget, keep its own records, and contract with instructional departments in the college for services related to hiring qualified faculty, developing courses, and evaluating the course offerings. The article provides a unique contrast to the more common approaches of funding off-campus programs.

813 Bogue, Jesse Parker. "Chapter Nine: Adult Education in the Community College." In Jesse Parker Bogue, *The Community College.* New York: McGraw-Hill, 1950, pp. 207–238.

For an annotation of the work in its entirety, please see no. 8.

814 Cohen, Arthur M., and Brawer, Florence B. "Chapter Ten: Community Education: Reaching Out with Extended Services." In Arthur M. Cohen and Florence B. Brawer, *The American Community College.* San Francisco: Jossey-Bass, 1982, pp. 251–282.

For an annotation of the work in its entirety, please see no. 12.

815 DeCrow, Roger. *Older Americans: New Uses of Mature Ability.* Washington, D.C.: American Association of Community and Junior Colleges, 1978. 32 pages. (ED 154 859; available in microfiche only)

Please see no. 177 for the full annotation.

816 Fuller, Jack W. *Continuing Education and the Community College.* Chicago: Nelson-Hall, 1979. 127 pages.

This publication addresses current and future issues confronting administrators of continuing education and identifies some innovative approaches to developing continuing education programs. It discusses the role of continuing education in the community college, with a focus on the lack of support for adult education programs, including specific examples and suggestions for developing an in-service continuing education program for faculty, a community leadership center, a literacy program, a women's program, management seminars, a program for the health care community, and a program for developing a continuing education facility. It serves as a reference for the community college administrator interested in developing continuing education programs for targeted audiences.

817 Gilder, Jamison. "Lifelong Education: The Critical Policy Questions." In Barry Heermann, Cheryl Coppeck Enders, and Elizabeth Wine (eds.), *Serving Lifelong Learners.* New Directions for Community Colleges, no. 29. San Francisco: Jossey-Bass, 1980, pp. 69–86.

The author presents an overview of policy questions concerning lifelong education in the community college, suggesting seven basic categories of effort needed to support lifelong education and proposing sharper definitions of functions as a means of increasing cooperation and expanding community linkage. She recommends local assessment of learning needs so that learning opportunities may be more precisely targeted, describes how funding mechanisms need to be adjusted to promote lifelong learning, and details the roles of labor, business, and industry. She concludes that current programs for adult learners (such as television courses or weekend seminars) have been developed in spite of restrictive policy frameworks imposed, for example, by legislation and board regulations, and calls for new policies to meet the growing demand for lifelong learning.

818 Miles, Leroy. "A Survey of Adult and Continuing Education Competencies Needed by Directors of Community Services and Continuing Education." *Community/Junior College Research Quarterly*, 1980, *4* (4), 319–330.

This article surveys a national sample of the directors of community college continuing education and community service programs, examining survey responses as to the official titles of the respondents, their years of administrative and teaching experience, their educational attainment, and the academic disciplines they studied in college. It also examines how the respondents ranked forty-two statements on the competencies required of continuing education or community service administrators. Among the findings is that the academic and professional backgrounds of the respondents had no effect on the perceived importance of adult and continuing education competencies.

819 Monroe, Charles R. "Chapter Eight: Adult Education and Community Services." In Charles R. Monroe, *Profile of the Community College: A Handbook*. San Francisco: Jossey-Bass, 1972, pp. 128–143.

For an annotation of the work in its entirety, please see no. 27.

820 Ohliger, John. "Integrating Continuing Education." *Continuous Learning,* 1970, *9* (3), 101–106.

This article describes the attempt of Selkirk College (British Columbia) to integrate adult and continuing education into the college's departmental structure, explaining that this integrated approach recognizes two types of adult education: (1) formal programming, in which qualified adults were invited to enroll in any credit class established for traditional-aged students, and (2) informal programming, in which regular departmental faculty members established noncredit workshops, seminars, or other learning opportunities in response to identified community needs. It cites an example of this informal programming and notes the difficulties encountered in gaining administrative understanding and support for the integrated approach. The article provides community service practitioners with a viable approach to involving the entire faculty in the community service function.

821 Richardson, Penelope L. "Lifelong Learning and Politics." *Convergence: An International Journal of Adult Education,* 1979, *12* (1-2), 95–104.

This article outlines strategies to be used by community college educators in defining, implementing, and promoting the concept of lifelong learning. The author notes that the term *lifelong learning* has been a catchall phrase attached to a variety of educational programs and urges community colleges to develop a clear agenda for lifelong education that will attract the support of local, state, and federal policy makers. She suggests that a combination of strategies should be used in promoting a solid continuing education platform through legislation, administrative regulations, judicial action, and political elections. She concludes with suggestions for promoting lifelong learning among policy makers, education interest groups, and the general public.

822 Thornton, James W. "Chapter Sixteen: The Curriculum: Continuing Education." In James W. Thornton, *The Community Junior College*. New York: Wiley, 1972, pp. 244–261.

For an annotation of the work in its entirety, please see no. 34.

823 Williams, Barbara B., and Atwell, Charles A. "Critics of Lifelong Learning." *Community Services Catalyst*, 1984, *14* (2), 5–8.

The authors argue that lifelong learning is coming of age as the population in the United States grows older and as adult developmental theory provides educators with a better understanding of adult needs. They suggest that the shift from an industrial to an information society, as well as other social changes, points to the development of lifelong learning as a dominant force in higher education and that community colleges are in a better position to provide this service than other agencies, including the military, business, and industry. The article provides insights into the rationale of those community college practitioners who would expand the curriculum well beyond traditional collegiate education.

824 Zusman, Ami. "State Policy Making for Community College Adult Education." *Journal of Higher Education*, 1978, *49* (4), 337–357.

Please see no. 422 for the full annotation.

Community Services and Community Development

825 Abbott, William. "College/Labor Union Cooperation." *Community and Junior College Journal*, 1977, *47* (7), 48–51.

This article utilizes a national survey of community colleges to study college cooperation with labor unions, reporting that college-union cooperative programs focus predominantly on apprenticeship training, job retraining, and skill upgrading and noting that more than half the respondents indicated an interest in forming work councils through which college personnel, employers, union leaders, and members of the public could develop and administer collaborative education and work programs. The author concludes that, in many cases, labor and community colleges are each waiting for the other party to make the first move in organizing cooperative relationships and implies that such cooperation requires college commitment in the form of a full-time labor coordinator.

826 Adams, Frank G. "Financing the 'College in the Community': A Model." *Community Services Catalyst,* 1983, *13* (3), 20–25.

Please see no. 812 for the full annotation.

827 Alfred, Richard L. (ed.). *Institutional Impacts on Campus, Community, and Business Constituencies.* New Directions for Community Colleges, no. 38. San Francisco: Jossey-Bass, 1982. 130 pages. (ED 217 944)

This sourcebook presents articles on the social and economic impacts of the community college, including discussions of social and economic gains experienced by community college students, the impact of community college programs on business and industry through the preparation of a trained labor force, how impact studies can be conducted to measure cost benefits to local communities, strategies that community colleges can use to improve their relations with state and federal agencies, and the relationship of faculty and staff morale to college impact on various constituencies. It concludes with a bibliography of relevant literature and serves as a useful source of background information for institutional researchers who need to conduct institutional impact studies.

★**828** Atwell, Charles A.; Vaughan, George B.; and Sullins, W. Robert. *Reexamining Community Services in the Community College: Toward Consensus and Commitment.* Topical Paper no. 76. Los Angeles: ERIC Clearinghouse for Junior Colleges and the National Council on Community Services and Continuing Education, 1982. 92 pages. (ED 220 138)

This publication examines the history, mission, role, and funding of community services and provides recommendations for the continued integration of such services within the community college. The authors argue that community college leaders have not clearly defined the role of the community service function in relation to other college missions and that, as a result, community service departments are not living up to their full potential. They call on community college leaders to come to a consensus as to the goals of community service programs and discuss ways of bringing them into the mainstream of the college. The work concludes with a sixty-one-item bibliography.

829 Brawer, Florence B. *Familiar Functions in New Containers: Classifying Community Education.* Topical Paper no. 71. Los Angeles: ERIC Clearinghouse for Junior Colleges, 1980. 40 pages. (ED 187 412)

This paper identifies various traditional and nontraditional educational delivery systems in an effort to provide a uniform system of definitions and categories for community services. It explores the changing role of community colleges over time and examines sundry definitions of adult education, continuing education, lifelong learning, community services, and community education. The author notes conflict and overlap in these definitions and presents a classification scheme for community college education based on the intentions and objectives of program participants.

830 Clary, Joseph R., and Iverson, Maynard J. *Maximizing Responsiveness to Industry by North Carolina Technical and Community Colleges. Occupational Education Research Project. Final Technical Report.* Raleigh: Department of Occupational Education, North Carolina State University, 1983. 52 pages. (ED 230 741)

This publication details the findings of a study conducted in 1981–82 to identify the elements that affect an institution's ability to respond to the training needs of local industries. It draws upon a literature review, input from a study advisory group, and interviews with college and industry personnel to identify nineteen elements that facilitate college responsiveness to industry needs, noting that the top six identified elements refer specifically to college commitment, policy, and/or activities, including reliability of the institution (to do what is promised); strong personal commitment of the college president to industry training; high-quality instruction; and quick response and follow-through by the institution. It provides the reader with insights into general policy considerations (albeit not into actual instructional delivery modes) that are correlated with successful college-business relationships.

831 Cohen, Arthur M. "Academic Planning in Community Colleges." *Planning for Higher Education,* 1979, 7 (5), 28–32.

Please see no. 514 for the full annotation.

832 Feldman, Marvin J. "Chapter Eight: Establishing Linkages with Other Educational Providers." In William L. Deegan, Dale Tillery, and Associates, *Renewing the American Community College: Priorities and Strategies for Effective Leadership.* San Francisco: Jossey-Bass, 1985, pp. 175–195.

For an annotation of the work in its entirety, please see no. 14.

833 Frankel, Joanne. *The Do Everything College.* Topical Paper no. 43. Los Angeles: ERIC Clearinghouse for Junior Colleges, 1974. 42 pages. (ED 094 814)

Please see no. 48 for the full annotation.

834 Gilder, Jamison, and Rocha, Jessica. "10,000 Cooperative Arrangements Serve 1.5 Million." *Community and Junior College Journal,* 1980, *51* (3), 11–17.

This article reports findings of a survey conducted to determine the nature of cooperative working relationships between local colleges and community-based groups. It examines the number of cooperative arrangements per college, the types of organizations that enter into these arrangements, the form that these arrangements take, and the sources of funding for such cooperative efforts.

835 Gleazer, Edmund J., Jr. "Chapter Five: A College for the Community." In Edmund J. Gleazer, Jr., *This Is the Community College.* Boston: Houghton Mifflin, 1968, pp. 80–99.

For an annotation of the work in its entirety, please see no. 16.

836 Gleazer, Edmund J., Jr. *The Community College: Values, Vision, and Vitality.* Washington, D.C.: American Association of Community and Junior Colleges, 1980. 190 pages.

Please see no. 18 for the full annotation.

★837 Gollattscheck, James F.; Harlacher, Ervin L.; Roberts, Eleanor; and Wygal, Benjamin R. *College Leadership for Community Renewal: Beyond Community-Based Education.* San Francisco: Jossey-Bass, 1976. 160 pages.

The authors contend that the Morrill Act, the GI Bill, and the comprehensive community college have been the three most important events in the history of higher education, because they made it possible for large numbers of students to attend and broadened the scope of collegiate programs. They suggest that the development of "community renewal" colleges committed to all aspects of community life could be a fourth step in the progressive history of increased educational access. They cite Metropolitan State University (Minnesota) and Florida Junior College as examples of community renewal institutions that are dedicated to individual and social development. The work includes illustrations of college interaction with various social, governmental, professional, educational, and neighborhood agencies.

838 Gottschalk, Kurt. "Can Colleges Deal with High-Risk Problems?" *Community College Frontiers,* 1978, *6* (4), 4–11.

The author argues that the community college does not fulfill its commitment to community development because college leaders deal exclusively with low-risk community problems that do not lead to conflict and criticism. He postulates that community problems are rooted in social inequalities but that representatives of the community power structure, rather than the poor and uneducated, are most likely to seek the services of the college. He concludes that colleges need to identify those aspects of community problems that are amenable to education and that the college should provide the knowledge needed by various individuals and groups to solve those problems.

839 Hankin, Joseph N., and Fey, Philip A. "Chapter Seven: Reassessing the Commitment to Community Services." In William L. Deegan, Dale Tillery, and Associates, *Renewing the American Community College: Priorities and Strategies for Effective Leadership.* San Francisco: Jossey-Bass, 1985, pp. 150–174.

For an annotation of the work in its entirety, please see no. 14.

840 Harlacher, Ervin L. *Effective Junior College Programs of Community Services: Rationale, Guidelines, Practices.* Occasional Report no. 10. Los Angeles: Junior College Leadership Program, School of Education, University of California, 1967. 75 pages. (ED 013 660)

This publication utilizes data from a national survey of staff at ninety-nine two-year colleges to examine factors that contribute to the success of community service programs in four areas: (1) community use of college facilities; (2) community educational services, such as workshops or speakers' bureaus; (3) cultural and recreational activities; and (4) institutional development activities, such as campus tours or alumni organizations. For each of these areas, it details the types of activities that respondents feel best meet the objectives of community service programming and the types of administrative procedures that respondents feel are conducive to program success. It draws from the study findings to provide readers with a checklist of critical program requirements related to goal setting, organization, planning, evaluation, and decision making.

★**841** Harlacher, Ervin L. *The Community Dimension of the Community College.* Englewood Cliffs, N.J.: Prentice-Hall, 1969. 140 pages.

The author defines community services as educational, cultural, and recreational services that are provided in addition to regular classes. He traces the growth of community service programs in community colleges and notes various program objectives: providing a center of community life, providing education for all age groups, assisting the community in solving its problems, and contributing to the cultural, intellectual, and social life of the college's service district. He points to problems in the development of community services, including staff support, coordination with other agencies, and program planning and funding. He treats community services as unique to community colleges while ignoring the contribution of university extension divisions.

842 Hodgkinson, Harold L. "Chapter Eleven: Establishing Alliances with Business and Industry." In George B. Vaughan and Associates, *Issues for Community College Leaders in a New Era.* San Francisco: Jossey-Bass, 1983, pp. 222–231.

For an annotation of the work in its entirety, please see no. 37.

843 Holcomb, Hope M. (ed.). *Reaching Out Through Community Service.* New Directions for Community Colleges, no. 14. San Francisco: Jossey-Bass, 1976. 122 pages. (ED 122 897)

This sourcebook presents fourteen articles and a bibliography on the community service function of the two-year college. It examines the historical development of the concept; a Florida study that produced a taxonomy for community services; patterns of financial support; programs in Florida and California; activities directed at special clients, including women, minorities, and senior adults; a model for managing community services in multicollege districts; and a nationwide study of Title I projects in forty-eight community colleges. It concludes that the major problems facing community services are finance, growth limits, management, academic standards, and the role of the instructors.

844 Howard, William R. "Community Transactions and the Marketing Process." In John A. Lucas (ed.), *Developing a Total Marketing Plan.* New Directions for Institutional Research, no. 21. San Francisco: Jossey-Bass, 1979, pp. 69–86.

The author describes institutional marketing from a community developer's point of view, arguing that college programs should be established in response to indigenous community needs. He outlines three steps in a community-based institutional marketing program: involving local constituents in planning groups, maintaining a dialogue between college personnel and local constituencies, and assessing community needs through surveys or community councils. He discusses barriers to the implementation of this marketing plan and weighs the desirability of colleges becoming agents of community development. He argues that community-based marketing is a proactive alternative to declining enrollments and retrenchment.

845 Jellison, Holly M. (ed.). *Interface Through Cooperative Agreements: Eleven Examples of How It Can Work.* Washington, D.C.: American Association of Community and Junior Colleges and National Center for Community Education, 1981. 64 pages. (ED 206 366; available in microfiche only)

This publication presents the texts of eleven cooperative agreements drawn up between community colleges and local education agencies (primarily school districts). Included are agreements for the joint operation of community services and adult education programs, shared facilities, and the development of a community education consortium for lifelong learning. The work provides a resource for community college administrators who wish to enhance their community education programs through cooperative efforts with area educational agencies.

846 Jellison, Holly M. (ed.). *Small Business Training: A Guide for Program Building.* Washington, D.C.: National Small Business Training Network, American Association of Community and Junior Colleges, 1983. 68 pages. (ED 229 072; available in microfiche only)

Please see no. 525 for the full annotation.

847 Jennings, Frank G. "The Two-Year Stretch: Junior Colleges in America." *Change in Higher Education,* 1970, *2* (2), 15–25.

The author takes issue with idealistic claims that community colleges can cure the nation's educational, economic, and societal ills, arguing that the uniquely American tendency to attack societal problems by adding a new type of institution to the educational landscape is reflected in the tremendous growth of community colleges and in the "boosterism" of their proponents, who maintain that the colleges can be all things to all people. He emphasizes that the community college needs to "match its pretensions with its performance" (p. 24) and define in more specific terms the outcomes it can effect in student learning. He draws upon Cohen's work in *Dateline '79* (no. 11) to suggest how this might be done.

848 Kapraun, E. Daniel (comp.). *Community Services in the Community College: A Bibliography.* Charlottesville: Center for Higher Education, University of Virginia, 1973. 26 pages. (ED 101 768)

This unannotated bibliography cites approximately 250 journal articles, monographs, and ERIC documents dealing with the community service function of the two-year college, categorizing the entries under broad headings: (1) background literature, (2) definition and scope, (3) organization and administration, (4) coordination, (5) research endeavors, (6) models of community service, (7) exemplary community service programs, and (8) issues for the 1970s. It serves as a thorough listing of the literature published during the 1960s and early 1970s (although some items from as early as the 1920s are also listed).

849 Karvelis, Donald S. "Bridging the Community Services Credibility Gap." *Community Services Catalyst,* 1980, *10* (3), 9-11.

This article studies the California community colleges to ascertain the depth of their commitment to the community service function and to assess the definitions of community services upon which they operate. The author finds that community service programs include cultural events, noncredit classes, workshops, seminars, public information services, public use of college facilities, speakers' bureaus, and programs designed for specific community groups. He emphasizes that community service advocates should explain the objectives of their programs, rather than continually discuss what the programs do and how they are accomplished. He argues that the community service function is extremely vulnerable in taxpayer revolts so long as community college leaders do not "identify and delineate the reasons for and results of each element in the community services programs" (p. 11).

850 Kopecek, Robert J., and Clarke, Robert G. (eds.). *Customized Job Training for Business and Industry.* New Directions for Community Colleges, no. 48. San Francisco: Jossey-Bass, 1984. 119 pages. (ED 252 267)

This volume presents eight articles on contracted, customized training for business and industry. It includes discussions of the issues involved with industrial training and an organizational model for delivering such programs, the similarities and differences between traditional degree programs and industrial training programs, customized programs for steel and other heavy industries, and ways to improve productivity and college-employer relations through worker education. It also lists components of successful training programs, including flexibility, relevance, and marketability. It serves as a useful sourcebook for administrators charged with the task of planning and operating a college program for contracted learning.

851 Lombardi, John. *Community Education: Threat to College Status?* Topical Paper no. 68. Los Angeles: ERIC Clearinghouse for Junior Colleges, 1978. 45 pages. (ED 156 296)

This paper provides a succinct analysis of the problems surrounding the expansion of adult basic education, continuing education, and community services, noting the varying definitions for each of these components and examining the difficulties involved in obtaining standardized enrollment data for community education activities. The author reviews the debate concerning public support for these educational services, concluding that there is a trend toward making them self-supporting, with remission of tuition and fees for disadvantaged, handicapped, and senior citizens. He explores the dilemma of how to reconcile the growth of below-college-level activities with the desire to maintain the community college's institutional association with higher education.

852 Mahoney, James R. *Community College Centers for Contracted Programs: A Sequel to Shoulders to the Wheel.* Washington, D.C.: American Association for Community and Junior Colleges, 1982. 77 pages. (ED 229 061; available in microfiche only)

This publication draws upon a survey of thirty-seven colleges to summarize the characteristics of special community college centers that contract educational services to business, industry, government, and other groups in the local community. It examines factors that have influenced the creation of such centers and draws a composite of the centers' goals, objectives, services, program development procedures, and contract and linkage approaches. It also discusses special administrative problems experienced by the centers in such areas as staffing, labor union resistance, and competition with state universities and consulting agencies that provide the same services. It concludes with advice for administrators who are interested in initiating or expanding contractual services and with case studies describing centers that have been established at fifteen community colleges.

853 Martorana, S. V., and Piland, William A. (eds.). *Designing Programs for Community Groups.* New Directions for Community Colleges, no. 45. San Francisco: Jossey-Bass, 1984. 114 pages. (ED 243 553)

This sourcebook presents eight essays that discuss the role of community colleges in responding to changing community needs. Topics discussed include the role of education in the renewal of community life; a model for developing college-community linkages; working relationships between special interest groups and community colleges; institutional leadership in local economic development; ways in which colleges shape and respond to federal and state interests; and the assessment of adult education needs. The book concludes with a review of selected literature processed by ERIC. It provides community service personnel with a review of current issues surrounding the college role in local community development.

854 Micek, Sidney S., and Cooper, Edward M. "Community Impact: Does It Really Make a Difference?" In Ervin L. Harlacher and James F. Gollattscheck (eds.), *Implementing Community-Based Education*. New Directions for Community Colleges, no. 21. San Francisco: Jossey-Bass, 1978, pp. 79–90.

The authors argue that if community-impact studies are to be meaningful, researchers must identify all the constituencies affected by a college, the array of impacts or outcomes that may result from college programs, and the different ways of obtaining community-impact data (such as survey questionnaires or interviews). They provide a framework for such comprehensive impact analyses by outlining (1) the specific types of constituencies that the colleges serve, including individuals, interest groups, community organizations, and other audiences; (2) the major categories of college impacts, including those that affect the local economy as well as those related to increased knowledge or skill levels; and (3) the major indicators of impact in each of these categories. They also discuss administrative and methodological considerations in the planning and development of impact studies. They provide a useful synopsis of factors to be considered in assessing college impacts.

855 Michaels, Dennis F., and Boggs, David L. "Community Services: Community College Faculty Perceptions and Participation." *Community/Junior College Research Quarterly*, 1980, *4* (2), 137–149.

This article surveys a sample of 300 full-time faculty in Ohio to study their perceptions of and participation in community service programs, finding that involvement in planning and teaching within the community service program is a key factor in how full-time faculty perceive community services: the greater the involvement, the more favorable the perception. It notes further that female instructors and younger faculty members with less teaching experience were more likely to support community service activities. The article lacks an examination of why faculty support or do not support the community service function but serves, nonetheless, to illustrate that faculty are divided on this subject.

856 Myran, Gunder A. *Community Services in the Community College*. Washington, D.C.: American Association of Junior Colleges, 1969. 60 pages. (ED 037 202)

The author considers the purposes and administration of the community service function and examines the scope of community service offerings, arguing that they are undertaken in cooperation with other community agencies in an effort to meet personal and community educational needs that are not met by formal certificate or collegiate degree programs. He also discusses (1) organization, staffing, and financing patterns; (2) requisites to effective leadership of community service programs; (3) the integration of the community service program within the college; and (4) linkages with community groups. He posits a large social role for the community college, arguing that the community service function is a means for the college to respond to local problems posed by urbanization, racial tensions, environmental pollution, poverty, and other social ills.

857 Nelson, Robert E., and Piland, William E. *Organizing Small Business Programs in Community Colleges*. Urbana: Department of Vocational and Technical Education, University of Illinois, 1982. 74 pages. (ED 219 517)

Please see no. 529 for the full annotation.

858 Nickens, John M. "Who Takes Community Service Courses and Why." *Community/Junior College Research Quarterly*, 1977, *2* (1), 11–19.

Please see no. 88 for the full annotation.

859 Ogilvie, William K., and Raines, Max R. (eds.). "Part Seven: Community Services." In William K. Ogilvie and Max R. Raines (eds.), *Perspectives on the Community Junior College*. New York: Appleton-Century-Crofts, 1971, pp. 383–435.

For an annotation of the work in its entirety, please see no. 29.

860 Parnell, Dale. "Will Belly Dancing Be Our Nemesis?" *Community Services Catalyst*, 1982, *12* (3), 4–5.

This article argues that, even though most recreational and hobby courses are self-supporting, they result in a negative public image for the college. It recommends limiting community service offerings to those that flow out of the regular college curriculum and link the regular faculty with the community and suggests re-examining the premise that the community college must provide any and all types of programs for which there is a demand. The author maintains that colleges should assist other community agencies in offering marginally educative activities and encourage their own faculty to present instructional modules on community problems such as toxic-waste disposal, energy conservation, economic survival, and improving intergroup human relations.

861 Reynolds, James W. "Community Services." In Nelson B. Henry (ed.), *The Public Junior College*. Fifty-fifth yearbook of the National Society for the Study of Education. Part 1. Chicago: National Society for the Study of Education, 1956, pp. 140–160.

For an annotation of the work in its entirety, please see no. 20.

862 Shipley, Kenneth E., Jr. "Coordination, Control and Community Services in the Community College." *Community Services Catalyst*, 1980, *10* (1), 7–11.

This article draws upon interviews at three community colleges in three mid-Atlantic states to examine the extent to which increased state control has affected the pattern of community services offered by two-year colleges. The author finds that, while state coordination and control have had little effect on the pattern of community services offered, statewide coordination has been positively related to the degree to which colleges emphasize accountability and improve their planning procedures for the community service program. He also reports that community service programs tend to be more responsive to funding sources than to community needs and that colleges that adhere closely to state-level agencies' community service policies are more likely to receive state funding for community services.

863 Sisson, Kathryn A. "Integrating Community Development into Community Colleges: A Consideration." *Journal of the Community Development Society,* 1983, *14* (2), 1–18.

The author draws upon a literature review to examine the integration of community development activities in community service and community education programs, discussing the roles such programs can play in instigating community development and citing several examples of how community colleges have organized to marshal local resources and individuals in solving area problems. She notes that college involvement in actual community development (as opposed to traditional community seminars and education) is not widespread and that there are financial and attitudinal barriers to the incorporation of community development in outreach programs. The article serves as an exhaustive review of the research to date on the role of community colleges as community development agencies.

864 Tyree, Lawrence W., and McConnell, Nancy C. *Linking Community Colleges with Economic Development in Florida.* ISHE Fellows Program Research Report no. 3. Tallahassee: Institute for Studies in Higher Education, Florida State University, 1982. 38 pages. (ED 226 785)

This report discusses the role of the community college in fostering and promoting economic development through linkages with business and industry. It presents a rationale for establishing such linkages, noting the advantages enjoyed by industry and citing examples in California, New Jersey, and the Carolinas. It examines demographic and economic changes in Florida, as well as legislative and administrative efforts to bring educators in contact with business, and suggests strategies for linking Florida's community colleges more closely with future economic development. It concludes with an annotated bibliography.

865 Welch, Timothy. "Accreditation." *Community Services Catalyst,* 1973, *4* (1), 11–20.

The author asks "What are community services?", noting that there is no clear statement or statutory definition. After a brief review of the standards set by each of six regional accrediting associations, he finds that only two accrediting agencies have community service standards of any significance and that only one distinguishes between community services at two- and four-year colleges. He suggests a list of possible community services appropriate for community colleges, urging such activities as community use of the college facilities, organization of noncredit short courses, workshops, conferences, and cultural events, and special services for the elderly. He concludes that whatever guidelines an accrediting association chooses, it needs to develop a clear statement of what constitutes community services in two-year colleges.

★866 Young, Robert B.; Fletcher, Suzanne M.; and Rue, Robert R. *Directions for the Future: An Analysis of the Community Services Dimension of Community Colleges.* Community Colleges Community Education Monograph no. 2. Washington, D.C.: National Center for Community Education, American Association of Community and Junior Colleges; Ann Arbor: Office of Community Education Research, University of Michigan, 1978. 70 pages. (ED 158 787)

This publication details findings of a nationwide survey conducted in 1976 to examine the status of community service programs at two-year colleges. It draws upon responses from 855 institutions (67 percent of the colleges surveyed) to profile the community service function in terms of (1) institutional commitment to community service offerings, (2) cooperation among colleges and other community agencies, (3) staffing, (4) the various titles under which community service programs are offered, (5) the effect of college size on the community service program, and (6) differences in community service offerings. It concludes with a list of general concerns and with descriptions of models of successful and unsuccessful community education programs. The work serves as a cursory overview of community service offerings in the mid 1970s.

11

The Collegiate Function

When junior colleges were first established in the early decades of the twentieth century, their primary task was the provision of liberal arts and general education curricula that would either provide a capstone education for those terminating their education at grade 14 or serve as a relatively inexpensive avenue to upper-division studies at the university. Early writers, including Lange (no. 23) and Koos (no. 22) fully expected many universities to eventually abandon lower-division studies and leave education at the 13th- and 14th-grade levels to the emerging junior colleges. Had this actually happened, the two-year colleges today might be totally collegiate institutions, charged almost exclusively with the responsibility of serving as a bridge between the high school and the university.

The universities and four-year colleges, however, did not jettison the lower division. Over time, particularly after World War II, the colleges added occupational, community, and remedial education functions that, by the late 1970s, challenged the preeminent position of the transfer curriculum in terms of enrollment and total college curricular effort. The transfer function, nonetheless, survived as a central component of the institution's identity, testimony to the long historical involvement of the two-year college in baccalaureate education, the reluctance of faculty and other members of the college community to break their ties to higher education, and the importance of the transfer function to minority and other disadvantaged students, for whom the community college provides one of the only available avenues to a college education. This chapter cites those works dealing with the college role in providing undergraduate education at the 13th- and 14th-grade levels. These works can be subdivided under three headings: liberal arts in the community college (nos. 867–910), transfer to and articulation with four-year institutions (nos. 911–948), and general education (nos. 949–961).

Liberal Arts in the Community College

The liberal arts, including humanities and sciences, form the cornerstone of the community college transfer curriculum. Several works explore the status of the community college liberal arts curriculum, including two sets of monographs produced by the Center for the Study of Community Colleges in the late 1970s and early 1980s. One set (nos. 874, 875, 878, 879, 881) stems from a national study of two-year college humanities programs and provides detailed information on the components of the humanities curriculum, the characteristics and teaching practices of humanities instructors, and the characteristics of students in humanities programs. One of these monographs (no. 879) provides short, discipline-by-discipline profiles of community college instruction in the areas of literature, foreign languages, philosophy, religion and ethics, music history and appreciation, art history and appreciation, history, political science, cultural anthropology, and interdisciplinary humanities. The second set of monographs stems from a national study of two-year college science education and includes in-depth analyses of instruction in interdisciplinary social science education (no. 871), mathematics (no. 872), biology (no. 885), earth and space science (no. 886), environmental science (no. 887), economics (no. 889), engineering (no. 891), psychology (no. 894), sociology (no. 895), chemistry (no. 900), physics (no. 901), and agriculture (no. 870). Each of these science monographs includes analyses of the types of courses offered within each discipline, the instructional materials and methods used in the classroom, and the instructional assistance available to faculty.

Of the remaining works dealing with the liberal arts curriculum or related topics, several themes are examined, including:

- the status of the transfer function in light of growing enrollments in the career, compensatory, and community service programs (nos. 868, 880, 883, 897);
- the characteristics of two-year college science teachers (no. 903);
- the university influence on the community college transfer curriculum (no. 906);
- the status of music education at the community college (no. 902);
- the problems encountered in establishing religious education programs at community colleges (no. 905);
- adaptations of the English curriculum to meet the special needs of nontraditional students (no. 892);
- changes in the humanities curriculum during the 1970s (nos. 888, 890, 899);
- the alienation of community college liberal arts faculty from the mainstream of professional associations that are controlled by colleagues at four-year colleges and universities (no. 898); and
- the challenges facing mathematics curricula at two-year colleges (nos. 862, 867, 908).

Most of these works, it should be pointed out, are descriptive and provide insights into the status of humanities instruction at particular times. More research is needed on how the liberal arts can be most effectively taught to the diverse students in community colleges.

Transfer to and Articulation with Four-Year Institutions

The transfer of students from community colleges to senior institutions has generated quite a bit of literature, especially in light of the evidence offered by Astin (no. 916) and Alba and Lavin (no. 911) that students starting their baccalaureate studies at a two-year institution are less likely to attain the baccalaureate degree than students who start as freshmen at four-year colleges or universities. A review of the literature on transfer reveals, among other subjects, three major themes:

- analyses of the barriers posed to transfer, such as unduly harsh transfer requirements at receiving institutions or the hidden fiscal penalties imposed on those who transfer from one institution to another (nos. 925, 941, 946);
- follow-up analyses of the academic success of students who do transfer (nos. 912, 913, 914, 928, 933, 934, 942, 948, 936, 938, 939, 940); and
- descriptive studies of articulation agreements between institutions (nos. 924, 930, 931, 932, 947).

Few of these works, however, address a major problem in studying student transfer: the limited and unreliable data that are available on (1) the number of entering students who actually intend to transfer and (2) the number of students who actually do transfer. Cohen (no. 922) and Cohen, Brawer, and Bensimon (no. 923) explore these limitations.

General Education

General education—that part of the curriculum that is designed to provide a common core of knowledge that can be put to use by students as they pursue their career and personal lives— is deeply rooted in the tradition of American higher education. But, while general education has been the subject of much exhortation, few substantive analyses of community college general education programs have appeared. Of those few studies that provide insights into actual practices rather than opinions on what should be, most underscore the failure of general education programs to live up to their full potential.

B. Lamar Johnson's *General Education in Action* (no. 954) is the classic work on two-year college general education. Johnson stresses that general education is action oriented, providing all students—regardless of major—with the knowledge needed to contribute to society as active citizens, make productive use of leisure time, become productive and reliable workers, and lead satisfying family lives. Subsequent authors, including Harrison (no. 952) and Hudson and Smith (no. 953), argue that Johnson's action-oriented curriculum never really took hold at most colleges and that what passes for general education in college catalogues is little more than a series of elective transfer courses that are designed to prepare students for further study at the upper-division level. Despite exceptions, such as the general education program at Miami-Dade Community College in Florida (see Lukenbill and McCabe, nos. 955, 956), general education as a defined, core curriculum—rather than a set of electives—has not taken hold at community colleges or, for that matter, at most institutions of higher education.

Sources of Further Information

Researchers seeking further information on the collegiate function should consult the ERIC data base, which includes, among other items, the following:

- descriptions of efforts undertaken at individual colleges to identify and assist potential transfer students;
- documents describing how the liberal arts are taught at individual colleges; and
- descriptions of general education curricula at individual colleges.

Numerous dissertations have also been written on various aspects of the collegiate function and can be found by consulting *Dissertation Abstracts International*. Further information on ERIC and *Dissertation Abstracts International* is provided in Chapter Thirteen.

Many of the general texts cited in Chapter Two also serve as useful sources of information on the collegiate function. Koos (no. 22) and Eells (no. 15) underscore the predominance of the collegiate function in the pre–World War II junior college curriculum. Subsequent works providing extensive analyses of transfer or general education include Bogue (no. 8), Henry (no. 20), Hillway (no. 21), Medsker (no. 25), O'Connell (no. 28), Medsker and Tillery (no. 26), Ogilvie and Raines (no. 29), Monroe (no. 27), Thornton (no. 34), Cohen and Brawer (no. 12), and Vaughan (no. 37).

Liberal Arts in the Community College

867 Albers, Donald J.; Rodi, Stephen B.; and Watkins, Ann E. (eds.). *New Directions in Two-Year College Mathematics.* New York: Springer-Verlag, 1985. 491 pages.

This volume presents twenty-two papers delivered at the Sloan Foundation Conference on two-year college mathematics in July 1984. Topics covered include the need for curriculum change, mathematics instruction in vocational/technical curricula, the influence of new technologies on student learning in mathematics, faculty renewal, and collaboration with secondary schools, colleges, and universities. The book also lists recommendations emanating from the conference concerning (1) making mathematics courses of immediate use to students rather than focusing on preparation for distant career goals, (2) collaborative efforts with other institutions, and (3) faculty development. It provides useful insights into the factors that shape the mathematics curriculum at two-year colleges and the concerns of mathematics faculty.

868 Baron, Robert F. "The Change from Transfer to Career Education at Community Colleges in the 1970s." *Community/Junior College Quarterly of Research and Practice,* 1982, 7 (1), 71–87.

Please see no. 687 for the full annotation.

869 Beckwith, Miriam M. *Integrating the Humanities and Occupational Programs: An Inventory of Current Approaches.* Project Report no. 12. Los Angeles: Center for the Study of Community Colleges, 1980. 8 pages. (ED 196 489)

Please see no. 743 for the full annotation.

870 Beckwith, Miriam M. *Science Education in Two-Year Colleges: Agriculture and Natural Resources.* Los Angeles: Center for the Study of Community Colleges and ERIC Clearinghouse for Junior Colleges, 1980. 62 pages. (ED 180 567)

This publication examines agricultural and natural resources education in two-year colleges as revealed in a nationwide study involving a review of the literature, an examination of 175 college catalogues and class schedules, and a survey of instructors. It discusses the number and types of courses offered in these curricular areas, course prerequisites, instructional activities, grading and testing methods used, and faculty opinions concerning course improvement. It concludes with summary statements pointing to the growth of agriculture and natural resources programs and the need to improve basic science and math prerequisites, communications skills of students, and the use of media in agriculture instruction. The work provides the most comprehensive analysis to date of this two-year college curricular area.

871 Beckwith, Miriam M. *Science Education in Two-Year Colleges: Interdisciplinary Social Sciences.* Los Angeles: Center for the Study of Community Colleges and ERIC Clearinghouse for Junior Colleges, 1980. 69 pages. (ED 181 955)

This publication presents the results of a nationwide study of anthropology and interdisciplinary social sciences education in two-year colleges, drawing upon a review of catalogues and course schedules from a sample of 175 two-year colleges—as well as from a survey of faculty—to examine the number and types of courses offered, course goals, instructional methods and materials used, class activities, student achievement criteria, enrollments, and instructor characteristics. It recommends that (1) interdisciplinary social science courses incorporate anthropological concepts and methods; (2) courses be devised to fit into vocational programs; and (3) anthropology be included in general education curricula. It provides the reader with a detailed analysis of how anthropology and interdisciplinary social sciences are taught at the two-year college.

872 Beckwith, Miriam M. *Science Education in Two-Year Colleges: Mathematics.* Los Angeles: Center for the Study of Community Colleges and ERIC Clearinghouse for Junior Colleges, 1980. 80 pages. (ED 176 386)

This work presents the results of a nationwide study of curriculum and instruction in mathematics at two-year colleges, drawing upon a review of catalogues and class schedules from a sample of 175 two-year colleges—as well as from a survey of faculty—to examine the number and types of courses offered, instructional methods and materials used, class sizes, desired student outcomes, instructor backgrounds, and the types of assistance that are available to faculty. Among the conclusions noted are that instruction usually takes place in a lecture mode and that most classes use standard textbooks that are not chosen by the instructors themselves. The author concludes that high attrition rates are indicative of a need for changes in the ways mathematics is taught at the community college.

873 Beckwith, Miriam M. "An ERIC Review: Integrating the Humanities and Occupational Programs: An Inventory of Current Practices." *Community College Review,* 1981, *9* (1), 57–64.

This article cites examples of how curriculum planners at community colleges have integrated humanistic content into occupational courses. It includes descriptions of efforts to (1) design interdisciplinary humanities courses for students in vocational programs, (2) develop specialized, nontransfer courses, such as "literature for technicians," (3) create humanities modules for inclusion in vocational courses, and (4) provide vocational instructors with consultation in the humanities and with humanities resource material. It serves as a useful guide to the variety of approaches that have been taken to make the humanities part of the vocational curriculum.

874 Brawer, Florence B. *The Humanities in Two-Year Colleges: The Faculty in Review*. Los Angeles: ERIC Clearinghouse for Junior Colleges and Center for the Study of Community Colleges, 1975. 52 pages. (ED 111 469)

Please see no. 195 for the full annotation.

★875 Brawer, Florence B. (ed.). *The Humanities in Two-Year Colleges: Trends in Curriculum*. Los Angeles: ERIC Clearinghouse for Junior Colleges and Center for the Study of Community Colleges, 1978. 162 pages. (ED 156 285)

This publication draws upon a literature review and a national survey of community college humanities instructors to examine curricular trends and faculty characteristics in each of several humanities areas: cultural anthropology, art history and appreciation, foreign languages, geography, ethnic studies, women's studies, social studies, history, literature, music history and appreciation, philosophy, political science, religious studies, and theater and film courses. It provides information on the types of courses offered, enrollment trends, and, in some cases, instructional techniques. It also examines the demographic characteristics of faculty, their educational backgrounds, their involvement in professional activities, and their instructional practices. The work is one of the few sources of information on the status of individual humanities disciplines at two-year colleges.

876 Brawer, Florence B. (ed.). *Teaching the Sciences.* New Directions for Community Colleges, no. 31. San Francisco: Jossey-Bass, 1980. 69 pages. (ED 191 543)

This sourcebook presents twelve articles focusing on the teaching of the natural and social sciences at community colleges, including essays that (1) recommend the investigative laboratory for the teaching of science, along with courses such as remedial science and home study; (2) emphasize the importance of teaching ethical decision making and incorporating wait time into science instruction; (3) report results of a nationwide study of instructional practices used in science courses; (4) suggest the use of modularized, individualized study and placement testing in the teaching of mathematics; (5) describe programs to reduce attrition of science transfer students and to increase the involvement of part-time students; and (6) identify new approaches to teaching general biology, psychology, and sociology. It serves as a review of instructional methods that can be employed by two-year college science faculty.

877 Brawer, Florence B., and Friedlander, Jack. *Science and Social Science in the Two-Year College.* Topical Paper no. 69. Los Angeles: ERIC Clearinghouse for Junior Colleges and Center for the Study of Community Colleges, 1979. 37 pages. (ED 172 854)

This paper draws upon a survey of instructors and a review of course catalogues to examine curriculum and instruction in two-year college social science, science, and technology programs, focusing on (1) enrollments, (2) types of courses available for transfer and occupational students, nonscience majors, and students in developmental programs, (3) average class sizes, (4) course objectives, (5) use of instructional media and class activities, (6) grading and examination practices, and (7) instructor characteristics. The authors suggest that science and social science faculty should design differing courses for transfer students, vocational students, and other diverse constituencies that attend two-year colleges.

878 Cantor, Harold, and Martens, Kay. *The Humanities in Two-Year Colleges: What Affects the Program?* Los Angeles: Center for the Study of Community Colleges and ERIC Clearinghouse for Junior Colleges, 1978. 55 pages. (ED 162 686)

The authors draw upon case studies at twenty community colleges to examine external and internal influences that affect the development of two-year college humanities programs. They find that external influences include state regulatory agencies and legislation (especially through funding reviews) and the humanities requirements of transfer institutions, while the most important internal influence is a strong president or board, other internal forces including program funding, incentives for faculty, curriculum development, humanities grants, and instructional resources. They conclude by arguing that the strength of a humanities program depends on the various interplays between these external and internal forces. The work serves as a concise review of the wide variety of factors—both inside and outside the institution—that affect program development at the community college.

879 Cohen, Arthur M. (ed.). *The Humanities in Two-Year Colleges: Reviewing Curriculum and Instruction.* Los Angeles: ERIC Clearinghouse for Junior Colleges and Center for the Study of Community Colleges, 1975. 101 pages. (ED 110 119)

This publication provides a discipline-by-discipline profile of the humanities curricula at two-year colleges. It includes chapters on foreign language instruction, literature, philosophy, religion and ethics, music history and appreciation, art history and appreciation, history, political science, cultural anthropology, ethnic studies, and interdisciplinary humanities. It finds that the humanities have a lower priority in the community college than vocational or remedial studies, arguing, however, that, because people still attend concerts and read the classics, the lack of emphasis on the humanities is probably not the result of waning interest in these areas. It suggests that new formats be employed in teaching humanities, including educational television and cooperative programs with libraries, museums, or other cultural agencies.

880 Cohen, Arthur M. "Student Access and the Collegiate Function in Community Colleges." *Higher Education,* 1985, *14,* 149–163.

This article examines how the declining prominence of the transfer function assigns community colleges to a peripheral role in the American education system. The author notes that the early junior colleges were easily accessible points of entry into higher education, because they focused on traditional instructional programs for grades 13 and 14. He argues, however, that subsequent emphases on mission expansion and open access have had deleterious effects on the institution's collegiate identity and that these effects are manifested in growing vocationalism, declining proportions of students who transfer, and a flat curriculum offering few sophomore-level classes. He concludes that community college leaders are caught in a dilemma posed by the need to maintain open access while at the same time preserving the collegiate integrity of the institution.

881 Cohen, Arthur M., and Brawer, Florence B. (eds.). *The Humanities in Two-Year Colleges: A Review of the Students.* Los Angeles: Center for the Study of Community Colleges and ERIC Clearinghouse for Junior Colleges, 1975. 64 pages. (ED 108 727)

Please see no. 67 for the full annotation.

882 Cohen, Arthur M., and Brawer, Florence B. "Chapter Eleven: Collegiate Function: New Directions for the Liberal Arts." In Arthur M. Cohen and Florence B. Brawer, *The American Community College.* San Francisco: Jossey-Bass, 1982, pp. 283–310.

For an annotation of the work in its entirety, please see no. 12.

883 Cohen, Arthur M., and Brawer, Florence B. "The Community College as College: Should the Liberal Arts Survive in Community Colleges?" *Change*, 1982, *14* (2), 39–42.

The authors note the decline of the transfer function and argue that, if the liberal arts are to survive at the community college, they must be reconstructed and integrated into other parts of the curriculum. They examine ways that the liberal arts could be incorporated into the three dominant community college programs: community education, compensatory education, and career education. They also urge the development of interdisciplinary liberal arts courses in light of the difficulties experienced by the colleges in maintaining a full array of sophomore-level specialized liberal arts classes. They conclude that failure to preserve the liberal arts in the two-year college would be a great disservice to community college students.

884 Dawson, George G. *Economics Education in Two-Year Colleges: An Overview and Summary of Research.* Research in Economic Education Report no. 3. Old Westbury: Center for Business and Economic Education, State University of New York, 1980. 111 pages. (ED 190 189)

This report draws upon an extensive literature review to analyze the research to date on economics education in the two-year college. It presents a critical analysis of the literature in three broad categories: (1) fact-finding studies designed to determine information such as course content, instructor characteristics, and type of department responsible for economics courses; (2) comparative studies designed to contrast economics education at two-year and four-year colleges; and (3) internal studies designed to measure the effectiveness of economics instruction. For each of these three categories, it summarizes the findings reached by authors, further research that needs to be conducted, and recommendations for improving research methodology. The work serves as an exhaustive review and guide to the literature.

885 Edwards, Sandra J. *Science Education in Two-Year Colleges: Biology.* Los Angeles: Center for the Study of Community Colleges and ERIC Clearinghouse for Junior Colleges, 1980. 116 pages. (ED 188 709)

This publication presents the results of a nationwide study of curriculum and instruction in biology at two-year colleges, drawing upon a literature review, a review of course schedules from a nationwide sample of 175 two-year colleges, and a survey of faculty to investigate the number and types of courses offered, instructional methods and materials used, course enrollments, grading practices, desired student competencies, instructor backgrounds, and faculty use of support services. Among the findings noted is that the growth of allied health occupational education has had a strong effect on the types of biology courses offered at two-year colleges. The work concludes with ten recommendations for changes in the biology curriculum that could make it more responsive to the diverse needs of community college students.

886 Edwards, Sandra J. *Science Education in Two-Year Colleges: Earth and Space.* Los Angeles: Center for the Study of Community Colleges and ERIC Clearinghouse for Junior Colleges, 1980. 87 pages. (ED 180 535)

This publication presents the results of a national study of curricula and instruction in earth and space sciences at the community college, drawing upon a review of catalogue and course schedules from a sample of 175 two-year colleges—as well as from a survey of faculty—to examine the number and types of courses offered, course prerequisites, course enrollments, grading practices, course objectives, desired student competencies, instructional methods and materials used, and instructor backgrounds. It concludes with eight recommendations for meeting the needs of two-year college students for earth and space science education. The work provides the most comprehensive analysis to date of two-year college offerings in the areas of geography, geology, astronomy, oceanography, meteorology, and interdisciplinary earth science.

887 Edwards, Sandra J. *Science Education in Two-Year Colleges: Environmental Sciences.* Los Angeles: Center for the Study of Community Colleges and ERIC Clearinghouse for Junior Colleges, 1980. 82 pages. (ED 180 558)

This work examines the interdisciplinary components of science instruction at two-year colleges as revealed by curriculum offerings in environmental science, integrated science, and the history of science. It draws upon a review of catalogue and course schedules from a national sample of 175 two-year colleges—as well as from a survey of faculty—to examine the frequency with which interdisciplinary courses are offered, class sizes, course prerequisites, classroom activities, instructional methods and materials used, course objectives, and instructor backgrounds. It concludes with summary observations pointing to the small percentage of colleges offering integrated science in vocational curricula, the lack of goal clarification in interdisciplinary offerings, and the value of interdisciplinary science in developmental education.

888 Friedlander, Jack. "The History Curriculum in Two-Year Colleges." *Community College Social Science Journal,* 1980, *3* (1), 45–49.

This article examines changes between 1975 and 1977 in the history curricula offered by a national sample of 178 community colleges, drawing upon class schedules and enrollment data for spring 1975 and spring 1977 to examine (1) changes in the types and frequency of history courses offered, (2) changes in the relative strength of history enrollments in relation to total college enrollments and in relation to total enrollment in humanities courses, and (3) changes in enrollment within specific history disciplines. The author determines, among other findings, that there was a 9.4 percent drop in history enrollments during the two-year period studied and that there was no effort on the part of history departments to offer nontraditional courses (beyond the usual U.S. history and world civilization classes) that would be of interest to the growing numbers of nontransfer students.

889 Friedlander, Jack. *Science Education in Two-Year Colleges: Economics.* Los Angeles: Center for the Study of Community Colleges and ERIC Clearinghouse for Junior Colleges, 1980. 86 pages. (ED 188 719)

This publication presents the results of a nationwide study of curriculum and instruction in economics at two-year colleges, drawing upon a review of catalogue and course schedules from a nationwide sample of 175 two-year colleges—as well as from a survey of faculty—to examine the number and types of courses offered, course goals, reading requirements, instructional methods and materials used, grading practices, types of students enrolled, and instructor backgrounds. The author suggests a number of recommendations on how economics education can be strengthened. He concludes that community colleges, by virtue of the diversity of their student populations, play a key role in determining the level of economic literacy in the United States.

890 Friedlander, Jack; Cohen, Arthur M.; and Brawer, Florence B. *Trends in Community College Humanities Education, 1977–1982.* Los Angeles: Center for the Study of Community Colleges, 1983. 11 pages. (ED 231 431)

This publication reports the results of a national survey conducted to identify changes in two-year college humanities programs between 1977 and 1982. It provides data (collected from a random sample of 172 community colleges) on (1) the addition of new humanities courses to the curriculum, (2) the recruitment of nontraditional students into humanities courses, (3) the types of interdisciplinary courses offered in the fall of 1982, (4) support for humanities faculty and programs, (5) frequency of media use in humanities courses, and (6) community service offerings in the humanities. It serves as a succinct analysis of current trends in community college humanities education.

891 Friedlander, Jack, and Edwards, Sandra J. *Science Education in Two-Year Colleges: Engineering.* Los Angeles: Center for the Study of Community Colleges and ERIC Clearinghouse for Junior Colleges, 1980. 80 pages. (ED 191 538)

This work presents the results of a nationwide study of curriculum and instruction in engineering education at two-year colleges, drawing upon a review of catalogue and course schedules from a sample of 175 two-year colleges—as well as from a survey of faculty—to examine the number and types of courses offered, course prerequisites, completion rates, grading practices, instructional methods and materials used, and the educational background and teaching experiences of faculty. It concludes with a number of recommendations that can be followed to provide engineering education for all community college students, not just those who wish to major in engineering or engineering technology.

892 Gibson, Walker (ed.). *New Students in Two-Year Colleges: Twelve Essays.* Urbana, Ill.: National Council of Teachers of English, 1979. 130 pages.

This volume presents twelve essays exploring theoretical and practical issues related to the teaching of English in community colleges. Topics covered include problems in teaching traditional literature to nontraditional students, the use of popular fiction in remedial courses, folklore as an aid to teaching, and composition and moral education. It also explores the concerns that underlie teaching activities, with a focus on humanistic approaches to writing, the English teacher's concern for rhetorical modes, the function of metaphor in discourse, and the value of semantic analysis. It provides the reader with a variety of perspectives on the English teacher's responses to special problems posed by community college students.

893 Glab, Edward, Jr. (ed.). *Problems and Prospects of Introducing Latin American Studies into the Community and Junior College Curriculum.* Austin: Institute of Latin American Studies, University of Texas, 1977. 34 pages. (ED 140 924)

This series of essays addressing issues related to the teaching of Latin American studies in two-year colleges includes discussions of (1) constraints militating against the addition of Latin American courses to the curriculum; (2) the interdisciplinary approach adopted for social sciences, humanities, and Spanish language courses at Tarrant County (Texas) Junior College; (3) deficiencies of present U.S. history courses and the need for an accurate and unbiased portrayal of Mexican-American history; and (4) administrative resistance to the institution of Latin American history courses. It is useful in understanding the difficulties of introducing an intercultural dimension into the two-year college curriculum.

894 Hill, Andrew. *Science Education in Two-Year Colleges: Psychology.* Los Angeles: Center for the Study of Community Colleges and ERIC Clearinghouse for Junior Colleges, 1980. 74 pages. (ED 181 972)

This publication presents the results of a nationwide study of curriculum and instruction in psychology at two-year colleges, drawing upon a review of catalogues and course schedules from a nationwide sample of 175 two-year colleges—as well as from a survey of faculty—to examine enrollments, course prerequisites, the types of courses offered, instructional activities, grading practices, course goals, and faculty characteristics. Among the findings are that (1) psychology offerings account for about six percent of all two-year college science courses, (2) general or introductory courses are the predominant type of psychology courses offered, and (3) instructional practices employed by faculty are similar to those used by their social science colleagues. The work includes a literature review and bibliography.

895 Hill, Andrew. *Science Education in Two-Year Colleges: Sociology.* Los Angeles: Center for the Study of Community Colleges and ERIC Clearinghouse for Junior Colleges, 1980. 57 pages. (ED 180 572)

This publication presents the results of a nationwide study of curriculum and instruction in sociology at two-year colleges, drawing upon a review of catalogue and course schedules from a sample of 175 two-year colleges—as well as from a survey of faculty—to examine the number and types of sociology courses offered, course goals, instructional methods and materials used, class size, and grading practices. It also examines class activities, desired student competencies, instructor backgrounds, and the instructional support services available to faculty. It draws several conclusions about the status of sociology in the community college, noting that a large number of persons receive their only exposure to the study of sociology through introductory courses offered at the community college.

896 Koltai, Leslie (ed.). *Merging the Humanities.* New Directions for Community Colleges, no. 12. San Francisco: Jossey-Bass, 1975. 105 pages. (ED 115 334)

This sourcebook presents ten articles on teaching humanities at the community college, examining the place of humanities in the overall college mission, the design of interdisciplinary humanities courses, an interinstitutional approach to faculty development for history instructors, the teaching of English, history, and other humanities courses for occupational students, and nontraditional instructional approaches. It also analyzes the preparation, in-service training, attitudes, and values of humanities faculty, as well as their approaches to instruction. It concludes that the humanities must continue to play an important role in community college education.

897 Lombardi, John. *The Decline of Transfer Education.* Topical Paper no. 70. Los Angeles: ERIC Clearinghouse for Junior Colleges, 1979. 37 pages. (ED 179 273)

The author argues that transfer education is losing its preeminence as the principal function of the community college, citing declining enrollment patterns in transfer courses and noting that other forces detrimental to transfer education include (1) the increasing demand for vocational education, (2) the growth of new curricular functions, such as continuing education, (3) the need to provide remedial education, (4) competition for students with four-year institutions, and (5) the aging of the student body. He concludes, however, that the reluctance of educators to break their ties with higher education and the increased demands for improved humanities curricula will assure transfer education a vital, albeit smaller, role at the community college.

898 McCormick, Albert E. Jr. "Two-Year College Instructors and the Sociology Profession: An Exploratory Investigation." *Teaching Sociology,* 1982, *9* (2), 111–126.

Please see no. 218 for the full annotation.

899 Marks, Joseph L. "Understanding the Dynamics of Change: The Case of the Humanities." *Community College Review,* 1981, *9* (1), 6–11.

This article tests the hypothesis that changing patterns of funding and enrollment during the 1970s were detrimental to the humanities curricula at two-year colleges. It draws upon descriptive statistics collected from a national sample of 142 public community colleges to correlate (1) changes registered in institutional funding and enrollment between 1971–72 and 1976–77 with (2) changing patterns in funding, enrollment, and staffing for humanities courses between 1975–76 and 1977–78. The author concludes that worsening financial conditions experienced by community colleges during the 1970s did not have a deleterious effect on the strength of the humanities in the community college curriculum, noting that other forces were at work to maintain the position of the humanities, including the inertia that supports well-entrenched programs even in the face of fiscal exigency.

900 Mooney, William T., Jr. *Science Education in Two-Year Colleges: Chemistry.* Los Angeles: Center for the Study of Community Colleges and ERIC Clearinghouse for Junior Colleges, 1980. 109 pages. (ED 187 397)

This publication presents the results of a nationwide study of curriculum and instruction in chemistry at two-year colleges, drawing upon a review of catalogue and course schedules from a nationwide sample of 175 two-year colleges—as well as from a survey of faculty—to examine the number and types of courses offered, course goals, instructional methods and materials used, evaluation techniques employed, the educational background and employment status of faculty, the assistance available to faculty, and instructor opinions as to how instructional effectiveness can be improved. It concludes with thirty recommendations for strengthening comprehensive chemistry programs at the community college. It includes an extensive literature review and bibliography.

901 Mooney, William T., Jr. *Science Education in Two-Year Colleges: Physics.* Los Angeles: Center for the Study of Community Colleges and ERIC Clearinghouse for Junior Colleges, 1980. 106 pages. (ED 191 534)

This publication presents the results of a nationwide study of curriculum and instruction in physics at two-year colleges, drawing upon a review of catalogue and course schedules from a sample of 175 two-year colleges—as well as from a survey of faculty—to examine course offerings, instructional methods, and instructor characteristics. It profiles the physics curriculum, noting the frequency of course offerings in seven areas: introductory courses for nonscience majors; physics for allied health and biology majors; physics for students in engineering technologies; preparatory courses for underprepared students planning to take engineering sequences; general, noncalculus physics; specialized courses, such as those offered in fire science curricula; and calculus-based courses. It also examines laboratory requirements, instructional materials, student evaluation criteria, faculty degree attainment, and faculty suggestions for improvement.

902 Music Educators National Conference. *Music in the Junior College.* Washington, D.C.: Music Educators National Conference, 1970. 57 pages. (ED 042 437)

This publication draws upon a review of the literature and a survey of 586 junior colleges to assess the role of music education in the two-year college. It provides a brief description of the junior college music department, focusing on its structural organization, the characteristics of faculty, and the efforts of faculty to promote music in the community. It also examines the role of music education in the junior college transfer, terminal, community services, and general education curricula. It concludes with an analysis of problems faced by music educators at the junior college, including the difficulty of establishing successful transfer programs in music and the tendency of the public to regard music education as a frill. The work serves as an insightful, though brief, analysis of the ways that music instruction fits into the diverse functions of the two-year college.

903 National Science Foundation. *Junior College Teachers of Science, Engineering, and Technology, 1967: Experience and Employment Characteristics.* NSF-69-3. Washington, D.C.: National Science Foundation, 1968. 98 pages. (ED 028 768; available in microfiche only)

This publication reports findings of a nationwide survey of junior college faculty who teach the natural and social sciences, engineering, and technology. It draws upon responses from 2,540 instructors to assess their demographic characteristics, educational and teaching backgrounds, professional affiliations, administrative and research duties, outside employment and current work on higher degrees, salaries, and career aims and degree of job satisfaction. Among the findings noted are that 85 percent of the respondents were men, 91 percent taught full time, and 20 percent of the part-timers were women. The work provides a comprehensive picture of junior college science faculty in the mid 1960s.

904 Oxford, Jacqulinn F., and Moore, David M. "Media Use and Instructional Methods in Community College Science Courses and Related Areas." *Community/Junior College Quarterly of Research and Practice,* 1982, *6* (3), 261–270.

Please see no. 597 for the full annotation.

905 Schmidt, Roger. "Religion and the Community College." *Religious Education,* January/February 1973, pp. 115–125.

The author calls for the development of religious studies programs at two-year colleges, arguing that these institutions lag behind four-year colleges and universities in the study of theology. He notes that religious studies programs have been slow to take on at community colleges because of fears that religion is too controversial, attitudes on the part of some faculty that religious beliefs are fallacious, and the belief that religion should not be studied in public institutions. He maintains that religious education is central to the liberal arts and that limited opportunities for the study of religion as an intellectual discipline are inconsistent with the community college's obligation to provide lower-division curricula that are on a parallel with courses offered at senior institutions.

906 Schroder, Ralph J. "Independence for the Junior College Transfer Curriculum." *Journal of Higher Education,* 1969, *40* (4), 286–296.

The author argues that junior college educators should take the lead in designing the lower-division curriculum rather than trying to conform to the lower-division requirements of four-year institutions. He maintains that community colleges simply do not have the resources to match the diverse array of general education and breadth requirements at senior institutions and suggests that the junior college transfer curriculum should provide for more generalization and less specialization. He describes a curriculum reform effort undertaken at Gavilan College (California), which requires transfer students to "major" in one of five broad areas: physical science, life sciences, social science, humanities, and physical education. He concludes that this broad, general educational approach to lower-division studies will produce students who—in the best tradition of the liberal arts—have the knowledge and self-discipline required for success in more specialized studies.

907 Seidman, Earl. *In the Words of the Faculty: Perspectives on Improving Teaching and Educational Quality in Community Colleges.* San Francisco: Jossey-Bass, 1985. 292 pages.

Please see no. 263 for the full annotation.

908 Stones, Ivan D.; Beckman, Milton W.; and Stephens, Larry J. "Attitudes Toward Mathematics, Level of Mathematical Competency, and Relative Gains in Competency in Two- and Four-Year Colleges: A Comparison." *Community/Junior College Research Quarterly,* 1980, *4* (3), 225–230.

This article compares the mathematics competencies and attitudes of students in precalculus courses at four-year colleges and two-year colleges in Nebraska. It uses a pretest-posttest design to compare gains made during one semester in each of ten math competencies: numbers and numerals, operations and properties, mathematical sentences, geometry, measurement, relations and functions, probability and statistics, graphing, mathematical reasoning, and business and computer math. It also compares the results of a math attitude questionnaire administered at the beginning of the semester. The authors note that there were no significant differences between the two-year and four-year college students in attitudes toward math. They also find that pretest-posttest competency gains for both groups were small and that the four-year college students achieved significantly higher gains in only one area (geometry). They conclude that precalculus math courses do little to teach or reinforce basic math skills.

909 Yarrington, Roger (ed.). *Strengthening Humanities in Community Colleges: National Assembly Report.* Washington, D.C.: American Association of Community and Junior Colleges, 1980. 125 pages. (ED 180 561; available in microfiche only)

This publication presents seven papers delivered at the 1979 National Assembly on the Strengthening of the Humanities. Issues discussed include the findings of national research on the humanities at two-year colleges; new approaches to humanities instruction; humanities-focused community forums; humanities and the world of work; a statewide effort to improve community college humanities instruction in Washington; and financial considerations in reinvigorating the humanities. The work presents a list of problem areas and recommended solutions that focus on the revitalization of community college humanities education.

910 Zoglin, Mary L. "Community College Responsiveness: Myth or Reality?" *Journal of Higher Education,* 1981, *52* (4), 415–426.

Please see no. 542 for the full annotation.

Transfer to and Articulation with Four-Year Institutions

911 Alba, Richard D., and Lavin, David E. "Community Colleges and Tracking in Higher Education." *Sociology of Education,* 1981, *54* (4), 223–237.

Please see no. 98 for the full annotation.

912 Anderson, Ernest F. *Three-Year Comparison of Transfer and Native Student Progress at the University of Illinois at Urbana-Champaign, Fall, 1973 Group.* Research Memorandum 77-9. Urbana: Office of School and College Relations, University of Illinois, 1977. 63 pages. (ED 149 820)

Please see no. 101 for the full annotation.

913 Anderson, Ernest F., and Beers, Philip G. *Two-Year Comparison of Transfer and Native Student Progress at the University of Illinois at Urbana-Champaign: Fall, 1977 Group.* Research Memorandum 80-6. Urbana: Office of School and College Relations, University of Illinois, 1980. 89 pages. (ED 203 955)

Please see no. 102 for the full annotation.

914 Anderson, Ernest F., and DeGray, Judith. *Comparison of Transfer and Native Student Progress at the University of Illinois at Urbana-Champaign, Fall, 1973 Group.* Research Memorandum 76-8. Urbana: Office of School and College Relations, University of Illinois, 1976. 45 pages. (ED 128 062)

Please see no. 103 for the full annotation.

915 Anderson, Ernest F., and Scholl, Natalie. *Factors Influencing the Choice of a Transfer Institution for Chicago Area Community College Students.* Research Memorandum 76-3. Urbana: Office of School and College Relations, University of Illinois, 1976. 77 pages. (ED 128 061)

This publication surveys a random sample of students enrolled in fourteen Chicago-area two-year colleges to determine the factors considered important by community college students in choosing a four-year college or university for eventual transfer. It notes, among other findings, that the interviewees preferred a four-year college that (1) offers programs in the students' major areas, (2) is located close to home, (3) has a high academic reputation, and (4) charges low tuition. It concludes with a discussion of the steps that should be taken by the University of Illinois to ensure that it will meet the needs of transfer students from community colleges. The work provides one of the few analyses of student opinions concerning the types of institutions at which they would like to complete their baccalaureate studies.

916 Astin, Alexander W. *Four Critical Years: Effects of College on Beliefs, Attitudes, and Knowledge.* San Francisco: Jossey-Bass, 1977. 293 pages.

Please see no. 104 for the full annotation.

917 Astin, Alexander W. "Chapter Six: Strengthening Transfer Programs." In George B. Vaughan and Associates, *Issues for Community College Leaders in a New Era.* San Francisco: Jossey-Bass, 1983, pp. 122–138.

For an annotation of the work in its entirety, please see no. 37.

918 Bird, Grace V. "Preparation for Advanced Study." In Nelson B. Henry (ed.), *The Public Junior College.* Fifty-fifth yearbook of the National Society for the Study of Education. Part 1. Chicago: National Society for the Study of Education, 1956, pp. 77–93.

For an annotation of the work in its entirety, please see no. 20.

★**919** California Community Colleges. *Transfer Education: California Community Colleges.* Sacramento: Office of the Chancellor, California Community Colleges, 1984. 110 pages. (ED 250 025)

This publication draws from a variety of sources to review information on transfer education in the California community colleges, examining (1) historical events surrounding the transfer function, (2) data focusing on trends in the number of community college students transferring to four-year institutions, (3) the representation of ethnic minorities among transfer students, and (4) the academic performance of transfer students at the University of California and the California State University. It also notes the gaps in what is known about community college transfer education. The work provides an in-depth quantitative analysis of how the transfer function has changed over time in the state with the largest number of community colleges.

920 Clark, Burton R. "The 'Cooling-Out' Function in Higher Education." *American Journal of Sociology,* 1960, *65* (6), 569–576.

Please see no. 965 for the full annotation.

921 Clark, Burton R. *The Open Door College: A Case Study.* New York: McGraw-Hill, 1960. 207 pages.

Please see no. 966 for the full annotation.

922 Cohen, Arthur M. *Counting the Transfer Students.* Junior College Resource Review. Los Angeles: ERIC Clearinghouse for Junior Colleges, 1979. 6 pages. (ED 172 864)

This paper examines why it is difficult to determine the number of students who transfer from two-year colleges to senior institutions. The author notes that, while most studies define transfer students as those who have taken courses at a two-year college and subsequently enroll in a senior institution, there is little agreement as to the number of units that must be taken before the student achieves transfer status. He argues further that data obtained by college-based researchers are often invalidated by low survey response rates and that nonreturning students and interstate transfers are difficult to trace. He also points out that variations in data-collection methods add to the confusion, as does the difficulty of tracing students who "stop in" and "stop out" of different types of postsecondary institutions. The work serves as a succinct analysis of the problems that make transfer data highly unreliable.

923 Cohen, Arthur M.; Brawer, Florence B.; and Bensimon, Estela M. *Transfer Education in American Community Colleges.* Los Angeles: Center for the Study of Community Colleges, 1985. 292 pages.

This publication reports the results of an effort undertaken by the Center for the Study of Community Colleges to gather and analyze data on twenty-four institutions taking part in the Ford Foundation's Urban Community Colleges Transfer Opportunities Program (UCCTOP). It describes projects initiated by each of the colleges to enhance transfer opportunities for minority students and also examines survey data related to (1) faculty attitudes toward the transfer function and the contributions that faculty make to enhancing transfer opportunities and (2) student characteristics that are predictive of transfer. It concludes with a consideration of the future of transfer education and offers recommendations concerning transfer policy, organization, and program content.

924 Darnes, G. Robert. *The Articulation of Curricula Between Two- and Four-Year Colleges and Universities.* Gainesville: Institute of Higher Education, University of Florida, 1970. 56 pages. (ED 045 063)

The author draws upon the experiences of educational planners in Florida to formulate recommendations for the coordination and articulation of curricula between public junior colleges and universities in Illinois. He examines efforts undertaken in Florida during the 1960s to (1) establish interinstitutional compacts on the articulation of general education and advanced placement credits, (2) mandate cooperative planning efforts with upper-division universities, (3) promote statewide interinstitutional research efforts, (4) assess the transferability of certain technical courses, and (5) conduct statewide articulation conferences in all subject areas. The work serves primarily as a planning document for community college leaders in Illinois, who—at the time the document was published—were investigating articulation mechanisms. It provides, however, insights into the history of the junior college articulation process in Florida.

925 Dearing, Bruce. "Broadening Transfer Opportunities." *Liberal Education,* 1975, *61* (2), 238–246.

The author explores barriers to transfer and suggests a national transfer policy for their elimination, arguing that the needs and goals of the transfer student should be of primary concern in the transfer process and that students should not be judged by the receiving institution merely on the basis of their transcripts or on the status of the college from which they are transferring. He notes the parochial tendency of receiving institutions to view native students more favorably than students transferring in and to adhere to strict transfer guidelines even if transfer students have to repeat course work they have already completed. He outlines seven suggestions for improvement, including the recommendation that institutions of higher education evaluate transfer students on the basis of attained competence.

926 Eells, Walter Crosby. "Chapter Nine: The Preparatory Function." In Walter Crosby Eells, *The Junior College.* Boston: Houghton Mifflin, 1931, pp. 248–282.

For an annotation of the work in its entirety, please see no. 15.

927 Gragg, William L., and Stroud, Patricia M. "Do Community Colleges Help Salvage Late-Bloomers?" *Community College Review*, 1977, *4* (3), 37–41.

This article examines the extent to which the North Carolina community colleges perform a "recovery" function by accepting dropouts from four-year institutions and preparing them for a successful return to the senior college. It draws upon data collected over a four-year period to note that, of the "reverse transfers" who enter the North Carolina community colleges, most had experienced academic difficulty at the senior institution and 75 percent entered transfer curricula rather than vocational programs at the community college. It finds that of those "reverse tranfsers" going into transfer curricula, however, only 19 percent eventually go on to earn a baccalaureate degree. It concludes with a discussion of the circumstances under which "reverse transfer" recovery is more likely and urges community colleges to include recovery as one of its major missions.

928 Illinois Community College Board. *A Statewide Follow-Up Study of Fall 1973 Transfer Students from Illinois Public Community Colleges (Phase III Progress Report).* Vol. 2, no. 11. Springfield: Illinois Community College Board, 1977. 54 pages. (ED 140 894; available in microfiche only)

Please see no. 113 for the full annotation.

929 Johnson, Alan, and Avila, Don. "Community Colleges: Miniuniversities or Opportunity Centers?" *Community/ Junior College Research Quarterly,* 1977, *1* (2), 109–116.

Please see no. 115 for the full annotation.

930 Kintzer, Frederick C. *Nationwide Pilot Study on Articulation.* Topical Paper no. 15. Los Angeles: ERIC Clearinghouse for Junior Colleges, 1970. 135 pages. (ED 045 065)

This publication presents state-by-state accounts of articulation efforts between two-year and four-year institutions, outlining, for each of the fifty states, the history of two-year colleges in the state, their educational philosophy, their articulation policies and procedures, their significant articulation problems, and their prospects for the future. It provides historians of the community college with a detailed insight into the scope of articulation procedures as of 1970.

931 Kintzer, Frederick C. (ed.). *Improving Articulation and Transfer Relationships.* New Directions for Community Colleges, no. 39. San Francisco: Jossey-Bass, 1982. 117 pages. (ED 220 146)

This sourcebook presents ten articles on articulation (services for the transfer student) and transfer (exchange of credits, courses, and curricula), discussing the decline in the transfer function, the special needs of transfer students, the role of the chief instructional officer in articulation, the need for greater communication between community colleges and proprietary institutions, and the obstacles to transfer posed by accreditation standards set for baccalaureate institutions. It also describes successful articulation and transfer programs, including a computerized advisement and graduation information service for transfer students and a program for transferring credit earned through prior learning experience. The work provides the reader with insights into areas that need to be addressed if articulation and transfer processes are to be improved.

932 Kintzer, Frederick C., and Wattenbarger, James L. *The Articulation/Transfer Phenomenon: Patterns and Directions.* Horizons Monograph Series. Washington, D.C.: Council of Universities and Colleges, American Association of Community and Junior Colleges; Los Angeles: ERIC Clearinghouse for Junior Colleges, 1985. 80 pages.

This publication draws upon an extensive bibliography to examine the status of articulation and transfer between two-year and four-year institutions. Individual chapters discuss (1) the enrollment of students in transfer programs and the performance and persistence of community college transfers at senior institutions; (2) patterns of statewide articulation and transfer agreements; (3) formal and informal transfer agreements established between institutions of higher education in other countries; and (4) factors likely to affect transfer in the future, such as increasing numbers of nontraditional students, the need to establish transfer relationships with corporate educational programs, and recent national efforts to enhance the transfer function. The work serves as an extensive review of the problems faced by community colleges in successfully moving students to senior institutions.

933 Knoell, Dorothy M., and Medsker, Leland L. *From Junior to Senior Colleges: A National Study of the Transfer Student.* Washington, D.C.: American Council on Education, 1965. 102 pages.

Please see no. 117 for the full annotation.

934 Levin, Bernard, and Clowes, Darrel. "Realization of Educational Aspirations Among Blacks and Whites at Two- and Four-Year Colleges." *Community/Junior College Research Quarterly,* 1980, *4* (2), 185–193.

Please see no. 158 for the full annotation.

935 Massachusetts State Transfer Articulation Committee. *Study of Massachusetts Two-Year College Students: Implications for Massachusetts Four-Year Colleges and Universities.* Amherst: Massachusetts State Transfer Articulation Committee, 1972. 43 pages. (ED 068 081)

Please see no. 83 for the full annotation.

936 Miller, Howard F.; Janawsky, Robin; and Katz, Adolf. *The Academic Achievement of Two-Year College Graduates in New Jersey Four-Year Colleges.* Research Report 77-2. Trenton: New Jersey State Department of Higher Education, 1977. 19 pages. (ED 143 397)

Please see no. 121 for the full annotation.

937 Monroe, Charles R. "Chapter Four: Transfer Programs." In Charles R. Monroe, *Profile of the Community College: A Handbook.* San Francisco: Jossey-Bass, 1972, pp. 59–66.

For an annotation of the work in its entirety, please see no. 27.

938 Moughamian, Henry; Lach, Ivan J.; Kohl, Peggy L.; and Wellman, Fred L. *A Statewide Follow-Up Study of Students Who Transfer from Illinois Public Community Colleges to Illinois Four-Year Colleges and Universities. Fall 1973 Transfer Students Followed Through Spring 1976.* Springfield: Illinois Community College Board, 1978. 61 pages. (ED 160 146; available in microfiche only)

Please see no. 122 for the full annotation.

939 Nickens, John. "The Effect of Attendance at Florida Junior Colleges on Final Performance of Baccalaureate Degree Candidates in Selected Majors at the Florida State University." *College and University,* 1970, *45* (3), 281–288.

Please see no. 124 for the full annotation.

940 Orfield, Gary, and others. *The Chicago Study of Access and Choice in Higher Education: A Report to the Illinois Senate Committee on Higher Education.* Chicago: Committee on Public Policy Studies, University of Chicago, 1984. 351 pages. (ED 248 929)

Please see no. 986 for the full annotation.

941 Parker, Paul C. "Access and Mobility in Higher Education: The Search for a Common Currency and a Gold Standard." *Liberal Education,* 1979, *65* (2), 120–134.

This article discusses barriers to transfer between institutions of higher education, arguing that the students' right to move from college to college is unduly repressed by arbitrary transfer policies that serve administrative purposes rather than student needs. It describes articulation efforts undertaken to overcome these barriers in Florida, including (1) a 1959 agreement permitting junior colleges to define their general education curriculum, with the guarantee that their students would be accepted for transfer at senior institutions; (2) a 1971 agreement defining the associate degree and making it a passport to the university; and (3) the establishment of a statewide articulation committee made up of community college and university representatives. It concludes with an outline of nine steps taken by the committee to improve articulation in Florida during the 1970s.

942 Phlegar, Archie G.; Andrew, Loyd D.; and McLaughlin, Gerald W. "Explaining the Academic Performance of Community College Students Who Transfer to a Senior Institution." *Research in Higher Education,* 1981, *15* (2), 99–108.

Please see no. 127 for the full annotation.

943 Sames, Richard W. "The Upper-Level Universities and the Community Colleges." *Liberal Education,* 1974, *60* (3), 348–358.

This article discusses the origins and future potential of the relationship between community colleges and upper-level universities (that is, those institutions that offer upper-division and graduate course work only). The author argues that traditional four-year institutions have inexcusably failed to assume a partnership role with community colleges and that upper-level universities were developed primarily in response to the resultant difficulties in curriculum development and transfer. He notes that both community colleges and upper-level universities provide nontraditional programs for previously unserved students and maintains that these two institutions—working together—will form an alternative to the traditional liberal arts colleges and land-grant universities. The article reflects the optimism that many educators felt for upper-level universities in the early 1970s.

944 Sawyer, James A., and Nickens, John M. "The Fulfillment of the Democratization Role of the Community College." *College and University,* 1980, *55* (2), 113–124.

Please see no. 988 for the full annotation.

945 Thornton, James W. "Chapter Fifteen: The Curricular Education for Transfer." In James W. Thornton, *The Community Junior College.* New York: Wiley, 1972, pp. 222–243.

For an annotation of the work in its entirety, please see no. 34.

946 Van Alstyne, Carol. "Higher Cost of Transfer: The Hidden Penalties." *Community and Junior College Journal,* 1974, *45* (2), 12–14.

The author notes that many college students start their baccalaureate education at community colleges in an effort to save money but argues that the hidden costs of transferring to a four-year institution negate any savings accrued at the two-year institution. She cites longitudinal data collected by the Cooperative Institutional Research Program to point out that students who transfer (rather than remaining in one college for four years) have their undergraduate careers unnecessarily prolonged. She uses the case of a hypothetical transfer student who enrolled initially at a low-tuition community college to demonstrate how the delay in degree completion—along with other specified hidden costs—adds unnecessarily to the cost of a college education. She calls for the elimination of barriers to transfer that impose a fiscal penalty on students.

947 Walton, Karen D. "Articulation: Transfer Agreements, Minimum Grades Acceptable on Transfer Courses, and Transferability of Associate Degrees." *Community/Junior College Quarterly of Research and Practice,* 1984, *8* (1–4), 169–184.

This article reviews data from a survey of 835 two-year and four-year institutions to determine the nature of transfer agreements, minimum grades acceptable on transfer courses, and transferability of associate degrees. The author finds that fewer than half of the colleges had written agreements regarding transfer of credit and that, of those agreements in existence, half were formal articulation agreements and half were simply lists of acceptable courses. She also notes that (1) the minimum grade accepted on transfer courses was a *C* in two-thirds of the institutions and a *D* in one-third; (2) over two-thirds of the four-year institutions accepted neither the associate of arts degree nor the associate of applied science degree without evaluating courses individually; and (3) only one-sixth of the four-year colleges accepted both degrees without individual course evaluation. The article provides useful insights into common transfer practices.

948 Wray, Frederick E., and Leischuck, Gerald S. "Predicting Academic Success of Junior College Transfers." *College and University*, 1971, *47* (1), 10–16.

Please see no. 133 for the full annotation.

General Education

949 Bogue, Jesse Parker. "Chapter Seven: General Education in the Community College." In Jesse Parker Bogue, *The Community College*. New York: McGraw-Hill, 1950, pp. 151–178.

Please see no. 8 for the full annotation.

950 Case, Chester H. "Chapter Five: Reformulating General Education Programs." In George B. Vaughan and Associates, *Issues for Community College Leaders in a New Era*. San Francisco: Jossey-Bass, 1983, pp. 100–121.

Please see no. 37 for the full annotation.

951 Cohen, Arthur M., and Brawer, Florence B. "Chapter Twelve: General Education: Developing an Integrated Curriculum." In Arthur M. Cohen and Florence B. Brawer, *The American Community College*. San Francisco: Jossey-Bass, 1982, pp. 311–341.

Please see no. 12 for the full annotation.

952 Harrison, J. Derek. "General Education in the Community College: A Recent View." *Journal of General Education*, 1973, *25* (2), 83–93.

This article traces the history of general education in the two-year college, reviewing classic studies such as B. Lamar Johnson's *General Education in Action* (no. 954). The author suggests that community colleges fall short of their self-imposed general education obligations and describes patterns of general education—including the distribution system, required courses, and a combination of these two—to illustrate that community colleges have not developed innovative general education progams to meet their special needs. He concludes that community colleges would be stronger institutions if their leaders could reach a consensus about the purpose of general education and about the means of implementing it in the curriculum.

953 Hudson, A. James, and Smith, Ralph B. "Does General Education Have a Future?" *Community College Review*, 1976, *4* (2), 57–63.

This article analyzes the catalogues of 103 California community colleges to determine the extent to which general education goals are reflected in actual course offerings. It compares course offerings with the general education goals articulated by B. Lamar Johnson (no. 954) in the areas of personal and social adjustment, citizenship, vocational adjustment, cultural heritage, problem solving, communications, home and family life, moral values, and creative activities. The authors conclude, among other findings, that few community colleges offer courses designed to achieve these general education goals, noting that the general education curriculum is instead composed of elective transfer courses that are designed to introduce students to a field of study. The article exposes the rift between the ideals of general education and actual practices.

★954 Johnson, B. Lamar. *General Education in Action*. Washington, D.C.: American Council on Education, 1952. 409 pages.

This publication details the findings of a landmark research effort undertaken in 1950–51 to identify and describe general education practices in the California junior colleges. It discusses common methods of including general education in the curriculum and describes general education practices in the areas of student counseling; psychology and personal development; health, physical education, and recreation; family-life education; communication skills; creative arts and the humanities; natural sciences and mathematics; and citizenship. It also discusses general education in vocational courses, administrative issues, the role of the library, and special problems. It suggests a large junior college role in the amelioration of social problems through general education.

★**955** Lukenbill, Jeffrey D., and McCabe, Robert H. *General Education in a Changing Society: General Education Program, Basic Skills Requirements, Standards of Academic Progress at Miami-Dade Community College.* Miami, Fla: Miami-Dade Community College, 1978. 98 pages. (ED 158 812)

This publication describes a general education program centered on core courses that are required for all degree-seeking students at Miami-Dade Community College. It details goals and objectives of the program and discusses (1) basic skills competencies required of all students; (2) the general education requirements for the associate in arts, the associate in science, and the associate in general studies degrees; (3) support services provided for students; and (4) enforced standards of academic progress. It describes the general education core, which requires students to take courses from five course clusters: communications, humanities, the social environment, the natural environment, and individual growth and development. The work serves as a detailed example of how one institution tackled the problem of defining and implementing general education.

956 Lukenbill, Jeffrey D., and McCabe, Robert H. "Getting Started: Straightforward Advice." In B. Lamar Johnson (ed.), *General Education in Two-Year Colleges.* New Directions for Community Colleges, no. 40. San Francisco: Jossey-Bass, 1982, pp. 83–98. (ED 222 236)

The authors explain how to launch a new general education program, using the experience at Miami-Dade Community College (Florida) as a model. They argue that most community colleges have general education course *requirements* rather than a comprehensive general education *program* built around (1) a rationale, (2) established goals, (3) courses and objectives for attaining those goals, and (4) program evaluation criteria. They detail the respective roles of faculty and administrators in planning such a program and describe how the planning process at Miami-Dade resulted in a comprehensive general education curriculum incorporating remedial courses, a structured student-flow model, and academic support services. The work is useful for community college practitioners seeking practical advice on the process of general education curriculum development.

957 Monroe, Charles R. "Chapter Five: General Education." In Charles R. Monroe, *Profile of the Community College: A Handbook*. San Francisco: Jossey-Bass, 1972, pp. 67–77.

Please see no. 27 for the full annotation.

958 O'Banion, Terry, and Shaw, Ruth G. "Obstacles to General Education." In B. Lamar Johnson (ed.), *General Education in Two-Year Colleges*. New Directions for Community Colleges, no. 40. San Francisco: Jossey-Bass, 1982, pp. 59–71.

The authors identify and discuss twenty barriers to the development of community college general education programs, grouping these obstacles into five categories: (1) intrinsic conflicts, such as the association of general education with the liberal arts and elitism; (2) organizational and delivery impediments, such as the tendency to organize curricula by traditional academic disciplines; (3) barriers imposed by staff, such as the lack of administrative support; (4) student-related obstacles, such as the heterogeneity of the student population; and (5) external and societal restraints, such as the specialization of the job market. They conclude with suggestions for overcoming these barriers. The work provides a clear delineation of the factors that explain the gap between the hopes of general education proponents and actual college practices.

959 Sorensen, Nathalie. *General Education in Canada's Community Colleges and Institutes: Report of a National Survey.* Toronto, Ont.: Association of Canadian Community Colleges, 1984. 51 pages. (ED 244 684)

This publication surveys Canadian faculty and administrators to study the general education component of community college programs and to ascertain opinions on how general education should be carried out. It examines responses related to the aims of college education, the organization of general education, the amounts and kinds of general education offered, general education policy and administration, extracurricular aspects, and the attitudes and performance of students, noting discrepancies between the aims of college education considered important by the respondents and the degree to which those aims are addressed in college curricula. The author recommends a review of general education in all community colleges, the implementation of faculty development programs, and the establishment of a national center for general education. The work provides the reader with insights into general education practices in Canada.

960 Thornton, James W. "General Education." In Nelson B. Henry (ed.), *The Public Junior College.* Fifty-fifth yearbook of the National Society for the Study of Education. Part 1. Chicago: National Society for the Study of Education, 1956, pp. 118–139.

For an annotation of the work in its entirety, please see no. 20.

961 Thornton, James W. "Chapter Fourteen: The Curriculum: General Education." In James W. Thornton, *The Community Junior College.* New York: Wiley, 1972, pp. 201–221.

For an annotation of the work in its entirety, please see no. 34.

12

Educational Opportunity and Social Mobility

One of the great debates in higher education is the degree to which community colleges serve a democratizing role in American society. Two-year college leaders such as Gleazer (no. 16) posit that the leitmotiv of community college education is the extension of educational opportunity to those who have not previously been served by higher education. Other scholars, including Goodwin (no. 967), argue that this extension of educational opportunity has served conservative, elitist functions, such as the provision of a screening mechanism for universities. Still others have examined the community college from a sociopolitical viewpoint and come to the conclusion that two-year institutions perpetuate an inequitable class structure.

The literature on the community college's social role is relatively small, but it has a wide audience and has stirred considerable controversy. The works in this literature can be subdivided under two broad and interrelated headings: the community college role in promoting educational mobility (nos. 962–974) and the community college role in promoting social mobility (nos. 975–991).

The Community College Role in Promoting Educational Mobility

Community colleges are seen as a low-cost avenue to the baccalaureate degree for large numbers of students previously

449

unserved by higher education. Several writers, however, challenge the claim that the two-year colleges extend educational mobility. Recent authors have stressed that fiscal constraints and increased calls for improved quality have brought open-door admissions policies under attack. Others have asserted that:

- students starting their baccalaureate education at two-year colleges are less likely to obtain the bachelor's degree than students who start at four-year colleges or universities (nos. 963, 962);
- educational access to urban, disadvantaged youth cannot become a reality if colleges retain traditional educational practices without developing new programs to meet the needs of nontraditional students (no. 969);
- equal educational opportunity will remain more a slogan than a fact if new teaching strategies are not adopted to meet the special needs of the large numbers of students with academic skills deficiencies (no. 972);
- the conservative backgrounds and attitudes of most community college faculty have thwarted the development of innovative programs for nontraditional students (no. 964); and
- the colleges facilitate a "cooling-out" function, whereby large numbers of students are gently and unobtrusively convinced that their aspirations for the baccalaureate degree are unrealistic and inappropriate (nos. 965, 966, 973).

The "cooling-out" process is perhaps the most famous of these criticisms and is detailed at length in the findings of Burton Clark's comprehensive case study of the first four years of operation at San Jose Junior College in California (nos. 965, 966). Under the "cooling-out" theory, community colleges serve as a societal safety valve that regulates the flow of the large number of young people who aspire to the limited number of prestigious jobs that require a college diploma. Clark posits that large numbers of less able junior college students are eased out of the transfer curriculum, sidetracked into the vocational curriculum, and thus provided with an alternative avenue to success and a means of avoiding the stigma attached to dropouts. Though the cooling-out theory is famous, few researchers have examined how this process is actually carried out. London (no. 970) suggests that it does not work as smoothly as Clark seems to believe. Alba and Lavin (no. 962) warn that little is known about the community college environment and its effects on students. Besides the need for more reliable data on the number of students who transfer (a point made in the introduction to the last chapter), additional research is needed on how the community college environment encourages or discourages transfer and upward educational mobility.

The Community College Role in Promoting Social Mobility

Several authors look at the community college from a sociological viewpoint, charging that two-year institutions serve as a separate educational track for lower-class youth. Among these authors are Corcoran (no. 978), Karabel (no. 982), Birenbaum (no. 975), Zwerling (no. 991), Pincus (no. 987), and Orfield and others (no. 986). They bring a variety of criticisms of the community college, including the assertions that:

- two-year colleges, in which lower-class and minority students are disproportionately represented, are second-rate institutions that do not provide the same educational opportunity as four-year colleges and universities;
- tracking continues within the two-year college in that minorities and lower-class students are disproportionately represented in the terminal, vocational programs that provide only modest economic benefits and limited social mobility;
- minority and lower-class students who do transfer are likely to attend four-year colleges that are less prestigious than those attended by white and higher-class students who transfer; and
- lower-class students are exposed to a hidden curriculum that teaches subservience to the upper classes.

Other writers, it should be noted, bring evidence suggesting that community colleges do not serve as a separate track for minority and lower-class students. Researchers utilizing data collected in the National Longitudinal Study of the High School

Class of 1972 (no. 976) note that there is a significant overlap in the socioeconomic and ability characteristics of students at two-year and four-year institutions. As for the overrepresentation of minority students in vocational programs, West and Shearon (no. 989) argue that this does not necessarily perpetuate class stratification, because some vocational programs actually lead to higher-status jobs than some transfer programs. Finally, Cohen and Brawer (no. 977) make the point that community colleges cannot lift an entire social class from one stratum to another; the colleges can only make it possible for individuals to move between groups. It may be unfair, then, to blame the colleges for the perpetuation of social inequalities.

The debate over the community college's social role is by no means settled. Further testing of the observations made by critics of the community college will require more observational study to determine whether college environments do indeed provide a class-based educational track that reinforces lower-class subservience. Better longitudinal data are also required to assess the mobility of students throughout the system of higher education.

Further Information on the Community College Social Role

Most of the literature on the community college social role is found in the educational and sociological journal literature. Information on how to find journal literature on this and other educational topics is provided in the next chapter. It should be noted that the general texts cited in Chapter Two—with the exception of Cohen and Brawer (no. 12)—provide few analyses of responses to the social critics of the two-year college.

The Community College Role in Promoting Educational Mobility

962 Alba, Richard D., and Lavin, David E. "Community Colleges and Tracking in Higher Education." *Sociology of Education*, 1981, *54* (4), 223–237.

Please see no. 98 for the full annotation.

963 Astin, Alexander W. *Four Critical Years: Effects of College on Beliefs, Attitudes, and Knowledge.* San Francisco: Jossey-Bass, 1977. 293 pages.

Please see no. 104 for the full annotation.

964 Cain, Rudolph A. "Equal Educational Opportunity and the Community College." *Journal of Negro Education*, 1982, *51* (1), 16–28.

This article argues that the conservative backgrounds and attitudes of most community college faculty have thwarted the development of innovative programs that are required to provide equal educational opportunity to the large numbers of nontraditional students entering two-year colleges. The author cites the lack of faculty commitment to the community college mission and discusses contributing problems related to (1) the lack of graduate school training for community college instructors, (2) poor staff development programs, (3) the need to increase the number of minority faculty, and (4) the university orientation of many faculty members. He concludes that failure to address these issues will perpetuate "the myth that educational opportunity is available to all citizens" (p. 28).

965 Clark, Burton R. "The 'Cooling-Out' Function in Higher Education." *American Journal of Sociology*, 1960, *65* (6), 569–576.

This article explains the "cooling-out" process in the junior college, whereby low-ability students who hope to attain the baccalaureate degree are redirected into vocational or other terminal curricula rather than dismissed from higher education altogether. The author notes how pre-entrance testing, orientation counseling, and feedback from instructors all play a role in subtly inducing the student to relinquish the bachelor's degree and "ease himself out of the competition to transfer" (p. 574). He stresses that such sidetracking serves as a safety-valve mechanism for society, giving large numbers of students an alternative avenue for success rather than branding them as failures.

★966 Clark, Burton R. *The Open Door College: A Case Study.* New York: McGraw-Hill, 1960. 207 pages.

This publication presents the findings of an intensive case study of the first four years of operation of San Jose (California) Junior College. The author examines the effects on the institution's developing character of three factors: (1) the college's administrative location within the organization of the public school system, (2) the open enrollment of underprepared students, and (3) administrative structure and personnel. He concludes that the character of the junior college is largely shaped by its "unselective-voluntary clientele," and he details institutional mechanisms used to gently guide academically underprepared students away from the transfer track and into alternative, terminal programs. (Note: This is the classic study leading to the development of Clark's "cooling-out" theory.)

967 Goodwin, Gregory L. "The Nature and the Nurture of the Community College Movement." *Community College Frontiers,* 1976, *4* (3), 5–13.

This article briefly reviews the history of the junior college, arguing that two-year colleges have served the conservative role of convincing large numbers of students that their aspirations for the baccalaureate degree are unrealistic and inappropriate. The author notes the heritage of this conservatism in (1) the early efforts of William Rainey Harper and others to relegate lower-division studies to junior colleges that would screen out less able students; (2) the terminal education and general education emphases of later junior college advocates, including Walter Crosby Eells and B. Lamar Johnson; and (3) the growth of vocational education in the

1960s and 1970s. He concludes that the democratic image of the community college is not totally warranted and that community college practitioners should be more self-critical.

968 Hyde, William. *A New Look at Community College Access.* Denver, Colo: Education Commission of the States, 1982. 194 pages. (ED 217 905)

This publication examines key questions related to the provision of educational opportunities by community colleges, discussing (1) the different meanings of educational access and how different implications for public policy stem from various definitions and standards; (2) data on the extent to which community college access has been achieved; (3) the limits of access within the context of financial constraints and conflicting needs; and (4) community college practices that influence access. It also discusses the likely importance of access in the 1980s, identifying the conventional arguments for continuing various educational programs and outlining the changing emphasis that policy makers are placing on access. It serves as an in-depth analysis of how access has been defined and how emphasis placed on access by educational leaders has given way to an emphasis on other concerns.

★969 Knoell, Dorothy M. *Toward Educational Opportunity for All.* Albany: Office of Executive Dean for Two-Year Colleges, State University of New York, 1966. 234 pages. (ED 011 454)

The author draws from a variety of primary and secondary sources to assess the need for a new type of two-year college that would expand educational access to urban, disadvantaged youth. She examines (1) the efforts of other agencies, institutions, and groups to provide disadvantaged youth with education and job training; (2) interviews with high school seniors and their parents; (3) the attitudes of two-year college faculty, administrators, and trustees; (4) the employment and education experiences of two-year college students who drop out to find work; and (5) six background papers. She concludes that new approaches to programming—not simply the construction of more campuses—are required to realize the goal of free universal education at grades 13 and 14.

970 London, Howard B. *The Culture of a Community College*. New York: Praeger, 1978. 181 pages.

This publication details a study in which participant observation was used to examine students and staff in a New England community college during one academic year. It outlines many observations related to social class, including the finding that most students were conservative, even though they were from low socioeconomic groups. It notes further that these students were fearful of the dissociation from family and peers that might result as they advanced in higher education and that they were therefore not readily acquiescent to demands placed on them by instructors. The work provides few policy recommendations but concludes that the "cooling-out" function articulated by Burton Clark in an early community college study (no. 965) does not work as smoothly as Clark seemed to suggest.

971 National Council of State Directors of Community-Junior Colleges. *Status of Open Door Admissions: Issues, Trends and Projects*. Committee Report no. 1. N.p.: National Council of State Directors of Community-Junior Colleges, 1983. 35 pages. (ED 230 214)

This publication reports findings of a national survey of state directors of community college education who were asked (1) whether the state had a formal commitment to an open-door admissions policy, (2) whether the commitment was in a written document, and (3) whether the policy had legal status. It concludes that the majority of responding states had a formal commitment to the establishment and maintenance of an open-door admissions policy but that there was a growing trend to curtail enrollments by means of the budgeting process. The work enumerates state-by-state responses, providing community college researchers with insights into how governmental commitment to open-door admissions is codified through statutory law, executive order, court ruling, administrative regulation, precedent, and practice.

972 Roueche, John E., and McFarlane, William H. "Improved Instruction in the Junior College: Key to Equal Opportunity." *Journal of Higher Education,* 1970, *41* (9), 713–722.

Please see no. 601 for the full annotation.

973 Shea, Brent M. "Two-Year Colleges and Inequality." *Integrated Education,* 1975, *13* (1), 38–43.

The author examines the community college role in reconciling the "inconsistency between the encouragement of achievement and the realities of limited opportunity" (p. 39), describing how institutional inputs (student backgrounds) and processes (the "cooling-out" function) operate as "a channeling mechanism by which student aspirations are adjusted to conform with labor market demands" (p. 40). He argues that this is a necessary task in a society characterized by a hierarchical occupational structure and that if community colleges did not perform this function, other educational institutions would.

974 Young, Robert B. "The Identity Crisis of the Community College: A Dilemma in Dialectic." *Journal of Higher Education,* 1977, *48* (3), 333–342.

Please see no. 55 for the full annotation.

The Community College Role in Promoting Social Mobility

975 Birenbaum, William M. "From Class to Mass in Higher Education." *Higher Education Review,* 1973, *6* (1), 3–16.

This article analyzes the gap between intentions and reality in the commitment to provide equal educational mobility for all social classes, noting, for example, that segregation by class and race is unacceptable and contrary to the stated aims of higher education but that such segregation occurs between different institutional types and within individual institutions themselves. The author utilizes the example of the City University of New York (CUNY) to argue that lower-class students are segregated in the university's community colleges and that these students are further segregated into two-year college vocational curricula that provide limited career and economic promise. He warns against complacent acceptance of the status quo and urges fresh attempts to restructure education to provide equal opportunity.

976 Clowes, Darrel A., and Levin, Bernard H. "How Do Two Year Colleges Serve Recent High School Graduates?" *Community College Review,* 1980, 7 (3), 24–35.

Please see no. 107 for the full annotation.

977 Cohen, Arthur M., and Brawer, Florence B. "Chapter Thirteen: The Social Role: A Response to the Critics and a Look to the Future." In Arthur M. Cohen and Florence B. Brawer, *The American Community College.* San Francisco: Jossey-Bass, 1982, pp. 342–365.

For an annotation of the work in its entirety, please see no. 12.

978 Corcoran, Thomas B. "The Coming Slums of Higher Education." *Change,* 1972, *4* (7), 30–35.

The author argues that community colleges do not enhance equality of educational opportunity and suggests reforms that might improve the educational experiences of two-year college students. He maintains that the availability of community colleges has (1) benefited middle-class students more than the poor, (2) restricted the range of institutional choice for those who cannot attend four-year colleges, and (3) segregated lower-class students into a relatively low-quality segment of higher education. He urges that a greater proportion of the educational dollar be earmarked for community colleges and suggests other reforms, such as the establishment of short-term residence facilities on campus. The article provides a middle ground between those who would leave the colleges unchanged and those who would abolish them altogether.

979 Dugger, Ronnie. "The Community College Comes of Age." *Change,* 1976, *8* (1), 32–37.

This article extols the potential democratizing effects of the teaching emphasis of the community college, tracing the low status of the community college to elitism, prejudice, and errors in the value system of higher education and contrasting the diverse, student-centered roles of the community college with the overemphasis that universities place on narrow research and the resulting neglect of classroom instruction. The author concludes that legislators should "shake off the mystique of the university" (p. 36) and allocate larger proportions of the higher education budget to community colleges. The article offers scant supporting data but serves as an example of the high hopes that many educators have for the community college as a democratizing agent.

980 Ericson, David P., and Robertshaw, Dianne. "Social Justice and the Community College." *Community/Junior College Quarterly of Research and Practice,* 1982, *6* (4), 315–341.

This article utilizes data collected in the National Longitudinal Study of the High School Class of 1972 to re-examine assertions in the literature that community colleges perpetuate class-based tracking. The authors find that community colleges do not in fact attract disproportionately large numbers of low-status, low-ability students and that social status is a very small determinant of who completes a two-year degree and who transfers to a baccalaureate program. They argue that the community college is a fairly meritocratic institution "that distributes its benefits on the basis of educationally relevant attributes" (p. 339). They conclude that, because meritocracy is intrinsically unjust, the situation in community colleges needs redress. They caution, however, that social justice at all costs may not be desirable, since it would conflict with other fundamental values, such as excellence and performance.

★**981** Goodwin, Gregory L. "A Social Panacea: A History of the Community-Junior College Ideology." Unpublished manuscript, 1973. 316 pages. (ED 093 427)

This work reviews the writings of major community college spokespersons from the beginnings up to the 1970s, showing that, although educational rhetoric has changed from one generation to the next, the basic mission of the institutions has remained consistent. It demonstrates that the early spokespersons reserved for the junior college the unique mission of training people for middle management, thus leaving elementary schools for the masses and universities for the professional elite. The author concludes that the ideals of community college spokespersons, though sincere, were elitist and undemocratic. The work provides historians of the two-year college with an important insight into the evolution of those institutional characteristics that would lead contemporary critics to the conclusion that community colleges perpetuate an inequitable class structure.

★**982** Karabel, Jerome. "Community Colleges and Social Stratification." *Harvard Educational Review,* 1972, *42* (4), 521–562.

The author takes the position that the community college contributes to social-class stratification, economic inequality, and inflation in the number of years of schooling expected of people in America. He traces the tracking of lower-class students into occupational programs and the forces impelling growth in vocational education within the institutions and predicts that community colleges will become ever more rigid as structures that track lower-class students into lower-class occupations. The article is useful as a classic example of a line of reasoning that sees the community college as a perpetuator of social-class inequalities.

983 Levin, Bernard, and Clowes, Darrel. "Realization of Educational Aspirations Among Blacks and Whites at Two- and Four-Year Colleges." *Community/Junior College Research Quarterly,* 1980, *4* (2), 185–193.

Please see no. 158 for the full annotation.

984 Moore, William, Jr. *Community College Response to the High-Risk Student: A Critical Reappraisal.* Horizons Monograph Series. Los Angeles: ERIC Clearinghouse for Junior Colleges; Washington, D.C.: American Association of Community and Junior Colleges, 1976. 60 pages. (ED 122 873)

Please see no. 160 for the full annotation.

985 Olivas, Michael A. *The Dilemma of Access: Minorities in Two-Year Colleges.* Washington, D.C.: Howard University Press, 1979. 259 pages.

Please see no. 162 for the full annotation.

986 Orfield, Gary, and others. *The Chicago Study of Access and Choice in Higher Education: A Report to the Illinois Senate Committee in Higher Education.* Chicago: Committee on Public Policy Studies, University of Chicago, 1984. 351 pages. (ED 248 929)

This publication draws upon a variety of data sources to assess the extent to which students in metropolitan Chicago have real access to higher education and choice among postsecondary institutions. It focuses particularly on the role of community colleges and concludes that (1) students from predominantly minority neighborhoods are tracked into community colleges rather than into more prestigious institutions, (2) the community colleges do not provide equal educational opportunity, (3) the community colleges are not highly successful in transferring students to four-year institutions, and (4) those students who do transfer—particularly minorities—are more likely to attend less prestigious four-year colleges. The authors argue, therefore, that predominantly black community colleges are "strongly connected with a system of separate and unequal education that proceeds from elementary school through college" (p. 205).

987 Pincus, Fred L. "The False Promises of Community Colleges: Class Conflict and Vocational Education." *Harvard Educational Review*, 1980, *50* (3), 332–361.

This article reviews the history and controversies surrounding the growth of community college vocational education, concluding that advocates of occupational programming have yet to demonstrate that employment and earnings benefits actually accrue to graduates. The author notes the lack of data on employment rates and incomes of recent graduates but argues that available statistics provide only modest evidence of the economic benefits of vocational education. He posits that nonwhite and lower-class students are more likely to attend community colleges than senior institutions and are more likely to be enrolled in the occupational programs than in the transfer programs. He concludes that vocational education in capitalist America does not and cannot change the fact that most lower-class and nonwhite young people are not destined to get the limited number of prestigious, well-paid jobs in the labor market.

988 Sawyer, James A., and Nickens, John M. "The Fulfillment of the Democratization Role of the Community College." *College and University*, 1980, *55* (2), 113–124.

This article analyzes the socioeconomic status (SES) of 3,172 Florida community college graduates to determine whether low-SES students are underrepresented among those who transfer. It compares transferring graduates with nontransferring graduates on the basis of sex, race, family income, parental schooling, and parents' occupations. It also examines (for those who transferred) the relationship between family income and distance of the senior institution from the students' homes. The authors conclude that low-SES students transferred in proportion to the numbers that graduated and tentatively question the validity of arguments that community colleges do not promote social mobility.

989 West, Russell F., and Shearon, Ronald W. "Differences Between Black and White Students in Curriculum Program Status." *Community/Junior College Quarterly of Research and Practice*, 1982, *6* (3), 239–251.

The authors examine the hypothesis that community colleges perpetuate social inequities because of the overrepresentation of minority students in vocational curricula. They argue that any examination of this hypothesis should consider the fact that some vocational programs actually lead to higher-status jobs than some transfer programs. They utilize enrollment data for 9,907 North Carolina community college students to (1) determine the specific majors or programs those students were enrolled in, (2) classify those programs on the basis of the socioeconomic status of the occupations to which they lead, and (3) compare the status rankings for black and white students. They conclude that status differences in the types of programs enrolled in by blacks and whites are not as great as past critics of the community college have maintained.

990 Zwerling, L. Steven. "Experiential Education at a Community College." In John Duley (ed.), *Implementing Field Experience Education*. New Directions for Higher Education, no. 6. San Francisco: Jossey-Bass, 1974, pp. 1–12.

This chapter describes an experiential program established at Staten Island (New York) Community College to raise student self-esteem and career aspirations. The author notes that the relatively low job aspirations of community college students (compared to four-year college students) are reinforced by internships in low-prestige job areas. He examines how the Staten Island program combats this problem through self-discovery seminars and individualized, off-campus internships that provide exposure to careers that students might not have thought attainable. This is one of the few works that go beyond the rhetoric of social mobility and provide a plan of action to operationalize the oft-stated goal of upward mobility for lower-class community college students.

★**991** Zwerling, L. Steven. *Second Best: The Crisis of the Community College.* New York: McGraw-Hill, 1976. 372 pages.

The author argues that the community college plays an essential role in maintaining the social and economic structure of the United States, maintaining that proof of this social function may be found in the facts "that community college students will come primarily from the lowest socioeconomic classes of college attendees, that the dropout rate among community college students will be the highest of any college population, and that these dropouts—or 2-year-college graduates for that matter—will enter lower-level occupations than equivalent students who attend higher status colleges" (p. 33). He traces and accepts Clark's thesis that the community college plays a role in convincing students that their failure to attain the baccalaureate degree and to achieve higher-status positions is their own fault. The work includes a critical bibliography in which writers on the community colleges are classified into several clusters according to the nature of their criticism. It is useful for understanding the community college's social role.

13

Additional Sources
of Information

As community colleges grew in number during the 1950s and 1960s, the literature on two-year college education expanded at an equally impressive rate. Besides the growing body of published monographs (most of which are listed in this bibliography), the two-year college literature available to today's researcher includes approximately 12,300 documents that have been added to the ERIC data base since 1966 and approximately 5,600 journal articles that have been published since 1969. The number of dissertations on subjects relating to two-year college education and administration also runs into the thousands.

Fortunately for the researcher, however, this large body of literature is well organized and easily accessible through a variety of library tools, including indexes produced by the Educational Resources Information Center (ERIC) and other information agencies. This chapter describes the types of materials that are made available through the ERIC system and discusses additional library resources that can be consulted to find journal articles, dissertations, government documents, and statistical information on two-year colleges.

Using ERIC to Find Information on Two-Year Colleges

Every researcher studying two-year colleges—or any other educational topic—usually becomes very familiar with ERIC, an information service funded by the U.S. Department of Education to build and maintain a collection and bibliographical data base covering all aspects of education. Founded in 1966, the ERIC system includes sixteen clearinghouses operated by universities or professional associations that keep track of the literature within their individual scope areas. The ERIC Clearinghouse for Junior Colleges (operated since 1966 by the University of California at Los Angeles) has primary responsibility within the ERIC system for acquiring materials of interest to two-year college practitioners or researchers; the ERIC Clearinghouses for Higher Education and for Adult, Career, and Vocational Education have also contributed materials dealing with two-year colleges to the ERIC data base.

Following are the addresses of the individual clearinghouses:

Adult, Career, and Vocational
    Education
Ohio State University
National Center for Research in
    Vocational Education
1960 Kenny Road
Columbus, Ohio 43210
(614) 486-3655

Counseling and Personnel
    Services
University of Michigan
School of Education Building,
    Room 2108
Ann Arbor, Michigan 48109
(313) 764-9492

Reading and Communication
    Skills
National Council of Teachers
    of English
1111 Kenyon Road
Urbana, Illinois 61801
(217) 328-3870

Educational Management
University of Oregon
Library, Room 108
Eugene, Oregon 97403
(503) 686-5043

Handicapped and Gifted
    Children
Council for Exceptional
    Children
1920 Association Drive
Reston, Virginia 22091
(703) 620-3660

Languages and Linguistics
Center for Applied Linguistics
1118 22nd St., N.W.
Washington, D.C. 20037
(202) 429-9292

Higher Education
George Washington University
One Dupont Circle, N.W., Suite
630
Washington, D.C. 20036
(202) 296-2597

Information Resources
Syracuse University
School of Education
150 Marshall Street, Huntington Hall
Syracuse, New York 13210
(315) 423-3640

Junior Colleges
University of California at Los
Angeles
Math-Science Building, Room
8118
Los Angeles, California 90024
(213) 825-3931

Elementary and Early Child-
hood Education
University of Illinois
College of Education
805 West Pennsylvania Avenue
Urbana, Illinois 61801
(217) 333-1386

Rural Education and Small
Schools
New Mexico State University
Box 3AP
Las Cruces, New Mexico 88003
(505) 646-2623

Science, Mathematics, and Environmental Education
Ohio State University
1200 Chambers Road, 3rd Floor
Columbus, Ohio 43212
(614) 422-6717

Social Studies/Social Science
Education
Indiana University
Social Studies Development
Center
2805 E. 10th St.
Bloomington, Indiana 47405
(812) 335-3838

Teacher Education
American Association of Colleges for Teacher Education
One Dupont Circle, N.W., Suite
610
Washington, D.C. 20036
(202) 293-2450

Tests, Measurement, and
Evaluation
Educational Testing Service
Rosedale Road
Princeton, New Jersey 08541
(609) 921-9000. Ext. 2176

Urban Education
Teachers College, Columbia
University
Box 40
525 West 120th Street
New York, New York 10027
(212) 678-3437

The types of materials collected by the clearinghouses and made available through the ERIC system fall under two broad categories: (1) unpublished documents, such as institutional research reports and conference papers, and (2) published journal articles. The scope and availability of these materials are discussed below.

Unpublished ERIC Documents. The ERIC data base includes a variety of unpublished materials that are of value to two-year college researchers and practitioners. This unpublished, or "fugitive," literature includes instructional materials, curriculum guides, literature reviews, legal and legislative materials, opinion papers, course and program descriptions, research reports, conference papers, state and federal documents, and state and national compilations of statistical data on two-year colleges. Much of this material is practice rather than research oriented and is particularly useful for those seeking information on how faculty and administrators at individual colleges have solved problems or developed programs. Several documents, for example, describe staff development efforts undertaken at various two-year colleges to integrate part-time or adjunct faculty into the college community. These items may prove particularly useful for those who are faced with the task of developing similar staff development programs and who wish to learn from colleagues' experiences at other institutions.

The researcher looking for ERIC documents on particular topics of interest has two options: a manual search of monthly editions of *Resources in Education (RIE)* or a computer search of the on-line ERIC data base. *RIE,* a reference tool available in thousands of libraries and education research centers nationwide, provides indexed lists of documents as they are acquired and processed by the ERIC clearinghouses. Each edition of *RIE* includes subject, author, and institution indexes leading the reader to appropriate document citations. Besides standard bibliographical information, such as author, title, and the name of the institution responsible for the production of the document, each citation provides an abstract of up to 200 words (see Exhibit 1). An on-line computer search is an alternative to manual searches of

Exhibit 1. Sample *RIE* Citation.

ERIC Accession Number—identification number sequentially assigned to documents as they are processed.

Author(s).

Title.

Organization where document originated.

Date Published.

Contract or Grant Number.

Alternate source for obtaining document.

Language of Document—documents written entirely in English are not designated, although "English" is carried in their computerized records.

Publication Type—broad categories indicating the form or organization of the document, as contrasted to its subject matter. The category name is followed by the category code.

ERIC Document Reproduction Service (EDRS) Availability—"MF" means microfiche; "PC" means reproduced paper copy. When described as "Document Not Available from EDRS," alternate sources are cited above. Prices are subject to change; for latest price code schedule see section on "How to Order ERIC Documents," in the most recent issue of RIE.

Clearinghouse Accession Number.

Sponsoring Agency—agency responsible for initiating, funding, and managing the research project.

Report Number—assigned by originator.

Descriptive Note (pagination first).

Descriptors—subject terms found in the *Thesaurus of ERIC Descriptors* that characterize substantive content. Only the major terms, preceded by an asterisk, are printed in the subject index.

Identifiers—additional identifying terms not found in the *Thesaurus*. Only the major terms, preceded by an asterisk, are printed in the subject index.

Informative Abstract.

Abstractor's Initials.

ED 654 321   CE 123 456

Smith, John D.   Johnson, Jane

Career Planning for Women.

Central Univ., Chicago, IL.

Spons Agency—National Inst. of Education (ED), Washington, DC.

Report No. — CU-2081-S

Pub Date — May 83

Contract— NIE-C-83-0001

Note — 129p.; Paper presented at the National Conference on Career Education (3rd, Chicago, IL, May 15-17, 1983).

Available from—Campus Bookstore, 123 College Ave., Chicago, IL 60690 ($3.25).

Language—English, French

Pub Type— Speeches/Meeting Papers (150)

EDRS Price—MF01/PC06 Plus Postage.

Descriptors — Career Guidance,* Career Planning, Careers, *Demand Occupations, *Employed Women, *Employment Opportunities, Females, Labor Force, Labor Market, *Labor Needs, Occupational Aspiration, Occupations

Identifiers — Consortium of States, *National Occupational Competency Testing Institute

Women's opportunities for employment will be directly related to their level of skill and experience and also to the labor market demands through the remainder of the decade. The number of workers needed for all major occupational categories is expected to increase by about one-fifth between 1980 and 1990, but the growth rate will vary by occupational group. Professional and technical workers are expected to have the highest predicted rate (39 percent), followed by service workers (35 percent), clerical workers (26 percent), sales workers (24 percent), craft workers and supervisors (20 percent), managers and administrators (15 percent), and operatives (11 percent). This publication contains a brief discussion and employment information concerning occupations for professional and technical workers, managers and administrators, skilled trades, sales workers, clerical workers, and service workers. In order for women to take advantage of increased labor market demands, employer attitudes toward working women need to change and women must: (1) receive better career planning and counseling, (2) change their career aspirations, and (3) fully utilize the sources of legal protection and assistance that are available to them. (SB)

RIE; the procedures and advantages of the computer search are discussed in a separate section below.

Once the researcher has identified those documents that meet his or her informational needs, the full text of those documents can usually be obtained in one of two ways. Approximately 650 libraries across the country make the ERIC documents available on microfiche. The documents can also be ordered from the ERIC Document Reproduction Service (EDRS), 3900 Wheeler Avenue, Alexandria, Virginia 22304. EDRS charges are based on the cost of reproduction and mailing.

It should be noted that some documents listed in *RIE* are not available in library microfiche collections or through EDRS. *RIE* citations clearly indicate when this is the case and provide the address of an alternative source from which the document may be obtained.

Journal Articles. A second monthly index produced by ERIC—*Current Index to Journals in Education (CIJE)*—provides access to articles published in over 700 education-related journals. Among these journals are several dealing specifically with two-year colleges or with higher education in general (see Appendix I). Like *RIE,* monthly editions of *CIJE* include author and subject indexes; each article citation also provides a fifty-word annotation. The types of articles indexed in *CIJE* range from substantive research reports (many of which are included in this bibliography) to opinion papers and descriptions of instructional and administrative practices at individual colleges. Unlike the documents cited in *RIE,* however, these journal articles are not available in ERIC microfiche collections or through the ERIC Document Reproduction Service. The articles can be obtained at most university libraries or through interlibrary loan. Copies of most of these articles can also be ordered by mail from University Microfilms International in Ann Arbor, Michigan. Ordering information is provided in each edition of *CIJE.*

On-Line Computer Searches of ERIC. Besides going to the library and looking through *RIE* and *CIJE,* the researcher can search the entire ERIC data base—both unpublished documents and journal articles—via a computer hookup to a data-base vendor. Using the vendor's command language and ERIC subject headings, it is possible to quickly retrieve citations to and abstracts of ERIC documents and journal articles that are specifically related to the researcher's topic of interest. Most libraries have fee-based computer search services for their patrons, and it is still common practice for the researcher to consult a librarian who will do the actual computer search. Such search services are particularly useful to researchers who have neither the computer equipment nor the expertise to successfully negotiate a computer search. Two data-base vendors, however, have developed special services for nonlibrarians who have microcomputers with telephone hookups and who prefer to do their own searching. Additional information on these services can be obtained by writing to either of the following: BRS After Dark, 1220 Route 7, Latham, New York 12110, or DIALOG Knowledge Index, 3460 Hillview Avenue, Palo Alto, California 94304.

Computer searching has several advantages. The most obvious of these is the time saved by searching on line rather than leafing through printed indexes. Another advantage is the wide range of search strategies that are available to the computer searcher. But computer searching is not without its disadvantages. Data-base vendors charge searchers by the amount of time spent on line and often by the number of citations that are printed off. In addition, computers cannot be used to browse serendipitously through the literature; the researcher who simply wants to see what is new in the two-year college field is better off browsing through the "Junior Colleges" sections of new editions of *CIJE* and *RIE*. A good reference librarian can usually advise the researcher whether it is more advantageous to use the printed indexes or to conduct a computer search.

Limitations of the ERIC Data Base. Of all the library tools available to those doing research in the social sciences, the ERIC data base and its indexes (*RIE* and *CIJE*) provide the most comprehensive coverage of the two-year college literature. ERIC has, nonetheless, two limitations that should be kept in mind. First, ERIC's coverage of unpublished documents extends back only through 1966, and its coverage of the journal literature goes back only to 1969. Researchers looking for material prior to those dates will have to use other reference tools. Second, while ERIC provides access to journal articles and unpublished documents, it does not provide substantial numbers of references to dissertations and published books. Other sources of information that can be used to complement the ERIC data base are discussed below.

Finding Additional Journal Literature About Two-Year Colleges

While ERIC's *Current Index to Journals in Education* lists most of the contemporary journal literature about two-year colleges, additional reference tools should be consulted to find (1) journal articles published before 1969 and (2) articles published outside of the education journal literature (for example, in journals that deal primarily with clinical psychology or with sociology).

Coverage of the education journal literature prior to the 1969 advent of *CIJE* is provided by the *Education Index*, a reference tool that has been published monthly by the H. W. Wilson Company since 1929. The *Index*, though still published today, is primarily valuable as a reference to journal articles written during the 1930s, 1940s, 1950s, and 1960s. Two-year college researchers should note that the *Index* provides comprehensive coverage of the *Junior College Journal* (now the *Community, Junior, and Technical College Journal*), which, from its inception in 1930 up through the mid 1960s, was one of the only journals devoted solely to two-year college education and administration. As a source of information on contemporary journal literature, however, the *Education Index* is rather weak; *CIJE* covers many more titles.

A small percentage of the literature on two-year colleges is published outside of the education journals that are covered by *CIJE* and the *Education Index*. Occasionally, psychologists and sociologists writing about the two-year college will submit their works to disciplinary journals such as the *Journal of Psychology* or the *Annals of the American Academy of Political and Social Science*. Two periodical indexes covering this literature are *Psychological Abstracts* and *Sociological Abstracts*. A search of the April 1985 edition of *Psychological Abstracts*, for example, yields a citation to an article entitled "Attributions for Success or Failure

Among Anglo, Black, Hispanic, and Native American Community College Students" (*Journal of Psychology*, 1984, *58*, 891–896). Though this article may be of potential value to a researcher examining the status of minority students at community colleges, he or she would not find it in *CIJE*.

It should be noted, however, that as far as the community college literature is concerned, there is considerable overlap between *CIJE*, on the one hand, and *Psychological Abstracts* and *Sociological Abstracts*, on the other. The 1984 editions of *Psychological Abstracts*, for example, cite twenty-two articles under the headings "Community Colleges" and "Community College Students." Only two of these articles, however, were published in journals that are not covered by *CIJE*. *Sociological Abstracts* provides even fewer citations to articles on the community college, but, again, there is overlap. The researcher should be aware, therefore, that, while *Psychological Abstracts* and *Sociological Abstracts* do provide important citations, their small numbers may not warrant the cost of the extra time involved in searching beyond *CIJE*.

Finding Government Documents on Two-Year Colleges

Thousands of government documents dealing with two-year colleges or higher education in general are produced annually, and a large (though undetermined) percentage of them are acquired by the ERIC clearinghouses and made available through the ERIC system. Should the researcher need further government information, however, three additional reference tools should be consulted: the *Monthly Catalog of State Publications*, the *Monthly Catalog of United States Government Documents*, and the *CIS/Index*.

State Documents. The increased state role in community college governance has been well documented, and this increased role, of course, has resulted in a growing body of report literature produced by state agencies and commissions. One way of keeping abreast of this literature is to consult the *Monthly Checklist of State Publications*, a reference tool produced by the U.S. Library of Congress. The *Monthly Checklist* provides, for each state, a listing of the latest documents produced by individual agencies, such as state higher education coordinating commissions or the headquarters of state community college systems. These documents range from in-depth research or statistical reports to simple outlines of commission hearings or committee meetings. The researcher should be forewarned, however, that the *Monthly Checklist* provides no subject index and that it is useful only as a listing of publications as they are acquired by the Library of Congress. Furthermore, a good percentage of the listed documents eventually find their way into the ERIC system, because the *Monthly Checklist* itself is used by ERIC personnel as one of the many sources used to find new documents for the data base. Finally, most of the documents cited in the *Monthly Checklist*— unless they are entered into the ERIC data base—never find their way into libraries outside their states of origin. Many of these documents must be requested on interlibrary loan or ordered from the state agencies responsible for their publication.

Federal Documents. Most federal documents on two-year colleges are eventually entered into the ERIC system. This is especially true of those reports produced by the various agencies of the U.S. Department of Education and by the agencies of other departments (such as Defense and Labor) that are in some way responsible for education and training. Those wishing to delve further into federal reports should consult the *Monthly Catalog of United States Government Documents* (commonly called the *MoCAT*), a thoroughly indexed reference tool that lists—by agency—most of the documents produced by the federal government. Besides documents that are likely to be found in the ERIC data base, the *MoCAT* can be used by higher education researchers to find information that is often of related or peripheral interest, such as the data provided in the census reports of the Department of Commerce. These federal documents—along with the *MoCAT* itself—can be found at those libraries that serve as depositories of federal government documents.

Another important source of federal information is the *CIS/Index*, a resource produced by the Congressional Information Service. The *CIS/Index* provides a thoroughly indexed listing of the documents and reports published by the U.S. Congress, including transcripts of committee hearings, research reports generated by the staff of Senate and congressional committees, and House and Senate reports. The *CIS/Index* is particularly useful for researchers interested in the testimony presented by community college leaders before various committees, such as the House Committee on Education and Labor or the House Committee on Science and Technology. Most of the documents referred to in the *CIS/Index* are made available through the Congressional Information Service on microfiche, and most of the libraries that subscribe to the *CIS/Index* have those microfiche on hand.

Statistical Information on Two-Year Colleges

Researchers often need hard data to answer questions such as "How many full-time students are enrolled in community college vocational programs?" or "What is the average faculty work load of community college humanities instructors?" For many of these questions, the researcher can turn to the state and national compilations of two-year college data that are available in the ERIC data base. Other sources of statistical information include the *American Statistics Index (ASI)* and the *Statistical Reference Index (SRI)*, both published by the Congressional Information Service. *ASI* is an index to federal government documents that include statistical summaries or data tables, and *SRI* is an index to state documents, university reports, and the publications of professional associations that likewise provide statistical information. Both provide numerous citations to and abstracts of documents that include data on two-year colleges; the abstracts describe the data presented in the documents and indicate the pages on which data tables are located. In addition, the documents cited by *ASI* and *SRI* are usually available at the libraries that subscribe to those indexes.

Among ERIC, *ASI,* and *SRI,* the researcher will find hundreds of documents providing statistical information on two-year colleges. Many are state statistical abstracts that are updated annually and that summarize enrollment and financial data collected by state agencies or professional associations in one-shot research studies. Despite the number of data sources available,

however, the scope of the data provided is surprisingly limited.
Most quantitative analyses or statistical abstracts dealing with two-
year colleges utilize data generated by the Higher Education
General Information Survey (HEGIS) and include information on
institutional revenues and expenditures, the demographic characteristics and enrollment of students, the number and demographic
characteristics of staff and faculty, and the number of associate
degrees awarded in academic and vocational areas. Data on
subjects *not* covered by the HEGIS surveys are found only in
scattered sources and are not often updated on a regular basis.
Such hard-to-find data include the number of students who are
enrolled in transfer as opposed to vocational curricula, the number
of community college students who already have a baccalaureate
degree ("reverse transfers"), the proportion of community college
expenditures devoted to vocational as opposed to collegiate
programs, and data on the characteristics of part-time community
services faculty. Another problematical area concerns data on
student outcomes, such as the number of students who successfully
transfer or the number of vocational students who successfully find
employment. Few documents present statewide or national
outcome summaries, and those that do (see nos. 98–133 in this
bibliography) suffer the limitations that are inherent in most
follow-up research studies. For many questions requiring data not
provided by the HEGIS surveys, community college researchers
cannot often rely on secondary data sources.

Directories Providing Information on Two-Year Colleges

Directories can serve as useful sources of statistical
information as well as ready-reference sources that provide the
names, addresses, and telephone numbers of individual institu-
tions. Of the many directories of colleges and universities in the
United States, three (as of this printing) are of particular value to
persons studying two-year colleges: D. Parnell and J. W. Peltason,
American Community, Technical, and Junior Colleges (9th ed.;
New York: Macmillan, 1984); *Community, Technical, and Junior
College Directory* (Washington, D.C.: American Association of
Community and Junior Colleges, published annually under

various titles since 1950); and *Directory of Administrators of Community, Technical, and Junior Colleges* (Washington, D.C.: American Association of Community and Junior Colleges, published annually since 1984). Of these directories, the *Community, Technical, and Junior College Directory* is the most valuable for historians of the two-year college. It has been produced since 1950, and copies of the *Directory* going back to 1955 are available as ERIC documents.

The reader should be aware, however, of several problems related to the use of directories. First, the directories often draw from different samples of colleges; some directories, for example, include two-year branches of state universities, while others do not. Second, only the *Community, Technical, and Junior College Directory* provides separate enrollment figures for credit and community service courses; the others do not make this distinction. Third, most of the data presented in the directories are derived from surveys and thus have the limitations that are inherent in all self-reported information. Finally, the scope and titles of two-year college directories change from year to year.

Dissertations

Scores of dissertations are written annually on two-year college education and administration. Most are listed and indexed in *Dissertation Abstracts International (DAI)*, a reference tool published by University Microfilms International of Ann Arbor, Michigan. *DAI* is produced in several sections, and the overwhelming majority of dissertations on two-year colleges are found in the "Humanities and Social Sciences" section. This section includes citations to and abstracts of theses written by those receiving doctorates in higher education as well as by Ph.D. degree recipients in sociology, psychology, political science, and other related fields. Copies of most of the dissertations listed in *DAI* and can be purchased from University Microfilms International.

Summary

The resources reviewed in this chapter and summarized in Appendix II can be used to find numerous items that complement the materials listed in previous chapters of this bibliography. These materials include descriptions of educational and administrative practices at individual colleges, state and national compilations of data on two-year colleges, legislative summaries and hearings, and doctoral dissertations. The ERIC indexes—*RIE* and *CIJE*—are the logical starting points for those searching the two-year college literature; of all the library resources available, *RIE* and *CIJE* provide the most comprehensive coverage of two-year college education.

Any literature search is made more efficient with the help of a reference librarian. The librarian can point out differences in the indexing and organization of available reference tools. He or she can also help the researcher find new books on community college education as they are published. Another source of help for two-year college researchers is the staff of the ERIC Clearinghouse for Junior Colleges; clearinghouse services include computer searches of the ERIC data base and consultation on further sources of information. Researchers with questions on information about two-year colleges are invited to contact the User Services Librarian, ERIC Clearinghouse for Junior Colleges, 8118 Math-Sciences Building, UCLA, Los Angeles, California 90024.

But, regardless of the scope of available information resources, researchers should bear in mind the limitations of most two-year college literature. As has been pointed out in Chapter One—and as is made evident in the scope of the materials listed throughout this bibliography—additional research is needed in three critical areas: (1) analyses of the two-year college environment and of the effect of that environment on students; (2) analyses of the outcomes of two-year college education in terms of student development and the well-being of the community; and (3) analyses of the effectiveness of alternative approaches ι instruction and college administration. Most of the literature of the past twenty years is descriptive, not analytical. While this descriptive literature serves the important function of chronicling the growth of two-year colleges and giving voice to the ideals of two-year college practitioners, the current environment of fiscal exigency and limited enrollments requires more evaluative, problem-solving analyses.

Appendix I

Journals

Community College Journals

American Mathematical Association of Two-Year Colleges Review. Garden City, N.Y.: American Mathematical Association of Two-Year Colleges.

Community College Review. Raleigh, N.C.: North Carolina State University.

Community College Social Science Journal. El Cajon, Calif.: Crossmont College.

Community/Junior College Quarterly of Research and Practice. Washington, D.C.: Hemisphere.

Community Services Catalyst. Blacksburg: Virginia Polytechnic Institute and State University.

Community, Technical, and Junior College Journal. Washington, D.C.: American Association of Community and Junior Colleges.

Journal of Developmental & Remedial Education. Boone, N.C.: Center for Developmental Education, Appalachian State University.

New Directions for Community Colleges. San Francisco: Jossey-Bass.

Teaching English in the Two-Year College. Greenville, N.C.: Department of English, East Carolina University.

Journals Dealing with Higher Education in General

Academe. Washington, D.C.: American Association of University Professors.

AGB Reports. Washington, D.C.: Association of Governing Boards of Universities and Colleges.

American Scholar. Washington, D.C.: Phi Beta Kappa.

CASE Currents. Alexandria, Va.: Publisher Services.

Change. Washington, D.C.: Helen Dwight Reid Educational Foundation.

Chronicle of Higher Education. Washington, D.C.: Chronicle of Higher Education.

College and University. Washington, D.C.: American Association of Collegiate Registrars and Admissions Offices.

College Board Review. Staten Island, N.Y.: College Board Review.

College Teaching. Washington, D.C.: Heldref Publications.

Educational Record. Washington, D.C.: American Council on Education.

Higher Education. Amsterdam, The Netherlands: Elsevier Science Publishers.

Higher Education Review. Croydon, England: Tyrrell Burgess Associates.

Innovative Higher Education: The Journal of Nontraditional Studies. New York: Human Sciences Press.

Journal of Higher Education. Columbus: Ohio State University Press.

Journal of Student Financial Aid. Washington, D.C.: National Association of Student Financial Aid Administrators.

Journal of the College and University Personnel Association. Washington, D.C.: College and University Personnel Association.

Liberal Education. Washington, D.C.: Association of American Colleges.

NACADA Journal. Seattle: National Academic Advising Association, University of Washington.

National Forum: Phi Kappa Phi Journal. Baton Rouge, La.: Honor Society of Phi Kappa Phi, Louisiana State University.

New Directions for Higher Education. San Francisco: Jossey-Bass.
New Directions for Institutional Research. San Francisco: Jossey-Bass.
Research in Higher Education. Albany, N.Y.: Agathon Press.

Appendix II

A Summary Look at Major Sources of Information on Two-Year Colleges

ERIC Materials

Resources in Education. Washington, D.C.: U.S. Government Printing Office (published since 1966).

This source provides access to a wide range of unpublished materials, such as institutional research reports, state and federal documents, conference papers, curriculum guides and course materials, state and national data summaries, and descriptions of programs and innovations at individual colleges.

Current Index to Journals in Education. Phoenix, Ariz.: Oryx Press (published since 1969).

This source indexes the education journal literature since 1969. It includes citations to journal articles ranging from simple descriptions of programs and innovations at individual colleges to summaries of large-scale research reports.

Sources of Additional Journal Literature

Education Index. New York: Wilson (published since 1929).

This index provides access to the education journal literature published since 1929. The number of journals covered by the *Index* is much smaller than the number covered by *CIJE,* but the *Index* remains the primary source of information on journal articles published before 1969.

Psychological Abstracts. Washington, D.C.: American Psychological Association (published since 1927).

This publication covers the psychology journal literature. It is useful for finding the small number of articles on two-year college education that have appeared in psychological journals not covered by *CIJE* and in finding articles dealing with the clinical psychology of college students and with various issues related to learning and testing.

Sociological Abstracts. San Diego, Calif.: Sociological Abstracts (published since 1953).

This source covers the sociology journal literature. It is useful for finding articles on the sociological aspects of two-year college education, though most of this literature is also indexed in *CIJE.*

Government Documents

Monthly Checklist of State Publications. Washington, D.C.: U.S. Library of Congress (published since 1910).

This source provides a monthly update of the latest documents produced by agencies in each of the fifty states. Many of the documents dealing with two-year colleges eventually are listed in *RIE* and made available through the ERIC system.

Monthly Catalog of United States Government Documents. Washington, D.C.: U.S. Government Printing Office (published since 1895).

This is a thoroughly indexed listing of the documents produced by the departments, agencies, and offices of the federal government. Many of the documents dealing with two-year colleges also find their way into the ERIC system.

CIS/Index. Washington, D.C.: Congressional Information Service (published since 1970).

This publication provides an indexed listing (with abstracts) of all documents produced by the U.S. Congress. It includes numerous citations to committee hearings on legislation affecting higher education in general and two-year colleges in particular.

Statistical Information

American Statistics Index. Washington, D.C.: Congressional Information Service (published since 1973).

This source indexes federal documents that include statistical summaries or extensive data tables. It is useful in finding data collected by the federal government on two-year colleges. Many of these federal sources are also listed in *RIE.*

Statistical Reference Index. Washington, D.C.: Congressional Information Service (published since 1980).

This publication indexes several types of documents that provide statistical information, including state documents, university reports, and the publications of professional associations. Many of these documents are also indexed in *RIE* and made available through the ERIC system.

Dissertations

Dissertation Abstracts International. Ann Arbor, Mich.: University Microfilms International (published since 1938).

This work provides access to the scores of dissertations produced annually on two-year college education and administration.

Directories

Parnell, D., and Peltason, J. W. *American Community, Technical, and Junior Colleges.* (9th ed.) New York: Macmillan, 1984.

This directory provides quick, ready-reference data on each two-year college, including college name, address, and telephone number; type of control; names of administrators; the calendar system used; admissions requirements; enrollment data; the type of housing available; the estimated percentage of entering students who transfer; the estimated percentage of entering students who have already attended a four-year college; the areas of study offered; the size of the library collection; and the annual tuition and fees charged.

Community, Technical, and Junior College Directory. Washington, D.C.: American Association of Community and Junior Colleges (published annually under various titles since 1950).

This work lists the nation's two-year colleges and provides, for each, the college name, address, and telephone, type of control, name of the president, the calendar system used, enrollment data, annual tuition and fees charged, and the number of faculty and administrators.

Directory of Administrators of Community, Technical, and Junior Colleges. Washington, D.C.: American Association of Community and Junior Colleges (published annually since 1984).

This publication lists the nation's two-year colleges and provides, for each, the name of the president and the names of the institution's top-level administrators.

Author Index

The following index includes the names of personal authors, as well as the names of educational institutions and agencies that are responsible for the publication of the works cited in this bibliography. The numbers in the index refer to entries in the bibliography, not to page numbers.

Subject Index

Subjects listed in this index are referenced to entry numbers and also to page numbers. Page numbers are given for topics that appear in the authors' introductions to chapters and sections in the book; they do not duplicate entry numbers. Entry numbers are in boldface type; page numbers are in roman type.